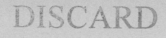

THE GROWTH OF
POLITICAL THOUGHT IN THE WEST

THE GROWTH OF POLITICAL THOUGHT IN THE WEST

FROM THE GREEKS TO THE END OF THE MIDDLE AGES

BY

CHARLES HOWARD McILWAIN

EATON PROFESSOR OF THE SCIENCE OF GOVERNMENT
IN HARVARD UNIVERSITY

COOPER SQUARE PUBLISHERS, INC.
NEW YORK
1968

PREFACE

This book is a serious attempt to set forth in moderate compass and with the greatest possible clearness the *development* of our ideas about the state and about government, beginning with the fifth century B.C. in Greece and extending as far as the end of the middle ages. The difficulties are great. Such an account should never lose sight of the *growth* of thought while engaged with the detail of its contemporary expression; it should keep the history of political ideas in closest touch with the actual political developments and the institutional growth, but without becoming a mere political or institutional history. It should also be perfectly clear, but with a clearness resulting not from avoiding the difficulties and technicalities of which political writings are full, but from a concise and well-ordered analysis of all essentials, expressed in the simplest and most straight-forward English. A book properly combining these qualities would be welcome to the special student and at the same time intelligible and helpful to the beginner in the subject. Conscious of these needs and difficulties, I have tried very hard to write such a book, but whether successfully or not, the reader must judge.

A large part of the section on Greek political thought was included in somewhat different form in the series of Beecher Lectures which I had the honor to give at Amherst College in 1930, and portions of the medieval chapters were the basis of a series given at Boston in the Lowell Institute in 1931; but no part of the book has been printed till now. On the earlier part of it the criticisms of Professors W. S. Ferguson and C. J. Friedrich have been of great help to me, and in preparing the volume for publication, the assistance of Mr. George S. Pettee is gratefully acknowledged. I am grateful also to Harvard University for a grant from the Milton Fund to further the work.

C. H. McILWAIN

CAMBRIDGE, MASSACHUSETTS
February, 1932

TABLE OF CONTENTS

vii

THE GROWTH OF
POLITICAL THOUGHT IN THE WEST

THE GROWTH OF POLITICAL THOUGHT
IN THE WEST

CHAPTER I

THE BEGINNINGS

"Man is born free and everywhere he is in chains. . . . What can make it legitimate?"[1] It is the central question of all political thought. For more than two thousand years men have been searching, as Rousseau searched, to find "if in the civil order there can be any rule of administration legitimate and sure";[2] to discover how it can be that so many millions endure as so often they do the rule and even the tyranny of a single one "who has no power that has not been given him, and no strength to hurt them save in their own willingness to suffer it."[3] For such power to be legitimate must also be sure. Dominion if it is to be justified at all must be "a condition of rational nature" as Wycliffe defined it,[4] and in reason permanent government must have a justification sufficient to explain the historical fact of its continuous existence among rational beings. "What is it that makes the state one? It is the union of its members. And whence comes the union of its members? From the obligation that binds them. . . . But what is the foundation of that obligation?"[5] There begin the differences of opinion. At one extreme among the answers that men have given to this great question is the absolute denial that reason gives the slightest justification for domination of any kind or in any degree exercised by one man or any number of men over others: all political superiority and all government are a mere usurpation of powers that can rightly belong to none. Such is

[1] Rousseau, *Du contrat social*, Liv. i, chap. i.
[2] *Ibid.*, Liv. i, Introduction.
[3] Étienne de la Boëtie, *Discours de la servitude volontaire, Œuvres complètes*, edited by Léon Feugère, pp. 9-10.
[4] Dominium est habitudo nature racionalis secundum quam denominatur suo prefici servienti. *De Dominio Divino*, edited by R. L. Poole, p. 4.
[5] Rousseau, *Lettres écrites de la montagne*, lettre vi.

I

the answer of the philosophical anarchists like Bakunin. As an ideal attainable by beings equally perfect in mind and character such a theory must always have a strong claim upon the idealist. The noble ideal of the freest scope for the law within unhampered by the trammels of the coercive law without has always appealed to liberal minds, even to those who have sadly admitted that it is an ideal that can never be reached. It implies a perfection never yet attained by men and possibly never attainable. They see as St. Paul did "another law" in the members, warring against the laws of the mind, and bringing us "into captivity to the law of sin"; [1] and hence the searchers for the *rationale* of political relations among men have in most cases been forced to limit their horizon to "men such as they are" and to laws "such as they may be." [2] But even within this more restricted sphere there has been the widest variance as to what is "the condition of rational nature." "To one it is force, to others paternal authority, to others the will of God." [3] Force alone is not enough for this. It must be a force justifiable by reason. Might must make right. And force to all save a few has never been accepted as the basis of government "legitimate and sure." It can neither explain nor justify the permanent political dominance of some over others. It cannot explain it, for even "the weakest," as Hobbes said, "has strength enough to kill the strongest" by stealth or in combination with others in like condition with himself.[4] Nor can it justify submission an instant longer than the force is actually able to compel it. The bond then must be one of law of some kind, a *vinculum juris*, and a people must be one held together as Cicero said by consent to law, *juris consensu*.[5] But to what law? the law of God, the law of a father of a family, a mere pact formally or informally accepted by the citizens, or something in some way compounded of some or of all of these? And under such a law where does "rational nature" require that the dominant power be lodged; in a single ruler, in a few of the best or the richest, in all the people acting as individuals or as a corporate whole? And how does this "rational nature" prescribe that this power shall be exercised, wherever lodged? May it be delegated, and if so, how,

---

[1] *Romans*, VII, 23.
[2] Rousseau, *Du contrat social*, Liv. i, Introduction.
[3] Rousseau, *Lettres écrites de la montagne*, lettre vi.
[4] *Leviathan*, part i, chap. 13.
[5] *De Re Publica*, Lib. i, cap. xxv.

and to whom; may it all be delegated or only a part, such as the administration rather than the formulation of law?

It is in the successive answers to these and to cognate questions that we find the material of the history of political thought. And most varied these answers have been, a diversity usually to be explained by their close and constant connection with actual political developments; but from the time when the restless curiosity of the Greeks, in its search for a single principle underlying the universe, first turned their minds inward and began to examine the principles of human conduct as well as outward phenomena, the subject of political obligation in some aspect or other has furnished one of the most absorbing of the objects of human speculation.

The beginnings of this speculation, it may be, are to be found long before the Greeks were interested in it, and certainly there were before that time long ages of actual government and even of government recorded in historical documents, but it was among the Greeks apparently that we find the first faint trickle of that particular stream of speculative thought upon the nature of political relations which has been flowing ever since over the European world and over all the lands whose culture is in origin European.

With Greece then we must begin a history of our own political thought at least, and in Greece with the oldest surviving evidence of an interest in the life of collective man.

At the outset it is worth remembering that our very word "political" comes from the Greek *polis*. It was the Greek city-state that furnished the data for the first systematic thought of our race on "civil relations." It conditioned the thinking of some of its most powerful and penetrating minds upon the perennial and still unsolved problems involved in these relations; and even today, after the lapse of more than two thousand years of development and change, we can think of these in large part only in the terms that Plato and Aristotle formulated in contemplation of the political life of those small but intensely interesting centres that had taken form before the fifth century B.C. about the Aegean. Whatever our modern laws may be, Rome is the source of our jurisprudence, and whatever our form of government, Greece has furnished us the main outlines of our political science. And the fact that the details of government under modern conditions have become so different from those peculiar to Aristotle only serves to bring into stronger relief their essential identity.

A great master of Roman law whom we have recently lost has said that one of its chief merits as a study today arises from the fact that its mooted questions turn for the most part upon points that are strange to our modern everyday life.[1] The same is true of the Greek speculations about the *polis*. We still use the term "political." We have not ceased to refer to the "body politic," and even in the language "of the street" we mean by "politic" somewhat the same difference that a Greek must have had in mind between the rustic and the more sophisticated city dweller, though we should scarcely speak of a "public spirited" man as "politic" or call one wholly absorbed in his own private and selfish interests "idiotic" as he probably deserves. In like fashion, when we speak of a man as "civil," or refer to another's "incivility," we are thinking in similar terms, though in a Latin form, and the same is true of "urbanity," after the adoption of Christianity in Rome of "pagan," and, among our own race, of "heathen."

But the differences between the ancient and the modern setting of these central principles are no less important than the identity of the principles themselves. This ancient city-state, with its 5040 citizens as Plato would have limited it and a territory that Aristotle thought too large if you could not see across it, may be identical in what constitutes the essentials of its "good life" with our modern national state with perhaps a million of population where the Greek one had a thousand and a square mile of territory to its every acre; but if we are ever really to appreciate this identity it can only be by a corresponding understanding of the inevitable differences that size and other equally important points of dissimilarity must make in the operation even of like principles in the political life of a little community like Corinth or Megara just after the Persian wars and of a modern nation like the United States or modern Germany. Only by a thorough mastery of the peculiarities of the ancient city-state can we ever come to feel the underlying sameness of their foundations and ours. It is the eternal character of these foundations that makes valuable for us the study of the Greek state and the Greek speculations concerning it; it is only by a consideration of the differences between

[1] P. F. Girard, *Manuel élémentaire de droit romain*, 5ᵉ éd., p. 5.

these states and our own that a true understanding becomes possible of the great principles common to both.

Possibly it was the very smallness of their units of government that led to one of the most characteristic of these differences between the Greek view of political life and ours. They made no such distinction as we do either between society and the state or between the state and the government. To Aristotle man is a "political animal," but when St. Thomas Aquinas expressed the same thought for the thirteenth century he had to say Man is a "*social* and political animal," [1] and Seneca had long before referred to him as *sociale animal*.[2] As puzzling to Aristotle as it seems exaggerated to us cooler Anglo-Saxons, must have appeared Rousseau's delirium on first putting to himself the question whether the arts and sciences had contributed to corrupt or to purify morals.[3] To Aristotle the idea of the state was less differentiated than to us. The state absorbed and included the entire collective activity of its citizens, a whole outside of which its members could not even be thought of, much less exist. Hence all social life is political life, possibly because in the city-state the political life was in fact so much more "social" than with us. Every act of man, therefore, in so far as it affects others is to Aristotle a political act, and ethics is only a part or rather an aspect of politics. In saying that man is a "political" animal he meant much more than we should mean by political. St. Thomas did not really change his meaning by adding the word social; he only made it clearer to his own century and to ours.

This concentration upon the *polis* as the be-all and end-all of its citizens may also be the explanation of Aristotle's strange ignoring of international matters, which has attracted attention and hostile criticisms ever since his day. Though he was of course acquainted with the Athenian Empire and had been the tutor of Alexander, to him the *polis* is so nearly coterminous with society, its good life so nearly approximates the highest good, that everything beyond its sphere may be omitted in a treatise on politics without any serious loss. The interest of Isocrates in the states of Greece

---

[1] *De Regimine Principum*, Lib. 1, cap. 1.
[2] *De Clementia*, 1, 3.
[3] "Unable to walk for shortness of breath I sank down under one of the trees of the avenue and there passed a half hour in such agitation that when I arose I found the whole front of my waistcoat wet with tears, though I had not been conscious of shedding any." (*Second Letter to Malesherbes*.)

as a whole was as much greater than Aristotle's as his keenness of analysis of each seems inferior.[1]

It is evident that the first prerequisite to an understanding of the earliest thoughts of our race about politics is a thorough knowledge of the nature of the *polis* that conditioned those thoughts and of the public life its citizens lived within it.   Thus and thus alone may we begin to understand the meaning of their own words and be able to go on from this to our later and most important task, an estimation of the significance of those thoughts for later ages including our own.

Putting aside the interesting question of origins, we may then ask what were the chief characteristics of the Greek city-state. In the first place it was a community (κοινωνία), a *res publica*, or in good old English, a true common weal or commonwealth.   It had something in common with the local units familiar to us and our ancestors for a thousand years and more, what we still speak of — now usually without understanding why — when we put ourselves "on the country" to be tried by a jury "of the vicinage." In the earlier history of our jury, before it was informed by the evidence of outside witnesses, it and the compurgators who preceded it derived their importance from the fact that they embodied the common knowledge, common opinions, and common life of the little district from which they came.   A suitor of an old English county court would probably have understood the "community" (κοινωνία) of the city-state far better than any modern city dweller, who usually knows nothing of his next door neighbor or of his doings and thoughts.   "Among simple men," as Mr. Zimmern finely says,[2] "far removed from the seat of government, and too poor and too busy to stir outside their native valley, neighbourliness takes the place of citizenship."   Our forefathers would have understood something of this neighborliness as the Greeks did, and the knowledge of it has not yet disappeared in the country.   But long before they were advanced enough to leave us any record of their thoughts our early English communities had lost, if they had ever had, another great characteristic that the Greek city retained to the end, its self-sufficiency (αὐταρκεία) or independence. Thus St. Thomas Aquinas had also to make it clear to his readers of the thirteenth century that Aristotle's ideas about the polity

[1] See Georges Mathieu, *Les idées politiques d'Isocrate* (1925), especially chap. v.
[2] *The Greek Commonwealth*, 2d ed., p. 92.

might be applied to provinces (*provinciae*) as well as to cities (*civitates*) in a way that it is clear Aristotle himself would not have admitted, and the authors of the celebrated *Defensor Pacis* in the fourteenth century tacitly applied all of Aristotle's observations upon the Greek *polis* to their own medieval *civitates* or *regna*. Most cities had in fact by that time become subject to kings and emperors and the "self-determination" so characteristic of the Greek cities could no longer apply to any but the larger unit of the province or the realm (*regnum*), save in the case of the few cities which enjoyed *merum et mixtum imperium*, and only in part even to them. The latter, which flourished down to modern times in Italy and Germany, are probably the closest modern parallel to the Greek city-state with its communal and its independent life. But it could be shown that though they shared with it a certain measure of independence, other aspects of their social and political life were widely different.

In most cases the *municipia* had in fact lost some of the vividness and vigor of their political life. It had become diluted by the loss of their separateness and independence. As Mr. Zimmern says again, "in all societies in all ages the law of the larger unit tends to be held in less esteem than that of the smaller, and progress consists in making the spirit of the smaller, with its appropriate ideas and customs, transmute and inspire the larger." [1] Thus the Greek ideas of the polity tended to lose some of their sharpness when applied to the larger unit of the province, the realm, or the Empire, or later to our own huge modern nation-states. As the seat of government became more remote, so the government itself gradually became further removed from the every-day lives of the citizens. They found themselves engrossed in their private concerns more than in their public duties. It became increasingly hard to "inspire the larger unit with the spirit of the smaller"; political life became more stagnant; and what Plato calls the "art of drawing pay" (ἡ μισθαρνητικὴ τέχνη) [2] was gradually replacing the zeal for public service. Our word "politician" ought to be a good translation of the Greek *politikos*, but it is not — and why? Such things as these make it easier to agree with Mr. Warde Fowler when he says that "The πόλις was in fact, in most respects though not in all, a more perfect form of social union than the modern State, and its history, if we were more exactly informed

---

[1] *The Greek Commonwealth*, 2d ed., p. 98. [2] *Republic*, p. 346.

about it, would be relatively easier to understand." [1] The vividness of the feeling of community, the approximation of neighborliness and citizenship, the living realization of a true *res publica*
or common weal, this was probably the deepest root from which
the ancient polity drew its life. We need not inquire into its
history, nor touch on the mooted question whether its unity
originated in kinship or in contiguity. It was there, and the
exceptional vigor of its political life was heightened by circumstances probably more favorable than have ever existed in the
world before or since.

Never has there been so close an approximation as in the Greek
city-state of the "political man" in the sense in which the Utili-
tarians created their "economic man," never has man been so
completely a "political animal." He had fewer temptations than
we have to be anything else. Religion and worship did not, as
they must now, draw him away from the affairs of his city, they
involved for him no division of his loyalty between "church and
state"; they were, on the contrary, probably more inseparably
connected with his "political" life and activity than any other
part of it, for the gods he worshiped — at least in the period when
civic life remained most vivid — were not "strange gods" but the
divinities who presided over his own fireside and his own city.
We cannot think truly of Athena without thinking of Athens, nor
can we understand Athens without Athena. The very establishment of their city and the constant preservation of its distinctive
character and welfare the citizens attributed to the particular
divinity who presided over it, and for that very reason the common
worship of that divinity naturally came to be in their eyes at once
the most striking manifestation of the common life they lived

[1] *The City-State of the Greeks and Romans*, p. 9, — "It is the unexhausted vitality, the
permanent inspiration, the eternal humanity of Greek political ideas which gives them their
claim to be restudied and restated in our own time." John L. Myres, *The Political Ideas of
the Greeks* (1927), p. 45. One cause of this vividness of the feeling of community in the
Greek city-state was the fact that so many of the inhabitants — free as well as slave — were
not citizens; yet this was not the only cause, nor the main one. It was far deeper than
that. Making all allowances for the large proportion of these non-citizens, the political
units of Greece still remain strikingly smaller than our modern political units and their
common life far more intimate. It is easy to overemphasize the difference between antique
and modern political units arising from the disproportion of citizens and residents. In
Massachusetts during the first half of the seventeenth century, for example, it may be
doubted whether the proportion of "freemen" to inhabitants was much greater than in
most Greek cities in the time of Aristotle. For the whole medieval period in western Europe
and later, those who would have been included within Aristotle's definition of a citizen — one
who rules and is ruled in turn — were actually but a very small fraction of the inhabitants
of any state. It was this, no doubt, which led Bodin to reject Aristotle's definition.

within their little commonwealth and the surest means of preserving
its distinctive character and institutions.

So Plato, in the opening words of his dialogue on the *Laws*,
begins with the question, "Tell me, Stranger, is God or a man supposed to be the author of your laws?" and Aristotle, in the part
of the *Politics* in which he in like fashion is constructing the best
state that conditions permit, is careful to provide not merely that
there should be public meals and public education, but that the
cost of divine worship should be borne by the whole state.[1]

But it was not religion alone that bound the citizen to his city.
The *polis* was in a sense his home, for he never, at least in the later
period of Greek development, allowed his household to draw him
away from the every-day association with his fellow citizens. For
him there was nothing quite comparable with the English love of
home to keep him from the market-place where his real life was to
be lived, and it was there that his days were actually passed.
Women's sphere might be the home, and silence their chief virtue,
but his place was in the assembly or the market-place. A woman,
says Aristotle, who was only as modest as a good man would be
considered a chatter-box,[2] and one of the bad features of extreme
democracy is that the wives of the poor cannot be kept from going
out of doors.[3] But for men he would provide in his best city a
market-place far away from the general mart of commerce, an
"upper market" not to be soiled by the wares of traffickers,
reserved for the citizens alone, in which those men of virtue could
spend their leisure time in talk,[4] a place from which "all goods for
sale are rigidly excluded, and all hawkers and hucksters with
their yells and cries and vulgarities. They must go elsewhere, so
that their clamor may not mingle with and mar the grace and
orderliness of the educated classes."[5] In such a market-place
the talk, we may imagine, would be in large part "small-town
talk," and provincial and personal enough no doubt; but even
today our own nearest approach to the *symposia* of the Greeks
would probably be found not in our crowded cities but about the
tavern stove, or in front of the "general store." A "village

---

[1] *Politics*, Bk. IV (old VII) chap. x. Probably the most striking appreciation of the great
importance of religion in the essential life of the city-state is to be found in Fustel de
Coulanges, *La cité antique*, translated into English as *The Ancient City*, by Willard Small.
In that interesting and valuable book, the author possibly overrates the relative importance
of the religious element, but it is desirable that its great significance should be emphasized.

[2] *Politics*, III, chap. iv.   [4] *Politics*, Bk. IV (old VII), chap. xii.

[3] *Politics*, VI, chap. xv.   [5] Xenophon, *Cyropaedia*, I, 2, 3.

Socrates" is conceivable though not very likely to appear in our modern life; a city one can scarcely be imagined. For our own part we now incline to accept Maitland's view of the actual crudity of our lowest local unit of the township in its early period, in preference to the rather grandiose interpretation of the Germanic school of half a century ago; and to a certain extent the same admissions should probably be made for the earlier and the smaller Greek city-states. They may indeed, in Aristotle's phrase, originally have come into existence merely to make life possible. But "they *existed* to make life good." Some of them were by no means small in the period after the Persian wars; and in all, the fact that, unlike our townships or our counties, they had no political superior tended to raise the personalities of their discussions far above the level of mere ordinary local gossip. Politics at all times have been personal and must always to a great extent remain so, however large the state. It was Aristotle's view that it becomes too large just so soon as these personalities can no longer be based on immediate personal contact. In a sense its very "pettiness" is its chief merit; and if it is borne in mind that the Greek city was no mere satrapy of a far away king, but an independent self-governing whole, we begin to see why the greatest political thinkers of all time were educated in such a school, small as it was; we fully understand for the first time what Aristotle really means when he says there can be no government where friendship is impossible and no political life where no leisure exists, and we can appreciate his feeling that if a state becomes too large it ceases really to be a state. For to the Greek, the city consisted primarily in the union of its citizens. It was no mere territory with a government. It was far more than that. The government was no less than the sum of the political activities of its citizens, and Aristotle was warranted in calling it, as he did, "a life" (ὁ βίος). The life of the citizens was its life, and that life was more nearly the whole of theirs than men in the varied distractions of our modern time can appreciate without an effort. To a Greek audience there seemed no straining for effect in Plato's famous figure in which he finds the mind of man depicted in the larger letters of the "constitution" of the state. None but a modern man could dismiss this as a mere "parallel" or "analogy." It was something far deeper. The mind of the state and the mind of its citizen are identical — the macrocosm and the microcosm. The citizen is not simply the counterpart of the state, nor the state of him. He *is* the state in little. "The life of the state is the life of the men composing it."[1] There is some idealization here, of course, but to the Greek it was certainly neither meaningless nor absurd as it seems to have been to the utilitarian mind of Grote.[2]

There are other features of the city-state, less important perhaps than its communal character and its self-sufficiency, but not without influence upon Greek political thought. Among these are the economic connection of the urban and the rural part of its territory, and the actual relations economic and social between the various "parts" of its population, estimated in terms of birth, wealth, occupation, or their respective shares in the privileges of citizenship.

Even in its mere physical aspect the Greek city-state has no exact counterpart in anything we know in modern times. Its territory included a rural and an urban part not distinguished from each other by any governmental line, nor always divided, as at Athens, by any physical one. It had some points in common with the medieval "nucleated village" and some familiar to us in the New England "town," but it was, even considered as a mere local unit, not quite the same as either. As Mr. Warde Fowler again says, "The Athenian State comprised all the free people living in Athens, and also those who lived in the Attic territory; but these last had their political existence, not as inhabitants of Attica, but as Athenians, as citizens of the πόλις of Athens."[3] It is their "political existence" that chiefly interests the student of political thought and this particular relation of the people to the soil had much to do with the emphasis always put in Greek thought upon the people rather than upon the territory of a state. So conceived the state of Athens was the sum of Athenian citizens, and her "constitution" the outward form of their corporate political life: it was no mere collection of territorial laws imposed by the state upon the residents within her boundaries, or within distinct sub-divisions of her territorial area. Solon's famous four classes were divisions of the people, not mere sections of the inhabitants.[4]

Obviously the details of these constitutional arrangements and

---

[1] R. L. Nettleship, *Lectures on the Republic of Plato*, p. 68.
[2] *Plato and the Other Companions of Sokrates*, vol. iii, pp. 46, 123 ff.
[3] *The City-State of the Greeks and Romans*, p. 8.
[4] Cicero gives an interesting account of these territorial aspects of the ancient city-state. *De Legibus*, II, 2.

of their growth even in the most important of the states of Greece must be left to the constitutional historian. At the same time they are an important part of the data from which we must reconstruct and attempt to explain one of the most significant and most difficult of the chapters in the history of political speculation. Without a comprehensive and an exhaustive knowledge of Greek history and Greek constitutionalism all hope of an understanding of Greek political thought is utterly vain.

For it is only after an open-eyed study at first hand of these details that we can expect even gradually to obtain for ourselves, and not as a mere echo from someone else, some appreciation of the essential life of the state that gave these details of government and administration their practical vitality and their influence upon the thought of the future; and such an appreciation is the only sufficient justification of the study of the variations of political experience and reasoning in any part of the world's history. Possibly we may not reach the same conclusions in all points as Aristotle, but we must follow the same general method he adopted when he examined more than one hundred and fifty actual constitutions in attempting to set forth the general principles underlying any. It is the greatest mistake to assume, as is sometimes done, that Aristotle in his theory of the state was entirely empirical. In all political thought there is hardly to be found a great figure more deductive in method than he, but it was a deduction from principles which had themselves been reached only by the most patient search into actual political conditions. And Plato even, who has been classed as the most deductive of all political philosophers, based his deductions upon a knowledge of Greek law and institutions that was almost encyclopaedic, as examination of his *Laws* will clearly show.

If, then, we are to understand the state as Plato or Aristotle, as Xenophon, or Thucydides, or Isocrates conceived it in essence to be, we must as our first task approach as nearly as now we may to their knowledge of what it actually was. The one characteristic, among the many they saw in the actual life of existing city-states, that seems to have struck them all as the most persistent and fundamental was the common life of the people; and so to Aristotle the necessary definition of any state comes to be "a community of citizens united by sharing in one form of government," [1] or as put

[1] *Politics*, III, 3, p. 1276 b.

in more ideal terms, "a community of well-being in families and aggregations of families, for the sake of a perfect and self-sufficing life," [1] while a great mass of people such as Babylon's population, though contained within a single wall, appeared to him to be "a nation rather than a state," [2] Corinth and Megara would not be one just because one wall surrounded them both, and even if one could enclose the whole of the Peloponnesus within such a wall, he could never thereby make it a "city." Plato also says, "so long as the city can grow without abandoning its unity, up to that point it may be allowed to grow, but not beyond it," [3] and the same idea lies behind the moving words that Thucydides puts into the famous funeral oration of Pericles, though the actual ideal of government was widely different from Plato's or Aristotle's.[4]

To all these the actual states of Greece were and every true state must be "not an organization but an organism," [5] but no organism in the crude physical sense posited by Bluntschli: "It is a moral organism." [6]

It is clear, however, that if we are ever to penetrate to the full meaning of their words we must know something beyond the mere political facts upon which Plato and Aristotle reasoned. We must add to that knowledge some understanding of the sources and principles of the general philosophy of which their politics formed a necessary and important part. This is the second great prerequisite to the study of Greek political philosophy.

The earliest Greek thinkers of whom any record remains looked to the external world for the central principle of all things, and even if our scanty knowledge of them were greater than it is, we should probably not be able to trace to them the first appearance of connected thoughts about the state. These could emerge only after man himself had become an object of intellectual curiosity and his conduct in isolation or in society. But by the fifth century B.C. these newer objects of thought had so come to dominate it all that Protagoras of Abdera, the first of the well-known Sophists so-called, born probably between the victories of Marathon and Salamis, in his famous aphorism, "Man is the measure of all things," [7] was apparently giving concrete expression of a

---

[1] *Ibid.*, III, 9, p. 1280 b.   [3] *Republic*, IV, p. 423.
[2] *Ibid.*, III, 3, p. 1276 a.   [4] Thucydides, Bk. II, chap. 35 ff.
[5] Butcher, *Some Aspects of the Greek Genius*, p. 52.
[6] A. C. Bradley, *Aristotle's Conception of the State, Hellenica*, p. 210.
[7] Plato, *Theaetetus*, 152.

view already widely current.[1]   The Sophists seem to stand for a transitional period in Greek philosophy in general rather than for any particular system of thought, some individuals to whom the name was applied inclining to one, some to another of the theories of the universe already known.   They may have belonged, as Grote thought, to no single school, but at all events they all shared to a considerable degree the general intellectual tendencies of their time, the most striking of which was its subjectivism.   In the more extreme this developed into a thorough-going skepticism, as in Gorgias of Leontini in Sicily, who taught that nothing exists, that if it did exist it would be unknowable, and that even if it could be known, such knowledge could never be communicated.[2] From the devastating effects of so complete a skepticism no branch of the traditional beliefs of the Greeks was immune.   It tended utterly to upset the accepted views of the origin of the laws of gods and men and to undermine the sanctions of both.   Laws are to be found indeed, but they differ from city to city and from country to country, some even enjoining what others forbid. Such laws can be neither commands of the gods nor manifestations of any principles seated in the nature of man : they are mere conventions artificially created at given times or places to meet particular needs.   Such was the view prevalent among the Sophists on the nature of law, though they were not always in agreement as to its authors, some believing it to be the result of a mutual compact among the many weak to protect them against the masterful few who by right of might ought naturally to dominate them. Others would have defined it as they defined justice to be the right of the strongest, as Thrasymachus does in Plato's *Republic*.[3]   All agreed, however, in denying that law was according to nature. Two examples may serve to illustrate their views on these important questions, each from a dialogue of Plato, who is, of course, not an entirely sympathetic reporter.   Possibly the clearest of all is in Plato's *Gorgias*, where Callicles is made to set forth the views of some at least among the Sophists, in the following words :

[1] "But at this period [in the time of Socrates] men gave up inquiring into the works of nature, and philosophers diverted their attention to political science and to the virtues which benefit mankind."   Aristotle, *De Partibus Animalium*, Bk. I, chap. 1, p. 642 a, translation by Ogle.

[2] Sextus Empiricus, *Adversus Mathematicos*, VII, 65 ff., extracts in Ritter et Preller, *Historia Philosophiae Graecae*, 7th ed., pp. 188–191 ; Zeller, *A History of Greek Philosophy from the Earliest Period to the Time of Socrates*.   English translation, vol. ii, p. 451 ff.

[3] P. 338 ff.

". . . the truth is, Socrates, that you, who pretend to be engaged in the pursuit of truth, are appealing now to the popular and vulgar notions of right, which are not natural, but only conventional. Custom and nature are generally at variance with one another. . . . By the rule of nature, that only is the more disgraceful which is the greater evil — as, for example, to suffer injustice; but by the rule of custom, to do evil is the more disgraceful. For this suffering of injustice is not the part of a man, but of a slave. . . . The reason, as I conceive, is that the makers of laws are the many weak; and they make laws and distribute praises and censures with a view to themselves and to their own interests; and they terrify the mightier sort of men, and those who are able to get the better of them, in order that they may not get the better of them; and they say, that dishonesty is shameful and unjust; meaning, when they speak of injustice, the desire to have more than their neighbors, for knowing their own inferiority they are only too glad of equality. And therefore this seeking to have more than the many, is conventionally said to be shameful and unjust, and is called injustice, whereas nature herself intimates that it is just for the better to have more than the worse, the more powerful than the weaker; and in many ways she shows, among men as well as among animals, and indeed among whole cities and races, that justice consists in the superior ruling over and having more than the inferior." [1]

A somewhat different but equally interesting view is expressed by the Sophist Thrasymachus in a well-known passage of the *Republic*: ". . . each government has its laws framed to suit its own interests; a democracy making democratical laws; an autocrat, despotic laws; and so on. Now by this procedure these governments have pronounced that what is for the interest of themselves is just for their subjects; and whoever deviates from this, is chastised by them as guilty of illegality and injustice. Therefore, my good sir, my meaning is, that in all cities the same thing, namely, the interest of the established government, is just. And superior strength, I presume, is to be found on the side of government. So that the conclusion of right reasoning is that the same thing, namely, the interest of the stronger, is everywhere just." [2]

---

[1] Pp. 482–483. The translation is Jowett's. See also pp. 491–492.

[2] Pp. 338–339, translated by Davies and Vaughan. The well-known passage in the *Clouds* of Aristophanes seems intended to attribute to the Sophists a similar view of justice: "What is justice? There's no such thing. . . . How! No such thing as justice? No;

In the dialogue which follows, Socrates finally manages so to entangle the Sophist in contradictions that he goes away in a huff, but at this point Glaucon and Adeimantus, professing to sympathize with the views of Socrates but to be unsatisfied by his reasons for them, demand a further justification, and in doing so themselves disclose opinions which Plato clearly desires here to present as views accepted generally by his own contemporaries. For this reason, if for no other, these views are of unusual interest to the historian of political thought. So Glaucon says, "To commit injustice is, they say, in its nature, a good thing, and to suffer it an evil thing; but the evil of the latter exceeds the good of the former; and so, after the two-fold experience of both doing and suffering injustice, those who cannot avoid the latter and compass the former find it expedient to make a compact of mutual abstinence from injustice. Hence arose legislation and contracts between man and man, and hence it became the custom to call that which the law enjoined just, as well as lawful. . . . Such is the current account, Socrates, of the nature of justice, and of the circumstances in which it originated."[1]

If such theoretical views as these were accepted generally as Plato intimates, it probably resulted, as it has usually resulted, from experience of existing conditions. To Callicles nature proves the right of the strongest, not only among individual men and among animals, but "among whole cities and races."

". . . We Athenians will use no fine words," Thucydides reports the Athenian envoys as saying to the magistrates of Melos in 416 B.C., ". . . you and we should say what we really think, and aim only at what is possible, for we both alike know that into the discussion of human affairs the question of justice only enters

---

where is it? With the immortal gods. If it be there, How chanc't it Zeus himself escap'd For his unnatural deeds to his own father?" A remarkable passage in Xenophon's *Memorabilia* seems to show that somewhat the same view was shared by no less a person than Pericles. To the question of Alcibiades as to what law is, he answers, "All those regulations are laws, which the people, on meeting together and approving them, have enacted, directing what we should do and what we should not do." But if these enactments prescribe bad things, or if a few enact them for the many, what then? "Everything," answers Pericles, "which the supreme power in a state, on determining what the people ought to do, has enacted, is called a law." Even "whatever a tyrant in authority prescribes, is also called a law." Probably no passage among the Greek sources comes closer to a statement of the modern theory of sovereignty than this. But if so, Alcibiades pertinently asks, "what is force and lawlessness?" "When I was your age," answers Pericles, "I was very acute at such disquisitions." "Would that I had conversed with you, Pericles, at the time when you were most acute in discussing such topics!" *Memorabilia*, I, 2, 40–46.

[1] Pp. 358–359, translated by Davies and Vaughan.

where the pressure of necessity is equal, and that the powerful exact what they can, and the weak grant what they must." [1] "As for the Gods, we expect to have quite as much of their favour as you; for we are not doing or claiming anything which goes beyond common opinion about divine or men's desires about human things. For of the Gods we believe, and of men we know, that by a law of their nature wherever they can rule they will. This law was not made by us, and we are not the first who have acted upon it; we did but inherit it, and shall bequeath it to all time, and we know that you and all mankind, if you were as strong as we are, would do as we do." [2]

Callicles, therefore, probably was no more cynical in theory than the Athenians in action, and Machiavelli in his *Discorsi* drew no more of his keen and callous maxims of political conduct from the Italy of his day than did this Sophist from the practices of his own time.

What these practices had thus taught the Sophists about justice, an ever increasing knowledge of distant "cities and races" seemed also to teach them about law. To the many who believed with Heracleitus that "nothing abides" there was little strange in this, and even to those who accepted the unchangeableness of the physical world, the striking contrast between this fixity and the endless varieties they found among men's laws and customs were a proof that the latter must be against nature and the result of mere convention. The history of Herodotus is filled with descriptions of such "outlandish" customs, and Aristotle mentions the strange rule of common ownership of land said to exist among some of the barbarians. [3] If law were natural, it would be everywhere the same. If one law were according to nature, anything that enacted the opposite could not be, and yet such differences between existing laws are actually to be found.

The Sophists' solution of this dilemma is the one to be expected

---

[1] Bk. V, chap. 89. Jowett's translation.

[2] Bk. V, chap. 105. These cynical words are of course those of Thucydides alone, but there is no reason to believe them to be essentially different in tone from the ones actually used by the Athenian envoys.

"As to the speeches which were made either before or during the war, it was hard for me, and for others who reported them to me, to recollect the exact words. I have therefore put into the mouth of each speaker the sentiments proper to the occasion, expressed as I thought he would be likely to express them, while at the same time I endeavoured, as nearly as I could, to give the general purport of what was actually said." Thucydides, I, 22. See *The Speeches of Thucydides*, by R. C. Jebb, in *Hellenica*, p. 266 ff.

[3] *Politics*, II, 5.

from the subjective and even skeptical character of the general
thought of the time in which they shared, a solution that every
addition to their knowledge of the non-Greek world seemed to
corroborate; and in the view of some of them that human laws
are the result of human compact, they anticipated one of the most
important of the political ideas of the later Middle Ages and
modern times. Their general conception of the nature of law
appears clearly in the Platonic dialogue *Minos*, in which the
interlocutor opposes to the view of Socrates that law is the discovery of that which is, the obvious fact "that neither do the same
persons always have the same laws, nor different persons always
different laws," in proof of which he cites, among other instances,
the sacrifice of human beings by the Carthaginians as a holy and
lawful act though condemned in Athens as unholy and against
law. "What else can law (νόμος) be," then, he asks, "if not
[merely] the things established by law (τὰ νομιζόμενα)?" But,
answers Socrates, if I asked instead what is gold, you would not
inquire, what kind of gold. For gold cannot differ from gold, so
far as it *is* gold. Nor can law differ from law, in so far as they
really are law. Law, (νόμος) therefore, cannot be merely the sum
of existing legal rules (τὰ νομιζόμενα), for some decrees are good
and some evil, but law cannot be evil. Hence all decrees cannot
be law, but those only that are good and consonant to law in its
true sense. Law, then, is the discovery of a good that exists, it
can be discovered only by those who are wise, and such above all
are statesmen and kings, whose writings relating to the state men
generally call laws. But it is the decrees only of the good and the
wise that we may *rightly* call laws, and one that is not right (ὀρθόν)
we shall no longer call lawful (νόμιμον); it becomes "unlawful"
(ἄνομον). "Therefore in all writings concerning the just and the
unjust, and in general concerning the regulating of a city and the
manner in which it is needful to administer it, while the right
(τὸ ὀρθόν) is a kingly law (νόμος βασιλικός) the wrong is not . . .
for it is unlaw." [1]

This dialogue sets forth in clearest terms not only the view of

---

[1] *Minos*, cap. IX, p. 317. The dialogue is generally believed to be no authentic work of
Plato, and Stallbaum, on grounds of content as well as of style, condemns it in unmeasured
terms. Plato's it may not be, but the whole line of argument seems Platonic, and its discussion of the important difference between "law" and "laws" is of the greatest significance,
and, as Dean Pound says, "gives us a clue to the juristic problems of the time." *An Introduction to the Philosophy of Law*, pp. 24–25.

law prevalent among the Sophists, but the reaction from the extreme subjectivism underlying that view for which the name of Socrates seems to stand in the history of Greek philosophy.[1] Possibly that reaction may also be seen in the *Antigone* of Sophocles, in the famous antithesis between Creon's statement that "whomsoever the city may appoint, that man must be obeyed, in little things and great, in just things and unjust,"[2] and the passionate cry of Antigone in answer: ". . . it was not Zeus that had published me that edict; not such are the laws set among men by the Justice who dwells with the gods below; nor deemed I that thy decrees were of such force, that a mortal could override the unwritten and unfailing statutes of heaven. For their life is not of today or yesterday, but for all time, and no man knows when they were first put forth. Not through dread of any human pride could I answer to the gods for breaking *these*."[3] The awful doom of Creon in the tragedy would seem to indicate that the sympathies of Sophocles were on the side of the "higher law" upon which Antigone relied. So, without doubt, were those of Socrates.[4] But Socrates himself left no written word, and aside from the profound statements in regard to law and justice and the nature of society

[1] "Socrates became the first to raise the problem of universal definitions." Aristotle, *Metaphysics*, Bk. XIII, chap. iv, p. 1078 b., translated by W. D. Ross. He "gave the impulse to this theory." *Ibid.*, Bk. XIII, chap. ix, p. 1086 b. His view of the universal character of law and justice is further illustrated by his colloquy with Hippias as reported by Xenophon in the *Memorabilia*, 4, 4, 19, in which he attributes to the gods those unwritten laws which men everywhere obey.

[2] Lines 666–667, translation by Jebb.

[3] Lines 450–460. Aristotle quotes this passage in illustration of the difference between a particular law (ἴδιος νόμος) and the common law (κοινὸς νόμος) which is according to universal nature (κατὰ φύσιν). *Rhet.*, I, 13, § 2, cited by Jebb. In another passage the same extract from the *Antigone* is adduced to illustrate the superiority over written laws (γεγραμμένοι) of equity (τὸ ἐπιεικές), that common (κοινός) law which "ever remains and never changes because it is according to nature" (κατὰ φύσιν γάρ ἐστιν); whereas the written law often changes. *Rhet.*, I, 15, § 6.

In interpreting these identifications by Aristotle of natural with common law it must be borne in mind that Aristotle's particular purpose in the *Rhetoric* is merely to set forth the artifices useful to a pleader. It is the practical effect on a large popular jury that he has in mind and his whole statement is colored by this, but it is none the less significant that he should have thought that such an appeal might secure a popular response. There must have been a fairly wide-spread popular acceptance of these views if it was ever advisable to appeal to them in addressing a jury of some hundreds of Athenians. The pleader, of course, should make his appeal to ideas which were the direct contrary where his case required it.

[4] Probably our most conclusive evidence of this is to be found in the *Apology*, the *Crito*, and the *Phædo* of Plato, together with the *Memorabilia* of Xenophon; in which the trial and death of Socrates are described. For him it was not permissible to evade the penalties even of a bad law if enacted by duly constituted authority, but if it were an evil law, a good man might not obey it with a safe conscience. It was the same with Sophocles. Antigone suffered death for her breach of Creon's decree, but her punishment was light compared with his.

and the state ascribed to him in the Platonic dialogues, surviving
evidence would rather lead us to think him less concerned with the
political side of human conduct than with the merely ethical; yet
there are grounds for the view that it was no other than he who
laid the broad foundations upon which the great political structures
of Plato and Aristotle were built. In defense of the Sophists
Grote has pointed out [1] that the debt owed them by Socrates was
very great. In a sense it was by a reliance on their own principles
that he was able to go beyond them, and it is common knowledge
that his enemies applied the very name of Sophist to him. In
fact it seems that he accepted the dictum of Protagoras that man
is the measure of all things, but that for him it was *man* rather
than *men*.[2] While admitting the right of self-consciousness to be
heard, its evidence was valid only because it was a consciousness
common to mankind. To the skeptical Sophist what each man
sees is the only truth possible for him, and there can be no norm
by which we can decide between this and its opposite when seen
by another. For to him not only is man the measure of all things,
but each man is the only measure.

It was the task of Socrates, as Schwegler says, through this
principle of free-will and self-consciousness to recover for mankind
by the same means by which the Sophists had destroyed it, a
veritable world of objective thought, "to set in the place of empirical subjectivity absolute or ideal subjectivity, objective will, and
rational thought." [3] This meant to reassert the positive value
and universal application of human ideas of justice and law, on
the evidence of human reason.

If such were indeed the real contribution of Socrates to the development of political thought there could in his day scarcely have
been a greater. We may be unable, on the available evidence, fully
to share the certitude of Schwegler on these points, or further to
believe that Socrates — or indeed even Plato and Aristotle after him
— entirely succeeded in overcoming the persistent dualism of the
knower and the known; but their mighty effort to do so must stand
for all time among the greatest achievements of the mind of man.

---

[1] *History of Greece*, chap. 67.

[2] Aristotle, who on this matter seems to follow Socrates and Plato, says that it is the distinctive mark of the virtuous man that he has the power of seeing the truth in all cases,
because he is, as it were, the standard and measure of things. *Eth. Nic.*, Book III,
p. 1113 a. See also *Ibid.*, Bk. X, p. 1176 a.

[3] *History of Philosophy*, translated by Stirling, p. 38.

Even in this, however, we shall probably never be able to estimate with any approach to certainty how much belongs to Socrates
himself and how much we must ascribe to his reporter and greatest
disciple; and in such circumstances it would seem better to leave
the master and pass at once in greater detail to the political thought
of the Platonic dialogues, laying aside the much disputed and
apparently insoluble problem of how many of the political ideas of
the Platonic Socrates were really those of Socrates himself and
how many were first formulated by Plato.

CHAPTER II

PLATO

If a correct interpretation of Plato's political thought depended solely on a close translation from Greek into English our problem would be much simpler than it is. We have no choice now but to use our own words in trying to express Plato's thought, but those words — with whatever care we choose them — can seldom give better than a distorted image of Plato's real conceptions. Try as we may we cannot wholly shake from them the accretion of centuries gathered since Plato's time in a political environment far different from his. "Politics" or "political" must mean for us something very different from his *politike* or *politikos*.

To explain such terms in our own words, it is not enough, then, to give the nearest equivalent, nor even to reconstruct in our minds the political life of the men of the past : we must add an appreciation of the subtle differences that time has made between our words and theirs, and make constant allowance for these. We must qualify at every turn, and paraphrase as well as mere translation will often be necessary.

One general tendency may be seen in these historical changes of meaning. Our terms are usually more differentiated than Plato's. "Political," for example, was for him about what "social" is for us, while our "political" has become so narrow in its meaning that he would have understood it only with the greatest difficulty. One could hardly imagine a stranger thing than a translation such as Plato might have made of *The Man versus the State*, unless it were a translation of the *Republic* by Herbert Spencer.

The breadth of Plato's politics was great enough to include our sociology as well as our "politics," much of our ethics, and even some of our theology. Competition with the family, the church, the trade union — to say nothing of international associations — has left our state a shrunken thing compared with Plato's — shrunken in its sphere but not in its size, or its power — and

22

"politics" has dwindled with it till it now includes no more than a few of the many phases of the "good life" that for Plato and Aristotle combined to require the legislator's care. To ignore these changes is to misunderstand and to misrepresent the real meaning of Plato. So when he and Aristotle speak of "the constitution" of a state, they still have a right to call it "a life," for it is rightly enough to them the state's whole being. From it any particular state derives all its distinctive character. It is the state's constitution in the sense in which we speak of a man's constitution — that condition of his whole body, which makes him physically what he is. But the constitution of our body politic we have so whittled away that little remains of it beyond a few bits of governmental machinery that we can change overnight without any serious modification of that good life for which men have always striven. In consequence, we have lost in theory if not in practice much of Plato's horror of *stasis* (στάσις), or division within a state, that lack of coördination which brings revolution and change of constitution in its train. Our politics in short are more progressive and less static than his; and largely because our changes in political form and constitutions are more superficial. We no longer conceive of them as going to the very roots of all social life as they did for the ancient world. It is all a part of this same progressive narrowing of political life and political conceptions which more than anything else makes the modern political world different from Plato's world and in like measure renders his world more difficult for us to comprehend.

These are difficulties affecting somewhat our reading of all ancient political writers; for Plato in particular a few added preliminaries would seem necessary before we can hope to enter into his full meaning. One is the probable effect upon his thought of the actual political developments of his time, another is the form and probable order of those of his dialogues most important for politics.

The life of Plato, an Athenian of aristocratic family (B.C. 428–347), covers one of the most important and most troubled periods in Greek history. Born in the midst of the Peloponnesian war, he was old enough to remember the rule of the Four Hundred at Athens, was a grown man at the war's disastrous end and the rule of the Thirty which ensued, was witness of the almost continuous wars and alliances of the years following, and before his death must have been aware of the lengthening shadow of Macedon. To this must be added his unfortunate experience of tyranny at Syracuse, after which, if Diogenes Laertius is to be believed, he took no active part in politics because the people of Athens had adopted a form of government of which he could not approve.[1] There are few direct references to these stirring events in his dialogues, but the political instability they indicate must have made a deep impression upon his mind, and probably contributed to his marked aversion to political divisions within a state and to his well-known dislike of both democracy and tyranny, on the one hand, and on the other to his inclination toward the sterner discipline of a state like Sparta and of the form of government most likely to perpetuate it; though, like Aristotle, he would have preferred to see this discipline directed to an end less exclusively war-like than Sparta's.

The almost endless disputes concerning the order, the relation, and the authenticity of the Platonic dialogues fortunately need not detain us long, for, while there is scarcely one of the dialogues which does not help to make clearer Plato's political views, these views may be indicated briefly, as they must be here, by special reference to the three of his dialogues most directly concerned with political life and conduct, the *Republic*, *Politicus*, and *Laws*; and fortunately in regard to these less uncertainty exists than in the case of some others. The authenticity of the *Republic*, Plato's greatest work, rests on contemporary evidence and is not questioned. It evidently comes from the period of his greatest intellectual power. A like authenticity may be granted for the *Laws*, the work of his old age and his last and largest dialogue, for Aristotle's direct testimony is scarcely questionable though it has been questioned. The *Politicus* is more doubtful, but probably came also from Plato's own pen, and apparently in the interval between the *Republic* and the *Laws*.[2]

Even if we confine our special attention to these three dialogues

---

[1] In the seventh of the surviving letters ascribed to Plato, the same aversion is expressed to the actual political conditions in Athens. On the authenticity of Plato's letters see R. Hackforth, *The Authorship of the Platonic Epistles*, 1913.

[2] Treatment of these points and of the interrelation of the dialogues is found in many places, notably in Zeller's *Plato and the Older Academy* (English translation) chaps. 2–4; in Grote's *Plato*, I, chaps. iv–vi; and in *Die genetische Entwickelung der platonischen Philosophie* by Franz Susemihl. The question of the effect upon Plato's meaning of the dialectical method he employed is not without importance, but too technical for treatment here. A discussion of it will be found in *Platon*, by U. von Wilamowitz-Moellendorff, vol. ii, chap. ii (1919); or in Grote's *Plato*, vol. i, pp. 94–112 (3d ed., 1875).

alone, however, it will be evident that they present somewhat different points of view in regard to the state, and it has been further maintained that these points are not consistent with each other but represent different periods of the author's mental growth, the *Republic* expressing an earlier enthusiasm for an ideal which later experience of actual conditions destroyed and replaced by the system found in the *Laws*, the work of a disillusioned old man. More recent students of Plato have generally been unable to accept Schleiermacher's view that all the dialogues are but parts of a general and consistent plan which existed from the first in Plato's mind; but a careful reading of the *Laws* would seem to make equally impossible this opposite view that the Plato of the *Republic* and the Plato of the *Laws* are men with essentially conflicting views about the state. Scattered through the later work may be found many statements that indicate the same ideal as in the earlier years, though the immediate purpose is a more practical one. It is true, such things as the community of wives and children are not repeated there though referred to with emphatic approval, but they were not proposed even in the *Republic* as a measure to be adopted in any possible state, and it seems to be a possible state that the *Laws* have in mind, as the *Republic* has not.[1] All things considered it seems truer to say that Plato's essential ideals never radically changed and that all his writings express with varying emphasis a general conception of politics whose main characteristics remain the same from the beginning to the end.

It is now time to try to set forth briefly what these characteristics are. To do so it is necessary to recall Plato's settled belief in the reality of the external world and its knowability and his conception of the nature of our knowledge of it. Through the causation of the founder of the universe, its uncaused cause, "the world

[1] "Whether there is now, or ever will be, this communion of women and children and of property, in which the private and individual is altogether banished from life, and things which are by nature private, such as eyes and ears and hands, have become common, and in some way see and hear and act in common, and all men express praise and blame, and feel joy and sorrow, on the same occasions, and the laws unite the city to the utmost, — whether all this is possible or not, I say that no man, acting upon any other principle, will ever constitute a state more exalted in virtue, or truer or better than this. Such a state, whether inhabited by gods or sons of gods, will make them blessed who dwell therein; and therefore to this we are to look for the pattern of the state, and to cling to this, and, as far as possible, to seek for one which is like this. The state which we have now in hand, when created, will be nearest immortality in the next degree; and, after that, by the grace of God, we will complete the third one. And, we will begin by speaking of the nature and origin of the second." (*Laws*, p. 739, Jowett's translation.)

became a living soul and truly rational," [1] and "the pattern of the universe contains in itself all intelligible beings." [2]

Man, therefore, is rational and his mind is but a part of the pattern of a rational world. What he may know of that world then is his soul's recognition of its own nature in the world about him. Sight is this recognition through the eye of our likeness to the world without — "there is a unison, and one body is formed by natural affinity," [3] "the eye and the appropriate object meet together and give birth to whiteness." [4] This sight was given us "that we might behold the courses of intelligence in the heaven, and apply them to the courses of our own intelligence which are akin to them, the unperturbed to the perturbed; and that we, learning them and being partakers of the true computations of nature, might imitate the absolutely unerring courses of God and regulate our own vagaries." [5] This knowledge is the recognition of the mind without by the mind within, "but mind is shared only by the gods and by very few men." [6] Few have seen the light and few eyes can bear it. These few are the natural rulers of mankind. Their rule is universal reason and it is higher than any fixed laws. The burden of the *Gorgias* is a defence of this view against the skepticism of the Sophists. Here appears the basis for Plato's unshaken conviction — shared by Aristotle — that men are by nature unequal, and of many other parts of his political faith besides. It is this theory of knowledge that alone explains the statement attributed to Socrates, that he cannot impart knowledge to another but only bring it to birth by his dialectic. It also makes clear the practical and active character of that knowledge, something far wider and deeper than the mere intellectual acquisition we usually mean, an active principle of virtuous action; and it accounts for the great part that education plays in the political scheme of Plato, and of Aristotle after him, and the character of that education. But it is noteworthy that, with all that environment and education may do, Plato believes as fixedly in rule by the "elect" as Calvin did in their exclusive salvation.

It is this essential inequality mainly that necessitates coercive government and keeps Plato's ideal from approximating that of the modern anarchistic idealist, with whom he has some points in common. He believes that a régime of law is necessary perhaps

---

[1] *Timaeus*, p. 30.   [3] *Ibid.*, p. 45.   [5] *Timaeus*, p. 47.
[2] *Ibid.*   [4] *Theaetetus*, p. 156.   [6] *Ibid.*, p. 51.

but certainly not preferable.[1] It is only the inferiority of the bulk of mankind to the true philosopher which imposes upon the latter the stern necessity of restraining these inferiors by rules imposed from without instead of leaving them as philosophers might safely be left to be governed by the law within. Such rules as these will be coercive laws for the vulgar many, but for the true philosopher they will be merely the dictates of his own reason. The result is aristocracy, an aristocracy of wisdom, government by philosopher kings. And in a very real sense Plato regarded these as kings *legibus soluti*, if the highest ideal of government were to be attained. For laws by their very definition are *general* rules: their generality is at once their essence and their main defect, because generality implies an average, and such rules can never meet the exceptions that are always arising, as can the unfettered discretion of an all-wise ruler. At best these rigid rules are a rough make-shift far inferior to the flexibility of that wisdom which alone meets the test of true justice, by rendering unerringly to *every* man *his* due, not the due of some "average man" who never existed nor can exist. For Plato, therefore, discretion if it is wise discretion is higher than the straight-jacket of the law, and it is only because all are not wise that laws are necessary. It is also because some are wiser than others that the discretion of the wiser must perforce become law for the less wise and aristocracy result. In a world of philosophers, we might assume that neither laws nor government would be needed. But Plato even in his most ideal moments cannot believe all men capable of this wisdom. There will always be some who must be content with the dim shadow of the truth on the prison-wall of their cave. Their own greatest good will be to be ruled at the discretion of the few who have seen the light. Only where these fail us must we have recourse to that second-best, a régime which stretches us all on the Procrustean bed of rigid law. There is nothing anywhere in Plato's writings to indicate that he ever gave up the higher ideal of wisdom unlimited, nor anything to prove that he ever believed

[1] In the discussion which follows I attempt to bring together in one account the materials scattered through all three dialogues. I have added references to separate passages usually only where they are found in other dialogues. The summary here given is not intended as a substitute for the reading of the three dialogues in question. It is hoped that it may be a help in understanding them, which it cannot be unless they are read in connection with it. The translations here given are usually those of Jowett's third edition of the *Republic*, though occasionally Davies and Vaughan's is used. For the *Politicus* and the *Laws* I have used Jowett's first edition.

that ideal actually attainable in any state on earth present or future. But attainable or not, this ideal affects all parts of Plato's thought about the state, and it is more important for us here than his more practical proposals.

Law then is wisdom shorn of its wings, but still it is wisdom, for the discretion of the wise from which it proceeds cannot but be founded in universal truth. Hence, with all its inevitable imperfections it is according to nature, and no mere capricious creation of men, varying from place to place, as the Sophists maintained. Thus Plato, while admitting that the rule of law is inferior as an ideal to the unhampered justice of a true philosopher, is led to make it the necessary basis of all good forms of actual government and by its presence or absence to pronounce them good or bad.

Though the art of the true ruler is "superior to law," or, as Plato elsewhere puts it, is in itself his law, the states that are based upon law, even while falling far short of this ideal, are "imitations" of it. Such states are only a "second best," but even this is preferable to the unhampered discretion of an *unwise* man, and after all it is better "to have the laws observed alike by one and all" than to be subject to the personal rule of one who has no knowledge, for the former will at least be "copies" of the wise administration of the true ruler so far as these admit of "being written down from the lips of those who have knowledge," while the discretion of a ruler who has no knowledge though it "imitate the truth," must "always imitate ill." And the sad fact is that the true ruler nowhere actually exists. If he did all must be subject to him. The state as it is is not like a bee-hive. It has no natural head recognized as superior in body and mind, and the many never have a real knowledge of any art. The royal or political art, the highest of all, will never be mastered either by the wealthy or by the mob. Therefore mankind are obliged as a last resort to meet and make laws and endeavor to approach as nearly as they can to the true form of government, and the nearest approach to this true form they can make is to do nothing contrary to their own written laws and natural customs. When the rich do so it is called aristocracy, when they disregard the laws it is oligarchy. In like manner, a king is either one who has wisdom, or one who "imitates" him by ruling according to law. Tyrants are false claimants to the wisdom of the true king, who on the basis of that claim substitute their own appetite or their own advantage for the law. And the rule of the many in the same way may be through law or without it. Even the best of all these are "untrue" forms of government founded on the letter rather than the spirit of true politics and the wonder is that states have been able to endure them without perishing, for any other art than that of government, if built upon such a foundation would be impossible. The lawless forms are infinitely worse. Thus Plato is led to recognize seven forms in all: the perfect but non-existent monarchy of a super-man — "among states what God is among men"; three "imitations" of this ideal form in which law becomes the basis respectively of monarchy, the rule of the few, or government by the many; and three lower forms corresponding to these, but without law. "Then the question comes — which of these untrue forms is least oppressive to live under, though they are all oppressive; and which is the worst of them." Monarchy is at once the best and the worst, the best if limited by law, the worst when a tyranny. The government of a few lies between the two extremes, whether it is according to law or without it, and the rule of the many is too weak to do any great harm or any great good, and is therefore "the worst of all lawful governments, and the best of all lawless ones."

In all this Plato apparently realizes, as Aristotle did, the important distinction between what the latter called legal or particular justice, and the greater whole of which this is but a part, universal justice.[1] In those states that "imitate" the ideal one, those in which the basis of government is law instead of the interest or appetite or ignorance of its rulers, justice is according to law, and it is therefore defective in proportion as that law itself fails in imitating the whole wisdom of an ideal ruler. It is faulty in proportion as the law on which it rests fails by its generality to reach that perfection of art ensured by the wisdom of the true king. But partial and defective as this particular or legal justice must be, it is, none the less, an approximation or an imitation — a "copy," of the true reason that is real and unerring. It is emphatically "according to nature," for it is a part, even though but a little part, of the rational pattern of the universe.

This is the basis of Plato's contention, oftentimes repeated with many variations in several dialogues, against the skeptical attitude

[1] *Nicomachean Ethics*, V, ii (Burnet's ed.). See Appendix I.

of the Sophists and their assertion that law and the justice it creates are after all not things of nature but merely the arbitrary and capricious creations of men, not always for the worthiest ends.

But this contention of Plato concerning the nature and origin of particular justice and of the whole fabric of law upon which it rests, explains them after all only by referring us back to universal justice as the basis of all, and such an explanation can never satisfy the inquiring mind unless this universal justice, the whole of which justice according to law is a part, can itself be justified in nature and reason. This mighty task is the theme of the greatest of all Plato's dialogues, the *Republic*.

If we wish to follow him through it with any success we must first know the meaning of his terms, or at least the chief one, the one usually translated "justice" (δικαιοσύνη). Is Plato after all in the *Republic* really talking about "justice"? So it is said and thus he has been translated. But by "justice" we nowadays usually mean no more than particular justice; the word's only meaning is a legal meaning, the meaning of Simonides which Plato expressly rejects at the opening of the dialogue — to render to each his due, an anticipation of Ulpian that gives one only what is legally his and rises no higher than to recompense evil with evil. But it is of *universal* justice that Plato is speaking now. He goes far beyond the law and has little patience with the "narrow, keen, little legal mind," [1] that would limit the moral life of man to the mere observance of legal rules. He rises above Aristotle, and even anticipates Christ in advocating the recompense of evil with good. *Dikaiosyne* would mean "righteousness" rather than mere "justice" if the former of these two words only had less of a theological flavor and of the negative implication of "sinlessness" that this involves. It properly includes within it "the whole duty of man," and no single English word conveys its whole meaning.

Plato does not minimize the difficulty of the task he has set for himself. He knows his thesis is opposed by the majority of men, and he fully recognizes the force of the arguments against it. In fact no one has ever stated those arguments with greater force and cogency than he himself has done. And he labored under a further difficulty of which his successors in later ages were free: there was no accepted revelation or revered tradition or writing to which he could appeal as authority for his views, but on the

[1] *Theaetetus*, p. 175.

contrary, in the highest authority there was, the poets, the life of the gods and their relations to each other and to men at every turn appeared to refute his whole argument.

It is this very difficulty perhaps that leads him to despair of winning assent without the aid of allegory and homely illustration, both favorite devices of his, and it is one of these illustrations that has been the occasion of the assumption so often made that this whole dialogue's main purpose was the mere delineation of the "government" of a state as it should be, the creation of an Utopia.

The famous figure of the large and the small letters is thoroughly in keeping with his usual method of argument and he uses this very figure in slightly different forms more than once in other dialogues. His opponents are sometimes made to object to this general method of procedure and to complain of his appealing "to the popular and vulgar notions of right," [1] of "always talking of cobblers and fullers and cooks and doctors, as if this had to do with our argument," [2] of continually "arguing about little and unworthy questions." [3] To one of these complaints Socrates drily answers, "I envy you, Callicles, for having been initiated in the great mysteries before you were initiated into the little." [4] For in reality it is the little that oftentimes alone can explain the great, provided the two are not different; and it is precisely "the greatest and noblest truths" with "no outward image of themselves visible to man," which are most in need of this mode of explanation, because "there is always less difficulty in fixing the mind on small matters than on great." [5]

Plato knows full well that the deepest truths of existence are beyond the power of the human mind to demonstrate. For such a demonstration must contain not merely the explanation of the facts taught us by experience; it must explain all the facts of all possible experience: it must exclude all alternative explanations, and the latter cannot be done because in our proof we can never go beyond actual and possibly incomplete experience itself. All we can do, therefore, is to exhibit as fully as possible the conformity of these great truths with actual experience and thus secure their *recognition* as the most probable explanation of the riddle of life and being, and for the purpose allegory and illustration are often more effective than a more rigorous deductive process, the more so since

[1] *Gorgias*, p. 482.
[2] *Ibid.*, p. 491.
[3] *Ibid.*, p. 497.
[4] *Ibid.*
[5] *Politicus*, pp. 285–286.

the bulk of mankind are destined never to see more than the dim shadow of truth upon the wall of their prison-house. "The higher ideas," Plato tells us, can therefore "hardly be set forth except through the medium of examples," and as with children learning to read, "Will not the best and easiest way of guiding them to the letters which they do not as yet know, be to refer them to the same letters in the words which they know, and to compare these with the letters which as yet they do not know, and show them that they are the same, and have the same character in the different combinations . . . ?" [1]

So in investigating "the real nature of justice and injustice," an investigation demanding "a keen sight," it may be better to adopt such a method as this: "Suppose we had been ordered to read small writing at a distance, not having very good eye-sight, and that one of us discovered that *the same writing* was to be found somewhere else in larger letters, and upon a larger space, we should have looked upon it as a piece of luck, I imagine, that we could read the latter first, and then examine the smaller, and observe whether the two were alike." But "We speak of justice as residing in the individual mind, and as residing also in an entire city, do we not?" "Well, a city is larger than one man." Then . . . Perhaps it "may exist in larger proportions in the greater subject, and thus be easier to discover: so, if you please, let us first investigate its character in cities; afterwards let us apply the same inquiry to the individual, looking for the counterpart of the greater as it exists in the form of the less." [2]

It must be evident that such a method of impressing upon the hearer or reader the reality of these "greatest and noblest truths which have no outward images of themselves visible to man" and are therefore probably not susceptible of complete demonstration, can be successful only where the more familiar letters actually do spell the very same words as the less familiar ones whose inner hidden meaning is the real object of the whole search. If these more familiar letters more easily seen in man's collective life in the state are in reality nothing more than a mere "analogy" to his inmost individual life, or only a parallel to it, then the whole search is hopeless, the figure meaningless, and the method entirely pointless; for an analogy or a parallel, as this has sometimes been called, implies only a comparison of two similar but different things,

[1] *Politicus*, pp. 277-278.   [2] *Republic*, pp. 368-369.

and it proves but little. This remarkable figure is far deeper and more pregnant in meaning than that, far more helpful, and infinitely more convincing, just because Plato meant by it no analogy, no parallel, but an actual identity. The large letters are *"the same writing"* as the small ones; each is a partial aspect of the same great whole; they both spell the same universal principles of life and conduct that control both the inward activity of the individual and his outward activity in dealings with others in the state; politics is but ethics "writ large"; they are not two distinct arts but one. They differ only in the fact that the great principles of action may be more easily detected in our outward public actions than in the inner recesses of the individual soul. Plato would have been the very last to subscribe to that political creed common in our own day and not unknown to his, which allows "reasons of state" to override the ordinary rules of morality and concedes to the state a moral code less rigorous than the one which governs the actions of private men.

And so the meaning of the great dialogue becomes manifest. It is no description of an Utopia, its primary purpose is not the delineation of a state at all, actual or ideal; it is no treatise on "politics" as we narrowly define that term : it is a search for the fundamental principles of all human conduct; concerned with "justice," it is true, but Plato's "justice" is the "whole duty of man." "Its name might suggest that it was a book of political philosophy, but we very soon find that it is rather a book of moral philosophy." Its "justice" is in reality, as Aristotle later said, "the whole of virtue shown in our dealings with others." "It is a book about human life and the human soul or human nature, and the real question in it is, as Plato says, how to live best." [1]

To say this, however, is not to deprive it of "political" value nor to render it less important for the history of political thought. Thus to understand it adds to that value, for it enables us not only to enter into the heart of the ancient view of social and political life : it helps us better to appreciate the deepest principles from which that life must spring as long as man endures. And to Plato that life, whether viewed in the individual or in the state, always presented itself as an art. It was active, not passive. The art of governing and the art of obeying, or, as Aristotle put it,

[1] Nettleship, *Lectures on the Republic of Plato*, pp. 4–5, citing Aristotle's definition of "justice" from *Eth. Nic.* V, 1, 15 and 20.

of "ruling and being ruled in turn" is an active principle of the soul. And so Plato not inaptly illustrates this by the other humbler arts of the shepherd, or the physician, or the navigator, and his frequent reference to such "little and unworthy questions" of which his opponents complained has a value and a significance likely to be lost on us who too often look on virtue as the mere avoidance of evil. Plato looked deeper and saw that true virtue means much more than that. To him it is, as Nettleship finely says, "that quality in an agent in virtue of which it does its particular work well," [1] and "wisdom" is "a specific form of virtue"; it also is active, not merely passive, and the wise man is he "who is master of the art of living." [2]

Such an art is not complete when we merely refrain from interfering with the appropriate acts of others. That we must do, but not leave undone our far more important task, assigned us by nature, of fulfilling to the utmost, by thought and action, by training and effort, those capacities for self-realization and for public service alike with which we are endowed. If living is an art, we must become the best artists we can. This is virtue, and "political" virtue is a large part of it. The "cobblers and fullers and cooks and doctors" are not so much beside the point after all. We in all our life, social and individual, should imitate in the sphere allotted us, the perfection the artisan achieves in the smaller sphere his capacities have assigned to him, and by the same means of ceaseless training and effort, by knowing what our true sphere is and achieving the highest possibilities it affords. And this can be done only if we remain strictly within that sphere, only if we know our own capacity and confine ourselves to our own peculiar task, and in all our dealings with others refrain from any interference with theirs. That state, then, is "just" in which each class does its own proper work, "and each of us also, if his inward faculties do severally their proper work, will, in virtue of that, be a just man, and a doer of his proper work." [3]

The *Republic* is concerned, first with establishing this general principle, and second, in determining, in the larger letters of the state, how this proper work is to be discovered and how best performed.

To accomplish the first of these purposes, the dialogue begins, as do most of Plato's dialogues, with an examination of current

[1] *Op. cit.*, p. 35.   [2] *Ibid.*   [3] *Republic*, p. 441.

but inadequate interpretations of the matters under discussion.
He examines the legalistic conception of justice drawn from
Simonides and finds it wanting, he dissects the Sophist view as
set forth by Thrasymachus and pronounces it vicious, and thus
far the familiar method of dialectic is sufficient to win an easy victory over his opponents. But the victory is too easy. All this
is child's play compared with what is to follow. Merely to disprove these obviously incomplete or erroneous conceptions can
never fully satisfy the earnest inquirer after the real principles of
the conduct of life. So here Glaucon and Adeimantus interpose
and demand a positive answer to the questions, what is justice,
and why should we practice it? Thrasymachus may be wrong
but a view not unlike his is the one usually practiced, it is taught
to the young, it seems even to actuate the gods if the poets are to
be trusted. These facts impose the burden upon any one disputing such a view not alone of proving that it is inadequate or
degrading: he must point the way to a view that is better and
truer. *Why* is it really preferable to suffer injustice rather than to
do it? *Why* is a reputation for justice, even if gained by actual
injustice not as great a good to be sought for as justice itself,
especially when the latter seems so often in life to bring in its train
nothing but suffering and misery? Is justice inherently so much
better than injustice that it is its own sufficient reward; or can
it be shown, in face of the apparent lessons of experience to the
contrary, that men are more truly blessed as a result of practicing
it? It is here that the real difficulty first appears, the difficulty,
if not the impossibility of demonstrating the reality of one of those
great truths which "have no outward images of themselves visible
to men." So it is at this point that Socrates in his attempt to do
so is forced to employ the figure of the letters, and the dialogue
for the first time becomes distinctly "political" in our narrower
sense.

The ideal is accordingly constructed in the "large letters" of a
city, composed, it is true, of materials familiar to any dweller in
the Greek city-state: its slaves, its partially and its fully qualified
citizens, its artisans, its men of war and of leisure, etc.; but one
in which the interrelations of these classes are assumed to be
regulated by principles of justice far higher than those found in
any actual state. If we can but see how these principles are applied
on this larger scale, we may have some hope of discovering some-

thing of "justice" in itself and the result of its operation on the lives of men.

Surprise has been expressed that Plato in this ideal construction should ignore to the extent he does all social and economic classes but the highest. It would be strange indeed to do this, if here, as is sometimes thought, he were giving a rounded description of an ideal commonwealth. But the strangeness vanishes if it is borne in mind that it is justice he is really attempting to descry, that this justice is knowledge in action, that such knowledge is possessed by the few, and that it must, therefore, be the governing or regulative power of these few alone in his state which will make that state good, and best secure the ideal life of all classes within it; just as justice in the individual also will preside over and regulate all the other emotions of the soul to secure by their harmony that perfect equilibrium which is found in sanity or health of body and mind alike.

The construction then begins. States first arose, we are told, out of the mutual supply of the needs of men which none could fully supply for himself unaided, and the barest possible notion of a state implies at least four or five such persons each furnishing to the others the food, the shelter, or the covering that together meet the bare necessities of the rudest life. In time the numbers increase, wants begin to multiply, a further division of labor follows with its differing modes of life, money comes into use, exchange is pushed beyond the boundaries, and inter-state relations gradually develop, unfriendly as well as friendly. At this point, therefore, a new class of warriors becomes necessary within the state to protect the rest in their varied pursuits from outside attack. These must fight in defence of the whole state, and of all its civilians, who are disqualified by their peaceful pursuits for defending themselves. Warfare is thus the first form of distinct public service. "It is strange at first sight that war, arising from luxury and self-aggrandisement, should be the point of departure for the introduction of the guardian class, and therefore of government and conscious morality. But both the theory of natural selection and the lessons of history seem to show that it is war which makes a nation." [1] The warriors, therefore, or "guardians" (φύλακες)

---

[1] Bosanquet, *A Companion to Plato's Republic*, p. 85, ". . . It is significant that it was from the common bond of mutual defence and the maintenance of a common camp of refuge, in an age of violence, that the Greek city-state and its citizens took their eventual nomenclature." J. L. Myres, *The Political Ideas of the Greeks*, p. 72. There is a sharp

are the first public servants; and they must devote themselves
entirely to this service just as all other classes must refrain from it
wholly, because each class will be more effective in doing the particular task in the general economy of the state for which it is
fitted by nature, if it confines itself to that task alone and is never
permitted to go beyond it. When, therefore, any youths in any
class of the people are found with a natural genius for warlike pursuits, they are to be enrolled among the guardians to be trained
throughout their whole lives for the service of the state alone, in
singleness of purpose to lay aside all thought of private gain or
even of a private life, and to find their highest and only happiness
in the full performance of their own special task, at once the
highest and the most exacting of all tasks, because it exists for the
sake of all the others. This is no doubt in large part a Spartan
ideal, but of a greatly idealized Sparta. The guardians are to be
the watch-dogs of the state, they must be enrolled from among
those whose traits are those of a good watch-dog, and their training
must be such as will develop these traits to the utmost. Like a
good dog they should be "dangerous to their enemies and gentle
to their friends," of "great spirit" but also of "gentle nature,"
and if either of these qualities be lacking they will be no true
guardians. Without courage they cannot protect the state, without gentleness, their power — for they must be stronger than all
the rest of the citizens — will degenerate into license and they
become "savage tyrants instead of friends and allies," no longer
guardians or watch-dogs, but wolves which "turn upon the sheep
and rend them."

Such a combination of gentleness and courage is rare, if not
impossible. A good guardian must "unite in himself philosophy
and spirit and swiftness and strength," and when these qualities
are found in this rare combination they must be strengthened in
every way by environment and education, lest "want of discipline
or hunger, or some evil habit or other" turn those who are the
stronger into wolves instead of watch-dogs, into tyrants instead
of kings, who for lack of true philosophy, with Thrasymachus and
the Sophists, would substitute the interest and advantage of the

criticism of this statement of Plato concerning the beginning of the state in Aristotle's
Politics, Bk. 6 (or 4 according to the older arrangement), chap. iv. He objects because Plato
omits in his enumeration of the necessary members in the primitive state the military and
administrative classes, and brings them in only at a late stage of the development. Aristotle
seems to imply that they must have been present from the very beginning.

stronger for the higher end always in the eye of the real physician
or shepherd or ruler, the interest of those committed to his care,
which is justice or righteousness in its only true sense.

The life of such a guardian must then be a life of philosophy, of
self-sacrifice, and even of asceticism, though an asceticism far
different from the type familiar in the Middle Ages. It will
require an inner spring of thought or action no less compelling
than that of the medieval mystic, and its full accomplishment will
necessitate a discipline no less rigorous than his. It is to this
discipline that the education of Plato's guardians is directed, and
the good life of the whole state will depend upon its thoroughness,
for the state will be what these guardians make it, its ideals will
be theirs. The other classes will be necessary to the life of the
state, this class alone can make that life good, for Plato believed
as strongly as Aristotle that the ruling class *is* the state. From
these considerations it becomes easier to see why the education of
the guardians alone absorbs practically the whole of Plato's attention, and why that education takes the form it does. In justice
to him it must also be borne constantly in mind that the state in
which it is found is an ideal one only. "Until kings are philosophers, or philosophers are kings, cities will never cease from ill:
no, nor the human race; nor will our ideal polity ever come into
being."

Almost the whole of the second and third books of the *Republic*
are taken up with the details of the education the guardians are
to receive.[1] But for the purpose intended environment and habit-
uation were no less important to Plato in the training of the
guardians than the positive forces of education; they must "be
such as will neither impair their virtue as guardians, nor tempt
them to prey upon the other citizens." Hence the most criticised
of all Plato's proposals, the community of goods and of wives and
children, described in detail in book five of the *Republic*.

In the first place, it should be noted that Plato in the *Republic*
is careful to exclude the discussion of the *possibility* of this provision,[2] and in the *Laws* it is reasserted as an ideal but not actually
incorporated in the state there set up.[3] It is merely a part of
those larger letters in which the nature of justice may perhaps be

---

[1] These should be read entire. A fine account of Plato's education for government is
given by R. L. Nettleship, *The Theory of Education in Plato's Republic*, in *Hellenica*, edited
by E. Abbott, p. 67 ff.

[2] P 458.   [3] *Ante*, p. 25, note 1.

discovered; an ideal only, admittedly existing nowhere and not proposed as an actual provision for any state present or future; nothing in fact but a necessary prerequisite, in "the best-ordered State in which the greatest number of persons apply the terms 'mine' and 'not mine' in the same way to the same thing," to the attainment of a justice that can only be truly appreciated and secured in a state where, if "any one of the citizens experiences any good or evil, the whole state will make his case their own." In short, it is to Plato only a means to the realization of that unity and harmony which are as necessary for the good life of a political community as they are for the healthful moral life of any man.

Aristotle, in his famous criticism of this provision, is not as much concerned as are most modern critics with its supposed immoral character or its ill economic results. His objections are aimed chiefly at the sort of unity obtainable by such means as this. To him the state is or ought to be "a plurality which should be united and made into a community by education." [1] He insists as strongly as Plato upon the necessity for unity. A whole there must be but it must be one consisting of reciprocal parts, it is the interaction of these parts alone that can ever in any real sense unite them, and there can be no such interaction if all the parts are exactly alike, for then there would be no lack in any that another need supply. Hands and feet and head are parts of a living body in large measure just because they are not identical. That body has a truer unity than a pile of exactly uniform bricks. In fact, such identity as the latter makes true unity impossible, and Plato's is in reality nothing but dead uniformity; the varied tones of the harmony have sunk into a dreary unison.

Aristotle's other criticisms are less fundamental and seem to be based in part on a failure fully to consider Plato's chief purpose in his ideal construction. This one goes to the very heart of the whole argument, and is for that reason far more significant and more penetrating than most subsequent objections. The latter too often ignore Plato's real purpose in the whole argument and thus overlook the fact that his was but an ideal "laid up in Heaven." [2]

[1] *Politics*, II, 5.
[2] In saying this I am not unmindful of Plato's arguments at p. 472 ff. of the *Republic* designed to show the practical nature of his great ideal. His main purpose was a practical one, the positive inculcation of virtue. But in showing that his ideal is practical, that it may and should affect our life and actions, he does not mean to say that every part of his ideal republic may be or should be put into actual use in any state that ever has existed or ever can exist upon earth.

An equal cause of misconception and hence of injustice to Plato is the identification of his communism with the particular modern economic communism developed in greater part only since the Industrial Revolution and as a result of it, an identification made sometimes by the supporters, sometimes by the opponents of modern capitalism. Aristotle objected because Plato's communism left the majority in a state untouched, and thus, by creating two states instead of one, made real unity impossible. He did not overlook the fact, as some modern interpreters have, that this communism affected only the governing minority. Nor is this the only or the most striking of the differences between it and modern economic communism. It was more a communion in deprivation than a community of goods, for the guardians were to have neither gold nor silver, nor lands nor houses; only the bare necessities for their life of war and service to the state were to be furnished them. Neither friends nor enemies of modern communism would be willing to attribute to it any such an ideal. In fact, that ideal came much nearer to that of medieval monasticism than to the goal of modern communism, notwithstanding the inevitable and fundamental differences between a régime designed to produce a class of warriors and statesmen and one whose aim was withdrawal from the evils of this world and the fixing of the mind upon the next.

It was spirit or courage that first marked out the young for enrollment among the guardians, and their education and environment were both to be regulated to foster this spirit and the wisdom which must direct its use and prevent its abuse. But courage and wisdom are two different traits whose distinctness Plato elsewhere recognizes; wisdom more than courage is the growth of age and experience, and government properly belongs directly only to it. This leads to a further differentiation within the class of guardians as a whole between the "elder statesmen," on the one hand, trained by years of war and discipline and now free from the distractions of active service for which their age unfits them, to turn their leisure and their accumulated wisdom to the task of government; and on the other, the younger warriors, still in active military service and only probationers as yet in the highest, the ultimate, and the most exacting of all forms of human endeavor, the just government of the whole state. Something like this is proposed in the *Laws* in the "Nocturnal Council" composed of older men, while the elders are referred to alone in the *Republic* as "governors" (ἄρχοντες), the younger only as "auxiliaries" (ἐπίκουροι).[1]

One of Aristotle's keenest criticisms of this rigid discipline remains to be discussed, and it is the more interesting because Plato seems to have anticipated it in one of the most interesting passages in the *Republic*. Socrates in the *Republic*, says Aristotle, "deprives the guardians of happiness, and says that the legislator ought to make the whole state happy. But the whole cannot be happy unless most, or all, or some of its parts enjoy happiness. In this respect happiness is not like the even principle in numbers, which may exist only in the whole, but in none of the parts; not so happiness. And if the guardians are not happy, who are? Surely not the artisans, or the common people." [2]

Again it is the defective character of Plato's unity to which Aristotle objects. Grote's criticisms, based on his own utilitarian views, are far less fundamental and not nearly so convincing.[3] He holds that Plato's whole political philosophy is self-regarding; that Plato's *eudaimonia* may be fully translated by our word "happiness"; that this happiness is really the main quest of the argument in the *Republic;* and, since the guardians may in no real sense be regarded as "happy," that the whole quest has therefore resulted in complete failure.

But let us see what reply Plato himself makes to such objections. To Grote's more superficial criticism the chief answer occurs at the end of book four, where, after the inherent nature of justice has been found, Plato turns briefly to the correlative question whether it is profitable. Virtue has been found through the larger letters of the state, to be "the health and beauty and well-being of the soul" and vice, its opposite, "the disease and weakness and deformity" of the same; but what is their comparative profitableness? That question has not yet been answered. But here Adeimantus interposes, "The question has now become ridiculous" (γελοῖον), since the real nature of justice and injustice has been disclosed. "When the bodily constitution is gone, life is no longer endurable, though pampered with all kinds of meats and drinks, and having all wealth and all power; and shall we be told that

---

[1] *Republic*, pp. 374 E, 412 B, 414 B. Cf. the notes to these passages in Adam's annotated edition (2 vols. Cambridge, 1902).

[2] *Politics*, II, 5.

[3] *Plato and the Other Companions of Sokrates*, vol. iii, p. 128 ff.

when the very essence of the vital principle is undermined and corrupted, life is still worth having to a man, if only he be allowed to do whatever he likes with the single exception that he is not to acquire justice and virtue, or to escape from injustice and vice; assuming them both to be such as we have described?" "Yes," says Socrates, "the question is, as you say, ridiculous." [1]

"Our opponent is thinking of peasants at a festival, who are enjoying a life of revelry, not of citizens who are doing their duty to the State. But, if so we mean different things, and he is speaking of something which is not a State." [2] Was a more trenchant condemnation of the extremes of utilitarian individualism ever put in so few words?

"The question, 'Why should I be moral?' if referred to consequences outside morality, is of course self-contradictory. . . . It now appears . . . that philosophy can only analyse the nature of morality and immorality, and not give external reasons for and against them, but also, that this is enough." [3] Virtue is in fact its own reward. This is one of those "greatest and noblest truths" which "have no outward image of themselves visible to man," and must, therefore, be set forth "through the medium of examples." [4]

Plato's *eudaimonia* is an active principle of the soul, a positive principle of moral action. It means the fullest realization of one's capacity for virtuous life and activity, and its emphasis is upon duty, rather than rights or absence of pain and discomfort. In the full performance of that duty individual man and communities of men will find the truest blessedness, and the highest and only real "happiness." One of the most striking modern parallels to this ideal is found — albeit in terms of Christian theology — in Calvin's Genevan catechism, — "What is the chief end of human life? To know God by whom we have been made men. What reason have you for saying this? Because He created us and placed us in this world that He might in us be glorified. And surely it is just that our life, of which He is the beginning, should be referred to His glory. What is in truth the highest good of man? That itself. Why does this appear to you as the highest good? Because, with it taken away our condition is more unhappy than that of any of the brutes. From this therefore we clearly see that nothing can be more unhappy for man than not to live

[1] P. 445 A–B.
[2] *Republic*, p. 421.
[3] Bosanquet, *op. cit.*, p. 171.
[4] *Ante*, p. 31.

for God. Yes so it is." [1] Grote's criticism of this ideal errs fundamentally in the assumption that Plato's whole philosophy is "self-regarding." To Plato the realization of one's self is not distinguishable from the devotion of one's life to others. The modern antithesis, the antagonism even, of egoism and altruism would have been as utterly meaningless to him as his own noble ideal seems to be to the hedonistic utilitarian.

The far more searching criticism of Aristotle is anticipated by Plato himself in the words of Adeimantus, who objects that the guardians themselves never can be truly happy, posted as they seem to be in the city "like mercenary troops, wholly occupied in garrison duties." To this, says Socrates, we shall reply, "that, even as they are, our guardians may very likely be the happiest of men; but that our aim in founding the State was not the disproportionate happiness of any one class, but the greatest happiness of the whole; we thought that in a State which is ordered with a view to the good of the whole we should be most likely to find justice, and in the ill-ordered State injustice: and, having found them, we might then decide which of the two is the happier. At present, I take it, we are fashioning the happy State, not piecemeal, or with a view of making a few happy citizens, but as a whole. . . . Suppose that we were painting a statue, and some one came up to us and said, Why do you not put the most beautiful colours on the most beautiful parts of the body — the eyes ought to be purple, but you have made them black — to him we might fairly answer, Sir, you would not surely have us beautify the eyes to such a degree that they are no longer eyes; consider rather whether, by giving this and the other features their due proportion, we make the whole beautiful. And so I say to you, do not compel us to assign to the guardians a sort of happiness which will make them anything but guardians." If this were applied to the lower classes in the state it would be bad enough, "but when the guardians of the laws and of the government are only seeming and not real guardians, then see how they turn the State upside down; and, on the other hand they alone have the power of giving order and happiness to the State. We mean our guardians to be true saviours and not destroyers of the State, whereas our opponent is

---

[1] *Catechismus Ecclesiae Genevensis* (1545), J. C. G. Augusti, *Corpus Librorum symbolicorum*, Elberfeld, 1827, pp. 464–465. In form the catechism seems to be modeled after the Socratic dialogue, and shows the influence of Calvin's early humanistic training.

thinking of peasants at a festival, who are enjoying a life of revelry, not of citizens who are doing their duty to the State: But, if so, we mean different things, and he is speaking of something which is not a State.   And therefore we must consider whether in appointing our guardians we would look to their greatest happiness individually, or whether this principle of happiness does not rather reside in the State as a whole." [1]

It is one of the signs of greatness in Plato as it is in Darwin that he never cries down nor tries to evade the most fundamental of the criticisms of his opponents.   In fact he frequently states them with greater force than those opponents themselves, and then meets them squarely, face to face, as best he may.   Thus having anticipated and met these objections, in the remainder of book four, Plato proceeds to the conclusion of the first and positive part of his great argument, the reading of the meaning of justice in the large letters of the good state which has now been constructed, or rather of its governing part, and the application of this justice so found to the individual soul.

This argument may be summarized in brief as follows: The State we have constructed, being rightly ordered, must be perfect — the *societas perfecta* from which political theorists in all ages have deduced the particular principles which they think ought to prevail.   If perfect, it must be perfectly wise, courageous, temperate, and just.   This four-fold enumeration of the moral virtues is assumed to be exhaustive and is the most formal, and from the point of view of modern psychology, far the least convincing of all the steps in Plato's reasoning, but not without significance for all that.   If, then, we can find in our state the first three of these moral virtues, the residue must be that "justice" which we have been seeking so long.   But we do find the first three of these in the state.   The wisdom has been found among those whom we were just now describing as perfect guardians, and the state over which they rule, being constituted according to nature, will be wise.   In like manner, there will be no difficulty in seeing the nature of courage, in discovering the class in whom it resides, or in assuming that they too give to the whole state the character of perfect courage.   Temperance may also be discovered, though not confined like the other two to the ruling class alone, in "the agreement of the naturally superior and inferior as to the rule of

[1] Pp. 420–421.

either" — "a sort of harmony" of all. And so the first three being obvious, the last of the four qualities which make a state virtuous must be justice, if only we could discover what that residue really is. But it has been "tumbling out at our feet" from the very beginning of our inquiry and we have never seen it — "the ultimate cause and condition" of all the others. Have we not found the greatest ruin of the state to be the meddling by one class in the business of another for which it is unfitted by nature? This, then, is injustice; but when the trader, the auxiliary, the guardian each does his own proper work and that alone, that is justice and will make the city just. A state was thought by us to be just when the three classes within it severally did their own business. And the just man, if we regard the idea of justice alone, will be like the just state. We may assume that he has the same principles in his own soul that we found in the state; and he may be rightly described in the same terms, because he is affected in the same manner, for if these qualities are found in the state where could they have come from if not from the individuals composing it? Injustice, then, must be a kind of strife between these three principles — "a meddlesomeness, and interference, and rising up of a part of the soul against the whole, an assertion of unlawful authority, which is made by a rebellious subject against a true prince, of whom he is the natural vassal." So the permanent condition of justice and injustice will be like the conditions of health and disease, being in the soul what health and disease are in the body. "The creation of health is the institution of a natural order and government of one by another in the parts of the body, while the creation of disease is the production of a state of things at variance with this natural order." And is not the creation of justice the institution of a natural order and government of one by another in the parts of the soul, and the creation of injustice the production of a state of things at variance with this natural order? "Then virtue is the health and beauty and well-being of the soul, and vice the disease and weakness and deformity of the same."

This concludes the first part of the investigation. Perfect justice has been found because the state in which it was sought was itself perfect. But its nature ought to appear no less clearly from the character of injustice, its opposite, as it is to be seen in an imperfect, or disordered state. The pathology of an unhealthy state, therefore, becomes the subject of the second part of the dialogue.

There are five forms of the soul, as there are five forms of the state. Virtue is one, but the forms of vice are innumerable. The particular form of the state in which virtue resides, has already been described. It may be called either monarchy or aristocracy, according as the rule is in one or more, but this is a mere matter of form : it will be a good state in either form if the ruler or rulers be trained in virtue and good government in the manner already set forth. The other three forms will all be more or less vitiated, because they will be found to depart in greater or less degree from the perfect model of the true aristocracy and injustice may therefore be found to some extent in them all.

These three lower forms are oligarchy, democracy, and tyranny. But these forms of government and in fact all states are what their citizens are. They grow out of human character and human character grows out of them. "As the government is, such will be the man." Hence, if there be five forms of government there will be five types of men who make them, and if we have been able to understand the soul of the perfect man from his government in the perfect state, we may also study the inferior natures of men through these inferior forms of their government and "the enquiry will then be completed."

Then follows a description, psychological rather than historical, of the gradual degrading of the state and of men, "the successive stages of decline of society and of the soul," as Nettleship happily phrases it. It is a progressive lowering of the ideals of life. First of all, timocracy replaces aristocracy. Honor rather than virtue becomes the supreme end of life and of the state. Then wealth replaces honor, and the oligarchic man, the typical citizen of an oligarchic state, comes to be the miser and the money-maker. Next comes democracy, "a charming form of government full of variety and disorder, and dispensing a sort of equality to equals and unequals alike," a government where freedom is unlimited, where "subjects are like rulers and rulers like subjects," and "everything is managed by the drones." Lastly comes tyranny, the worst form of all, brought in by the excesses of democracy, and the cycle is complete. "The best and justest is also the happiest, and this is he who is the most royal man and king over himself . . . the worst and most unjust man is also the most miserable, and . . . this is he who being the greatest tyrant of himself is also the greatest tyrant of his state."

From all this, Plato's own political preferences become reasonably clear. Aristocracy, whether of one or more is best and most just because it is wisest. Among the rest, tyranny is worst, because lust and passion have completely replaced wisdom, and between them oligarchy and democracy, while less unjust than tyranny, are both debased.

The criticism of democracy is probably the most interesting of all this part of the argument because it indicates Plato's attitude to the general course of political development in his own day in Greece, especially in Athens, and also because of democracy's importance to us in our own time. Democracy, Plato believes, comes as a reaction from oligarchy, and under it insolence is termed breeding, anarchy liberty, waste magnificence, and impudence courage. In such a state "the master fears and flatters his scholars and the scholars despise their masters and tutors; young and old are all alike; and the young man is on a level with the old, and is ready to compete with him in word or deed; and old men condescend to the young and are full of pleasantry and gaiety; they are loth to be thought morose and authoritative, and therefore they adopt the manners of the young." "The last extreme of popular liberty, is when the slave, bought with money, whether male or female, is just as free as his or her purchaser; nor must I forget to tell of the liberty and equality of the two sexes in relation to each other." Even "the horses and asses have a way of marching along with all the rights and dignities of freemen; . . . all things are just ready to burst with liberty." And how sensitive the citizens become! "They chafe impatiently at the least touch of authority, and at length, as you know, they cease to care even for the laws, written or unwritten; they will have no one over them." "Such my friend . . . is the fair and glorious beginning out of which springs tyranny."

There are in this indictment, no doubt, some shrewd thrusts at the existing government in Athens, and elsewhere Plato is even more outspoken.

In the *Politicus* he intimates that if democratic principles were carried to their logical conclusion all the arts must utterly perish beyond recovery and human life, bad enough already, become unendurable.[1] Many persons, he declares in the *Laws*, would say that legislators ought to impose such laws as the mass of the

[1] P. 299.

people will be ready to receive; but this is just as if one were to command gymnastic masters or physicians to treat or cure their patients in an agreeable manner.[1] Democracy, he says elsewhere, and oligarchy and tyranny as well, cannot be called a government at all, for not one of the three exercises a voluntary rule over voluntary subjects; "They may be truly called states of discord, in which the government is voluntary, and the subjects always obey against their will, and have to be coerced; and the ruler fears the subject, and will not, if he can help, allow him to become either noble, or rich, or strong, or valiant, or warlike at all. These two are the causes of almost all evils."[2] The Athenians, he thinks, now have less moderation than in former times;[3] their freedom and absence of all superior authority is greatly inferior to the limited government existing at the time of the Persian wars.[4]

I should like to know, says Socrates, in another dialogue,[5] "whether the Athenians are said to have been made better by Pericles, or, on the contrary, to have been corrupted by him; for I hear that he was the first to give the people pay, and made them idle and cowardly, and encouraged them in the love of talk and of money."[6] "You praise the men who feasted the citizens and satisfied their desires, and people say that they have made the city great, not seeing that the ulcerated and swollen condition of the State is to be attributed to these elder statesmen; for they have filled the city full of harbors and docks and walls and revenues, and all that, and have left no room for justice and temperance. And when the crisis of the disorder comes, the people will blame the advisers of the hour, and applaud Themistocles and Cimon and Pericles, who are the real authors of their calamities."[7]

Scarcely less important for the history of political thought as a whole though possibly less interesting to us today than this acute, albeit unfavorable, description of democracy, is Plato's remarkable picture of the nature of the tyrannical man and of the tyrannical state where his ideals of government have free scope. This is the last stage in human degradation, moral and political, and its delineation in book nine of the *Republic* is one of the most remarkable parts of this master-work of genius, to which no mere summary can do adequate justice.

---

[1] P. 684.   [4] *Ibid.*, p. 698.   [7] *Ibid.*, pp. 518–519.
[2] *Laws*, p. 832. [5] *Gorgias*, p. 515.
[3] *Ibid.*, p. 693. [6] *Ibid.*

In this condemnation of all forms of government that fall short
of the perfection of aristocracy, particularly in the dislike for the
tendency toward democracy to which no political observer in
Greece in Plato's day could shut his eyes especially if he were an
Athenian, Plato seems not to have been alone. Aristotle, as we
shall see, though he qualifies his criticisms more than Plato, is in
general agreement in condemning the excess of democratic liberty
in substituting absolute for proportional equality and the employment of the lot as it was practiced in Athens, and one biassed
writer of the time tells us that "in every country the better class
of the people is adverse to a democracy." [1] "If you want a really
good government," says the same author, "you must first see the
wisest men make laws for the people; and then the good must
punish the bad, and consult for the interests of the commonwealth,
and not permit madmen to offer counsel and harangue and address
the public assemblies. In such an excellent state of things, however, the lower classes (ὁ δῆμος) would soon fall into servitude." [2]

But it is time to turn to the speculations of a greater than this
"old oligarch," whoever he was, and deal with the political philosophy of Aristotle himself.

[1] Ἀθηναίων Πολιτεία, chap. I, § 5. This short treatise, apparently by some member of
the aristocratic party at Athens or by one of the émigrés, was formerly thought by some
to be the work of Xenophon, and it is usually included in editions of his minor works.
[2] Ibid., § 9.

CHAPTER III

ARISTOTLE

The *Politics* of Aristotle, says Zeller, "is the richest treasure that has come down to us from antiquity," and "the greatest contribution to the field of political science that we possess." [1] Of the same book, Dr. A. E. Taylor declares: "No Aristotelian work is quite so commonplace in its handling of a vast subject as the *Politics*." "In truth his interest in these social questions is not of the deepest." [2]

Which shall we believe? Possibly it would be better to defer any answer until we have examined the book itself, and before that can be done to attempt briefly to clear the path so far as we may of a few of the obstacles that stand in the way of an understanding of it. For while there may be a difference of opinion about the importance of the *Politics*, there can be very little concerning its difficulty: it is, if not the most important, by far the most puzzling of the classics of political philosophy. Some of these difficulties have been noticed already, those which are always inherent in the thought and language of men of more than two thousand years ago; but in the case of Aristotle there are still greater hindrances of a special kind which make harder the task of obtaining a complete grasp of his ideas about the state.

First among these is the peculiar form of most of the surviving writings attributed to the pen of Aristotle, the *Politics* included, which often renders it difficult if not impossible to trace the whole course of his argument or even at times to be sure of its outcome. The *Politics*, as well as many others of the Aristotelian writings as they now stand, is full of cross references of an extremely puzzling kind. At times they cite the discussion of a subject which apparently has received no treatment whatever in the text as we have received it, at other times there will appear in what,

---

[1] E. Zeller, *Aristotle and the Earlier Peripatetics*, English translation, vol. ii, p. 288.
[2] *Aristotle*, p. 85.

50

on good evidence seems to be an earlier part of the treatise, a clear reference to a part that now comes later, and the whole book is marked by abrupt changes of the subject, parenthetical statements, and promises of later discussions which are never fulfilled. Some of these references have led some modern editors to discard entirely the order found in the manuscripts of the different parts or "books" into which the treatise had been divided, apparently after Aristotle's death, and it may be said that their true order is still in part no better than a matter of conjecture, though certain points may now be considered as established. It seems probable too that some of the treatises — and the *Politics* is one of these — are unfinished in the form in which we have them, apparently omitting important parts of the discussion, which were never completed, or have been lost; and there are occasionally to be found even statements that seem to be inconsistent with the argument in which they are incorporated or at least out of place there. If to all this it be added that none of the surviving manuscripts of the works of Aristotle most important for his political philosophy are of a date earlier than the twelfth or thirteenth century, and that among these there are so many variants and corruptions that in many cases the true reading can at most be only a matter of conjecture, we may have some conception of the causes of the varying views still held of the real meaning of many of Aristotle's most important political statements.

These extraordinary peculiarities have received many varying explanations in modern times. It has been thought, for instance, that these books are really notes of Aristotle's lectures taken down by his pupils and preserved in the Lyceum, while others think they are the rough notes made by Aristotle himself. Some believe that we have here several series of lectures, originally delivered at different times, and put together at some later period to form consecutive works. Such subsequent alterations, and others of a like kind, some consider to be mainly the work of Aristotle's successors or of their pupils in the Lyceum, while to others they appear more probably to be the result of the strange history of the transmission of the Aristotelian manuscripts and of the changes made by much later editors at Rome or Alexandria. These certainly are grounds enough for all our difficulties and uncertainties, but possibly one or two points may be considered as probably established at least.

It seems safe to say that the form of these writings is somewhat

owing to their connection with Aristotle's actual teaching in the
Lyceum, possibly as students' notes, but far more likely as the
notes of the master himself; and that what we have may be a
patch-work, made up later, composed in part at least of portions
of two or more series of notes for lectures on the same general
subjects but possibly delivered by Aristotle in different years, and
occasionally including parts of separate and more elaborately
polished treatises now lost. One striking fact at least seems to be
established: there were certain works of Aristotle in general
circulation in his own day, but not one of these is to be found among
the ones attributed to him which we now have, with the possible
exception of the "Constitution of Athens," found in Egypt less
than half a century ago. On the other hand, none of the treatises
that pass today as the work of Aristotle, with this one exception,
seem to have been known to his own contemporaries or to the
Greeks after his death, outside the small circle of pupils who may
have studied them in the Lyceum. The most probable explanation
of these strange facts would seem to be that the manuscripts of
the Lyceum by a happy fortune have been preserved to our own
day while the "published" works have been lost.[1]

It is from these writings then, and in such a form, but from the
Politics in particular, that Aristotle's political philosophy must
be drawn, but their full meaning cannot be fully appreciated without some knowledge of the background of the author's life and
mind, and at least a brief consideration of the system of which
the political philosophy was an integral part.

Aristotle was born B.C. 384 in the Thracian peninsula of Chal-
cidice, at Stagira, a city of Greek tradition and culture, of an
influential family, his father being the physician and intimate of
the Macedonian king. From his eighteenth year to his thirty-
seventh, he was a pupil of Plato in the Academy, and this was the
factor most important in the shaping of his philosophy, political
and other. But on Plato's death in 347 B.C. Aristotle withdrew
from Athens not to return for some thirteen years, three of which
were spent at the Macedonian court as tutor to Alexander the
Great, then a boy between thirteen and sixteen years of age.

---

[1] For a valuable discussion of these peculiarities in the surviving works of Aristotle see
Richard Shute, *On the History of the Process by which the Aristotelian Writings arrived at their
Present Form*, Oxford, 1888. A convenient account of the history of their transmission is to
be found in Zeller, *Aristotle and the Earlier Peripatetics*, vol. i, chaps. ii and iii (English translation by Costelloe and Muirhead).

What he accomplished in the twelve years of his second stay in Athens seems almost incredible in extent and importance, for it was then that practically all his surviving works were produced; but in the end he was forced to flee from the city in order, as he said, not to "give the Athenians a second chance of sinning against philosophy," and died soon after in 322.

This life of sixty-two years spanned one of the most important and most disastrous periods in Greek history. Aristotle could easily remember the fall of Sparta and the establishment of the short-lived Theban supremacy at the battle of Leuctra in 371. Shortly before the beginning of his second residence in Athens the battle of Chaeronea had been fought and lost and with it Greek independence in 338, and in 323, only a few months before the close of his own life, had come the news of the death of his former pupil, the great Alexander.

Actual references to these tremendous events are fewer perhaps than we might expect in Aristotle's writings, but between the lines the deep impression they made can often be read. The great days of the Greek city-state were plainly over, as we now know, and as Aristotle knew too, for he frequently laments the degeneracy of the times; but notwithstanding this, his *Politics* seems clearly to have been intended by its author primarily as a Statesman's Manual, a text book [1] for constitution-makers, and the constitutions they are advised there to make — or to patch up — are invariably of the old familiar types. There is no reference to the changes that Aristotle must at times have suspected to be inevitable in Greece, especially after the battle of Chaeronea, no recognition among governments of great territorial states except to condemn them as the result of an Asiatic slavishness, and apparently no feeling whatever that the Greeks as a whole, though the only race capable of virtue or deserving of freedom, should ever achieve a political unity to correspond with their racial integrity. Instead of the latter, Aristotle's preliminary political studies for the most part included a collection and summary statement of the political changes that had occurred and of the political conditions which actually existed in more than one hundred and fifty of the separate little city-states about the Aegean and beyond,[2] though we

---

[1] A. E. Taylor, *Aristotle*, p. 72.

[2] The Ἀθηναίων Πολιτεία is divided into two parts in this way. The statement above is based on the assumptions that the *Constitution of Athens* is one of Aristotle's constitutions and that the rest of the constitutions were probably arranged on the same general plan as

know that he had also extended these investigations to some of the barbarian institutions as well.[1]

His estimate of existing political conditions based on these studies was not high nor was his expectation of their future hopeful. His investigations seemed all too clearly to show that practically all the states of Greece had already drifted or were rapidly drifting, even where they were not being driven, under a mob rule that respected no rights and was bound by no laws, or into the hands of a narrow oligarchy whose will was their only law, forms, both of them, which differed from tyranny itself only in the accident that it was the many or the few rather than one by whom the citizens were arbitrarily misruled.

These political investigations are important for us both for their result and for their method. Their result appears in the qualified political fatalism which Aristotle shares with most of his contemporaries, a view that contrasts strangely with the optimism of nineteenth-century democracy and its cheerful expectation of indefinite human progress,[2] but one that possibly we who have seen the Great War can understand somewhat better than our grandfathers could have done. The method seems so commonplace to us now that we see little to remark in it. It is the method any sound investigator would follow, the collection of all available facts as the first step in his investigation. But Aristotle lived before our days of *questionnaires*, and "surveys," and before the general use or even the recognition of a scientific method. It was he, probably more than any other, who led the way to the application of that method to the facts of political life, though he never thought his task complete as some of our modern collectors of their so-called "data" sometimes appear to do, with the mere gathering together of a mass of unrelated and undigested, if not indigestible, "facts." It is indeed on the application of this method to the state that some modern historians believe to rest Aristotle's chief title to fame as a political philosopher.

It is, says Oncken, in the application to politics of the methods derived from the investigation of nature that "the epoch-making

this single surviving one. The sources of our own knowledge of these constitutions outside the recently-discovered "Constitution of Athens" are indicated and discussed by Zeller, *Aristotle* (English translation), vol. i, p. 101, note. A fine account for English readers of the *Constitution of Athens* is to be found in the *Introduction* to his edition of it by the late Sir J. E. Sandys, London, 2d ed., 1912.

[1] Rehm, *Geschichte der Staatsrechtswissenschaft*, p. 72.
[2] See J. B. Bury, *The Idea of Progress*, London, 1920.

merit" of the *Politics* lies,[1] and it must be the same thing which Sir Frederick Pollock has chiefly in mind when he says it was Aristotle who "made the capital advance of separating ethics from politics," [2] for in almost everything but method Aristotle was in reality as far from separating ethics and politics as Plato before him. "He never contemplates a study of the individual's good apart from politics, the study of the good of the society." [3] Zeller's statement is admirable: "*Ethics* and *Politics* may be said to be related to one another as the pure and the applied part of one and the same science." [4]

If, then, Aristotle's method is so all-important, that method itself must be understood before we may hope to understand its application to politics, and this will unavoidably entail a brief examination of the main lines of Aristotle's philosophical system, particularly in those parts which affect most closely the relations of men in society. For it is the application to man of this method which Aristotle had already successfully applied to the phenomena of nature, and his correlation of the results so obtained with the general system of thought whose main principles he had learned from Plato, that constitute the central problem, the true greatness, and the main difficulty of the Aristotelian political philosophy; and Aristotle was the first resolutely to face the difficult problem of reconciling the facts of a democracy which he did not try to ignore, with a philosophy of justice which utterly condemned the central principle on which that democracy rested, the doctrine of the right of the majority to rule.[5]

It was his biological studies that enabled him to take "the first step" [6] in his solution of this problem. "There is," he says, "a fixed measure of magnitude for a state as well as for all other things, animals, vegetables or instruments." [7]

Not that these are alike in all respects, however, for the sciences that concern some are practical, involving the practical reason, while others are theoretical and fall within the sphere of the theoretical reason. It is essential then to know Aristotle's basis of distinction of these sciences if we are to understand the relation

[1] *Die Staatslehre des Aristoteles*, vol. i, pp. 12–13.
[2] *An Introduction to the History of the Science of Politics*, London, 1900, p. 15.
[3] A. E. Taylor, *Aristotle*, p. 73.
[4] *Aristotle* (English translation), vol. ii, p. 137, note.
[5] H. Rehm, *Geschichte der Staatsrechtswissenschaft*, pp. 60, 61.
[6] *Ibid.*, p. 61.
[7] *Politics*, Bk. IV (VII in the old order), chap. iv.

of politics to either of them. The division he several times makes
is a three-fold one. Sciences are either theoretical, productive, or
practical [1] and politics is one branch of — or rather *is* — the third
of these.

Ethics, says the author of the *Magna Moralia*, is "a branch of
nothing else than state-craft (πολιτική), . . . and as a whole it
seems to me that the subject ought rightly to be called, not Ethics,
but Politics;"[2] and a study of ethics is "a political inquiry,"
Aristotle says, for politics comprehends and makes use of all the
other practical sciences, its end being nothing less than "the true
good of mankind."[3] But it *is* a practical science, and as such
must be distinguished from a productive one, such as building or
sculpture, but above all from pure theory.

This division of the sciences takes us at once into the heart of
Aristotle's philosophical system, for its basis is concerned with
the ends of all human activity, as well as the subject-matter of
the different sciences and the faculties of the mind by which each
is apprehended. Even for an understanding of the politics alone,
a short excursion into metaphysics becomes inevitable.

The end of politics "is not knowledge but action";[4] it "is concerned with nothing so much as with producing a certain character
in the citizens, or in other words, with making them good";[5] but
the end of pure science is knowledge. Politics, therefore, has to
do for its subject-matter with the voluntary actions of men, and
these actions may vary. "Probability is the very guide of life,"
as Bishop Butler said, and there is a sense in which Aristotle would
have agreed. In ethics and politics "we must be content to arrive
at conclusions which are only generally true,"[6] for "of accidents
that are not essential according to our definition there is no demonstrative knowledge."[7] But scientific knowledge, on the other
hand, is not concerned with things even true and real which can
be otherwise than they are.[8] There can be no scientific treatment "of the accidental."[9] Politics, therefore, is concerned with
the contingent, theoretical science only with the absolute and the
invariable.

---

[1] For a discussion of Aristotle's division of the sciences, see Zeller, *Aristotle* (English Translation), vol. i, p. 180 ff.

[2] *Magna Moralia*, Bk. I, chap. i, p. 1181 a–b.

[3] *Ethica Nicomachea*, Bk. I, chap. i.   [5] *Ibid.*, Bk. I, chap. 10.

[4] *Ibid.*   [6] *Ibid.*, Bk. I, chap. 1.

[7] *Analytica Posteriora*, Bk. I, chap. 6, p. 75 a.

[8] *Ibid.*, Bk. I, chap. 33, p. 88 b.   [9] *Metaphysica*, Bk. VI, chap. ii.

But how comes it in the universe that there is this difference between the variable or the accidental with which politics is concerned and the absolute and invariable which alone can be the object of scientific knowledge? It is at this point that Aristotle's biological studies came in to affect his answer, whether that answer applied to physical nature or to the product of man's activity in creation or action. "For just as human creations are the products of art, so living objects are manifestly the products of an analogous cause or principle, not external but internal, derived like the hot and the cold from the environing universe."[1] "Reason forms the starting point, alike in the works of art and in works of nature." Nay, in the works of nature "the good end and the final cause is still more dominant than in works of art."[2] And this nature Aristotle elsewhere defines as nothing but "the genesis of growing things" — "the essence of things which have in themselves as such, a source of movement."[3]

The essential nature of any created thing, then, is the idea implanted in it — the form inextricably imbedded in its matter which is constantly striving to realize itself in that thing's growth, which *is* realized when that growth is complete and its "limit" or term is reached in the full unfolding of the form or idea with which it started, when "becoming" develops into being, and potency grows into full actuality. A thing's end is its nature. This is Aristotle's formula for the universe — the growth of ideas from potency into actuality; and the formula applies to the state as well as to the productions of art or to the works of physical nature. Thus the form of the oak is potentially present in the life of the acorn and determines every stage of the development between, but the true nature of that organism at any stage can best be seen in its full unfolding, at the end of the process. Potency can only be learned through actuality. And in a true sense, therefore, in the sense of its essential being and "knowability," though not, of course, in the order of its progressive development nor even of men's sensuous perception of it, the oak is really prior to the acorn.[4]

[1] *De Partibus Animalium*, Bk. I, chap. i, p. 641 b.
[2] *Ibid.*, p. 639 b.
[3] *Metaphysica*, Bk. I, pp. 1014 b–1015 a.
[4] Aristotle's ideas upon these fundamental questions are illustrated in almost all his works. A few especially important statements are to be found in the following places: (The references to pages are to the great edition of Aristotle's works published by the Prussian Academy, whose paging is indicated in most modern editions and in some translations. The

These things condition the whole of nature and all our knowledge of it, they apply to the heavens above and the earth beneath,
and they are as true of the state as of a hive of bees. As the oak
is prior to the acorn, so the state is prior to the family, Aristotle
says in the *Politics*. But how can it be so, how can we say that
ends are thus realized, when we look about us and see the manifest
abortions, the deformities, the monstrosities, the failures, in nature
and in art and life ? To be specific, what good end could we possibly discover in the development of man's political life toward a
thing so deformed in Aristotle's eyes as the lawless domination of
the vulgar herd over the wise and the virtuous, as it exists in the
later Athenian democracy? The answer lies in the refractory
character of the material. Everything consists of form and
matter. The form is constantly struggling to impress itself upon
the matter, but if the wax be imperfect, then the result also must
be imperfect, however good the die may be.

This is true everywhere, the contingent is never absent, potentiality never reaches full actuality except in God who is complete
actuality since He is pure reason without matter; and in the
sphere of human conduct, of ethics and politics, where things may
always be other than they are this is peculiarly true, the contingent is always with us; and the reason for this is not far to seek.
The wax refuses to conform to the die. Men are the materials of
the state and men are refractory materials. They constantly
tend to obstruct the realization of the true end of man, the consummation of perfect virtue and happiness in the good life, by
the substitution for it of something lower, the mere life of an
animal or something even worse than that; and thus the state,
at once the highest form and means of that good life, degenerates
into a "city of pigs" where *mere* life is the end, or into something lower still, a tyranny in which the unbridled will of one or
of a few or of the many exploits the whole state against its true

translation has been taken from *The Works of Aristotle*, translated into English under the
editorship of J. A. Smith, and W. D. Ross, Oxford, the Clarendon Press).

De Partibus Animalium, pp. 639 a–642 b.

Metaphysica, pp. 981 a, 982 a–b, 992 b, 994 b, 996 b, 1006 a, 1006 b, 1008 b, 1010 a–b,
1011 a, 1012 b, 1013 a, 1014 b, 1015 a, 1018 b, 1019 a, 1022 a, 1023 b, 1024 b, 1025 b,
1026 a–b, 1027 a, 1028 a, 1029 b, 1032 a, 1033 b, 1034 a, 1035 b, 1036 a–b, 1037 b, 1038 b,
1039 b, 1040 a–b, 1041 b, 1043 a–b, 1045 a–b, 1046 a, 1047 a–b, 1049 b, 1050 a–b, 1051 a–b,
1052 a, 1053 b, 1055 a–b, 1057 a–b, 1058 a, 1062 b. et seq., 1064 a–b, 1065 a–b, 1069 b,
1070 a, 1072 b, 1078 b, 1079 b, 1080 b. et seq., 1086 b, 1087 a, 1090 b.

Analytica Posteriora, pp. 71 a–72 a, 72 b, 75 a–b, 77 a, 81 a–b, 87 a–88 b, 89 a, 99 b–100 b.

Categoriae, p. 14 a–b.

interest and choice and rules for the selfish advantage of the ruler alone.

The *Politics* of Aristotle — and the *Ethics* as well — is a practical hand-book. It is primarily a guide to constitution-makers, and therefore concerned with states, with citizens as members of states, with men as citizens, and with the conduct of men collectively and individually. Its "end is not speculation and knowledge but action." The chief purpose of the book — if it is a single book and has a single purpose — is to furnish to the "legislator" the rules by which polities as good as possible may be actually set on foot, or existing ones made as good as conditions ideal or actual will admit. But even action implies some knowledge. No constitution-maker can go to work intelligently to make or to mend a constitution unless he has some knowledge of what a constitution should be, "men being what they are and laws as they may be." He must, as Aristotle says, "try to learn the principles of legislation," and for this will need not only experience but some knowledge too, both of men and things.[1]

But what kind of a knowledge will this be, and how shall the statesman acquire it, if it touches only the accidental and the contingent within which the "principles of legislation" seem to fall? It cannot be scientific knowledge, for scientific knowledge is only of the absolute and invariable, never of the contingent or accidental. Practical science seems then to imply not only an end and a subject-matter different from those of theoretical science, but a kind of knowledge peculiar to itself. This, according to Aristotle, is the practical reason (φρόνησις), and it requires a different faculty of the mind from that by which a knowledge of the absolute is apprehended.

No doubt the most fundamental of the differences between Aristotle and Plato consists, as is generally assumed, in Aristotle's repudiation of the Platonic "idea" — or his conception of the Platonic idea — as something separate from the particular in which it is always found, and in his own counter-assertion that "no universal exists, apart from individuals";[2] but in the field of politics specifically, the results of this difference would seem on the whole to be of no greater significance, and certainly are of no greater practical importance, than those which follow from this sharper separation by Aristotle of the speculative and the practical

---

[1] *Ethica Nicomachea*, Bk. X, chap. x.   [2] *Metaphysica*, p. 1040 b.

reason as two distinct processes carried on by two separate faculties of the mind.   As a result of it, the contingent rather than the
absolute becomes the legislator's study, that study consists in a
deliberation upon means rather than a contemplation of ends, and
it requires not so much wisdom as prudence.   Politics has come
down from heaven to earth.

"While a carpenter and a geometrician both want to find a right
angle, they do not want to find it in the same sense; the one wants
only such an approximation to it as will serve his practical purpose,
the other, as being concerned with truth, wants to know its nature
or character." [1]   With Aristotle the legislator has certainly become
more of the carpenter than Plato's legislator was, and apparently
also a good deal less of the geometrician.   Induction, or Aristotle's
explanation of the means of our apprehending truth, which he
regarded as a power within the human soul enabling it to "system-
atize" the results obtained from individual objects through sense
perception, may either go forward to the apprehension of the universals from which all scientific knowledge must be demonstrated,
or it may stop in this humbler sphere of the practical reason with
only such an "approximation" to truth as is needed by the prudent
man to guide him aright through the changes of human life, or
by the legislator in his search for means to make that life good.
With this hasty glance at the philosophical setting of the state in
Aristotle's thought, we must turn our attention to the state itself
and to those writings of Aristotle in which it is treated more at
length.

Aside from scattered statements in many of his works and two
or three important chapters in the *Rhetoric*, these writings are confined to the *Ethics* [2] and the *Politics*, but these two are undoubtedly

---

[1] *Ethica Nicomachea*, Bk. I, chap. vii.

[2] Of the three "Aristotelian" books on Ethics, the *Magna Moralia*, the *Nicomachean*,
and the *Eudemian Ethics*, the first is now regarded as not the work of Aristotle.   The other
two are still the subjects of dispute, but the more general opinion seems to be that Aristotle
is the probable author of the *Nicomachean Ethics*, while Eudemus, one of his pupils in the
Lyceum, wrote the similar treatise which bears his name, incorporating, of course materials
obtained from Aristotle.   The greatest difficulty in regard to them, however, arises from the
fact that of the ten books of the *Nicomachean Ethics* and the seven of the *Eudemian Ethics*, three
(*i.e.*, Books 5–7 of the *Nicomachean*, and 4–6 of the *Eudemian Ethics*) are common to both
treatises, one of these books containing the important treatment of justice.   This inevitably
raises the question whether, supposing Aristotle to have written the *Nicomachean Ethics*
and Eudemus the *Eudemian*, these three common books were originally the work of Aristotle
and were borrowed by Eudemus, or *vice versa*.   There still exists on this point the greatest
difference of opinion.   Whoever wrote these books, however, the ideas contained in them
are, in all their main outlines, thoroughly Aristotelian.   The subject probably most important for politics which is independently discussed in both works is friendship.   On this they

but two parts of one great subject in Aristotle's mind, the art of making or of mending constitutions, and must be studied together if either is to be fully understood. The *Politics* itself, though somewhat arbitrarily separated in our manuscripts into eight books, seems to be roughly divisible into three distinct parts or discussions, related to each other and not inconsistent, but very different in point of view and manner of treatment. A statement of this by Wilamowitz may serve as the basis of the division and order to be followed here: It is clear, he says, that in the *Politics* we have first "a common foundation" (Books I, II, and III in the old, or traditional order) "upon which arise two constructions *independent*" of each other, of which one contains an "explanation of the nature of constitutions, the distinctions between, and the changes within them" (Books IV, V, and VI), the other, "the principles underlying the best state" (Books VII and VIII, in the old order).[1]

The emphasis here placed on the independent character of the discussions in Books IV, V, and VI and in Books VII and VIII is highly important. If confusion and inconsistency are sometimes found in modern interpretations of Aristotle's political views, as often as not their cause lies in the unfortunate attempt to weave together into a single web these two independent parts each different from the other in the ends they have in view and in their method of treatment.

In the part which treats of the nature of constitutions and their distinctions and divisions, the approach is almost entirely empirical, absolute justice gives way to relative justice as defined by the constitution of the state itself, the best state and the ideas of Plato recede into the background, and Aristotle seems more modern in point of view than anywhere else in his political writings. It is this portion, if any, that warrants Sir Frederick Pollock in attributing to Aristotle the separation of ethics from politics, and to some it is the most enduring part of his work; but on the whole it may be doubted whether in its value it will compare with the masterly statement of general political principles in Book III.

Sharply contrasting with it is the treatment of the best state

frequently supplement each other, the *Eudemian Ethics* often containing important statements not found at all in the *Nicomachean* and of course *vice versa*. I have the general impression that the political aspects of friendship receive somewhat more emphasis in the *Eudemian* than in the *Nicomachean Ethics*, and a very definite impression that equality does.

[1] U. von Wilamowitz-Moellendorff, *Aristoteles und Athen*, vol. i, p. 355.

and its education in the books numbered seven and eight in the older order. Nowhere else, as Wilamowitz says, is Aristotle so Platonic as here. His best state is, in fact, little but the state of Plato's *Laws* over again, with the same or only slightly differing regulations of the family and of the various classes of the population. Empiricism is forgotten, it is constructed by Aristotle with as complete disregard of existing conditions as by Plato.[1] In this part of the *Politics* some find evidence of its being an independent work, more highly polished than the rest and possibly "published" separately before it was incorporated in the longer treatise, but others reject such a view.

On this general basis, then, we may suppose Aristotle to have followed an order somewhat as follows:

First there is an introduction setting forth the place of "legislation" in the classification of the sciences (*Nicomachean Ethics*, Book I), followed by statements and definitions of its object and subject-matter (Book II); then an enumeration and discussion of the separate moral virtues (Books III–IV), which "will be useful in legislation" since it is the legislators' main end to make men good. Following this is the important treatment of justice in book five; then a return to the separate virtues, this time in reference to the principle of the mean (Books VI–VII), after which the *Ethics* closes (Books VIII–X) with the significant discussion of friendship, which "forms the link between Ethics and Politics";[2] for "it seems that friendship or love is the bond which holds states together."[3] . . . "It is thought to be the special business of the political art to produce friendship."[4] The first three books of the *Politics* contain a definition of the state, an examination of alternative definitions, and a discussion of the principles underlying it on the basis laid down by Plato but with important modifications, then follows Aristotle's construction of his own best possible state (taking Books VII and VIII before IV, V, and VI as most modern editors do), next the empirical portion referred to above, and finally a short discourse on revolutions, their cause and cure. This general order is implied in the present discussion of

---

[1] "Sehr ins blaue," Wilamowitz, *op. cit.*, p. 356.
[2] Zeller, *Aristotle* (English translation), vol. ii, p. 137. See also *Ibid.*, pp. 193, 201–202.
[3] *Ethica Nicomachea*, Bk. VIII, chap. i. "Every association seems to involve justice of some kind and friendship as well." "All associations are, as it were, parts of the political association." *Ibid.*, chap. xi.
[4] *Ethica Eudemia*, Bk. VII, chap. 1.

Aristotle's political ideas, but cannot be followed exactly, nor can any but the most significant and important points be included.

There is, of course, no single key that unlocks all the doors of Aristotle's political thought, but the one that opens most is to be found in the very first paragraph of the *Politics*. The state is "a kind of *koinonia*." "It is that *koinonia* which is supreme over all others and embraces them all."

If we could but see all the shades of meaning in that word *koinonia* (κοινωνία) and could understand in the sense that Aristotle meant it just what those others are which the political *koinonia* includes, and the precise way in which it does include them all and is at the same time above them all — if we could do that we should know the basis of Aristotle's whole theory of the state. For the *koinonia* is the focus of it all, and this definition with which the *Politics* opens furnishes at once the link between ethics and politics — and therefore between the treatises in which they are respectively treated — and the theme of the first three books immediately to follow, the fundamental principles of all civil relations. It points us backward to those other bonds that hold men together, especially to the bonds of justice and friendship with which the books of the *Ethics* are so largely concerned; and it leads us forward to the *polis*, that whole of which these others are but parts, the end toward which they all move, which is their consummation.

What, then, is the political *koinonia;* but before that, what is a *koinonia?* It is plainly not the unity to which Aristotle believed the state had been reduced by Plato in the *Republic*. He criticises that conception in no measured terms as fundamentally false;[1] a state in that way may become so much of a unit that it ceases to be a state.[2] Nor is it, apparently, the same as the legal entity which we term a corporation. Aristotle seems as far from personifying his state as the English, who to this day have had to personify — or, as Maitland says, to "parsonify" — their king and make him a corporation sole, just because they have been as unable as Aristotle — though for a far different reason — to conceive of their state in its entirety as a single "person."[3] The state

---

[1] *Politics*, II, 5.   [2] *Ibid.*, II, 2. See *ante*, p. 39.
[3] See Rehm, *Geschichte der Staatsrechtswissenschaft*, p. 76 ff.; Newman, *The Politics of Aristotle*, vol. i, pp. 283–284. Aristotle cannot be said to be entirely clear of ambiguity on this point. There are statements of his made in the later parts of the *Politics* which seem necessarily to imply some idea of corporateness, but opposed to these are some very definite assertions.

then is "a kind of association," if we may so translate Aristotle's *koinonia*, though no unity in Plato's sense, and least of all a legal unity or artificial person. It is a *functional* unity of varied and reciprocal parts made one by the pursuit of a common aim in which their nature, their habits, and their training lead them all to join.

So far as the "legislator" may effect such a unity — and to a certain extent he may — the method he must pursue to attain it "is to retain the essential plurality of the state and to make it a community or a unit by education." [1]

An understanding of the full meaning of *koinonia* implies a re-living in imagination of the every-day life of Aristotle's contemporaries in the Greek city-state, and a re-thinking of their common thoughts, for the idea of it was so familiar to his audience that Aristotle in no place takes the trouble to describe it at length, though he was, as Mr. Newman says,[2] "the first to fix the conception" of it, and uses it as the basis of his definition not only of the state but of the family, the phratry, the colleges of priests, the relationships of men in trade and even of those between sportsmen or club-men or friends.

The *koinonia* has at times been called a "fellowship," a "participation," a "reciprocity," a "community" or "communion," a "partnership," a "share-holding"; and no doubt has in it something of all these and more. Friendship, one of its most important manifestations, Aristotle defines as "a living together" of men, a form of their common life; and in this we may possibly find as full an expression of its meaning as any other, if we bear in mind that *living* together is more than mere *being* together and the common life that results a life of men and of no less than men. It must be a common participation not in mere life but in something higher, especially in thought and conversation — "what we mean when we speak of living together in the case of men," . . . not, "as in the case of cattle, merely occupying the same feeding-ground." [3] "Some people," he says, "are companions in drinking, others in gambling, others in gymnastic exercises, or in the chase or in philosophy, and each class spends its days in that for which it cares more than for anything else in life; for as it is their wish to live with

---

[1] *Politics*, II, chap. v.
[2] *Op. cit.*, vol. ii, p. 97.
[3] *Ethica Nicomachea*, Bk. IX, chap. ix. An excellent modern analysis of the *koinonia* is given by Newman, *The Politics of Aristotle*, vol. i, pp. 41–44.

their friends, they do the things and participate in the things which seem to them to constitute a common life (συζῆν)." [1]

"The activity of friends . . . is realized in living together. It is only reasonable, therefore, that friends should desire community of life." For "friendship is a *koinonia*"; [2] but "friendly agreement is not about all things, but only about things that may be done by those in agreement and what relates to their common life." [3]

The books of the *Nicomachean* and *Eudemian Ethics* which treat of friendship and justice are full of statements which further illustrate the meaning of this central conception of Aristotle's thought about society and prepare us for his application of it in the *Politics* to the *polis*; but they can only be summarized here in briefest fashion.

The forms of association just referred to are all more or less voluntary and result from a sort of compact, but there are others which develop within the household, such as the association of father and child which is a *koinonia* analogous to that of a king and his subjects, or the one that binds together husband and wife in a relationship resembling aristocracy, or brother and brother in an association which implies numerical equality and is thus most like democracy. Of all the household relationships, only that of master and slave fails to rise to the level of a *koinonia*, because it is not a relationship between men, the slave as slave being a mere instrument of his master rather than a man. [4] "In the household first we have the sources and springs of friendship, of political organization, and of justice," for "man is not a lonely being, but has a tendency to partnership with those to whom he is by nature akin." [5]

In all the relationships created by this natural kinship of men, friendship of some kind is a necessary element; and as this friendship is impossible without agreement, the friendship of any association implies virtue in some degree, for "bad men cannot agree" on anything that touches their common life. But agreement is out of the question unless there be a real equality of some kind

---

[1] *Ibid.*, Bk. IX, chap. xii.   [2] *Ibid.*   [3] *Ethica Eudemia*, p. 1241 a.

[4] This exhibits Aristotle's theory of slavery at its worst. His admission that a slave may be a man is a tacit confession that the rigid logic which makes him a mere instrument is a failure when confronted with the real facts of life. In the *Politics*, he seems aware of this in admitting that there may be a kind of *koinonia* between master and slave. *Politics*, Bk. I, chap. xiii.

[5] *Ethica Eudemia*, p. 1242 a.

between the friends, the equality of brothers, for instance, or of traders, or comrades, in which their equality is mere numerical equivalence such as exists in a democracy; or the higher kind of equality which exists between father and son, or in the aristocratic or best form of government, where it is proportionate and not numerical.

And all these characteristics of friendship are equally true of justice, for justice is fully as essential as friendship to the existence of any *koinonia*. "Every *koinonia* rests on justice," for "justice involves a number of individuals who are partners, and the friend is a partner either in a family or in one's scheme of life." Justice will, therefore, exhibit the same varieties as friendship. "Whatever be the number of species of friendship, there are the same of justice and partnership," and like friendship it will necessarily imply an equality that may be either numerical or proportional. The legislator and the magistrate are *par excellence* "the guardians of justice," and in that part of justice especially which includes the distribution of honors and offices in the state, the fairness of the proportion they establish in the constitutions and laws they make or administer will be the test of the excellence and the stability of the whole state.

We pass, therefore, from the *Ethics* to the *Politics*, from the first part of Aristotle's definition of the state to the second. The first part was concerned with the *koinonia*, the second deals with the political *koinonia* "that embraces all the others and is above them all."

But in what sense and in what manner may it be said that the state embraces all the varied associations of which we have just been speaking, and how can it both include and be above them? In the answer that Aristotle gives to this fundamental question we may see the clearest traces of his biological studies, and the influence of his general philosophical system which owed so much to those studies. In a word, the state embraces all the other forms of human association in the same way that the whole of anything else in nature comprises all of its parts. A whole *always* implies two things : "that from which is absent none of the parts of which it is said to be naturally a whole," and its comprising all these parts in such a way "that they form a unity." [1]

---

[1] *Metaphysica*, Bk. V, chap. xxvi. For most of the statements which follow, see *Ibid.*, Bk. VIII.

The syllable *ba*, for example, contains both *b* and *a*, but *ba* is not the same as *b* and *a*; there is in it in addition a "principle" which makes it something which is more than the mere sum total of its elements, though these elements must all be present. A syllable is not constituted by letters plus juxtaposition, nor a house by bricks which are merely set together. There must in addition be a something which makes of the one a syllable, of the other a house; and this is the essence of each, it is the "ultimate principle of its being." "In the case of all things which have several parts and in which the whole is not, as it were, a mere heap, but the totality is something besides the parts, there is a cause of unity." The true distinction is between the matter and the form, both of which must always be present, but these are not related to each other in "a mere communion or connection or participation": they are "one and the same thing, the one potentially, the other actually." "That which is one is indivisible," and in a real sense the "whole" of anything is prior to the parts of which it is composed. The end toward which it tends is immanent in it from the first, though its manifestation appears only at the last; and that end is the full performance of its natural function. So "the parts of an animal are in some sense prior to the concrete animal but in another not." "It is not a finger in *any* state that is the finger of a living thing, but the dead finger is a finger in name only"; nor is it "a hand in *any* state that is part of a man, but the hand which can fulfil its work, which, therefore, must be alive; if it is not alive it is not a part." And in the political association likewise, the whole is "prior" to its parts, the *polis* is prior to the family and the village, though later in time, and all the smaller associations which combine to make a state, unless they are infused with the beginnings of the principles of virtue, of friendship, and justice which come to their full flower only in the state, are strictly not living parts at all, but mere *disjecta membra* devoid of any spark of life and incapable of doing their natural work. No household can ever be a real household, nor any other form of association, a true association — nor can an individual ever be a complete man even — if there is no state of which it is a living functioning part.

These less developed forms of association are steps toward the state, but their growth is incomplete, potentiality has not fully passed into actuality. In the state and in it alone is found the

"end" or "limit" of the principle which unites them.[1] They were
created for the mere maint nance of life and their activities are
restricted to that lower ideal.   They have neither the capacity,
nor the leisure, nor the virtue which are necessary to the fulfilment
of man's supreme good and highest happiness.   The state was
first formed in these inchoate shapes only "to make life possible";
it remains and advances toward its final goal of making "life good."
The undeveloped forms, therefore, are but "parts" that have no
life apart from the life of the whole and no meaning but in reference to it; they are neither self-sufficing, nor truly free.   The
polis, in which their partial life is consummated in the good and
complete life of man, alone has *autarkeia;* they have none.[2]

The state then is a whole, but a whole composed of differing
parts, made one not by their being exactly the same, as Aristotle
thought Plato made them, but by a universal principle inherent
in them all which unifies them without reducing them to uniformity.   But this whole is a "natural" whole, as "natural" as
any of the "parts" comprised within it, as fully "according to
nature" as man's body, composed of members which function
together to make him a man.

The state is man's natural "destination,"[3] because "man is by
nature a political animal";[4] or rather the converse, as Aristotle

---

[1] I use "limit" here in Aristotle's sense, not in our usual one.   "Limit" (τέλος), he says,
"means the last point of each thing, *i.e.*, the first point beyond which it is not possible to
find any part, *and the last point within which every part is.*" *Metaphysica*, p. 1022 a.   "What
more incongruous juxtaposition could have been conceived than that of *finis* with *telos*,
translating 'performance' by 'boundary,' and correlating *principium* with *finis*, 'commence-
ment' with 'extremity.'"   J. L. Myres, *The Political Ideas of the Greeks*, pp. 165–166.

[2] On the meaning of *autarkeia*, see the admirable note of Bradley, *Hellenica*, p. 194.
. . . . "In many ways 'freedom' seems to answer best to αὐταρκεία: freedom not merely
in a negative sense, but in that in which it is said that the truth makes men free."

[3] This apt term is used by A. C. Bradley, *Aristotle's Conception of the State*, *Hellenica*,
p. 195.

[4] Aristotle's phrase, πολιτικὸν ζῷον (*Politics*, Bk. I, chap. ii, p. 1253 a) is usually translated "political animal," and I have retained it therefore.   In the oldest Latin version, of
the thirteenth century, it appears as *civile animal* and this is adopted by Victorius and later
by Giphanius.   Seneca speaks of man as *sociale animal* (*De Clem*, 1, 3).   Saint Thomas in his
De Regimine Principum, Bk. I, chap. i, uses the expression *animal sociale et politicum*, and
both Welldon and Jowett employ the phrase "political animal" as the English equivalent
of πολιτικὸν ζῷον.   There is, however, a good deal to be said against this in favor of the
phrase used by Saint-Hilaire, *un être sociable*, and the use of the word "being" rather than
"animal" as our nearest English word for Aristotle's ζῷον.   Τὸ ζῷον includes all living things,
everything with a "soul."   "Being" might then be objected to here because it includes, in
its strictest sense, things without life, but notwithstanding this, it seems preferable to
"animal" on account of the implication in the latter of something "bestial" which is lacking
in Aristotle's τὸ ζῷον.

While men and all animals are therefore alike in having a "soul" or principle of life,
Aristotle sharply distinguishes the animate from the inanimate, animals from plants.   And

himself would have preferred to put it: We know man to be a political animal because his natural destination is the state.

"It would be misleading, on his view, to say that man produced the State because he wished to satisfy certain primary needs; those primary needs and instincts are the stirring in him of that immanent end or idea which is expressed in the state." [1]

"To say that the State secures or is the end of man is with Aristotle not a *proof* that it is natural: it is simply equivalent to describing it as his nature." [2] He objects to Plato's conclusions in many points, but could have found no fault with his master's method of searching for the nature of man in the "larger letters" of the state. His own position towards the question practically amounts to a denial of the antithesis between nature and law,[3] which is to say that law is "according to nature."

To strengthen this contention a short historical sketch is given of the growth from the household through the village to the state, not primarily for the sake of that history itself, but in order to show that the state must be natural if it is the outgrowth of the household which presumably even the Sophists would admit to be according to nature.

In the examination of the household which follows Aristotle sets forth some of his most important economic ideas and among other things elaborates his theory of slavery, but the last of these subjects alone can be briefly noticed here. His contention as usual is with Plato and with the Sophists. Against the view set forth in the *Politicus* [4] that a small state and a great household will be essentially the same and the government of both but "one science" whether its name happen to be royal, political, or economical, he

he distinguishes no less sharply between man who alone has reason, and mere animals which have not. To speak of man as an "animal," therefore, seems to revert to the idea of Ulpian who seems to reduce nature to instinct instead of confining it for political relations to reason as Aristotle does, for the state to Aristotle is not the primitive but the final stage in the development of man's "nature," and that nature is best exemplified by the highest form of man's development, not the lowest. The departure from Aristotle's true meaning is more the fault of the translators into English than of the makers of the earlier Latin versions. Our word "animal" has in it probably somewhat more of the meaning of the Latin *bestia* than of the Latin *animal*. The Latin *animal* is not far from Aristotle's true meaning, the English *animal* is very much farther from it. It is an instance, on the part of our English translators, of transliteration instead of translation. I owe the original suggestion of this point to my colleague, Professor C. J. Friedrich.

[1] A. C. Bradley, *op. cit.*, p. 201.

[2] *Ibid.*, p. 198. I have never found anything written on Aristotle's political theory superior to Mr. Bradley's admirable essay.

[3] Bradley, *op. cit.*, p. 191.

[4] P. 259.

insists on an absolute difference in kind between a political government over citizens free by nature and a household rule whose subjects are naturally slaves; but against the Sophists he maintains that this slavery is as much the natural destination of the slave as the state is of the free.   If by nature man is a political animal so the slave is nothing more than a domestic animal, a mere chattel, a bit of "animate property," "an instrument of action separable from the possessor."   Government and slavery, like the *polis* and the household may be different in kind from each other, one proper solely to man as man, the other the only fitting goal of the slave; but neither of them rests on force alone, and the status of the slave as fully as that of the free citizen is according to nature.   Servitude may, no more than government, be truly considered as the result of compact or convention.

Slavery, in short, is only one more manifestation of the general rule of nature that whenever several parts combine to form a whole, there invariably appears a subordination of some of these parts to others, a relation of ruler and subject of some kind, as of man over man, of man over the beasts, the soul over the body, or the reason over the appetite; and if this subjection is natural, it is just.   Indeed it is more than that.   For all who are natural slaves "as truly as for the body or for beasts, a life of slavish subjection is *advantageous*." [1]

But how are we to know which individuals ought to be slaves and which free ?   Certainly not by the mere fact that some happen to have the legal status of slaves.   For these "legal" slaves were made so in most cases as the result of the accident of birth, or of capture in war which could in no way affect their status in nature or justice unless might makes right.   It must be confessed that Aristotle in no place clearly indicates how a true slave may be known from a free man, but it is something that his definition excludes from slavery a large proportion of those whom the law of his day included.   In this, therefore, he deserves the credit of being more liberal than the law or the practice of his time even in Athens where these were in advance of some other parts of Greece; but even with all such allowances, it is rather difficult to see the moral or intellectual value of a distinction which gives to a man the status of a beast while admitting that he has not ceased to be

---

[1] *Politics*, I, chap. v.   This is one of the main sources of the medieval theory of "dominion."

a man. "If," as Professor Barker has admirably said, "the slave can be treated as a man in any respect, he ought to be treated as a man in all; and the admission that he can be regarded as a man destroys that concept on of his wholly slavish and non-rational (one might say non-human) character, which was the one justification of his being treated as a slave." [1] The utter hollowness of such a theory as this becomes evident if judged either by the facts of life or by the rules óf Aristotle's own logic, and it is clear from his statements that some of his contemporaries were far in advance of him on this point not only in condemning as unjust the actual slavery of the time, but in rejecting as untrue the whole conception of any such an inequality as could ever warrant a subordination of one man to another to the extent of making him the mere instrument of the other's will. In his attempted designation of the ones who are by nature fitted for this subordination, Aristotle nowhere draws any valid line between manual workers who are free and those who are slave. The life of both classes was such that neither had the leisure that Aristotle considered requisite for the cultivation of the virtue of a citizen or even of a free man. Under his definition of slavery some of the actual slaves in Athens probably ought to have been free, and many members of the *Ecclesia* certainly ought to have been slaves. For he believed leisure to be necessary for citizenship and in so far he was right. He, however, would have solved the practical problem by denying citizenship to all without leisure; the Athenians reversed the procedure and attempted to ensure leisure to the people by payments from the treasury. Both saw that some leisure is necessary, if not for virtue, at least for the fulfilment of the duties of citizenship, and one of the soundest demands of the workers in modern times is their insistence upon the right to the enjoyment of leisure enough to be men and citizens. The political safety of the future depends upon their getting it. If Aristotle was wrong, it was not in feeling that the citizen to be a citizen must have leisure. That was true, and it is still true. His real mistake, as our own history is gradually teaching us, was in denying that the manual worker ever could have that leisure, and therefore in declaring him forever shut out from the higher things of the mind and the real life of the state. The true solution lies not in denying him the citizenship for which a lack of leisure must unfit him, but rather in

[1] *The Political Thought of Plato and Aristotle* (1906), p. 366.

achieving an economic order which in itself will ensure that leisure without retarding the necessary work of the world. It is hardly to be expected that Aristotle should have seen clearly a problem whose solution we are now after more than two thousand years only just beginning seriously to face. Aristotle in many places betrays the prejudice of his time — and one that still survives — against the classes whose pursuits were "practical" rather than "liberal." Even a musician or a sculptor if he became too expert was in danger of being thought unfree. To become a "professional musician" was to sink into the class of mere technicians, and no doubt it was this same prejudice that in part accounts for his hostility to the Sophists who were willing to receive pay for their teaching. But are we ourselves wholly free of it? Handel was punished for wishing to become a musician and Berlioz had to jump out of a window to do so, nor is the time so far distant when a physician or a barrister could not bring suit in court for his fees. It may be more favorable circumstances and sad experience rather than greater insight that enable us to appreciate as Aristotle could not that labor itself does not debase a man nor deprive him necessarily of the leisure requisite for a free and political life or for "liberal" pursuits.

Since our brief sketch is mainly concerned with the positive features of Aristotle's political views, we shall pass over Book II of the *Politics* containing his interesting criticisms of the ideal states of other men and of the actual governments of Sparta, Crete, and Carthage, and turn at once to Book III.

Of all the parts of Aristotle's political thought, the discussion of the general principles underlying all civil relations in Book III of the *Politics* is the most fundamental, and in some respects the most enduring.

It is less original and less modern perhaps than his treatment of actual polities in the later books, and much more dependent than that upon the ideas of Plato; but it deals in a way that has never been surpassed since, if it has ever been equalled, with those general principles which must always underlie the political life of man as long as states endure in any form.

For this discussion, all that precedes is an introduction, the treatment of the less comprehensive associations in the *Ethics* and the first book of the *Politics*, and the examination of existing theories and polities in Book II. It is the natural sequel to them all, but there is one thing in it that appears at the very outset for which these earlier discussions have scarcely prepared us. From the definition of the state with which the *Politics* opens we might naturally have expected that the treatment to follow would be a study of the relations of the supreme association with the less developed associations comprehended in it which the *Ethics* describes. We should anticipate a study of the state as an association of associations as Althusius seems to have regarded it, in which the primary political unit would not be an individual but a natural group. The fact is entirely otherwise. Aristotle shifts his emphasis in Book III from the household to the individual. The parts of the state with which he has to do here are mainly individuals grouped together, not in the "natural" association of the household (or of the village to which for some reason he never gave any attention), but as classes held together by the fact of their being rich or poor. As Mr. Newman says, "The State seems rather to be adjusted to the σπουδαῖος [good man] than the σπουδαῖος to the State,"[1] the relation of kinship seems to count for less in comparison with the political relation than in the *Ethics*,[2] the "material state" tends to take the place in the discussion of the "intellectual state."[3] We are surprised to find Aristotle beginning his treatment of general political principles, not with the household, but with the citizen.

"The *polis* is a *koinonia* of free men,"[4] and its "constitution" (*politeia*) is "a certain ordering" (τάξις τίς) of its inhabitants,[5] but to be an inhabitant of it is not necessarily to be a citizen.[6] Without some bond of association even the freemen within a wall — to say nothing of slaves or foreigners — could no more form a city than a mere pile of bricks can constitute a house. Some inner formative principle of life is as necessary to merge neighbors in a true political community as it is to form a particular syllable of its separate letters.

There must be a common object of all their lives if citizens are ever truly to "live together" as members of a *koinonia* instead of merely feeding together like the cattle in one field. That object, Aristotle says, is "the safety of the *polity*,"[7] and by this he means nothing less than a common devotion to the central principle of

[1] *The Politics of Aristotle*, vol. ii, p. 399.　　[2] *Ibid.*, p. 395.
[3] A. W. Benn, *The Greek Philosophers*, 2d ed., pp. 323-324.
[4] *Politics*, III, chap. vi.　　[6] *Ibid.*
[5] *Ibid.*, chap. i.　　[7] *Ibid.*, chap. iv.

the community's life, the vital spark that must glow in the breast
of every citizen if he is to be a living member of the *polis* and not
like a severed finger or a foot of stone, its mere inaminate tool or
a positive encumbrance. One incapable of such devotion never
can be truly a citizen. In this we have Aristotle's conception
both of citizenship and of the *politeia* or "constitution." "The
constitution" to him means this principle of unity that makes the
citizens one, like the harmony that comes of different tones properly
blended.

In fact it is nothing less than the soul that animates the whole
of the body politic, and a full understanding of its nature is impossible to one who has no knowledge of Aristotle's discussions of the
relation of the soul and the body.[1] But to anyone it must be
obvious that by *politeia* Aristotle means something that we never
mean by our "constitution" and by citizen (πολίτης) one whose
character is almost a stranger to modern political thought.

To make clear the true nature of the *polis* then, the first thing
to do, as in the investigation of every other compound thing, is
to make a study of its parts. We must at the outset "investigate
the conception of the citizen; for the state is composed of a number
of citizens," and this is no easy task because the world is not agreed
in its definition of a citizen and in actual fact many who are citizens in a democracy would elsewhere be denied that status in an
oligarchy.[2] It is the old problem that crops up everywhere in
nature. "The form remains, the function never dies,"[3] but in
this imperfect world it never reaches its full perfection, the lump
is never fully leavened, the true citizen is found only in the ideal
state and the ideal state exists nowhere upon earth. Does this

---

[1] The soul Aristotle believed to be the animating principle of all living things, from the
vegetable to man. As such, every living creature is a compound of varying parts unified and
vivified by its soul, which can never be absent from any part so long as that part lives and
is a part. It is this soul that makes it a real functioning part of the whole, for everything
consists in the function it performs, its function is its life; the soul therefore is distinguishable from the body but never separable from it; they are really two aspects of the same thing,
one as form, the other as matter. The soul is the vital principle that distinguishes living
things from dead. The state, therefore, as a thing of life, must have such a principle and
it must be found in its every part; and one who for any reason cannot know and cannot do
the work of a member of the body politic is thus marked out by his nature to be its instrument only, not a citizen but in reality a slave of the state, related to it as the domestic slave
is related to his master. Aristotle, *De Anima*, especially Bk. I, chap. i, Bk. II, chaps. 1–4.
The edition by R. D. Hicks, Cambridge, 1907, contains text, English translation, notes,
and an excellent introduction. Another valuable summary is in Zeller's *Aristotle*, English
translation, vol. ii, chaps. x–xi.

[2] *Politics*, III, 1.

[3] Wordsworth, *Sonnets on the River Duddon*.

mean, as the Sophists say, that he has no existence even for thought? Are the *polis* and its citizens, like the law, nothing more than what the caprice of men chooses to make them, varying indefinitely and with no objective standard by which they may be called good or bad? Even if they are not — and Aristotle holds with Plato that they are not — their true character can be apprehended only by induction, through the sifting out by the mind of man, from their partial and imperfect manifestation in particular states, of those eternal principles that are constantly striving to work themselves out in our common life but nowhere reach their goal. His purpose, he says, at the opening of Book II of the *Politics*[1] is to find "the best of all forms of political association for persons whose life is capable of approximating most nearly to an ideal," to discover "what is right and what is expedient"; and for this, "the inquiry we undertake will seem to be due to the imperfection of all polities now existing or proposed": it will not consist in an attempt "to find some new form of polity seeming to indicate a desire to display our own cleverness at any cost" — an obvious and undeserved slap at Plato.

It follows then that the definition of the citizen will actually be determined by each particular polity and will vary from one to another. May we from these reach any political principles of universal validity?

Certain things seem to be clear. In the first place, mere residence does not make a citizen. The universal practice in Greece with its metics and its slaves here comes in to reinforce Aristotle's *a priori* conclusions. Neither does the mere enjoyment of private rights and their protection by the laws. Persons having these are universally treated in the same way as "children who are too young to be entered on the register of the *deme* or as old men who are exempted from civil duties."[2] They have no part in the active life of the state. They are bearers of rights, but not of duties, and it is only the participation in its positive functions that can make anything truly a part of any living whole. Furthermore, these are rights possessed equally by members of different states whose association is based merely on commercial treaties between the states. Such a form of association does not make them common members of either state. "There is nothing by which a citizen in the absolute sense is so well marked off as participation in judi-

[1] Chap. i.   [2] *Politics*, III, chap. i.

cial power and public office." [1]   True, polities vary in character
and this is a definition which may fully apply only to citizens of a
democracy.   It may or it may not exactly fit some other existing
forms of polity where the duration of judicial and deliberative
office is limited by the laws of the state, as in the case of the Ephors
in Sparta, for instance, instead of being unrestricted in time as in
democracies; but this is a minor matter.   It is also a fact that in
some actual states a citizen is defined for practical purposes as one
descended from citizens on both sides, but the difficulty here is not
so much to determine whether such a person is a citizen as whether
he ought to be, and, if he ought not, whether he does not cease to be.

Notwithstanding all these facts, we may say in general that a
citizen is "one who enjoys the privilege of participation in deliberative or judicial office.   He and he alone is, according to our
definition, a citizen of the state in question; and a state is, in general terms, such a number of persons so qualified as is adequate
for a self-sufficing life." [2]

But one or two incidental questions now arise to which some
answer must be given.   One of these consists in determining the
point at which a given state disappears and another takes its place.
Does this happen if all the inhabitants move to a new site, or when
some revolution alters the city's form of government?   And if the
state consists of its citizens, and these as we know are constantly
giving way to new generations of men, are we not faced also with
the problem which puzzled the ancient philosophers, whether one
can step twice into the same river?

The true answer to all such questions cannot long remain in
doubt if we keep in mind what a state really is.   If a *polis* is as
has been shown a *koinonia*, it is a *koinonia* of citizens under a
"constitution," and it must follow that when this constitution
changes its character, the *polis* itself ceases to be the same that
existed before; just as a chorus in comedy totally changes its
character and becomes in reality a different chorus if later used in
tragedy, although the members may remain precisely the same.

This is equally true of the state.   It is to the *politeia* or "constitution" that we must look : if that changes, the state is changed,
if it remains unaffected, the state persists through all other alterations of place or constituent members.   The *polis* is a *koinonia*,
and the *koinonia* is embodied in the *politeia*.

---

[1] *Politics*, III, chap. i.   [2] *Ibid.*

Like considerations will affect our answer to another important question. Is the virtue of a good man and that of a good citizen the same thing? In an ideal state these two would of course be identical, but in every actual one, since it is an imperfect state, the virtue of its citizens will be only a partial and not a complete virtue because the definition of virtue will be in terms of that state's constitution only, and because the common aim in which its citizens share will fall far short of the highest good of man, and will never look beyond the limited ideals of life and justice which give that form of polity its distinctive character. The virtue of a democratic citizen is not that of an oligarchic, and both are far below that of the complete man.

But if the polity or constitution (πολιτεία) is so all-important in fixing the character of the *polis* we must know exactly what a polity is. Aristotle's central thought on this subject may be expressed in three propositions concerning it, and if we can fully understand their terms, most of his political ideas will be clear to us.

They are these:

The *polity* determines the character of the *polis*.

The *politeuma* determines the character of the polity.

The polity is a certain ordering of the inhabitants of the *polis*.

In modern terms as nearly equivalent as possible we might put the first and second of these thus: The "constitution" makes the state what it is. The nature of the ruling class (πολίτευμα) determines the nature of the constitution.

In a remarkable passage, Aristotle sums it all up by saying, "The polity is an ordering of the *polis* in respect of its offices and especially in respect of the one supreme over all others. For the supremacy is everywhere in the governing class of the *polis*, and the governing class is the polity." [1]

But the first of the propositions above, "the constitution makes the state," is obviously not true of any modern state. "To us," says one editor, "the sentiment here expressed will appear outrageous: — that the English nation might be superseded by another race and yet that so long as the same constitution was preserved, there would still remain the same state." [2]

At first sight, it is undeniable, such a statement as Aristotle's does seem "outrageous." But most of our repugnance is the

---

[1] *Politics*, III, 6.
[2] *The Politics of Aristotle*, Bks. I–V, by Susemihl and Hicks, p. 366, note.

result of an unwarrantable reading into Aristotle's terms of a
meaning that never fully attached to them till modern times, and
then only as the result of the growth of the great racial states we
know today.   In justice to him it must be remembered that when
he said that "the 'constitution' is the state" and that the state
changes its identity when the constitution changes, he never had
in mind anything even remotely approaching another race's
"superseding" the English nation, as is proved by the whole tenor
of the *Politics*.   He was thinking of the Hellenic race only, and of
nothing beyond the changes that had occurred before and might
occur again within the institutions peculiar to it.   The parallel
above is greatly overdrawn.   Illustrations taken from foreign in-
vasion or the period of the Persian wars were needless and nothing
to Aristotle's real purpose.   He could well remember more than
one instance of revolutionary change within Athens itself in which
one class of the people had driven another from power and replaced
suddenly and with violence all the existing forms and ideals of
government by others of their own which were equally Greek but
radically different in almost every way.   Such were his changes
in the "constitution."   To compare these to the conquest of England by an alien enemy is little better than a travesty of Aristotle's
thought, but it is a mistake even more serious to identify the Greek
politeia from which his examples are drawn with the thing we
usually have in mind when we speak of the English or the American
"constitution."   What Aristotle meant by the term might be
made clearer if we should add to his statements given above another that may at first sight seem no less strange : "It is inevitable
that the canons of good and bad must be the same for the *polis*
and the polity, *for the polity is as it were the life* (βίος τίς) *of the
polis*." [1]   The polity, the constitution, he seems to say, is the state,
because the polity is in reality its life.

What writer on modern government would ever be tempted to
make such an assertion !   Yet Aristotle both made and meant it,
and nothing he ever said about the state was more characteristically
Greek.   Plato had referred to the *politeia* as an "imitation" of our
life,[2] and Isocrates called it "the soul of the polis." [3]

---

[1] *Politics*, VI (IV), chap. xi.   [2] *Laws*, Bk. VII, p. 817.
[3] "For the soul of a city (ψυχὴ πόλεως) is nothing else than the polity." *Areopagiticus*,
14.   See also *Panathenaicus*, 138.   For reference to these passages and to the one above
from Plato's *Laws*, I am indebted to Mr. W. L. Newman, *The Politics of Aristotle*, vol. i,
pp. 94, 210.

As Mr. Newman says, "Each constitutional form exercised a moulding influence on virtue; the good citizen was a different being in an oligarchy, a democracy, and an aristocracy. Each constitution embodied a scheme of life, and tended consciously or not, to bring the lives of those living under it into harmony with its particular scheme," and he aptly cites as a parallel Burke's contrast between the French Revolution as "a revolution of doctrine and theoretic dogma" like nothing since the Reformation, and those revolutions brought about in Europe "upon principles merely political." [1]

The summary of these matters by Mr. Greenidge is so good that I venture to repeat it in part : With respect to the terms "state" and "constitution," he says, "it will be observed that where we possess two abstract or semi-abstract terms the Greeks had only one. This is not an accidental difference. To us the 'state' is an abstraction which should, when used in its strict sense, express the whole of the national life, the 'constitution' expressing but a part of it. To the Greek the constitution (πολιτεία) is the city itself (πόλις) from an abstract point of view; it professes, therefore, to express the *whole* of the national life. This idea, which underlies the constructive theories of Plato and Aristotle, and which has given rise in modern times to the strange notion that Greek society 'subordinated the individual to the state,' is only a fiction in the sense that it was a theory which did not always square with the facts of political life. As a genuine theory, the realisation of which was consistently pursued by philosophers if not by legislators, it runs through the whole of Greek political thought." The *politeia*, he further says, "is an expression of some particular life that the state has elected to live, some particular theory of existence which it has determined to put into force. But different theories of life are represented invariably by different classes of society, and thus, when a new theory is adopted, it means that a new class has risen to the top in political affairs. This class will be τὸ πολίτευμα, *the* privileged class for the time being; and hence the question 'What is the πολιτεία ?' will be answered when we can reply to the question 'What is the πολίτευμα ?'

"πολιτεία, therefore, meant to the Greek something more than 'constitution' or 'government' means to us. It was not merely a convenient form of organisation under which men lived. Aristotle,

[1] *The Politics of Aristotle*, vol. i, p. 210.

as an historian, realised, as perhaps only a Greek could realise, that
with every change of constitution the balance of power was entirely
shifted.   Classes of individuals which had been kept in the background now came forward and showed themselves sovereign; the
beliefs and interests of one class had given place to the beliefs and
interests of another; a change in constitution was a change of
creed, and the sovereign class could force its subjects to bow down
to the political creed of the day.   In most Greek states there was
little or nothing of the compromise, the principle of mutual political
concession, which is such a striking feature in Roman history and
in that of our own country.   When the balance of power had swung
over, everything went with it, and the change was thorough and
radical." [1]

From this it becomes equally evident what Aristotle meant when
he said that the governing class *is* the polity.   His term *politeuma*
(τὸ πολίτευμα) is not used always in the same sense throughout
the *Politics*, but its meaning here in book three is clear enough :
it is the individual or the class (defined in terms of wealth or social
status) in whose hands rests the power of ordering the state according to its own peculiar views, ethical, social, political and economic.
The supremacy (τὸ κύριον) enjoyed by such a class enables it to
dispose on its own principles all the inhabitants of the *polis* and
so to order the magistracy that these principles will be practically
enforced over all.   Dissentients will be coerced by fear or force,
by ostracism or even death, till the entire *polis* conforms outwardly
at least to the whole political, social, and economic creed of its
masters.   So long as their supremacy lasts their ideals of life and
government will be enforced by political machinery of their choice,
the *politeuma* will in actual fact be the *politeia*, and the *politeia*
truly enough "the soul" or "the life" of the *polis*.   The whole of
Greek political history is a commentary on these statements of
Aristotle.   He was but putting in abstract terms the common
experience of his time, and there was scarcely a city in Greece but
had witnessed more than once the changes he describes here.

It is natural to identify this supreme power (τὸ κύριον) with
our modern sovereignty, as Susemihl does,[2] and the class enjoying
it with our "sovereign"; but this is very questionable.   For
modern sovereignty is a legalistic conception, the outgrowth of the

[1] A. H. J. Greenidge, *A Handbook of Greek Constitutional History*, pp. 4-6.
[2] *The Politics of Aristotle*, by Susemihl and Hicks, p. 381 n.

ideas of Roman law, and their application to modern nation states; Aristotle's discussion of "supremacy" here is nothing but "an ethico-political appraisal" of the relation of the "political koinonia" to other lesser associations of men. It is of no manifestation of the supreme authority in the state defined in terms of law that he is thinking,[1] but of an actual supremacy in an economic and social class ensured by physical superiority.

It follows that revolution was to Aristotle much more of a "political" change than a legal one. It was a reversal of ethical, social, and economic standards rather than the mere subversion of the legal basis of the state which we usually mean by it, and this change took place when the supremacy passed from one social class to another.

It is evident, therefore, that for Aristotle the most significant factor in politics is the character of the class possessing the supremacy — he considered the very identity of the state to depend on it — and naturally, as a consequence his classification of polities will also be based upon it. The details of this classification are not always consistent throughout the *Politics* and they are often "difficult to follow," [2] but in general Aristotle seems to have been influenced by the traditional order in his primary classification of polities according as the supremacy was in the hands of one, of a few, or of the many. This was in accord with the rule laid down in *The Parts of Animals*,[3] where he says that the best method of classification is "to attempt to recognize the natural groups, following the indications afforded by the instincts of mankind." But in indicating the actual marks by which these groups may be distinguished from each other, Aristotle, like Plato, is often forced by the consistency of his theory to give to old terms meanings very different from the ones apparently in current use.

The customary definition of oligarchy seems to have been just what the word implies, simply the government of a few, and of democracy, nothing but the supremacy of the whole body of citizens (ὁ δῆμος), both merely quantitative distinctions without regard to the character of the rulers; but to Aristotle this is a mistake analogous to a grouping of animals together because they happen to be wild or tame, not because they are mammals, or

[1] Rehm, *Geschichte der Staatsrechtswissenschaft*, pp. 81, 101-102; Jellinek, *Allgemeine Staatslehre*, 2d ed., pp. 421-25.

[2] Ross, *Aristotle*, p. 252.

[3] Bk. I, chap. 3, p. 643 b.

fishes, or the like.[1] "The small or large number of the class supreme in a state is only an accident of oligarchies on the one hand, and democracies on the other, owing to the fact that the rich are few and the poor numerous all the world over . . . The really distinctive characteristics of democracy and oligarchy are poverty and wealth." [2] It is wholly the character, not the number of the ruling class by which it must be distinguished from others. This, in some ways, seems more Platonic than Greek, but to anyone who has considered the nature of Aristotle's *koinonia* it must appear inevitable. The specific quality employed in distinguishing oligarchy and democracy is an economic one, the possession of wealth, and this is a result of the depraved nature of both. For the nobler forms of aristocracy and true monarchy the quality is correspondingly higher, ethical rather than economic; but in every case the basis is a qualitative one, and this is in part a heritage from Plato.

Nor is it the only point in which this great third book discloses Aristotle's immense debt to Plato. It comes out even more clearly in the discussion of the difference between good and bad polities and of the differing conceptions of justice in the various forms of the state. To take the first of these, a good or a bad polity — and this means a good or a bad state — can be adjudged so only by comparison of its quality with the quality of an ideal polity, and this will be a comparison of the essential principle of its *koinonia*, the purpose of its corporate life, with the true end of man, the *summum bonum*. The object of any *koinonia* is the common advantage, and when a polity is so framed as to secure it, it is a normal polity; when, on the other hand, its constitution looks only to the private interest of the ruling class, whether this consist of few or many, then the end of the association is thwarted and such constitutions must be considered perversions (παρεκβάσεις).[3]

Of course no constitutions in existence do fully secure the common good; it is even wrong to speak of different kinds of democracy and oligarchy as "good and bad," as Aristotle thinks Plato does in the *Politicus*, for all forms of both are "wholly vitiated," and the most we dare do is to call some less bad than others;[4] for the

---

[1] "We must proceed in the same way as if it were our purpose to ascertain the different species of animal. We should begin in that case by specifying the organs *indispensable* to any animal. . . . Hence if we take all the possible combinations of these organs, they will produce different species of animals. . . . It is the same with the polities in question." *Politics*, VI, chap. iv; *De Partibus Animalium*, I, 3.

[2] *Politics*, III, chap. viii.   [3] *Politics*, III, chaps. vi and ix.   [4] *Politics*, VI, chap. ii.

purpose of the association in both oligarchy and democracy scarcely goes beyond mere material prosperity and security against injury, its law is little more than a mere covenant, and its virtue the barest fragment of complete virtue. Now a true state is not merely a local association, nor one whose only purpose is the prevention of injury or the promotion of trade; such associations as that are not states at all. " It is an association of households and families in well-living with a view to a complete and self-sufficient existence," whose true object "is not merely a common life but noble action." No existing forms of government by the few or the many attain more than a very small measure of this, yet we may not rightly call any of them complete perversions unless the exploitation or spoliation of the whole state by the class in control has become the chief end and purpose of their constitutions.

Thus we get three normal forms of polity: Kingship, Aristocracy, and a third for which Aristotle has no distinctive name except *Polity* (πολιτεία) used in a special sense; and three other forms, each a perversion of one of the normal ones, tyranny, oligarchy, and democracy. Monarchy which exists for the good of all is kingship, the government of a few in the interest of all is aristocracy, and the control over the state by the masses, if for the common good, we may call a *Polity*. And, since the only form of virtue ordinarily attainable by the masses is military virtue, the third of these forms in practice amounts to a supremacy of the military class, under a constitution in which political privilege is enjoyed by all who bear arms. Tyranny is a perverted form of monarchy in which the good of the monarch is alone consulted, oligarchy, the rule of a few for the good of the wealthy, democracy, a supremacy of the masses for the good of the poor; and not one of the three really subserves the interests of the community as a whole.

Varieties of polity such as these must of necessity also imply corresponding differences in the definition of citizenship and in the principles upon which the distribution of office and privilege is made. These states in other words cannot but have varying creeds of distributive justice, and in any particular one the justice will be "according to the polity." But since nearly all the states of Greece had come in one way or another by Aristotle's time to adopt some form of oligarchy or democracy, his discussion of these varying ideals of justice is mainly a comparison of the merits of oligarchic and democratic distributive justice. For an understanding of it — one of the most valuable parts of the *Politics* — a clear idea of his general conception of "distributive justice" is necessary.

Complete justice is the whole of moral virtue from the point of view of one's relation to others.[1] Political justice is such "as exists among people who are associated in a common life with a view to self-sufficiency and enjoy freedom and equality," [2] as distinguished from the form of it existing in any other association, such as the "economic" or the commercial; and for politics the more important part of it is that which consists "in the distribution of honor or wealth, or any other things which are divided among the members of the *koinonia*." [3] This is "distributive justice" and it is "a sort of proportion." [4] "That which is just then in this sense is that which is proportionate." [5] But proportionate to what? In an ideal state it would be really proportionate to virtue, in the "vitiated" forms of democracy and oligarchy, wealth becomes the practical test of this virtue, and therefore in both, the ideas of justice incorporated in the constitution are incomplete and partial, for "legal" or partial justice is a relative term and varies with the polity. "Oligarchs and democrats," he says, "agree in this, that they both adhere to a certain principle of justice; but they do not advance beyond a certain point or put forward a full statement of justice in the proper sense of the word. Thus the one party [the democrats] hold that justice is equality; and so it is, but not for the world, but only for equals. The others [the oligarchs] hold that inequality is just, as indeed it is, but not for all the world but only for unequals." [6] The mistake of each is in assuming that its partial justice is absolute and universal, "for the oligarchs, if they are superior in a particular point, viz: in money, assume themselves to be superior altogether; while the democrats, if they are equal in a particular point, viz: in personal liberty, assume themselves to be equal altogether." [7] The oligarchs would be right if wealth were the true and only end of the political *koinonia*, the democrats would be right, if the state were bound to look no further than the mere equal enforcement of private rights.

Both views have a limited amount of truth, for both these ends are necessary for mere existence, but since the real object of the

---

[1] *Ethica Nicomachea*, V, 3.
[2] *Ibid.*, V, 10.
[3] *Ibid.*, V, 5.
[4] *Ibid.*, V, 6.
[5] *Ibid.*, V, 7.
[6] *Politics*, III, 9.
[7] *Ibid.*

political *koinonia* is not merely to live but to live *well*, both are defective in that they contain but a fragment of the moral purpose that must be the spring of true justice. And "a state which is not nominally but in the true sense of the word a state must devote its attention to virtue." [1] To neglect it is to reduce the political *koinonia* to a level little higher than the common field in which animals feed together — it is unworthy of men; and its law and "justice" become a mere covenant securing no more than "a mutual protection of rights," whereas a state is a "*koinonia* of families and villages in a complete and self-sufficing life," a life of "felicity and nobleness." [2]

But which of these two "vitiated" and fragmentary conceptions of justice is "less bad" than the other? On abstract principles ought the many poor or the few rich to be supreme, assuming that nothing better than either may be attained? Actually this will be determined by the law of each polity and this in turn will be dictated by the ruling class. Justice will be relative to the polity. To the Sophists this practical answer is all that we may or need expect. The law ought to be supreme. But Aristotle is too much of a Platonist to be satisfied with such an answer. "On that hypothesis," he says, "if the law is oligarchical or democratical, what difference will it make to the difficulties we have raised?" What should be the character of the laws "*if rightly enacted*"? The claim of the oligarchs is the familiar one, that political power ought to be proportionate to one's "stake in the country." "They have a larger interest in the soil and the soil is natural property"; [3] besides they as a class are more to be trusted than the masses in commercial transactions.

But, as Aristotle shrewdly observes, such reasoning as this might justify a supremacy in one man, if he were richer than anybody else, provided we were to take the individual as the political unit; and if, on the other hand, our unit is to be a social or economic class, then the claim of the masses might be assumed to outweigh that of the oligarchs, because the many are *collectively* superior in wealth and even in virtue to the few, and should be the better judges in political matters as they are of musical or poetical compositions. The company at a dinner will be better and more proper judges of the dinner than the cook. Not only so, but the masses are less liable to corruption than the few, just as a large

[1] *Politics*, III, 9.   [2] *Ibid*.   [3] *Politics*, III, 13.

amount of water will be less corrupted than a little, if impurities
be mixed with it.   The best working solution for the "legislator"
in the circumstances — and Aristotle always has him in mind —
is the one adopted by the great legislators of the past, such as
Solon, for "it may reasonably be argued that the existing state of
things is right"; and that is to empower the whole body of the
citizens (ὁ δῆμος) to elect officers of state, but to confine the tenure
of these offices to those with a fairly high property qualification.[1]
The citizens as a whole may also participate in deliberation (τὸ
βουλευόμενον) and in judicial functions, but the higher offices of
administration should be restricted in their tenure.   It is somewhat
analogous to the perennial question of government by experts
versus government by the people, and Aristotle fully appreciates
the strength of both sides of the argument, but he points out one
flaw in the oligarchic claim in noting the fact that it is not *any*
kind of superiority that should entitle one to office but only the
kind which would ensure effective government, that which "enters
into the constitution of a state."   Superiority in flute playing does
not necessarily go with nobility of birth or beauty of person, nor
eligibility to office in the state with wealth, if truly considered.

All this discussion brings up one last difficulty both theoretical
and practical, which Aristotle faces in his comparison of democracy and oligarchy.   It is really the difficulty of determining
whether our political unit is to be an individual or a class.   The
individualist argument would seem to upset the claims of both
oligarchs and democrats, for on this basis an outstanding individual ought to be supreme over both.   The practice in Greece was
otherwise; the collective class rather than the individuals composing it actually exercised political authority, and the question is
whether this is defensible in theory.   Suppose, for instance, there
are in a state a few persons whose individual merit entitles them
rightly to be supreme, but whose number is so small that they
could never effectively maintain such a supremacy.   What then?
The common interest of all requires a stable rule to which all must
conform.   Therefore, virtue alone is not enough in a ruling class.
It must be accompanied by the ability to put it in practice,[2] for
the life of the whole state must be embodied in the "constitution."
But these individuals are too weak in numbers to mould the state
to their views.   Must they, then, conform to the views of their

---

[1] *Politics*, III, 11.   [2] *Politics*, IV, chap. iii, p. 1325 b.

inferiors though more numerous ? It would be absurd to treat them
as the mere equals of the others, for "legislation can be applicable
to none but those who are equals in race and capacity." These
men are too good to be the citizens of a democracy. They are
like Gods upon earth, and are "themselves a law." Democratic
states met this problem by ostracism, thus "cutting down or ban-
ishing the citizens who overtop the rest." Aristotle admits the
fact that ostracism had often been abused in practice when used
for factional ends, he concedes that the "legislator" would do
better to make it unnecessary if he can, but he also recognizes in
the theory of it "a sort of political justice," and in cases of
necessity would even urge its occasional use in the interests of the
state as a whole, because the *koinonia* to be effective in securing
the end of its existence must have that end shared alike by all
its members.

There is undoubtedly some wavering from one point of view to
another on these matters in the different parts of the *Politics*, and
unfortunately we seldom have any warning when it is about to
occur; nevertheless, it may be said generally that the "parts" of
the state, which Aristotle usually has in mind as primary political
units, are collective classes of the citizens or of the inhabitants
conceived somewhat in mediaeval fashion as *universitates*, rather
than the separate individuals we normally think of today. The
Middle Ages implied unanimity in the *universitas*, even if they did
not always actually get it; Aristotle implies it in a *polis* dominated
by such a class or *universitas*. He would have accepted the spirit
though not the letter of the French maxim, *Un Roi, une foi, une
loi*. The state must be a *koinonia* of "like persons" (τῶν ὁμοίων).[1]

The difficulty referred to above arising from the presence in a
polis of anomalous persons — "anomalous" literally — is one
characteristic of perverted polities, and the remedy of ostracism is
just with reference to the polity though scarcely just in an absolute
sense. But even in the best polity a similar situation might arise
in the appearance of an individual of such preëminent virtue that
it would be equally absurd to remove him or to rule him by alternation in office. Only one course is possible in such a case — to
render him the willing obedience to which his relative merit rightly
entitles him, and this brings us to kingship, the last subject
treated in Book III.

[1] *Politics*, IV (VII), chap. viii.

The discussion of kingship opens with an interesting sketch of the history of the institution and of the various kinds of it which had appeared in Greece and elsewhere, but the chief theoretical point is the treatment of the question dealt with in Plato's *Politicus*, whether in any state possible among men "it is more advantageous to be subject to the best man or to the best laws." [1] In answer to that question Aristotle urges the impartiality of law compared with human judgments swayed by human emotions. "To invest the law with authority, is, as it seems to invest God and intelligence only; to invest man is to introduce a beast, as desire is something bestial, and even the best of men in authority are liable to be corrupted by anger." Law is "intelligence without passion." [2]

There are, however, cases where the laws cannot decide and the question remains whether these should be determined by one individual or by all the citizens, but even here, Aristotle, for every state but the best, would normally prefer to vest the power of decision in the whole body. But after all the proper form of government for any people in reality depends on their character, for some are fitted for aristocracy and some for a *Polity*. And if in like manner it were possible that a people should be capable of yielding the obedience of freemen to those whose virtue fits them for command as political rulers, and if persons so fitted should emerge, then it would be natural and proper and advantageous for all gladly to become subject to these, "not on the principle of alternation but absolutely." This if it were possible would be the highest of all polities, for in it the virtue of a citizen and of a man would be the same, and "the same principle and the same means which serve to produce a good man would serve also to constitute a state governed by an aristocracy or a king."

Book III of Aristotle's *Politics* is a statement of general political principles. The rest of the treatise so far as it has survived consists mainly of two parts, in one of which these principles are applied in an imaginary state constructed as in Plato's *Laws* in the way which to Aristotle seemed the best available, "men being as they are and laws as they may be," with certain conditions assumed "of an ideal kind," but none of them exceeding the bounds of possibility. [3]

The point of view in the other part is so different that one naturally suspects that it may come from a set of lectures given at

[1] *Ante*, pp. 27–29.   [2] *Politics*, III, 16.   [3] *Politics*, IV, chap. iv.

another time and more under the influence of the actual constitutions which Aristotle had collected. If the attempt made above to set forth Aristotle's general political principles has been in any measure successful, a shorter summary of this two-fold application of them which follows may be enough, and within it the chief attention will be directed to the second part which contains some of Aristotle's most acute and original political observations. ¶

Aristotle's best possible state is simply the one in which, assuming the most favorable conditions, the principles of Book III may be most nearly approximated; and this, he thinks, is a *polis* neither too rich nor too poor, secure from attack and devoid of the desire for great wealth or wide expansion of trade or territory, homogeneous, virtuous, and cultured, a defensible unambitious community self-sufficient but not aggressive, "great" but not large; a tight little independent city over which the supreme power will rest in a true aristocracy whose members rule and obey each other in turn in maintaining for themselves a life of freedom from mercenary pursuits devoted to the achievement of the highest possible measure of culture and virtue, of well-being and true happiness attainable by each and by all; while the work necessary to the state's mere material existence will be performed by those whose natural lack of virtue disqualifies them for the higher life and for political functions but does not unfit them for manual toil under the direction of their moral, intellectual, and therefore political superiors. These lower classes (βάναυσοι) are necessary elements of the *polis*, but, politically speaking, scarcely "parts" of it in an organic sense, whether they be legally free or slave.

Such a state Aristotle constructs in books four and five in the order now usually preferred by editors. "Weimar," says Mr. Taylor, "in the days when Thackeray knew it as a lad, would apparently reproduce the ideal better than any other modern state one can think of"; [1] but in reality we can think of no community in our modern political world anywhere which reproduces more than a few of the characteristics which made Aristotle's ideal polity what it was. For the realization of this ideal a favorable environment is necessary and Aristotle describes it at considerable length, but more important than that is the development of habits of virtue among the citizens, as one might expect from the great importance that habit assumes in Aristotle's ethical theory and

[1] A. E. Taylor, *Aristotle*, p. 85.

the prominence of that theory in his political system. In such a state, therefore, the "legislator's" main business will be the training of the citizens in these habits, with the result that a large part of the treatment of the ideal state is devoted to the subject of the education for citizenship, only a part of which has apparently survived.

It would seem more profitable here to pass this by and turn to the other application of Aristotle's political principles, in which the "legislator" is advised how to apply them, not with the freedom possible under ideal conditions, but under the serious restrictions imposed by the actual state of Greek political life and institutions in Aristotle's own day; for it is here that we find the most practical part of his political writings and in addition a large amount of invaluable historical information. This part of the work is more constitutional and less purely political than the rest, because the reforms the "legislator" should adopt must be such in any particular state as will be fitted to its peculiar polity if they are ever to be practical or successful at all.

For it is not enough that the statesman know the principles of politics and how he should apply them under conditions as he would have them. Most writers on politics have been content with this — apparently another thrust at Plato — but more is needed. The best polity is beyond the reach of most people; they must be given "the best under the actual conditions," [1] "such a polity as the majority of states are capable of enjoying." [2]

The varieties and characteristics of polities of this kind, the means of bettering them, and the best ways of preserving them, therefore, constitute the remainder of the *Politics*. And these polities — in every case some form of tyranny, oligarchy, or democracy — are all more or less depraved. Even the best of them, the combination of oligarchy and democracy to which Aristotle applies the term "Polity" in a special sense, is a debased form of constitution, though probably the highest and most permanent that "the majority of states are capable of enjoying." Since a polity is really the system of the offices of state, the variety of these polities is a result of the fact that every state is made up of a number of differing parts, and there will be as many kinds of polity as there are possible combinations of these parts in their constitutions, just as there will be as many different species of animals as there are

[1] *Politics*, VI, chap. i.   [2] *Ibid.*, chap. xi.

combinations of organs necessary to their existence. The study of these polities properly begins then with a study of their parts. These are the husbandmen, the mechanics, the commercial class, the hired laborers, the military class, the propertied class, the executive magistrates, the deliberative body, the judicial body, as Aristotle enumerates them in one place; and oftentimes the functions of one of these classes may be performed by another, as soldiers, for example are sometimes husbandmen, or the same persons may constitute the military, the agricultural and artisan classes and also make up the deliberative and judicial organs of the government. But "it is impossible that the same persons should be poor and rich," and therefore it is usually said that the poor and the rich are the parts of a state "in a preëminent sense."

On this basis it is correct to say that a democracy is a polity in which the supreme power is in the hands of the free citizens (ὁ δῆμος), that is, in the poor who are in the majority; while an oligarchy is one in which it rests with the propertied class who are a minority of the citizens; but in actual fact we may observe several varieties of each of these, according to the amount of participation under particular constitutions of these different economic classes in the higher functions of government. Thus the general principle of democracies is that all the citizens are equal whether rich or poor, but in some of them the constitution may restrict public office to those with a small property, in others to the descendants of citizens, in others to the citizen body; while in the extreme form the masses (τὸ πλῆθος) simply govern without any constitutional check and enforce their arbitrary decrees without regard to any constitutional law whatever, a form of government which cannot be called constitutional at all. Similar differences may be found among oligarchies, and in the extreme ones, the oligarchs, like the masses in an extreme democracy, are a law unto themselves and exercise a tyrannical rule.

It remains to speak of the best and the worst of actual states, "Polity" and tyranny. A Polity is "a fusion (μίξις) of oligarchy and democracy," [1] a combination of the two forms in the application of the oligarchic principle of wealth to some parts of the arrangements of office, the democratic principle of equality to others; but it is a *fusion*, not the balancing and checking of one class by another which Polybius regarded as the secret of the per-

[1] *Politics*, VI, chap. viii.

manence of the institutions of the Roman state. A tyranny is a
form of monarchy under which there is "an irresponsible exercise
of rule over subjects, all of whom are the equals or superiors of the
ruler, for the personal advantage of the ruler and not of the subjects. In this case, therefore, the obedience is not voluntary, for
no free person submits willingly to such a rule." [1]

All these varieties of constitution the "legislator" must know,
but how far may he or should he make changes in them, and in
what direction?

In a word, he should establish and should devise means of
perpetuating, so far as he can, such a constitution as will secure the closest approximation to virtue of which any particular
state is capable, and since virtue is a mean, this will consist
in the avoidance so far as possible of the extremes of both democracy and oligarchy, and in practice will amount to the lodgment of
the supremacy in the class which lies between the very rich and
the very poor. Practically, it will involve the fusion which characterizes a "Polity," and its success will depend upon the numbers
and strength of this intermediate class and upon the amount of
their participation in the government. If possible, they should be
stronger than the very poor and the very rich together, or at least
than either of them, and to make their rule permanent it is requisite
"that the part of the state which desires the continuance of the
polity should be stronger than that which does not." [2] To bring
about these objects, in as great a measure as possible, it is advisable
in general "to fee the poor" for participation in government, and
to "fine the rich" for non-participation, but in this it is essential
to keep in mind the different departments of government, for the
rule is not to be applied indiscriminately. These departments
are three in number, the deliberative (τὸ βουλευόμενον περὶ τῶν
κοινῶν), the executive, and the judicial. The deliberative body
is the supreme organ in the state.[3] It is supreme in all such questions as of war and peace, of the formation and dissolution of
alliances, of laws, of sentences of death, exile, or confiscation, of
elections of officers of state and their responsibility. It is a general
characteristic of popular government that all the citizens exercise
this deliberative power in all cases; when its exercise is confined

---

[1] *Politics*, VI, chap. x.
[2] *Ibid.*, chap. xii.
[3] *Ibid.*, chap. xiv, p. 1299 a–b. See Rehm, *Geschichte der Staatsrechtswissenschaft*, pp. 99–
101, an admirable discussion.

to certain citizens the state is oligarchic. But sometimes this deliberative function or a particular part of it is performed not by all but by a select body or person. In such cases the nature of the polity will depend on the laws governing eligibility to this body, the mode of election to it, and the conditions of the franchise. Thus, for example, that state will be a "Polity," in which some deliberative functions rest with officers chosen by suffrage and others with those chosen by lot; it will be an oligarchy if the deliberative body may perpetuate itself.

These and many other things the "legislator" must have in mind, but above all he should remember that his task is not finished when he has established his polity. More important than that is the provision he must make, the precautions he must take, for its security and its permanence. "It is easy enough for people to endure for a single day or two or three days under any form of polity." Chief among these precautions is education. Just as training in habits of true virtue is the surest foundation of the ideal state or aristocracy, so the strongest guarantee even of a debased one lies in "the education of the citizens *in the spirit of the polity*," democratically if the laws are democratical, oligarchically if they are oligarchical; [1] in making sure "that the part of the population which is favorable to the polity shall be stronger than the part which is not." [2] This is above all other things necessary because "the main cause of the dissolution of Polities and aristocracies alike is a deviation from their proper principles of justice in the constitution of the polity itself." [3] But there are other possible precautions of a more specific kind, and the legislator will be enabled to take them only if he knows the peculiar risks to which each form of polity is exposed, one kind in a democracy, another in an oligarchy, and under a tyranny dangers different from either.

In Aristotle's practical advice for the avoidance of the last of these his critics have found one of their chief points of attack. History teaches that tyrannies have been the shortest-lived as well as the worst of all forms of government, he says, and if they are to be prolonged the best way is for the tyrant to "wear the appearance" of a king, to *seem* to rule in his subject's interest, even though his aims are selfish, "to play a part" in pretence which if done sincerely would make him a true king. But this good advice is preceded by a section in which other less creditable methods are

---

[1] *Politics*, VIII, chap. ix.　　　[2] *Ibid.*　　　[3] *Ibid.*, chap. vii.

described with the acuteness if not with quite the cynicism of a Machiavelli. The sum of them all is "to prevent mutual confidence among the citizens, to incapacitate them for action, and to degrade their spirit." [1]

"The systems of Plato and Aristotle were splendid digressions from the main line of ancient speculation rather than stages in its regular development." [2] And yet no detailed study of the political part of that speculation can today do other than centre upon the political writings of Plato and Aristotle. We have, it is true, a few other writings of a distinctly political nature, such as the *Cyropaedia* of Xenophon, the short *Constitution of Athens*, formerly attributed to him, or the *Areopagiticus* of Isocrates, but the number of these is small and the whole sum of the information they yield slight compared with the contributions of Aristotle's treatises and Plato's dialogues. There is also further incidental evidence scattered through the writings of the dramatists, the orators, and the historians, and this is often of the greatest value, but the fact remains that Plato and Aristotle are the chief source of our knowledge not only of their own theories of the state, but of those of their predecessors and their contemporaries whether in agreement with theirs or not. It is to them above all that we must look if we wish to visualize the political life of Greece or to reconstruct its political creeds, though in so doing constant allowance needs to be made for the influence of their own personal views and of the consistency imposed by their respective philosophic systems. Their stock of political conceptions was typical of contemporary thought; it is rather in their unique combination of these and in their emphasis that the distinctive genius of Plato and Aristotle appears.

But Plato had withdrawn from public affairs because of his distaste for the excesses of democratic Athens — a dislike that was no doubt mutual. Aristotle believed that flight alone could save him from the fate of Socrates, and further proof is not wanting within as well as beyond the writings of both that many of their political preferences were far from being shared by the men of their time. Isocrates, for example, was more complaisant than either, though he looked back with equal longing to the sounder times of Cleisthenes. Plato more than once hints that Sophist views had a wider acceptance than his own, and Thucydides in the famous funeral oration of Pericles gives evidence of admiration for a

---

[1] *Politics*, VIII, chap. xi.   [2] Benn, *The Greek Philosophers*, 2d ed., p. 327.

régime for which Plato and Aristotle have little but condemnation. This view of Thucydides may be a better indication of the general attitude toward democracy, taken in the fifth century in Athens at least, if not in Greece as a whole, than the criticisms in the *Republic* and the *Politics*.

"Our government," says Pericles, "is not copied from those of our neighbors : we are an example to them rather than they to us. Our constitution is named a democracy, because it is in the hands not of the few but of the many. But our laws secure equal justice for all in their private disputes, and our public opinion welcomes and honours talent in every branch of achievement, not for any sectional reason but on grounds of excellence alone. And as we give free play to all in our public life, so we carry the same spirit into our daily relations with one another. . . . Open and friendly in our private intercourse, in our public acts we keep strictly within the control of law. We acknowledge the restraint of reverence ; we are obedient to whomsoever is set in authority, and to the laws, more especially to those which offer protection to the oppressed and those unwritten ordinances whose transgression brings admitted shame. Yet ours is no work-a-day city only. No other provides so many recreations for the spirit — contests and sacrifices all the year round, and beauty in our public buildings to cheer the heart and delight the eye day by day. Moreover, the city is so large and powerful that all the wealth of all the world flows in to her, so that our own Attic products seem no more homelike to us than the fruits of the labours of other nations.

"Our military training too is different from our opponents'. The gates of our city are flung open to the world. We practice no periodical deportations, nor do we prevent our visitors from observing or discovering what an enemy might usefully apply to his own purposes. For our trust is not in the devices of material equipment, but in our own good spirits for battle. So too with education. They toil from early boyhood in a laborious pursuit after courage, while we, free to live and wander as we please, march out none the less to face the self-same dangers. . . . Indeed, if we choose to face danger with an easy mind rather than after a rigorous training, and to trust rather in native manliness than in state-made courage, the advantage lies with us; for we are spared all the weariness of practising for future hardships, and when we find ourselves amongst them we are as brave as our plodding rivals. Here as elsewhere, then, the city sets an example which is deserving of admiration. We are lovers of beauty without extravagance, and lovers of wisdom without unmanliness. Wealth to us is not mere material for vainglory but an opportunity for achievement; and poverty we think it no disgrace to acknowledge but a real degradation to make no effort to overcome. Our citizens attend both to public and private duties, and do not allow absorption in their own various affairs to interfere with their knowledge of the city's. We differ from other states in regarding the man who holds aloof from public life not as 'quiet' but as useless; we decide or debate, carefully and in person, all matters of policy, holding, not that words and deeds go ill together, but that acts are foredoomed to failure when undertaken undiscussed. For we are noted for being at once most adventurous in action and most reflective beforehand. Other men are bold in ignorance, while reflection will stop their onset. . . . In a word I claim that our city as a whole is an education to Greece, and that her members yield to none, man by man, for independence of spirit, many-sidedness of attainment, and complete self-reliance in limbs and brain.

"That this is no vainglorious phrase but actual fact the supremacy which our manners have won us itself bears testimony. No other city of the present day goes out to her ordeal greater than ever men dreamed; no other is so powerful that the invader feels no bitterness when he suffers at her hands, and her subjects no shame at the indignity of their dependence. Great indeed are the symbols and witnesses of our supremacy, at which posterity, as all mankind today, will be astonished. We need no Homer or other man of words to praise us; for such give pleasure for a moment, but the truth will put to shame their imaginings of our deeds. For our pioneers have forced a way into every sea and every land, establishing among all mankind, in punishment or beneficence, eternal memorials of their settlement.

"Such then is the city for whom, lest they should lose her, the men whom we celebrate died a soldier's death: and it is but natural that all of us, who survive them, should wish to spend ourselves in her service." [1] With this higher estimate of democracy, the modern view of Freeman is in full agreement. "A fair examination of Grecian history will assuredly lead us to the conclusion

[1] Thucydides, II, 37–41. The translation is the one given by Zimmern, *The Greek Commonwealth*, 2d ed., pp. 200–204.

that this mob clothed with executive functions made one of the best governments which the world ever saw. . . . The Democracy of Athens was the first great instance which the world ever saw of the substitution of law for force." [1]

There is another important aspect of the difference between Aristotle's political views and those of some at least of his contemporaries. In only one place in the *Politics* does he speak with the slightest enthusiasm for any political unit greater than the *polis*. In Book IV he says that if the Greeks were united in a single polity, they would be capable of universal empire,[2] but the whole tone of his treatise seems to prove that this unification is for him impossible if not undesirable. In striking contrast is the glowing praise of Isocrates for Athens in the *Panegyricus*, his enumeration of her great services to Greece in the past, and his earnest appeal for a new unification of Hellas under her leadership against Persia. He seemed to see, and others like him, as Aristotle shows little sign of seeing, that the freedom of Greece was no longer possible if she remained politically divided; but there is no conclusive evidence that he foresaw any better than Aristotle the real quarter in which the total overthrow of that freedom was already preparing.

The fact is that the state of Aristotle's ideal belonged to the past; and the Macedonian conquest not only destroyed that state forever, but it had the further effect of turning men's thoughts, whether they would or not, out of the old channels into others that were new, in politics and in philosophy generally.

The magnificent attempts of Socrates, Plato, and Aristotle to solve the mysteries of existence and knowledge had amounted to no proof. Some of their profoundest assertions remained unproved because in their nature unprovable, and after Aristotle speculation rapidly fell back into the subjectivism that characterizes all later phases of Greek thought.

"The bloom of Greek philosophy was short-lived, but not more short-lived than the bloom of national life. The one was dependent on the other, and both were due to the action of the same causes." [3]

"Greek philosophy, like Greek art, is the offspring of Greek political independence." [4]

[1] E. A. Freeman, *The Athenian Democracy, Historical Essays*, 2d Series, p. 131.
[2] Chap. vii.
[3] Zeller, *The Stoics, Epicureans and Sceptics* (English Translation), p. 10.
[4] *Ibid.*, p. 15.

With Plato and Aristotle, Greek philosophy had reached its zenith, but much else was already in decline, especially religion, and political life. The loss of freedom completed the work. Not that intellectual life ceased; it may have become even more diffused, but it had lost much of its vigor and it was driven into different channels. In the first place, the relative importance of politics in the sum of human knowledge declined with the decline of actual self-government. Men retreated into themselves. Ethics though more emphasized than ever ceased to be a part of politics, and the interest in the latter fell off accordingly. Society and state ceased to be equivalent terms, and the individual apart from the state became one of the chief objects of contemplation; there was gradually emerging an individual who was something more than a citizen, a society that was wider than any possible political unit, and a humanity more extended than any single race: individualism and cosmopolitanism are the most marked of the newer aspects of political philosophy.

In part these may be considered to be the results of the inability of Plato and Aristotle successfully to bridge the gulf between the knower and the known, they are undoubtedly in one sense the reappearance of separate views that the Socratic philosophy had tried but without success to merge in a higher unity and thus far they may have been inevitable. But their reappearance was undoubtedly hastened and their extension greatly furthered by the decline of political activity and political interest which followed the loss of independence.

When Greeks alone were free and independent it was easy enough to assert as Aristotle had done that they alone were worthy of the higher types of political life; now that they are levelled with barbarians in a common subjection to a foreign power it is difficult to do so. Man has become a citizen of the world rather than of any particular city and that world a brotherhood of mankind under a law universal and uniform. All men are naturally free, and if slavery is not actively opposed it is not because slavery is according to nature but only because man's outward status has become less important to him than his inward life.

There is, says Dr. Carlyle, "no change in political theory so startling" as the change from the theory of Aristotle to the later philosophical view represented by Cicero and Seneca,[1] and that

[1] R. W. and A. J. Carlyle, *A History of Mediaeval Political Theory in the West*, I, p. 8.

change came in large part in Hellenistic Greece, though we must go back to the earliest Greek philosophers for its beginnings.

But it is a change, notwithstanding all its importance, of which the surviving record is slight. The political works of this epoch, such as they were, have been lost, and what little is to be known of them must be pieced together from fragments and references in writers some of them as distant as the period of the later Roman Empire and even further.[1] The one writing which forms probably the most important exception is the history of Polybius.

Polybius was first and foremost a historian and a philosophic historian. His philosophy of history is a rather fatalistic belief in cycles of national growth and decay which may be retarded in their development as Lycurgus retarded the decay of Sparta by the excellence of the constitution he gave her, but never really changed in their course. Much of this no doubt comes from Plato with whose works he was familiar, as well as with Xenophon, Thucydides, and apparently some of the constitutions and other writings of Aristotle, though of course he never saw the *Ethics* or the *Politics*. It is this background of Greek culture and constitutional theory and history that accounts for the significance in the development of political thought of Polybius' account of the Roman constitution in the second century B.C., and of his estimate of its comparative merits and its influence on the growth and permanence of Roman power. As a practical statesman himself he had little sympathy with the ideal polity of Plato, which, compared with existing constitutions, was as a mere lifeless statue instead of living breathing men.[2] And actual constitutions like nations or men, have their infancy, maturity, and period of senile decay. "There is in every body, or polity, or business a natural stage of growth, zenith, and decay; and . . . everything in them is at its best at the zenith."[3] The real reason why Rome was ultimately

[1] For a valuable account of the political conditions of the time and of the reaction of political ideas to them, particularly the ideas of monarchy, the deification of monarchs, the encroachment of the large state on the *polis*, and the growth of individualism and cosmopolitanism, see Professor W. S. Ferguson in the *Cambridge Ancient History*, vol. vii, chapter 1. The bibliography appended to this chapter gives a useful list of modern monographs. See also chap. ii of the valuable introduction of Professors Sabine and Smith in their translation of Cicero's *Republic: On the Commonwealth*, Marcus Tullius Cicero, translated with notes and introduction by George Holland Sabine and Stanley Barney Smith, Columbus, Ohio, 1929.

[2] Bk. VI, chap. 47. Of this book, from which most of the political observations of Polybius come, only certain portions have survived.

[3] *Ibid.*, chap. 51.

victorious over Carthage in the Hannibalic war is to be found in the fact that "the political state of Carthage was on the decline, that of Rome improving." [1]

There is little original in the classification Polybius gives of the different forms of polity. He seems practically to identify democracy with Aristotle's *Polity* and the unchecked rule of the masses which to Aristotle was democracy in its extreme form, he calls mob-rule or ochlocracy (ὀχλοκρατία). Like Aristotle he believes the most permanent of practical constitutions — and therefore the best — to consist in a mixture, but with him it is not the mixture of oligarchy or "aristocracy" with democracy, defined by law, as in Aristotle's *Polity;* but a mixture of monarchy, aristocracy, and democracy as found in the Consuls, the Senate, and the People of the Roman constitution. It is rather gratuitous to charge him as Rehm does with a misunderstanding of Aristotle, since it seems certain that he was unacquainted with the *Politics,* but it is undoubtedly true as Rehm has pointed out, that there is a fundamental difference between the checks and balances within the highest governmental organs of the state which to Polybius constitute the greatest merit and the secret of permanence in the mixed constitution of Sparta and to a smaller extent of Carthage, but above all of the Roman state, on the one hand; and on the other, the *fusion* of political *principles* which characterized the government under the supremacy of the middle class in Aristotle's *Polity* as set forth in Book III of the *Politics.* [2]

The chief importance of Polybius for the development of political thought as a whole, is not in his classification of polities, nor in his cyclical theory of their growth and decline, both of which are borrowed.

It lies in his theory of the mixed constitution as distinct from a state of mixed principles only, one in which the supreme governmental authority is compounded of several distinct organs, each set off against the others by the constitution, in which the co-operation of these different organs is essential, and therefore where one of them by withholding it may check and obstruct the action

---

[1] Bk. VI, chap. 51.
[2] Rehm, *Geschichte der Staatsrechtswissenschaft,* pp. 136–137. In one passage at least, in the more practical part of the *Politics,* it is true, Aristotle seems to have in mind the governmental organ, as Polybius does, when, at the end of chap. xiv, of Bk. VI, he speaks of the deliberative body (τὸ βουλευόμενον) and the supreme authority (τὸ κύριον) as exact equivalents.

of the rest. Such a system of checks and balances or separation of powers Polybius believed to be the secret of the Spartan polity of Lycurgus, but it was in the Roman constitution that he found its finest exemplification. The greatest significance of his speculations lies in the emphasis which he seems to have been the first to place upon this principle, whether such be regarded as a merit or whether we agree with Mommsen that there is hardly "a more foolish political speculation than that which derives the excellent constitution of Rome from a judicious mixture of monarchical, aristocratic, and democratic elements, and deduces the successes of Rome from the excellence of her constitution." [1]

[1] *History of Rome* (Dickson's translation), vol. iv, p. 247,

CHAPTER IV

ROME

In the general development of political thought the importance of Rome is very great but this importance results from no striking originality, nor from any considerable new Roman contribution to the world's stock of political ideas; it is owing almost wholly to the great practical part that Rome played in laying the legal and political foundations of the western world, and in her transmission of ideas learned from Greece to the rising peoples of western Europe which were brought within the sphere of her culture as a result of the marvelous extension and duration of her dominion. For the most part these ideas were those of the Hellenistic period. "Plato and Aristotle, to say nothing of the sages before Socrates, remained without material influence on the Roman culture, although their illustrious names were freely used, and their more easily understood writings were probably read and translated." [1] Their transmission by Rome to the West is a part of the obscure but important history of the gradual assimilation by the western world of Roman culture, but more especially of Roman jurisprudence through which Rome's influence on political thought has been chiefly exercised.

Of the great intellectual impact of Greece upon Rome in the Hellenistic period there is abundant evidence both external and internal, and it may have begun much earlier. Pomponius, a jurist of the time of Hadrian, cites a current opinion that the Twelve Tables were first suggested to the Romans by Hermodorus, an Ephesian exile in Italy, and Pomponius himself says the tables were based on laws obtained from Greek cities. [2] If this be true, and the traditional date of the Twelve Tables

---

[1] Mommsen, *History of Rome*, IV, p. 197. This is a considerable exaggeration, at least so far as Plato is concerned, but it is undoubtedly true that his views in their Roman form have been greatly modified in some important respects by the philosophical tendencies of the Hellenistic period, especially by Stoicism.

[2] *Digest*, 1, 2, 2, 4.

correct,[1] we have evidence of a considerable transmission of legal ideas as early as the middle of the fifth century B.C. A further possibility of early Greek influence upon Roman conceptions of law and politics appears in the existence and extension of the ideas of Pythagoras in Magna Graecia and some contact of the Romans with them as indicated by their accounts of the legislation of Numa Pompilius, but for this our historical evidence is scarcely sufficient to render it any more probable than the reciprocal influence of Roman ideas on Pythagoras.[2]

The question of Rome's debt to Greece in these matters passes out of the realm of conjecture with the extension of Roman influence toward the East after the second Punic war. After this time we have numerous references in authentic sources to the presence of Romans in Greece and of Greeks in Rome, as hostages, ambassadors, or slaves;[3] and in time, notwithstanding the opposition of conservatives like Cato, it became the fashion in Rome to have Greek tutors in the household or to send young men to Greece to be instructed by famous philosophers there.

Probably the most direct influence of this influx of Greeks and of Greek ideas upon political thought in Rome and upon Rome's part in its general development results from the fact that this new philosophic impulse came at the very time when the political expansion of Rome was presenting for solution the unavoidable problem of the status under Roman sovereignty of her new dependencies and of their systems of law. It was through the channel of Roman law mainly that the political thought of the Greeks ultimately passed to the West in the early Middle Ages, and this

[1] For the controversy as to the date of the Twelve Tables, see Ettore Pais, *Storia di Roma*, I, pp. 550 ff., II, 546 ff.; Édouard Lambert, *La question de l'authenticité des XII Tables* (*Nouvelle revue historique de droit français et étranger*, 1902); P. F. Girard, *Mélanges de droit romain*, pp. 1–64. Pais and Lambert, though in disagreement as to the dates they propose, agree in rejecting the traditional one. Girard defends it. For a summary of the controversy, see Kipp, *Geschichte der Quellen des römischen Rechts*, 3d ed., p. 34 ff. For Hermodorus of Ephesus, see Zeller, *Pre-Socratic Philosophy* (English translation), II, p. 99, note 3; Arthur Fairbanks, *The First Philosophers of Greece*, pp. 50–51; John Burnet, *Early Greek Philosophy*, 3d ed., pp. 130–131, 140–141. Hermodorus was a friend of Heracleitus, was banished from Ephesus, and the date makes it entirely possible that it may have been he who first suggested the XII Tables. Burnet seems to accept it as a fact, Zeller is more skeptical. *A History of Eclecticism in Greek Philosophy*, p. 6, note 2.

[2] Zeller, *Pre-Socratic Philosophy* (English translation), vol. i, pp. 518–521; *Eclecticism*, p. 6, note 2. For a discussion of the possible influence of Pythagoras upon Numa and the references to it in early writers, see Schwegler, *Römische Geschichte* (2d ed.), vol. i, pp. 560 ff.

[3] For a summary of these, and references to the sources of our information, see Zeller, *Eclecticism*, pp. 5–17.

result was largely determined by the philosophic training of the jurists of the later Republic. The Roman lawyers, Dr. Carlyle insists, were "not, properly speaking, philosophers, or even political philosophers," [1] and this is unquestionably true of the great jurists of the classic period of Roman law in the second and third centuries A.D., but to the early formative period in that law's history the statement does not truly apply. It was the jurists of this earlier period who gave to Roman law its philosophic content and most of its political importance and they did so precisely because they were men who looked far beyond mere law, men in most cases thoroughly trained in the philosophy of the day, frequently in Greece itself.[2] And their activity happened to come just at the time when such broad views as theirs had the greatest chance of influencing future development. There is a time in the legal history of every nation developing and expanding as Rome was in the last centuries before the Christian era, when the problem of what its "common law" is to be presses for settlement and will not wait. The outcome may be the "reception" of a foreign system, such as Germany's in the fifteenth and sixteenth centuries; or it may be the formation of one constructed in the main of local materials as in England some three centuries earlier, but the factors which determine the result are much the same in all cases. Consolidation of a nation's territory or jurisdiction, especially when it comprehends neighboring tribes or districts, cannot but raise at once the question of the relation of its law to theirs, and the answer cannot long be delayed. A "common" system of some sort must arise to meet this practical need and the actual content of this system will in every case depend upon the conditions existing when the need appears. If at the crisis a developed superior legal system lies ready to hand it may be appropriated as Roman law was in Germany; if the need happens to emerge before the medieval revival of Roman law, as in England, it may be met by the creation of a common system from native materials within reach; which system shall be the "common" one in each case depends on the particular circumstances of that case. Rome met this problem at a time relatively early in her legal history, when the influence of Greek political philosophy was strong and her own law still plastic

---

[1] *A History of Mediaeval Political Theory in the West*, vol. i, p. 35.

[2] For proofs of this statement, see Paul Krüger, *Geschichte der Quellen und Litteratur des römischen Rechts*, 2d ed., §§ 4–9, with the references he gives.

and much more susceptible to such an influence from without than it later became after its rules had developed and hardened into a technical science so exacting as to demand a study which necessarily excluded the other branches of knowledge. ⎞Thus it was that the early Roman jurists could and did fuse these Greek philosophic principles with the local laws of the Italian peninsula to form their growing system of jurisprudence, and for some of them this fusion may gradually have taken the shape of a more or less complete identification of the *jus gentium*, a "common" system distilled in practice from the varied local laws of Rome [1] and of the neighboring tribes lately made subject to her, with the *jus naturale* which the Stoic philosophy had taught them to consider as a system "common" to all mankind. Such a fusion as this of philosophic ideas and the actual rules of law, it is true, could never have been originally made by later jurisconsults such as Ulpian or Papinian, but it is far from improbable in the case of a Mucius Scaevola, a Tubero, or a Rutilius, steeped in the philosophy of Hellenistic Greece.

As a consequence Greek doctrines of political relations and law were combined with principles drawn from Italic custom to be handed on together at a later time to the newer peoples of western Europe as the basis of their law and politics. This combination and this transmission together constitute the chief rôle of Rome in the drama of the growth of western political ideas, a rôle second to none in practical importance.

The political doctrines thus infused into Roman law by the early jurists, as has been said, were not exactly those of Plato and Aristotle, but the later much modified forms which flourished in Greece when Rome's eyes were first steadily turned in that direction. But the Roman bent was practical rather than truly philosophic and in Roman hands doctrines drawn from rival schools tended to be thrown together to make a working political creed rather than a system consistent in all its parts. To say that the Romans were eclectics is to admit their lack of originality but also to account for their real importance in the history of thought.

"Stoic apathy, Epicurean self-contentment, and Sceptic imperturbability" all contributed to the creed of educated Romans of

---

[1] Karlowa points out in answer to Puchta that the *jus gentium* must not be thought of as excluding the laws of Rome itself. *Römische Rechtsgeschichte*, vol. i, p. 456. English readers, usually under the influence of Sir Henry Maine's brilliant generalizations, are particularly likely to overlook this fact. See Maine's *Ancient Law*, chap. iii.

the later Republic, but on the political side the contribution of
the Stoics seems to have outweighed the others. The Stoic creed
as Mommsen says "was really better adapted for Rome than for
the land where it first arose." "The leading feature of the system
came more and more to be its casuistic doctrine of duties. It
suited itself to the hollow pride of virtue, in which the Romans of
this period sought their compensation amidst the various humbling
circumstances of their contact with the Greeks." [1]

And there were other and higher considerations as well, which
commended the political views of the Stoics to the Roman world.
The Stoic doctrine of the brotherhood of man and the citizenship
of the world was not ill-suited to a state that seemed destined to
bring all races within its political control, nor was the Stoic belief
in a universal law binding upon all entirely strange to a people
under whose eyes the *pax Romana* was already growing by leaps
and bounds towards its ultimate inclusion of all the known western
civilized world and more.

It is Cicero who best exemplifies for us these characteristics of
Roman thought under the Republic, and among his writings
especially the fragmentary *De Re Publica* and *De Legibus*.[2] These
two works owe their form and general subject-matter, as well as
their names, to Plato's *Republic* and *Laws*, though philosophically
they are often more Stoic than Platonic and the laws referred to
generally Roman instead of Greek.[3] In Cicero's *Republic*, therefore, as in Plato's, the nature of justice is the main theme, and
the book is aptly referred to by St. Augustine as a keen and powerful defence of justice against injustice, in which Cicero sets forth
the views of the Stoics in its favor against the destructive arguments of Carneades, in the manner of Socrates and his opponents
in Plato's *Republic*. Public, says Scipio in the dialogue, means

---

[1] Mommsen, *History of Rome*, vol. iv, pp. 201, 204.
[2] The edition of both used here is by C. F. W. Mueller, Leipsic, 1910.
[3] There is also now an edition of the *De Re Publica* and the *De Legibus* with English translation in the *Loeb Classical Library* edited by C. W. Keyes, London and New York, 1928.
The translations given here are in some important points not in accord with those of Professor Keyes. The edition of the *Republic* in English by Sabine and Smith is accompanied
by valuable notes and an introduction which sets forth admirably the chief points in Cicero's
political thought and relates it to the thought of the past. *On the Commonwealth*,
Marcus Tullius Cicero, Translated with Notes and Introduction by George Holland Sabine
and Stanley Barney Smith, Columbus, Ohio, 1929. For a careful and detailed account of
the sources of these two works see Johannes M. Galbiatius, *De Fontibus M. Tullii Ciceronis
Librorum qui Manserunt de Re Publica et de Legibus Quaestiones*, Milano, 1916. If we had
the last portion of the *De Legibus* in which Cicero discussed the *jus civile* of Rome it would
more than compensate for the lost books of Livy's history.

"of the people." *Res publica* is *res populi*, but a "people" is "not an assemblage of men brought together in any fashion whatever, but an assemblage of many, associated by consent to law and by community of interest," [1] and the prime cause of their coming together is not weakness but rather a sort of natural affinity for each other; for they are gregarious by an instinct that is inborn. "Therefore every people which is such an assemblage of the multitude as I have explained; every state which is a disposition (*constitutio*) of the people; every republic, which as I have said is a thing of the people, must be directed according to some plan (*consilium*) if it is to be permanent, and that plan must in the beginning always be referred to that as its cause which was the cause of the being of the state itself." In the next place this direction must be entrusted to one person or to certain chosen ones or it must rest with the multitude and with all. When the supreme authority over all matters is in the hands of one we call that one a king and the form of his republic a kingdom. When it is in the hands of chosen persons, that state is said to be ruled at the will of the aristocracy. And that state is popular (*popularis*) — for so they call it — in which all things are in the people. "And any one of these three varieties, *if it holds to that bond which originally bound men to each other in the association of the republic* (si teneat illud vinclum, quod primum homines inter se rei publicae sociatate devinxit), though not perfect nor in my opinion the best, yet it is tolerable, so that one of the forms may be superior to another. For a just and wise king, or chosen and eminent citizens, or the people itself — though this is the least worthy — it seems may be capable of maintaining a stable rule if no violence or self-seeking prevent. But in kingdoms the subjects are too much deprived of common right and of participation in counsels, under the domination of an aristocracy the multitude can scarcely be a sharer in liberty when excluded from all common counsel and power, and if all things are under popular control, even a just and moderate one, yet the very equality is evil since it recognizes no gradations of merit." All three of these unmixed forms of government therefore have seri-

---

[1] Est igitur, inquit Africanus, res publica res populi, populus autem non omnis hominum coetus quoquo modo congregatus, sed coetus multitudinis juris consensu et utilitatis communione sociatus. *De Re Publica*, I, 25. Scipio again expresses the same idea in his famous dream, with which the *Republic* closes: "Nihil est enim illi principi deo, qui omnem mundum regit, quod quidem in terris fiat, acceptius quam concilia coetusque hominum iure sociati, quae civitates appellantur." *De Re Publica*, VI, 13.

ous defects, "and so there is a fourth kind of republic which I consider greatly preferable, one moderated and mixed of the three." [1]

Of the three, kingship is far the best but better even than kingship is a form of government composed of all three forms equated and tempered.   Such a mixed constitution contains a large measure of equality, "of which freemen cannot be easily deprived for any length of time," and it has also the merit of great stability. "So I decide," says Scipio, "I believe, I affirm, that of all republics, none can be compared in its nature, or its disposition, or its scientific perfection, with the one which our fathers received from their ancestors and have handed down to us." [2]   So he approves the view of Cato who compared the short-lived constitutions made by individuals such as Minos, or Theseus, Solon, or Cleisthenes, with the Roman, "established not by the genius of one man but of many, nor for the life of one man but for many ages."

Cato was wont to say that no genius ever existed so great that nothing escaped him, and even if any such had existed, all genius combined in one could never at one time comprehend all things without the aid of experience and the lapse of time.   Therefore for the object proposed, it would be more to the purpose, he thinks, to set forth "our own republic in its growth and maturity, now firm and strong," than to create one in imagination as Socrates does in Plato's *Republic*.[3]   For this reason Cicero's *Republic* is far different from Plato's, more local and much more historical in treatment.   For example, Cicero's abstract conception of tyranny is deeply affected by the actual or supposed facts of the expulsion of the Tarquins, and his views on this matter had considerable influence on later thought.   After setting forth the traditional story he asks, "Do you see, therefore, how a king has been transformed into a master, and how, through the fault of one man, the form of the republic has been altered from a good one into the very worst? For it is the master over a people whom the Greeks call a tyrant. The name king they apply to one who like a parent consults the good of his people and preserves those over whom he rules, a form of republic doubtless good under the most favorable conditions of life, as I have said, but liable nevertheless to the worst of perversions.   For no sooner did this king alter into an unjust master

---

[1] *De Re Publica*, I, chaps. 25–29 *passim*.
[2] *Ibid.*, 45–46.   [3] *De Re Publica*, II, chap. 1.

than he forthwith became a tyrant, than whom no animal more
foul and loathsome to gods and men or more detested can be
imagined; who, though he have the figure of a man, outdoes the
most monstrous of beasts in the excess of his vices." For who
could truly call him a man, who desires no community of right
between himself and his subjects, or even between him and the
whole race of man, who spurns the society of mankind? ". . .
Brittle indeed are the fortunes of a people if they depend upon the
will or the caprices of one man." This, then, is the origin of
tyranny among the Romans, which differs from that represented
in Plato's *Republic* in this, that it was not the seizing of a new
power by Tarquin, but the unjust employment of one he already
had, which completely overthrew this form of regal state.[1] "It
is most true that without the highest justice no republic under any
conditions can be maintained." [2]

But is this justice according to nature? The old contention of
the Sophists remained; it had been ably restated by Carneades,
and this view is now set forth with all the old arguments by Furio
in the dialogue, and so forcibly that Lactantius later declared that
Cicero was unable to answer it. The right we are seeking is
merely civil, it has nothing to do with nature; if it had, like heat
and cold the just and the unjust would be the same everywhere
and for all. The proof that they are not so lies everywhere.
Xerxes ordered the burning of the temples at Athens because the
Persians believe it impious to try to confine within walls the gods
whose house is the whole world; the Cretans and Aetolians consider highway robbery honorable, and even within a single city a
thousand changes might be shown to prove that no law is invariable and many harmful. If the just should obey the laws, which
laws must they be? Can anyone admit that there is a difference
among laws and still hold that good men by nature follow a justice
which really exists and is not merely assumed? Each nation in

---

[1] *De Re Publica*, II, chaps. 28–29. The bitterness of these words may be the result of
Cicero's hatred of Caesar. Compare the scarcely veiled references to him in the *De Officiis*
written later (Bk. II, chaps. 1, 7, 8, 24, Bk. III, 2, for example), and the outspoken hostility in
Cicero's letters. The *De Re Publica* was written between 54 and 52 B.C. and the *De Legibus*
begun in 52 but left unfinished. In Cicero's discussion of these matters, one may possibly
see indications of the famous distinction clearly drawn by Bartolus in the fourteenth century
between a tyrant *sine titulo* and one *exercitio*, a difference that lies behind almost the whole
of the great controversy about monarchy in the sixteenth century when religious differences
within states had come in to give a new and vastly significant meaning to acts of royal
oppression.

[2] *De Re Publica*, II, chap. 44.

actual fact ordains as law only what is expedient for it as Carneades proved. There is no justice; if there were, it would be the height of stupidity — to injure one's self in consulting the interests of others. Let the Romans if they wish to be just restore what they have seized from other peoples and sink back into the state of poverty and wretchedness from which their conquests raised them. There can be no advantages to one state which are not disadvantages to another. Those are called tyrants who have the power of life and death over the people, but they prefer to call themselves kings; when a few through wealth or birth control the republic it is faction, but is called aristocracy; if all are governed by the will of the people it is termed liberty but is nothing but license.

But since one fears another, man against man, and order against order, and no one dares trust to himself, a kind of pact is joined between the people and the magistrates, and it is only from this that arises that thing which Scipio so praised, a united form of state; "for neither nature nor volition is the mother of justice, but defencelessness." [1]

Wisdom prompts us to enlarge our wealth and power, justice urges us to spare others and respect their rights and goods. Wealth, power, and honors, public and private, are the rewards of following the promptings of wisdom; while the just man, pillaged and in chains, is reduced to the last extreme of poverty and misery. "Who, then, is so mad as to be in doubt which he should choose? And what is true of individuals is true of peoples. There is no state so stupid as not to prefer ruling unjustly to serving justly." [2]

We have little but fragments left of the answer of Laelius to this, but it was probably much the same as Plato's and it no doubt expressed the views of Cicero himself. How, he asks, could one call tyranny a form of republic when all are oppressed by the cruelty of one, and there is neither a bond of law (*vinculum juris*) nor consent and association of the assemblage, which alone can make them a people? A tyranny is not a vitiated republic: it is no republic at all. Nor may a state be truly called a republic when it is wholly in the power of a faction, as of the thirty in Athens or the rule of the Decemvirs just before their fall.

But a popular state, where all things are said to be controlled

[1] *De Re Publica*, III, 13.
[2] *De Re Publica*, III, chaps. 8–20 *passim*.

by and under the power of the people, and the multitude inflicts
punishment at will, and seizes and holds or destroys as it pleases,
surely that must be a republic, since there the people are everything
and we have agreed that a republic is a thing of the people.   By
no means, says Laelius.   "There is nothing I should more unhesi-
tatingly deny to be a republic than that."

We refused to admit that Syracuse was a republic when a
tyranny, or Agrigentum, or Athens, or this city under the Decemvirs, nor is there any greater reason to apply the name republic to
a state under the domination of the multitude, since the assemblage
is no people under Scipio's definition if not restrained by consent
to law (*nisi qui consensu juris continetur*), but as much a tyrant
as if it were one man, and even more horrid, because no beast is
more hideous than that which wears the face and bears the name
of the people.[1]

The quotations or paraphrases above include some of Cicero's
principal surviving statements regarding political institutions,
their origin and nature, and the part played by justice in them.
His conception of law appears to be the Stoic one, and it is set
forth at length in the *De Legibus* as well as in one remarkable passage from the *De Re Publica*, preserved by Lactantius; and since
it is by the existence of a "bond of law" (*vinculum juris*) that a
true republic is to be distinguished from other inferior groups of
men, Cicero's conception of the nature of law assumes great importance in his general view of the state.   "True law," he says, "is
right reason consonant with nature, diffused among all men, constant, eternal; which summons to duty by its command and
hinders from fraud by its prohibition, which neither commands
nor forbids good men in vain nor moves bad ones by either.   To
make enactments infringing this law, religion forbids, neither may
it be repealed even in part, nor have we power through Senate or
people to free ourselves from it.   It needs no interpreter or ex-
pounder but itself, nor will there be one law in Rome and another
in Athens, one in the present and another in time to come, but one
law and that eternal and immutable shall embrace all peoples and
for all time, and there shall be as it were one common master and
ruler, the god of all, the author and judge and proposer of this
law.   And he who obeys him not shall flee from himself, and in
spurning the nature of human kind by that very act he shall suffer

[1] *De Re Publica*, III, chaps. 31–33.

the greatest of torments, though he escape others which men consider pains."[1]

Now therefore, after consideration in the manner of Plato of men's natural endowments and the nature of their association, it remains to go on as Plato does in his *Laws* to this law which is so closely connected with these. For this we shall not look as men usually do to the Praetor's edict nor to the Twelve Tables as our predecessors did, but we shall draw it from the fundamental principles of philosophy. For it is not the details of legal rules or practice that we have undertaken to discuss but nothing less than the source of universal law and of enactments. The nature of law must be made clear and that must be derived from the nature of man; and enactments must be considered by which states ought to be ruled as well as the *jura civilia* in which the rights and commands of peoples have been actually set forth and described, not omitting those of our own people.

The wisest of men have defined law as the supreme reason seated in nature which enjoins what must be done and forbids the contrary, and that reason when fixed and elaborated in the mind of man, as *lex*. And so they have considered prudence to be law, since it is its province to command right action and to forbid the contrary, and they think its name is derived from the Greek word meaning to give to each one what is his, but I think it comes from our own word "to gather" (*legendo*) for as they place the emphasis in law upon fairness we place it on the choosing (*dilectus*) and no doubt there is something of each of these in law. But properly speaking, as it seems to me and to others as well, the beginning of law must be derived from *lex*, and that is the potency of nature, the intellect and reason of a prudent man, the measure of right and wrong. In popular language it is customary to call that law, which enacts as written rules what it pleases in commanding or forbidding, as the unlearned apply it, but we should look for the beginning of the establishment of law in that highest law which was born ages before any written law or even any state had been founded. Man is the only animate thing created by God as a sharer in reason, and what is more divine than reason, which when it develops and becomes perfect we call true wisdom ? Since, then, there is nothing higher than reason and it exists both in man and in God, the partnership in reason of man with God is first. If

[1] Lactantius, *Institutiones Divinae*, VI, 8; Cicero, *De Re Publica*, III, 22.

reason is common to both, so is right reason, and if right reason is law, by law as well we must believe that men are joined with the gods. Moreover, between those in communion of law there is also a community of right, and they who have these things in common must be thought of as belonging to the same state, as they are obedient to the same authority and power. And these much more so, for they are obedient to the celestial disposition of the divine mind and to mighty God. And so this whole world must be regarded as a single state common to gods and men. Virtue man shares with God : it is the likeness of man to God. We are born to justice, and right exists not by opinion but by nature, as will be clear if we but look at the association and relations of men with each other. For the likeness of all men to each other is far greater than their differences in mind and thought, in virtue, and even in their vices.

What nation exists that does not honor kindness, and hate the proud and the cruel ? Reason has by nature been given to all men, and if so, right reason, and law, and if law then right. "For there is one law by which the society of men is held together, and one *lex* has established it. That *lex* is right reason in commanding or forbidding, and one who disregards it is unjust whether it has ever been written or not." But if justice is no more than a compliance with the written laws and institutions of peoples, and if, as some say, all things must be measured by utility alone, then let every one neglect and break the laws if he can, when he thinks it is to his own advantage. If it is not of nature, there is no justice at all, and what has been established on account of utility, by that utility is destroyed. If right is not to be confirmed in nature, all virtues will be destroyed along with it. How can liberality exist, or love of country, or piety, or the desire to deserve well of another ? "For these all arise from our natural propensity to love men, which is also the foundation of right." If rights were established only by ordinances of the people or decrees of princes, or decisions of judges, then it would be right to pillage, to commit adultery, to falsify wills, if such things were approved by the votes or decrees of the multitude. It is not for hope of reward that men do right. If so we should praise a man for being crafty rather than good. One who looks about him must see that man is in reality a citizen of the world as of one great city. We have all learned by heart the Twelve Tables, and we have been used to call other things of this kind "laws," but we must remember that all the power these have to enjoin rightful acts or to forbid wrongful ones is older than peoples or states and coeval with the God himself who rules heaven and earth.   Reason, springing from the nature of things, which impels us to good and recalls us from evil, did not become law when it was written, but when it was made; and it was made at the same time as the mind of God.   The varying rules appointed for peoples according to the needs of the time have the name of laws more by favor than by right.   Every law which *rightly* bears the name is good.   How many things there are enacted among peoples to their harm and danger which no more deserve the name of law than if enacted by highwaymen!   "Law, then, is a distinction between things just and unjust, expressing that original and fundamental nature of all things to which the laws of men are conformed which inflict penalties on the wicked and defend and protect the good." [1]

From hence too is the power of the magistrate, that he rule and prescribe things right and useful and conformable to the laws. For the laws control the magistrate as the magistrate controls the people, "and it may be truly said that the magistrate is a speaking law, the law a silent magistrate." [2]   And nothing is more suited to the right and condition of nature (by which I mean law) than authority (*imperium*), for without it no household nor state can endure, not even the whole race of men, nor the nature of things, nor the world itself.   For as the magistrate is subject to God so the seas and lands are subject to the magistrate and the life of men conforms to the commands of the supreme law.[3]

The study of the state begins with a study of human nature and by that nature men are equal; all men and all races of men are capable of virtue; it is vice and wrong-doing, not nature, that produce inequality.   Dr. Carlyle has rendered a great service in

---

[1] *De Legibus*, I, chaps. 5–24; II, 4–5 *passim*.

[2] Vereque dici potest magistratum legem esse loquentem, legem autem mutum magistratum.   It was apparently a prominent part of the Hellenistic conception of kingship that the king was law personified, that is a "living law" (νόμος ἔμψυχος).   It was natural for the Romans after the expulsion of the kings to continue to ascribe a similar character to the magistrates who temporarily performed the offices once performed by their kings.   For an interesting account of this conception of kingship, which the author believes to be Hellenistic, drawn from the extracts preserved by Stobaeus, see Erwin R. Goodenough, *The Political Philosophy of Hellenistic Kingship, Yale Classical Studies*, vol. i, pp. 55–102, 1928, with the extracts there given and the references to modern monographic material.   Some of these apparently Hellenistic ideas regarding kingship may possibly have had their origin in Persia or other parts of the East, as Mr. Goodenough thinks.

[3] *De Legibus*, III, 1.

emphasizing the fact that this is the most important difference between Cicero and the greatest of the Greek philosophers. It is as he has said "The dividing line between the ancient and the modern political theory." We are "at the beginnings of a theory of human nature and society of which the 'Liberty, Equality, and Fraternity' of the French Revolution is only the present-day expression." And he has shown that this turning point lies in the period between Aristotle and Cicero.[1] The idea of the equality of men is the profoundest contribution of the Stoics to political thought, that idea has colored its whole development from their day to ours, and its greatest influence is in the changed conception of law that in part resulted from it. To Cicero law is coeval with man. Man as man shares it with God, and by nature he shares it equally with other men of whatever race or city, and this before the foundation of any state or the establishment of its *jus civile*. True, this in essence may be the same as the theory of Plato and Aristotle. The Stoics and the Roman jurists after them defended the objectivity and the natural character of law against their opponents much as Socrates and Plato and Aristotle had done against the Sophists, but the belief in equality has made in effect a new theory of it. To Plato only the few can ever bear to look at the light, though the light is there; the bulk of mankind are not capable of it, they must be content with the dim shadow of truth on the wall of the prison in which they are chained for life, and for Plato knowledge and political virtue are not separate things. Therefore it is "natural" to man and it is best for him to be ruled by his natural superiors, and aristocracy becomes the form of government suited to the nature of the vast majority of men. And Aristotle fully agrees, so far as political results are concerned. Citizenship implies equality indeed, but it is not numerical equality but proportional. Some are born to subjection as others are to rule, and as a principle of nature. It is not too much to say that Locke's theory of the rights of man as man antecedent to and independent of the state has been implicit in political thought ever since the Stoics and as a result of Rome's transmission of Stoic conceptions of equality.

For Aristotle only a beast or a god can subsist outside a state, and even many men who are in a state are scarcely of it, because they are "naturally" rather beasts than men. For Cicero on the

[1] *A History of Mediaeval Political Theory in the West*, vol. i, p. 9.

contrary "this whole world must be thought of as one great state common to gods and men," and "there is one common equal rule of life among men." If anyone disobeys this rule, a rule made at the same time as the mind of God, "before any written laws or any state had been founded," such a one "spurns the nature of man" itself. The ideas of Aristotle and Cicero about these things may have had a common origin but they have become poles apart in their influence on political thought.

It is in this newer conception of law that the departure from the inequality of antique thought has had its greatest influence upon later ideas of the state. For to Cicero this law common to all men and to God and as old as time is also the source of the state itself, — a state is nothing else than "a partnership in law" (juris societas).[1]

Not only is Cicero's law different, then, from Plato's or Aristotle's; his whole theory of the state is far more dependent on law than theirs, a theory of rights in a sense with which the Greeks were unacquainted; and this legalistic character, apparently of Roman and not Greek origin, confirmed by the later Roman jurists, was handed on by them to remain one of the distinguishing marks of western political thought almost to our own day, if it is not so still.

The authors of Justinian's *Institutes* defined a private obligation as "a bond of law" (juris vinculum),[2] and Cicero nearly six centuries before referred to "the bond (vinculum) that first bound men together in the association of a republic," [3] also as a "bond of law." "Law (lex)," he says, "is the bond of civil society" (civilis societatis vinculum), and *jus* is equivalent to *lex;* [4] for what is a state but "a partnership in law" (juris societas)? Law is coeval with God, though we knew it through the nature of man who shares it with God, and in that eternal law the state itself has its origin, for the state is "an assemblage of men associated in consent to law." To Cicero, then, the state is not "prior" to the individual, not even in thought, as with Aristotle. Society and the state are no longer equivalent terms. He can speak of society as a wider thing than any political unit and an older, and he can

---

[1] Quid est enim civitas nisi juris societas? *De Re Publica,* I, 32.
[2] *Institutes,* 3, 13, pr.
[3] . . . illud vinclum, quod primum homines inter se rei publicae societate devinxit, *De Re Publica,* I, 26.
[4] Quare cum lex sit civilis societatis vinculum . . . . *Ibid,* I, 32.

think of man as something more than a mere "part" of a state, lifeless as a foot of stone if separated from it, and even inconceivable but in reference to it. Man may have a real existence before he enters into any state, he *has* had an existence before states were or any of their laws; and if so, it is possible to think of him as in some ways independent of a state's existence, and it is conceivable that he may have "rights" with which it has nothing to do. We are plainly in the presence of the beginnings of "modern" political thought.

To Cicero, apparently, the "consent to law" in which the "partnership" of the republic consists, does not necessarily imply a definite "compact"; but there is one passage in which he represents the opponents of Scipio as practically anticipating even that famous theory, a part of it almost in the very terms of Hobbes himself — "But since one fears another, and no one dares trust to himself, a sort of compact (*pactio*) is made between the people and the powerful men, and it is from this that exists that form of united state which Scipio was praising." [1]

But whether formed by definite "pact" or not, it is significant that Cicero's state is founded in consent, and that this to be effective, must be the consent of the whole people (*populus*), a theory which formed the central principle of the Roman republican constitution and survived the establishment of practical despotism in the Empire to pass into the common thought of Europe in later centuries.[2] Furthermore, the state so founded is for Cicero no collection of men united merely *politically* by common aims and common ideals: it is a *populus* welded together by a bond of *law* into a corporate body with supreme legal authority, and this remains just as true whether the state happens to be a kingdom, an aristocracy, or a democracy; for all these are but differing forms of administration not of sovereign power. All three are varieties of *res publicae*, and a *res publica* is *res populi*. The Greek political notion of a *politeuma* was utterly foreign to the legalistic thinking of Rome. To a Greek, thinking politically, an oligarchy or a king *was* the state; to a Roman thinking in terms of law, it was "the proper business of the magistrate" — a king even, as well as others — "to understand that he impersonates the state,

---

[1] *De Re Publica*, III, 13.
[2] See Rehm, *Geschichte der Staatsrechtswissenschaft*, pp. 149-150. "The assembly of the people is the state; not merely the organ of the *populus*, but the *populus* itself."

to maintain its due dignity and honor, to conserve its laws, to administer its rights, and to bear in mind the things committed to his trust." [1] All the elements of the modern legalistic conception of sovereignty seem to be present here in their entirety and present for the first time, though Bodin's claim may be conceded that no philosopher or jurisconsult before him had exactly defined it.[2] The analogy between this bond of law (*vinculum juris*) thus arising from consent, which for Cicero creates a state, and the private obligations which later jurists defined by the selfsame phrase, is so striking as to suggest a possible connection between the two. The state is a *vinculum juris* and so is an *obligatio*. Obligations may arise from wrongful actions (*ex delicto*), and it was a prevalent theory in the early middle ages that the state itself had first appeared after the fall of man as a consequence and a remedy for his sin. Other obligations are created by a definite agreement (*pactum*) of parties (*ex contractu*) as the compact theory would create the state, and in still other cases an agreement is presumed and an obligation incurred by acts unaccompanied by any express pact (*quasi ex contractu*). The last of these seems to come nearest to the "consent to law" in which for Cicero the "bond of civil society" (*civilis societatis vinculum*) consists. But in every one of these cases it is the bond of *law* (*vinculum juris*) not the act of the party which creates the obligation. The agreement of two persons, for example, is itself no contract, though the bond of law may make a contract out of it : as in the commonwealth a "consent to law" exists or is assumed. It would be misleading to press this analogy too far, but the Roman mind was legalistic, the Roman state theory was largely the work of jurists from its beginning to its end, and so many of these Roman law ideas are actually found in the wake of the Roman Empire in early medieval speculations concerning the state that the fact can scarcely be a mere coincidence.

Between the writings of Cicero and those of the great Roman

[1] Cicero, *De Officiis*, I, 34, Est igitur proprium munus magistratus intelligere se gerere personam civitatis debereque ejus dignitatem et decus sustinere, servare leges, jura describere, ea fidei suae commissa meminisse. See Rehm, *op. cit.*, pp. 150–152, where this passage is quoted from Cicero and some of the points set forth above established. Cicero's phrase *se gerere personam civitatis* is very significant. The magistrate "wears the mask of the state." He impersonates it as an actor does any particular character by the mask he wears. His decrees are the voice of the law sounding through the mask of his official person. The magistrate is a living law because he bears the character (*persona* or *caput*) of the state. See Heumann, *Handlexicon zu den Quellen des römischen Rechts*, s. v. *Persona*.

[2] Bodin's *De Republica*, I, 8.

jurists preserved in Justinian's *Digest* come a large number of writers whose works here and there illustrate the state of contemporary political thought, poets, historians, and moralists, but none seem to contribute much that is actually new with the possible exception of Seneca, who died by his own hand at Nero's order in 65 A.D. His writings may be considered as the highest and the completest statement of Stoic views regarding the state in the early imperial epoch, but there is little in them to indicate much significant advance beyond his predecessors except perhaps his elaboration of the idea of the primitive innocence of mankind in the early ages of the world before there were states or other forms of dominion over men or external things. His belief in such a condition involved a further theory of the later degradation of mankind and the growth of certain human institutions either as a result of this fall from innocence itself or as the outgrowth of a coercive power which that fall made necessary. In Seneca, then, we have apparently the earliest complete surviving expression of some theories that later played a very considerable part in the historical unfolding of political thought. We have, for example, in the idea of a state of men's primitive innocence and their subsequent loss of it, a theory which in the hands of later Christian writers might easily be combined with the Biblical account of the fall of Adam to color all their thinking about the state, slavery, and property during the early middle ages. The profoundest of the results of this tendency and one of the earliest, was the added emphasis which in time was placed on the difference not merely between the *jus naturale* and the *jus civile,* but even between the *jus naturale* and the *jus gentium.*[1]

Many, possibly most, of the jurists of the second century A.D. if Gaius may be considered typical of them, seem still to adhere to a contrary view, and identify the philosophic law of nature and the actual *jus gentium;* but a generation later Ulpian and others set forth in unmistakable terms the idea, not merely that the two

---

[1] Cicero had emphasized the first of these differences and Hildenbrand argues convincingly that he had distinguished scarcely less clearly between the *jus naturale* and the *jus gentium. Geschichte und System der Rechts- und Staatsphilosophie,* pp. 560–581, especially pp. 572–577. Such a distinction would be a natural result of the subjectivism which Stoic doctrine shared with opposing schools of thought. If this distinction tended to disappear among the Roman jurists, as the later evidence of Gaius might seem to indicate, this must have been in part the result of factors in Rome extraneous to Greek philosophy, the outcome of local conditions, rather than a mere deduction from the original doctrines of Stoicism, which in some of their aspects would seem to discourage instead of to favor such a tendency.

are distinct, but that the *jus gentium* was of later historical origin and its actual content the result of strife and war.[1]   It was the views of Ulpian rather than of Gaius that later jurists followed on this point, as the *Institutes* of Justinian show, with the result that the weight of the Roman law was ultimately added to the influence of the philosophic views of Seneca to combine with *Genesis* in forming the theories generally accepted in the earlier middle ages on the question of the origin and nature of social institutions such as slavery and government.

Here and there among the early Christians leanings are to be found in the direction both of communism and anarchy, which must have been strengthened by a view like Seneca's that mankind while still uncorrupted knew no dominion of one man over another, political or economic, and later Roman legal writers tended in part to confirm it in theory if not in practice.   The result was that these human institutions came to be regarded as the result of sin, and it was possible for some to go even farther and regard them as sinful in themselves.   At least they were not original.   They had a historical origin.   They were man-made all of them, and if they have a divine sanction it is at most only as a remedy for sin.   The sinless had not needed them and never do need them.   Thus it appears that Seneca's ideas, though Stoic in origin, tended at a later time to veer around through this idea of the fall of man toward a view not unlike that of the older skeptics, that the state is not a natural but a conventional thing; and Seneca's writings indicate one of the streams that later united in the thought of the early Church fathers to form the usual view of the early middle ages, that slavery is only an external, accidental status, historical in origin, and against nature in character; that government may not be far different from it in origin at least; and that private property ought to be limited to the *use* of external goods, charity to be enforced as a duty, and poverty encouraged as a virtue.   Seneca's view is in some ways

[1] It is scarcely safe to assume, as is usually done, that the identification of the *jus naturale* and the *jus gentium* because made by Gaius, *must* be typical of his time even for lawyers. It is true, his textbook of law was the one most used, but its popularity did not result from the few general statements on the *jus gentium* with which it begins, but from the masterly summary of the *jus civile* which constitutes all the rest.   These opening statements about the *jus gentium* may not be of greater significance than the lip-service to the law of nature in what Sir Frederick Pollock aptly calls " the ornamental part " of Blackstone's *Commentaries* which precedes the author's complete acceptance of the doctrine of the omnipotence of Parliament.   Sweeping generalizations on this subject, such as Sir Henry Maine's, are based after all upon contemporary evidence very small indeed in amount.

strangely like Rousseau's *Discourse on the Origin of Inequality among Men.*[1]

The philosophic basis of Roman law is Greek and it was laid in the Republican period, but the particular principles of the law itself are Roman, worked out step by step with patient thoroughness by generations of magistrates and jurists. As the poet says of the English constitution they were "broadening down from precedent to precedent," slowly expanding to meet changing social and economic needs in a sure and gradual development scarcely matched in the whole history of human institutions for the length of the process or the permanence and solidity of the result. "It may be said that the Romans have fixed for all time the categories of juristic thought." [2] Cato might have boasted of the permanence of Roman private law with even more justice than he did of the Roman Republic and for the same reason: it was established not by the genius of one man but of many, nor for the life of one but for ages. The Greek genius produced a theory of the state and of law, Rome above all developed a scientific jurisprudence; but aside from its contributions, to political philosophy she added but very little. A permanent legal system such as Rome's or England's must be a gradual evolution, a conservative development based on precedent, and the work of innumerable hands, the product not so much of individual genius as of collective administrative ability, and of this the brilliant restless mind of Greece seemed impatient. It is dangerous to generalize about racial characteristics, and Greece had little chance to develop the political solidarity necessary for a great permanent system of jurisprudence. Particular states like Athens, and probably others if we knew more of them and their institutions, had gone some distance in that direction, but it is the fact, whatever the reason, that Greece produced, and in the circumstances could produce, nothing comparable with the Praetor's edict, Rome certainly produced no political philosopher comparable with Aristotle. Greek political philosophy — whatever the reason may be — was largely the work of exceptional individuals; the Roman constitution was the work-

[1] For a brief but adequate account of Seneca's political ideas, see Carlyle, *A History of Mediaeval Political Theory*, vol. i, chap. ii. Dr. Carlyle points out one important difference between Seneca and the ideas of the eighteenth century. For Seneca the primitive condition of mankind was one of innocence rather than perfection, an undeveloped stage of culture to which it was certainly not possible and probably not desirable to return. *Op. cit.*, pp. 23-24.

[2] E. Cuq, *Les institutions juridiques des Romains*, 2d ed., vol. i, p. xxiv.

ing system of a capable people; and naturally the former tended
to emphasize aristocracy; the central principle of the latter was
the sovereignty of the *populus*. Rome's influence upon the growth
of political thought is thus radically different from that of Greece,
but it is in its way scarcely less important.

From what has just been said, it is evident that we must expect
to find among the Roman juristic writings the evidence of what
men were actually thinking about the state, rather than any
striking innovations or important individual contributions to that
thought. And this is especially true of the first important jurist
of the classic period of Roman law whose work has survived in
its original form. Gaius was no original thinker, he was not even
a great jurist, but he was what is probably more important for our
search, the author of the best concise handbook of existing law, and
the most popular one of his day. For this reason his statements
may perhaps be a more trustworthy indication of the current political ideas underlying the law of Rome in the second century A.D.
than the novel generalizations of keener minds. "Whatever any
people itself has established as law for it," Gaius says, "this is confined to it alone and is called the *jus civile*, as a kind of law peculiar
to the state; whatever, on the other hand, natural reason has
established among all men, this is observed uniformly among all
peoples and is called the *jus gentium*, as a kind of law which all
races employ. And so the Roman people employ a law partly
peculiar to themselves and partly common to all men." [1] The two
divisions of *jus* made here are according to origins, but he proceeds
to make a further classification of it as it exists in Rome, on the
basis of the source of its authority, into *leges, plebiscita, senatus
consulta, constitutiones principum*, edicts of magistrates having
legal authority to issue them, and the responses of the learned in
the law. "*Lex*," he further says, "is what the *populus* commands
and has established," a plebiscite is now what the *plebs* commands
and has established (the *populus* being all the citizens, the *plebs*,
all except the patricians), but only since the passage of the *Lex
Hortensia* which gave it binding force equal to *lex*. What the
Senate ordains likewise "gains the position of *lex* (*legis vicem*

---

[1] Gaius, *Institutiones*, i, i . . . "quod quisque populus ipse sibi jus constituit, id ipsius
proprium est vocaturque jus civile, quasi jus proprium civitatis; quod vero naturalis ratio
inter omnes homines constituit, id apud omnes populos peraeque custoditur vocaturque jus
gentium, quasi quo jure omnes gentes utuntur. Populus itaque Romanus partim suo proprio,
partim communi omnium hominum jure utitur."

optinet) — though this has been questioned;" and a constitution
of the *Princeps* is what the Emperor by decree, edict, or letter, has
ordained; "nor has it ever been doubted that this should hold the
place of *lex*, since the Emperor himself receives his *imperium* by
a *lex*" (nec umquam dubitatum est, quin id legis vicem optineat,
cum ipse imperator per legem imperium accipiat). Only one more
short statement need be included: "Slaves are in the power of
their masters, and this power is of the *jus gentium*, for we may
observe among all races uniformly that a power of life and death
over slaves rests in their masters." [1] But it is followed immediately by the assertion that "it is not permissible now for Roman
citizens or any others under the sovereign authority of the Roman
people (*sub imperio populi Romani*) to indulge in excessive or
causeless harshness towards their slaves," two imperial constitutions are cited which impose particular restrictions upon masters,
and such a constitution, Gaius declares, is "rightly made" (*recte
fit*), for we should not make evil use of our right. These few sentences, considered together with the author's significant omission
of certain other statements about slavery made by later jurists,
constitute the chief indications given by Gaius of the political
thought of his time.

Among other things they seem to point to an existing belief that
the law of nature and the *jus gentium* are one and the same in
content, character, and origin, merging with the *jus civile* in Rome
to form a part of her law, no matter what the form of its promulgation may be; that any particular rule or institution is proved to
belong to the *jus gentium*, if we can find all nations employing it;
and that slavery is such an institution of that law in force everywhere, although full exercise of the rights under it may be an "evil
use" of them which enactments of the *jus civile* may "rightly"
curb. This recognition by Gaius that one admitted right under
the *jus gentium* "established by natural reason among all men,"
may at the same time be an abuse which a particular state ought
to limit by its own law, is a curious inconsistency that has received
scant attention, but it is the sign of a small breach in an older legal
theory which in a generation or two was to widen into the settled
belief that the *jus naturale* and the *jus gentium* are totally separate
from each other in origin, in nature, and in content, and that
slavery as an institution is "against nature."

[1] Gaius, *Institutiones*, 1, 52.

Another sign of the transitional character of the political thought of the time of Gaius appears in his discussion of *lex* and the relation of other kinds of enactment to it. "The imperium of the Roman people" is the authority from which comes the binding force of enactments of whatever kind, directly in the case of *leges* made by the *populus* itself, indirectly as in *plebiscita* which have "the place of *lex*" only because the whole *populus* by a *lex* have conferred on the *Plebs* the authority to make them. Decrees of the Senate have similar force, Gaius thinks, and for the same reason, though he hints at existing doubts of this, because no definite *lex* could be pointed to by which the *populus* had conferred the power; and the inconclusive reason suggested later in the *Institutes* of Justinian would hardly seem a valid answer to all such doubts. But no doubts of this kind could possibly exist concerning the imperial constitutions, because every emperor received his authority by a lex that was definite and known. This clear statement by Gaius that the *populus* is the source of all legal authority is of the highest importance, and it is not without significance that it continued to be the central principle of the Roman constitution to the very end, even after it was weakened into a mere theory of origins by the growth under it of a practical absolutism that was complete.

Between the writings of Gaius in the second century and the issuance of the great law books of Justinian in the sixth a few Roman legal writings are known to us from sources independent of Justinian's collections, chiefly parts of the treatises on the private law or imperial constitutions, but none of these is much concerned with the theory of the state, with the possible exception of an occasional imperial law included in the *Theodosian Code*. Our knowledge of the development of political thought in this period is derived almost entirely from legal writings included by Justinian's commissioners in the compilations or summaries of the sixth century. But it is important to bear in mind two things about these writings. Though set forth in their surviving form in the sixth century, some of the most important were originally written much earlier, the bulk of them in the third century, a few earlier, and some later. Secondly, the commissioners were required to make such alterations in these before publication as were necessary to bring them into line with the law of Justinian's time, and this was actually done, though apparently as sparingly as possible. It is mainly from these sources and with these limitations that we must reconstruct the history of Roman political thought from the third to the sixth century A.D. Of Justinian's books, the *Digest* is probably the most important as the source of earlier political thought. It consists of a vast number of extracts from legal writings extant in the sixth century, fortunately with the book, the treatise, and the name of its author, appended to each extract. The largest single contributor to it was Ulpian, one of the leading Roman jurists of the third century, and it is among the extracts from his writings that probably the largest number of statements of third century political thought are to be found, though a few of the most important of them come from the writings of other jurists of the same general period or near it. Scarcely less important than the *Digest*, at least for the ideas of the later Empire, was the students' manual issued in the same year, 533 A.D., with a title and a general order of treatment identical with those of the *Institutiones* or *Institutes* of Gaius. The amended *Code* promulgated the next year includes a few imperial constitutions of political interest, as do also the "new constitutions" issued from time to time during the remaining thirty years of Justinian's reign. From all these, together with incidental statements in non-legal writers, and an occasional inscription, such as the important *Lex de Imperio* of Vespasian,[1] most of the political ideas of the imperial epoch must be drawn.

"Justice," in the opening words of Justinian's *Institutes*, "is a constant and perpetual disposition of the will which renders to each one what is his right." This important definition is taken by the authors of the *Institutes* from the *Rules* of Ulpian written in the third century and included in Justinian's *Digest*.[2] The significant statements immediately following come from the same source: "Jurisprudence is the knowledge of things divine and human, the perception of the just and the unjust." "The precepts of law are these: to live uprightly, to injure no one, to render to each his right." "Jus," Ulpian had said in another book,[3] "is so called from *justitia;*" it is, as Celsus says, "the art of the good and the fair." [4] "The word *jus*," declares Julius Paulus, another great jurist contemporary with Ulpian, "is used in many senses; in one

---

[1] Printed in *Textes de droit romain*, edited by P. F. Girard, 5th ed., pp. 107–108; Bruns, *Fontes Juris Romani Antiqui*, 7th ed., pp. 202–203.

[2] *Digest*, I, 1, 10, pr.

[3] His *Institutes*, *Digest*, I, 1, pr.

[4] Celsus was an important Roman jurist of the first and second centuries A.D.

that is termed just which is invariably fair and good, as is *jus naturale;* in another for what is advantageous to all persons or to most in any particular state, as is the *jus civile,* and in our own state *jus* is applied no less properly to the *jus honorarium,* and the praetor is said to administer right even when he gives an unjust decision, regard being had not to what the praetor has actually done but to what he ought to do." [1]

Law is either public, concerned with the gods or the state; or it is private, pertaining to the interests of private individuals. The latter is threefold, deduced from rules of nature, of nations, or of a particular nation. "*Jus naturale,*" the first of these three, "is what nature has taught to all animals, for this law is not peculiar to man but common to all animals, whether brought forth upon the earth, in the sky, or in the sea. From it comes the union of male and female which we call marriage, and the procreation and training of offspring, for we see that other animals as well as man are acquainted with this law." [2] Examples of it are our "obligations to the gods and the duty of submission to parents or country" [3] or "the right to repel violence and wrong, for it is according to this law, that an act done for the protection of one's person is held to be rightful, and since nature has established a kind of kinship between us, as a consequence it is impious for one man to lie in wait for another." [4]

"The *jus gentium* is the law employed by men in nations, and that it departs from natural law is evident from the latter's being common to all animals, while the *jus gentium* is common only to men in relation to each other." [5] Manumission of slaves, for example, had its origin in the *jus gentium,* "for by the law of nature all would have been born free and manumission would therefore be unheard of since slavery itself would be unknown. But after servitude came in "through the *jus gentium* the benefit of manumission followed. And though we should have been known by one natural name as men, under the *jus gentium* three classes appeared, freemen, slaves, and a third class of freedmen who had ceased to be slaves." [6]

[1] *Digest,* 1, 1, 11.
[2] Ulpian, *Institutiones, D,* 1, 1, 2–3 ; *Institutiones,* 1, 2, pr.
[3] Pomponius, *Enchiridion, D,* 1, 1, 2.   Pomponius flourished in the first half of the second century A.D.
[4] Florentinus, *Institutes, D,* 1, 1, 3.
[5] Ulpian, *op. cit., D,* 1, 1, 1, 4.
[6] Ulpian, *Institutes, D,* 1, 1, 4.

"By this *jus gentium* wars were introduced, nations marked off, realms established, rights of ownership distinguished, bounds set to fields, houses built, traffic, purchase and sale, letting and hiring and all sorts of obligations instituted, except a few introduced under the *jus civile*." [1]

"The *jus gentium* is common to the whole human race. For, urged on by custom and human needs, tribes of men established certain rules for themselves; wars arose and as a result the taking of captives and reducing them to servitude which are contrary to natural law. For by natural law from the beginning all men were born free. And from this *jus gentium* also all contracts were introduced, such as purchase and sale, letting and hiring, partnership, *depositum*, *mutuum*, and others without number." [2]

"All people who are ruled by laws and customs employ a law partly their own, partly common to all mankind, for what each people has established as law for itself, that is peculiar to the state and is called *jus civile* as pertaining to that state alone; but what natural reason has established among all men, this is observed among all peoples uniformly, and known as the *jus gentium*, as of a law used by all nations. And so the Roman people employ a law partly peculiar to them, partly common to all men." [3]

"The *jus civile* is a law which neither departs entirely from natural law or the *jus gentium* nor wholly follows it; and so when we add anything to or subtract it from the common law (*iuri communi*), we create a law of our own, that is the *jus civile*." [4]

The *jus civile* is of two kinds, written and unwritten. The written law or *lex*, according to Papinian, generally conceded to be the greatest of Roman lawyers, is a command of general application, a resolution of learned men, a restraint of offences whether committed voluntarily or in ignorance, a common covenant of the Republic. [5] The characterization comes from an oration attributed to Demosthenes, and it is given in Greek in the extract immediately

---

[1] Hermogenian, *Juris Epitomae, D*, 1, 1, 5. Hermogenian flourished in the first half of the fourth century A.D.

[2] *Institutes* of Justinian, 1, 2, 2.

[3] Gaius, *Institutiones*, 1, 1. Quoted *verbatim* in Justinian's *Institutes*, 1, 2, 1. See *ante*, p. 122.

[4] Ulpian, *Institutes, D*, 1, 1, 6, pr.

[5] *D*, 1, 3, 1; The passage, attributed to Demosthenes, is from the first of the two orations *adversus Aristogitonem*, now considered spurius.

ensuing, taken from the *Institutes* of Marcian, a jurist of the time
of Caracalla, followed by another from Chrysippus.[1]

Justinian's *Institutes* give the same list of the forms of written
law at Rome as given by Gaius,[2] *leges* proper, *plebiscita*, etc., and
we need note only the differences in statement.   One or two of
these differences, however, are significant.   Where Gaius expresses
the opinion that decrees of the Senate obtain the place of *lex*, but
hints at existing doubts of this,[3] the authors of Justinian's *Institutes*
venture to give a reason.   "Since the Roman people has grown
to such a size that it would be difficult to call it together in one
place for the ordaining of law, it has seemed fair to consult the
senate instead of the people." [4]   But its decrees nevertheless are
law, "and also" — the most famous of all Roman political maxims
— "what the *princeps* has pleased to ordain, has the force of law,
since by a regal law enacted concerning his *imperium*, the people
has conceded to him and conferred upon him the whole of its
imperium and *potestas*." [5]   A part of one such regal law, apparently
in form of a decree of the Senate, conferring the *imperium* and
potestas upon Vespasian in 69–70 A.D., was found on a bronze
tablet unearthed in Rome in the fourteenth century.[6]   But over
against this most famous of all the dicta of Roman public law
must be set a pronouncement scarcely less noteworthy of Theodosius and Valentinian in 429 A.D.   "It is a worthy voice (*digna vox*)
of reigning majesty for the *princeps* to profess his obligation to the
laws; so our authority depends upon the authority of law.   And
in very truth, for sovereignty to submit to law is greater than
[arbitrary] rule.   And by the word of the present edict we declare
that we do not suffer its being allowed us." [7]

Written law however does not exhaust the *jus civile*.   There is
also the law that arises without a writing "because custom has
approved it, for immemorial custom approved by consent of those
who use it supplies the place of law." [8]

"Natural Laws, which are uniformly observed among all nations,
being established by a kind of divine providence, remain always

---

[1] *D*, 1, 3, 2.   [2] *Ante*, pp. 122–123.   [3] *Ante*, pp. 122–123.   [4] *Institutes*, 1, 2, 5.
[5] *Institutes*, 1, 2, 6.
   "Sed et quod principi placuit, legis habet vigorem, cum lege regia quae de imperio ejus
lata est, populus ei et in eum omne suum imperium et potestatem concessit." This new
wording comes from Ulpian's *Institutes* with unimportant changes. *Dig.* 1, 4, 1. Compare
it with the earlier statement of Gaius, *Institutes*, 1, 1, 5, *ante*, p. 123.
   [6] P. F. Girard, *Textes de droit romain*, 5th ed., pp. 106–108.
   [7] *C*, 1, 14, 4.   [8] *Institutes*, 1, 2, 9.

firm and unchangeable, while those established for itself by any
state soever are always liable to change either by tacit consent
of the people, or by a later enactment." [1]

To these general pronouncements about law one single significant passage from the *Institutes* concerning slavery must be added,
the statement taken from Florentinus: [2] "and the freedom from
which men are called free is one's natural faculty of doing what
is permissible for anyone to do provided he be not prevented by
force or by law. Servitude, on the other hand, is a constitution
(*constitutio*) of the *jus gentium* by which one is made subject,
against nature, to the dominion of another."

The impression left by these extracts as a whole is certainly not
one of great originality or philosophic depth. The indiscriminate
eclecticism of the writers of Justinian's *Institutes*, for example, per-
mits them to include within one small title both Ulpian's assertion
that the *jus gentium* "departs from the law of nature," and the
declaration of Gaius that it includes "what natural reason has
established among all men." These two positions may, it is true,
not be wholly inconsistent. Patristic theory later made brave
efforts to reconcile some aspects of them, not entirely without
success, and Seneca had already suggested an explanation that
may have influenced Hermogenian and the other jurists who
ascribed war and servitude as well as government and a considerable portion of the law of obligations to an actual though possibly
prehistoric "departure" from the primitive simplicity of the
earliest times. But among the jurists themselves the attempt to
reconcile such apparent inconsistencies is usually either altogether
absent, or so feeble as to create the suspicion that they scarcely
appreciated the existence of any important problem to be solved.

Notwithstanding the apparent inability to see or to resolve these
differences, the statements in Justinian's books may be taken as
evidences of certain marked tendencies in the course of political
thought in the Roman Empire. We seem to see generally, though
possibly not invariably, a growing feeling that all parts of the legal
and political institutions of men are not primitive, that some of
them which are obviously in use everywhere are even "against
nature." Such institutions have, in other words, a historical
origin, though it probably belongs to the period before recorded
history, and the causes which produced them are to be found not

---

[1] *Institutes*, 1, 2, 11.   [2] *Institutes*, 1, 3, 1-2: *D*, 1, 5, 4.

in men's higher propensities, but in such lower ones as cruelty and avarice. They originate in a departure from primitive innocence and as the departure becomes greater and more widely extended they grow along with it, till at length they are seen to be a part of the particular law of every people and as common to all mankind as the primitive nature from which they have "receded." We are back in much the same position as the Sophists, that political institutions are the result of men's conventions, not the outgrowth of their inherent nature; and the beginnings of this divergence from Plato and Aristotle lie far back in the course of political speculation, they were Greek before they were Roman, and may be traced to the Epicurean and other schools of thought whose doctrines the Romans eagerly received together with Stoicism but never entirely reconciled with it.

At all events under the Empire the majority of men seem to have come to accept the view that some legal and political institutions do not orginate in nature and are therefore not natural even though universal. In some ways they seem to go even beyond the Sophists, whose favorite point of attack upon the "natural" character of these institutions was the fact that men were not in agreement about them. There could be no "law," because men in different places actually employed laws that were in opposition and contradiction one to another, while fire burns alike in Persia and in Greece. To the Roman some institutions had become "against nature" even though they were in full operation among all peoples.

For Ulpian this contradiction between nature and universal custom is explained by the assumption that "nature" is an animal instinct which man shares with the lower creatures, while any legal or political institution found among men which departs from it, if universal, must be attributed to the *jus gentium*. This explanation seems to have appealed to few of Ulpian's successors but the compilers of Justinian's *Digest* and the authors of his *Institutes*, but notwithstanding this it may have had some influence on subsequent political thought. "No philosopher, so far as I know," declared Vinnius in the seventeenth century, " and no jurisconsult, has asserted that *jus* is something that applies to the brutes, except Ulpian alone, from whom Tribonian took it." [1]   To Ulpian never-

---

[1] Arnoldi Vinnii, *In Quatuor Libros Institutionum Imperialium Commentarius*, Antverpiae, 1721, p. 13.   The statement is not supported by all the facts.

theless appears to belong the somewhat doubtful distinction of being one of the authors of the identification of the *political animal* or "being" and the beast (*besta*) or *lower animal*, and it was not a long step beyond when the "lower order" of men were collectively called by some not a beast merely, but a *noxious* beast (*belua*), "a monster" not unlike Cicero's tyrant who "outdoes the most monstrous of beasts in the excess of his vices," [1] except that it is "a monster with a hundred heads." The influence of such ideas upon the later development of the theory of tyrannicide is hard to estimate but it may have been considerable. The tyrant under that theory was an enemy of mankind and it was the duty as well as the right of anyone to "knock him in the head." Like the medieval *utlagatus* or outlaw, he "bore the head of a wolf," was beyond the law, and might be attacked with impunity. Moreover, since the application of the Darwinian hypothesis to ethics and politics in our own day, the naturalistic theories of Ulpian have again assumed an importance in general political thought which they lacked for centuries, and must therefore not be left out of the reckoning, whether we regard ethics and politics as a development of organic evolution or a departure from it.

But "*Jus* does not apply to brutes," says Cujas in the sixteenth century in a note to these assertions of Ulpian's, "nor can they suffer *injuria* . . . since brutes are without either reason or law." Then unfortunately he tries to save Ulpian's face by adding a distinction which seems dangerously close to a quibble, and leaves totally out of account institutions of the *jus gentium* such as slavery which the Roman jurists considered flatly *against* nature. So he continues, "But if men by reason do the same things which brutes do by incitement of nature, they do them under the law of nature. If all men do by reason things which brutes do not do, they do them under the *jus gentium*, which is itself called the law of nature, the good and the fair, the natural equity, natural reason, *lex naturalis* and nature. Those things which are done, not by all, but by a certain multitude of men assembled in one place and for public utility, they are done under the *jus civile*." [2]

But after all it is not Rome's individual jurists or philosophers so much as the creators — mostly unknown — of her general system of public and private law and its administration, who entitle

---

[1] *Ante*, p. 109.
[2] Jacobi Cuiacii, I. C., *Ad Libros Quatuor Institutionum Dn. Justiniani Notae.*

her to her deservedly large place in the general history of political thought. The constitutional doctrines concerning the basis of the Emperor's authority, and the ideas political and religious that gathered about his person or his office, had effects upon both the theory and the practice of monarchy in the later western world probably more profound and more lasting than those brought about by the hesitating interpretations put on Greek political ideas by Roman jurists, and they were effects produced by causes certainly more distinctly Roman than the latter. Among these causes none is of greater significance than the Roman constitutional doctrine that the Emperor really wields the power of the *populus*.

Differences of opinion have existed and some still exist among later authorities, concerning a number of points connected with the so-called *lex regia*, by which this power was acquired, but only a few of these points are matters directly affecting the course of political thought. The Roman jurists are in general agreement in asserting that by this *lex* the people conferred on the Emperor the whole (*omne*) of its *imperium* and its *potestas*. *Imperium* and *potestas* both are legal and technical terms; they are not popular ones; and each of them includes some particular portion of the authority exercised by the magistrates under the Republic, not vaguely conceived power or influence, but a concrete and definite piece of constitutional authority established by law. It is lawyers' terms with which we are dealing here, not philosophers'; and a thousand years later when one of these same words, *potestas*, is used by Bodin as the equivalent of *majestas* or modern sovereignty, it is still the *potestas* of the Roman lawyers that he has in mind. To Bodin "sovereign" *potestas* was as much a *legal* power as the tribunician *potestas* was to Gaius, for though unlike Gaius he was a great political philosopher, he had been a jurist before he was a philosopher and to the end remained a profound student of the law of Rome both private and public. In fact the whole prevailing legalistic cast of most modern political thought has Rome for its origin, and by Roman law modern thought must therefore in part be interpreted, especially that most legalistic portion of it, the idea of supremacy within a state, which since Roman times we have been conceiving not so much in terms of social or economic control as Aristotle thought of it, but rather by reference to the constitutional form in which it acquires an authority recognized as legally binding. As long as sovereignty constitutes a part of political speculation, the Roman *potestas* and *imperium* and the law by which the Emperor got them must remain an indispensable part of any historical treatment of politics. Wide differences of opinion exist among the greatest modern legal historians concerning the relation of *imperium* to *potestas* and the precise extent of the latter, but no jurist ancient or modern has ever doubted that both these terms always had a technical and a strictly legal meaning and referred not to actual but to lawful authority. It seems clear also that in the sixth century A.D., and probably by the third, the Roman jurisconsults were unanimous in believing that by these two terms the whole of the sovereign authority of the *populus Romanus* was included and transferred to the Emperor. Whether such a transfer was revocable or irrevocable, the classical jurists did not stop to inquire, fundamental as the question is, because it did not occur to them, or appeared beyond doubt, or — more likely still — because these were discussions it was decidedly safer to leave untouched at that time; but in the thirteenth century that question was broached in the glosses on these passages of Justinian's books and the differences of opinion on this point furnish one of the most interesting points in medieval juristic thought for the historian of political ideas.

In Roman constitutional theory therefore, the evidence leaves little doubt that the sovereign power was regarded as an emanation from the *populus,* and when exercised by a *princeps* or *imperator,* that this authority was his by delegation of the people. The Emperors themselves were not only careful to preserve Republican forms, but have left evidence in unofficial as well as official utterances, of their own acceptance of this constitutional theory of monarchy.

The influence on subsequent development of this constitutional attitude toward politics, or rather of this legalistic conception of the constitution of a state, has been incalculable; and though some inklings of it may be seen in the more practical parts of Aristotle's *Politics,* its full development comes first in the Roman state.

One of the developments directly traceable to this legalism has caused endless confusion in political thought and no little irritation to minds of the type of Jeremy Bentham's, the increased importance of fictions in the theory of the state. In politics as in law, the Romans seem in some ways more progressive than the Greeks, if by that word we mean gradual growth contrasted with sudden change.   In Greece both legal and political changes were more likely to be sudden, open, fully understood, and at times even marked with violence; in a word they were revolutionary and often traceable to definite individuals.   In Rome this characteristic is less marked in law and politics alike.   There were certainly civil commotions enough at Rome, but a *formal* continuity persisted through them all, as St. Augustine says.   Outwardly the Romans when compared with the more progressive Greek states such as Athens seem more conservative, more prone to conceal a necessary change by the retention of old forms and names even after the thing itself had altered.   In short, they employed on a scale apparently unapproached before, the aid of *fictions*.   This has long been understood in the history of Roman private law, and von Ihering and Sir Henry Maine have given classical expositions of it; [1] but in the field of public law and of political speculation this characteristic of the Roman mind is scarcely less important, though its effects have in general been less frequently noticed.   In this way, to take but one of the many illustrations furnished by almost every branch of the private law, a new conception of the family entirely replaced the old agnatic family with its *manus* and its *patria potestas*, completely revolutionizing the whole law of domestic relations;   and yet this great change, which required many generations for its development, was far along toward its completion before the rules of the old strict law based upon the ancient patriarchal family were openly discarded.   Thus for generations, a great gulf was left yawning between two systems existing side by side but representing stages of culture ages apart, the older still entrenched in legal rules which had never been abrogated, the newer given actual validity by fiction or under the authority of the magistrate's *imperium*.   In this way there long existed in almost every branch of Roman private law conditions widely at variance with rules still prescribed by the old *jus strictum*, and much of the growth of the science of jurisprudence is the result of the gradual accommodation of the one to the other.

It would have been strange if the public law had been left untouched by a habit of thought that appears so strongly in every relation of private life, and there is much evidence that it was not untouched.   Except for its duration the *consular imperium* looks

---

[1] R. von Ihering, *Geist des römischen Rechts*, four volumes incomplete and diffuse but monumental; Maine, *Ancient Law*.

very like that of a King — both Polybius and Cicero speak of the consular power as monarchical — and the foundation of the principate on the authority of the Republican magistracies is notorious, though it would have looked strange indeed to Aristotle. Thus there grew up in Rome a variance between the law of the constitution and the actual facts under it, without a parallel in Greece, but familiar enough to any student of modern constitutional history.

There can be no question where the legal sovereignty rested in Republican Rome. It rested with the people alone, and yet it requires but little study of the history of the period to see that for most of that period the actual exercise of this sovereign power was in the hands of the Senate. The most authoritative enactments of law (*leges*) were in the constitutional theory within the competence of none but assemblies of the whole people, but the *rogatio* by which such enactments must be initiated was in the hands of a magistrate whom the Senate *in fact* controlled. By such means the Senate might and in practice continually did influence the exercise of sovereign powers to which it could lay no legal claim whatever.[1] There is almost the same difference between law and fact in Rome under the Republic as the student of modern history finds between "the fundamental laws of the French monarchy" and the practical absolutism of a Louis XIV or between the laws and the conventions of the modern English constitution. All are the result of a spirit of legalism and legal conservatism which has never ceased to mould the political institutions and thought of the West since Roman times, but can be only dimly discerned before.

The same spirit and the same difference between law and fact serve to explain the real character of the *Principate*. In theory the people still remain sovereign. They alone can enact *leges*.

---

[1] It might thus be said in the modern language, that the people had the "authority," the Senate the political "power." Sovereignty lay in the People, its exercise was conditioned by the Senate. Cicero states this concisely in a passage of the *De Legibus*. "For the actual situation is such that, if the Senate dominates in matters of public policy, and all support whatever it has decreed, and if the rest [of the citizens] suffer the republic to be guided by the advice of the principal order, then from the balancing of right may be preserved that tempered and harmonious constitution [described above] *since the sovereignty is in the people, the actual authority in the Senate*" (quom potestas in populo, auctoritas in senatu sit). *De Legibus*, III, 12. I have ventured practically to transpose *potestas* and *auctoritas* in the translation because in modern English "authority" seems closer to the *legal* sovereignty apparently meant here by Cicero's *potestas* while his *auctoritas* is nearer to our actual political "power" than to our legal sovereignty or authority.

The Emperor's constitutions are not laws, they have only "the force of law" (*vigor legis*).   And yet the *Princeps* is in fact supreme, and that fact is well understood.   The lawyers go on repeating the *formulae* of the Republican constitution and these are still good law, but the historians and the rhetoricians are beginning to speak a different language and what they say is probably equally true if properly understood.   To strict constitutionalists like the lawyers the *Imperator* was no more than a military leader, and the *Princeps* merely the state's first citizen.   The *imperium* and the *potestas* which underlay the Emperor's authority theoretically included no powers which the people had not conferred upon some magistrate or other in the time of the Republic; and yet from the time of Augustus himself it seems to have been accepted, with only an occasional protest, that this overwhelming concentration of authority in the hands of one man was not only inevitable, but complete and permanent.   For the rhetorician and the philosopher the fact of monarchy was becoming more important than the theory of republicanism, especially if he were a Greek.   In law the *lex regia* which clothed the Emperor with the *imperium* and *potestas* of the people, like its predecessors the *leges curiatae* by which like powers had been entrusted to the magistrates under the Republic, conferred these powers under very distinct limitations.   The single surviving law of this kind, granting authority to Vespasian in 69–70 A.D., includes only such distinct immunities and powers as had before been granted to Augustus, Tiberius, and Claudius.   Vespasian is to be bound by no law of which any of these predecessors was free, and such enactments as were binding on the rogation of any of these predecessors, are declared to be equally binding if made on his rogation; but there is no statement that the Emperor is either free of all law whatever, or that every expression of his will has the binding force of a *lex* or a *plebiscitum*.   Furthermore, such grants of authority as these *leges regiae* contain were made to the Emperor for his life, and lapsed with his death.   They were temporary and had to be renewed, and they conferred no right upon his family.

Yet in the face of these undoubted constitutional principles the Julian house had succeeded to the throne as a matter of fact, as long as heirs apparent survived, and the powers actually exercised by the Emperors under these strict legal limitations were those of a monarch, and coming to be very generally recognized as such.

Rome was, in the words of Gibbon, "an absolute monarchy disguised by the forms of a commonwealth"; [1] but the disguise was so transparent, that the keener eyes scarcely could have failed to see the reality beneath the appearance. The only satisfactory explanation of the people's contentedness with a situation so anomalous is the existence of a belief on the part of their natural leaders that security from civil strife was compensation enough for the loss of self-government in everything but name, and "Augustus was sensible that mankind is governed by names." [2]

The old names indeed survived, but there is evidence in plenty that the real situation was not misunderstood by some at least. Seneca's *De Clementia* addressed to Nero in the prince's younger and better days, is a stirring appeal for the exercise of mercy, whose entire force is dependent on the underlying assumption that Nero's power is supreme and practically without limit, except in his own inward control over his actions. The need for mercy in the guidance of his will is fundamental just because the possibility of an arbitrary exercise of that will is limitless. "I have been chosen," he represents his prince as saying, "to act in the place of the gods upon earth, the arbiter of life and death to nations, what fortune and what station each should have has been placed in my hands to determine. Whatsoever Fortuna wishes to have given to each mortal, by my mouth she makes it known. In my responses peoples and cities find cause for rejoicing. No part ever flourishes except by my will and my favor. These many swords which my peace keeps sheathed, at my nod shall be drawn. What nations should be utterly destroyed, what transported, what given liberty or deprived of it, what kings and cities created, whose head encircled by the royal diadem, all belong to my jurisdiction." [3] The Emperor, Seneca says, "is the bond by which the republic is held together," its "breath of life," [4] its very soul.[5] Few punishments are necessary, for "in one who is all powerful," it is not how much he has done that is considered, but how much he may do.[6]

The rhetorical exaggeration of such statements must be considered, but similar views are found in many another writer especially in the eastern part of the Empire. Among these none

---

[1] The best account of the imperial constitution is probably still in the second volume of Mommsen's *Römisches Staatsrecht* (1877–1887).

[2] *Decline and Fall*, chap. iii.

[3] *De Clementia*, Lib. I, cap. i.

[4] *Ibid.*, cap. iv.

[5] *Ibid.*, cap. v.

[6] *Ibid.*, cap. viii.

is more significant perhaps than Dio Chrysostom of Prusa in
Bithynia, the friend and admirer of Nerva and Trajan, in his four
orations on Kingship and one on Tyranny,[1] in which he sets forth
the ideal monarch in terms almost identical with Seneca's. Another is the oration *To Rome* (Εἰς Ῥώμην) by Aelius Aristides of
Smyrna delivered at Rome in the year 154 A.D., which Professor
Rostovtzeff has called "the best general picture of the Roman
Empire in the second century, the most detailed and the most
complete that we have." [2]

The author follows Polybius in praising the mixture of monarchy,
aristocracy, and democracy in the Roman state as Dio Chrysostom
did before him, and he sees clearly that the *princeps* has become
the head and centre of the system, who, notwithstanding the constitutional powers of the people and the Senate, exercises the completest monarchical power, free of the vices of tyranny, and "of
greater than regal majesty." [3]

To these and other Greek writers, the Emperor embodies the
majesty of the Roman state and that state in the person of its
head is regarded and spoken of as "the savior" of Greece. This
feeling was no doubt stronger outside Italy than within it and more
distinctly expressed, if not more widely extended, in the Greek
part of the Empire than in the West. What Mommsen says of
Dio may be true in a measure of Aelius and other such Greek
eulogists of the Roman state. They are probably expressing views
current in Bithynia rather than those held in Italy,[4] and there were
reasons, which Aelius makes clear in some of his other orations,
why such views as his should make a stronger appeal in Asia Minor
than in the West. Rome and her Emperor in a very true sense

---

[1] περὶ βασιλείας and περὶ τυραννίδος, *Dionis Prusaensis quem vocant Chrysostomum
quae extant omnia*, edidit J. de Arnim, Berlin, 1883, vol. i, pp. 1–79, 83–95.

An excellent account of Dio Chrysostom is given by the late Sir Samuel Dill in his *Roman
Society from Nero to Marcus Aurelius*, London, 1920, pp. 367–383, where references may be
found to the most important passages concerning monarchy. Professor Rostovtzeff gives
another, *The Social and Economic History of the Roman Empire*, Oxford, 1926, pp. 114–118,
520–521.

[2] *The Social and Economic History of the Roman Empire*, p. 125. The most modern text
of Aelius Aristides is that of Bruno Keil, *Aelii Aristidis Smyrnaei quae supersunt omnia*,
vol. ii, Berlin, 1898, but the remarkable edition of Samuel Jebb, Oxford, 1722, is still of
great value. The most detailed modern account of the political views of Aelius Aristides
is given by André Boulanger, *Aelius Aristide*, Paris, 1923 (doctoral thesis). Comments and
references of great value are to be found in *Das Kaisertum*, by Ludwig Hahn, Leipzig, 1913,
especially chap. III, and in Professor Rostovtzeff's *Social and Economic History of the Roman
Empire*, pp. 125–129.

[3] Εἰς Ῥώμην, edited by Jebb, I, p. 223.

[4] *Römisches Staatsrecht*, vol. ii, pt. ii (3d ed.), pp. 752–753, note.

appealed to these men as "Saviors" of Greece. True liberty, they are never tired of saying, has only come to Greece with the *pax Romana*. They have given up altogether Aristotle's ideal of the self-sufficient city-state, which had not saved Hellas from the fatal divisions that brought on her fall. The world is one great state, and Rome by virtue of her might is its proper head. Under Rome's stern but even rule the municipalities have been secured from attack from without, from abuses of governors, and from dissensions among themselves. The whole world prays that the Roman rule may last forever, says Aelius Aristides.[1] Far-seeing Greeks felt that the *pax Romana* had saved them from themselves, as many an intelligent Indian feels that British rule has saved India; and in no part of the modern British Empire is the King in title an Emperor except in India. Probably in no part of the Roman world was the Emperor to such an extent the embodiment of the majesty of Rome as in the East and for reasons much the same, though it was natural that provincials everywhere should exalt him more than the inhabitants of Italy. "The true prince will be the father of his people, surrounded and guarded by a loving reverence, which never degenerates into fear. His only aim will be their good. He will keep sleepless watch over the weak, the careless, those who are heedless for themselves. Commanding infinite resources, he will know less of mere pleasure than any man within his realm. With such immense responsibilities, he will be the most laborious of all." [2]

Many statements such as these are to be found in the writings of philosophers, rhetoricians, and historians, particularly in the eastern part of the Empire, and especially from the Antonines to Theodosius. Compared with the former struggles for power, Rome has given to Greece "the sweetest peace," Aelius declares.[3] Democracy is a noble, but an impractical ideal, Appian thinks.[4] Rome, says Libanius, has driven away enemies, who govern by strange laws.[5]

---

[1] Εἰς 'Ρώμην, § 89 (Keil's edition), cited by Hahn, *Das Kaisertum*, p. 24.

[2] Dill, *Roman Society from Nero to Marcus Aurelius*, p. 378, summarizing Dio Chrysostom.

[3] Εἰς 'Ρώμην, § 69 (Keil's edition), cited by Ludwig Hahn, *Das Kaisertum*, p. 25. This book gives the best general account of the monarchy under the Roman Empire. Its concluding sentences may be forgiven on account of the excellence of the rest. The few references to contemporary writers given here are in large part taken from the many valuable ones to be found in this book.

[4] Hahn, *op. cit.*, p. 28.

[5] *Ibid.*, p. 31, note 1.

It was natural that this feeling should find a centre in the office and the person of the Emperor, and many things contributed to such a result.   Among them the prominence of the proconsular imperium among the legal sources of the Emperor's authority was probably less obvious to Greeks than his increasing practical activity in the final determination of judicial cases on appeal, the fact that imperial constitutions were fast monopolizing the field of legislation, which now included the whole colonial world, and the increasing personal interest of the Emperors after Hadrian in securing an honest and effective administration in the provinces by abolishing the earlier abuses introduced by the Roman oligarchy.   In men prepared for it by the traditions of Alexander and his successors, facts like these might easily lead to the feeling that the Emperor was Rome incarnate, and to their ascribing to his office or to his person all the benefits they received from the effectiveness of Roman law and administration.   Their feeling for the Emperor was not unlike the feeling of the French in the sixteenth and seventeenth centuries that their king was the living embodiment of French nationality.   Themistius speaks of the Emperor as a living, breathing law, a refuge for men from the rigidity of existing law.[1] "Liberty is never sweeter than under a pious King," declares the Romanizing Greek Ammianus Marcellinus.[2]

To men bred in a literature full of demi-gods and heroes of divine lineage the deification of the Emperor was a further step of no great difficulty, whether the heroes were Theseus and Minos or Romulus and Numa.   "Faithful devotion is due to the Emperor as to a present and corporeal god" says Vegetius in the fourth century.[3]   For Greeks, even for all provincials, this was possibly somewhat easier than for Romans, and it may have been a recognition of this difference that led Augustus to permit temples to be dedicated to him in the provinces, while he forbade it in Rome. But even if this were so, it is clear that the successors of Augustus met with fewer such obstacles.

In Rome the Emperor was usually *divus* not *deus*, and even the former word was applied to him after his death, but the Orient popularly drew no such fine distinctions.   For it the Emperor was a "present god" and *basileus* as befitted the successor of Alexander

---

[1] Hahn, *Das Kaisertum*, p. 32, note 2.
[2] Quoted by Hahn, *op. cit.*, p. 34, note 3.
[3] *Epitoma Rei Militaris*, II, 5, quoted in Hahn, *op. cit.*, p. 22, note 6.

or of the Pharaohs and Ptolemies.[1] Whether any real depth of
religious feeling is indicated by such expressions may well be
doubted, especially when used by men in the literary tradition of
Polybius, to whom, somewhat as to Machiavelli, the chief value
of religion was as an aid to the state. But for all that, the idea
is of the greatest importance politically, and it was strengthened
by the feeling of gratitude for Rome's great services in protecting
their peace and respecting their culture. Hahn goes so far as to
say that "the cult of the Emperor is the expression of the gratitude of the peoples and the provincials for deliverance from the
age-long curse of civil war." [2] This *Kaiserkult* soon became for
them a type of *staatsalmacht* so nearly identical with the imperial
authority itself, that a denial of one was felt to be a denial of the
other.[3]

Such a feeling, for local reasons, may have been more vivid and
more widely diffused in the East than in the West, but there is
evidence that it was by no means confined to that portion of the
Empire. Even in the East the application of such ideas to the
Roman Emperor is rare before the time of Hadrian, who seems to
have been the first of the emperors to feel clearly and to make his
subjects feel that he was ruler over the whole Empire and not
merely over Italy; and before that time Seneca, by birth a Spanish
provincial but a resident of Rome, had expressed an ideal of
monarchy not widely different from that of Dio Chrysostom or
Aelius Aristides. The *Panegyric* addressed to the Emperor Trajan
by Pliny the Younger yields to none of the Greeks in its delineation of the Emperor as the ideal and all-powerful monarch.[4] It
is true he praises the Emperor on account of his respect for the
ancient constitutional rights of the Senate and People in a way not
usual among the Greeks, but his picture of actual imperial authority is drawn in much the same lines as theirs. Before the middle
of the second century, at least, it seems that the acceptance of
such views was becoming general in both West and East.

The cult of the Emperor seems from our modern point of view
more an expression of political than of religious feeling. It was
one of the main props of imperial authority and as such cultivated
by Emperors, and by all supporters of the imperial régime. Ves-

---

[1] Hahn, p. 19. [2] *Ibid.* [3] *Ibid.*, pp. 20—21.
[4] C. Plini Caecili Secundi *Panegyricus Traiano Imperatori Dictus*, ed. R. C. Kukula,
Leipsic, 1912.

pasian, for example, was a careful preserver of the ancient ritual notwithstanding his famous remark on his death-bed that he felt himself becoming a god.[1]   Such a remark may indicate a certain amount of religious skepticism but it is not to the same extent an evidence of political cynicism.   The force of the feeling that the faith as well as the government should express the unity of a people did not begin with the Roman Empire nor did it end with it.

But it was easier to maintain under the conditions existing in ancient times than it is now, and it was natural that the emperors should foster it as the strongest centralizing tendency in an empire composed of so many peoples, different in race and in almost all cultural traditions; nor does this in itself imply a cynical "exploitation" of religion in the interests of the state, nor even necessarily a skeptical indifference to religion itself.   Such a misjudging of Roman imperial policy is scarcely justifiable in a modern world which still cherishes ideas of "divine right" in holes and corners.

The feeling of loyalty to a person long survived the Roman Empire even in states with a tribal or racial solidarity, as a natural as well as a useful adjunct in welding subjects together.   And at times and places when this solidarity was lacking history has often shown it supplying the only refuge from complete anarchy, as appears in those centuries of European history which we call "feudal."

Excluding all ideas of divine right, Bagehot three quarters of a century ago essayed to show the practical political value of the sentimental attachment of subjects to a king even in a small compact realm like present day England.   In a vast, scattered, decentralized, political unit like the modern British Empire some such focus is an undoubted benefit, and almost a necessity.   For the Roman Empire the Emperor was such a focus, and it was inevitable that attachment to him should take a religious form impossible under modern conditions, but entirely consistent with the ideas and traditions of the time.

Among these traditions probably none was more important than the survival of the ancient Roman tribal religion.   The legendary accounts of the founding of the city that formed a part of it, the divine origin of its early kings, the supposed communication

[1] "'Vae,' inquit, 'puto, Deus fio.'"   Suetonius, *Vespasian*, cap. xxiii.

between Numa and the Gods, the close interweaving of *fas* and *jus* in the whole early development of law, public and private, the alleged divine origin of the Julian line itself; all these and many other parts of the received tradition tended to link the old religion with the institution of monarchy, and they furnish the explanation of the scrupulousness with which Augustus and most of his successors preserved the ancient forms and ceremonies and were so careful to retain the old priestly offices among the parts of the older constitution which were united to form the legal basis of the principate. Every emperor from Augustus to Valentinian was *Pontifex Maximus*, even though the later ones called themselves Christians.[1] As Sir Samuel Dill says, "The emperors from Augustus found religion a potent ally of sovereignty. . . . Yet it may be doubted whether . . . the emperors were not rather following than leading public opinion."[2] The fact is that to keep such an ally they had to adapt themselves to the great religious changes that swept over the western peoples as a result of their growing knowledge of the East and the introduction of new cults, such as that of Isis from Egypt and especially the worship of Mithra from Persia. There were few obstacles to such a policy of accommodation because these newer cults, instead of hindering the apotheosis of the emperor which had begun with the new monarchy, were in every way suited to bring nearer its complete consummation. As a result they lent valuable support to the growing absolutism of the emperor and in turn the later pagan emperors as a rule identified themselves with them, and favored every measure for their extension. So great was the influence of these eastern ideas on the development of the Emperor's power that Cumont sees in the absolutism of the later Empire the triumph of the Orient over the spirit of Rome, of the religious idea over the legalistic conception of monarchy.[3] Possibly the more moderate statement of Dill may be preferable: "The influence of Egypt and Persia lent its force to stimulate native and original tendencies to king-worship, and to develop the principate of Augustus into the theocratic despotism of Aurelian and Diocletian";[4] but it is noteworthy none the less,

[1] For an excellent account of this and of later phases of the relation of the Roman religion and the Roman monarchy, see Dill, *Roman Society from Nero to Marcus Aurelius*, Bk. IV, chaps. iii–vi.

[2] *Op. cit.*, p. 537.

[3] *Mithra*, I, 282, quoted by Hahn, p. 56, who disagrees and attributes the development largely to strictly Roman causes.

[4] *Roman Society from Nero to Marcus Aurelius*, p. 616.

that the deification of kings was fully developed and common in Greece long before it became an accepted fact in the Roman Empire.

For the history of political ideas, the concrete effects of the existence of such a "theocratic despotism" are probably more important than the difficult question of its origins. Some of these effects were so profound and have been so lasting that the whole subsequent history of monarchy in state and church alike is inexplicable except in light of them.

When the Empire became definitely and officially Christian, it was, of course, impossible to continue to claim divinity for its head, but the establishment of Christianity was a gradual process in which the monarchy lost some of the characteristics it had acquired in heathen times and in part from heathen cults, but retained others in a more or less modified form. The *jus sacrum* remained a part of the *jus publicum* and under the control of the Emperor as head of the state. Some parts of the Imperial titles, scarcely consistent with the new religion, were not dropped at once, including the title of Pontifex Maximus, and a few not at all. Even after the emperors had ceased to be pontiffs, they retained much of their ancient authority in matters of religion, merely allowing churchmen to exercise the *potestas ordinis* while they themselves kept the whole of the *potestas jurisdictionis* in their own hands. Constantius claimed and exercised the power of determining the doctrine of the Church and of punishing as a heretic anyone who dared to disagree with him.[1] Here the principle *cujus regio, ejus religio* was in full force and here it had its beginning. Moreover the *regio* still included the whole of Christendom. It is not strange that later emperors who still claimed to be Roman, and kings who called themselves emperors within their own kingdoms, should find, as they did, some of their strongest arguments against the Papacy in the great body of Roman law that was taking form at this time and under these conditions in the writings of the jurists and the constitutions of emperors.

But it is the same period also that marks the beginnings of an

[1] Book XVI of the *Theodosian Code* is filled with imperial laws defining orthodoxy and heresy, regulating the Church, depriving apostates of Roman citizenship, etc. See also *Theodosian Novels* XVII and XVIII (ed. Mommsen and Meyer); Justinian's *Code*, I, 1–13; and the many novels of Justinian referring to the Church and the clergy, especially the *Praefatio* and *Epilogus* of Novel VI. For an account of this legislation and the conditions which caused it, see Boissier, *La fin du paganisme*. See also A. Bouché-Leclercq, *L'intolérance religieuse et la politique* (1917), especially pp. 329–36.

ecclesiastical organization whose constitution and laws were later gradually to develop into a great rival body of law, so massive that for centuries it stood able to defy all attempts of secular rulers to make an effective breach in it.

It is true that under the early Christian emperors, the whole machinery of the Church was under the Emperor's control and that this control was often acquiesced in by the leaders of the Church itself. Nevertheless the relations between Church and Emperor were different from anything that Greece or Rome had ever known before. The difference lies in the nature and history of Christianity itself, and in part in the nature of the Jewish religion out of which it developed.

The first commandment of the Decalogue, "Thou shalt have none other gods before me," accepted by Jews and Christians alike, enunciated a principle foreign to both Greek and Roman habits of thought. It made the religion of Jews and Christians an exclusive religion, unwilling and unable to accommodate itself to other cults, a phenomenon which the Romans, unable to understand, naturally attributed to a hatred of mankind. But there was one fundamental difference that finally emerged between Jews and Christians. As Gibbon says, "The Jews were a *nation;* the Christians were a *sect.*" [1] The exclusiveness of Jews led them to despise and to withdraw from other peoples and their beliefs, the exclusiveness of the Christians' faith, no longer tied to any race or nation, urged them on to make proselytes from other religions and to wage aggressive war against all false gods. The Jewish faith was exclusive, the Christian religion was both exclusive and militant. This unique character of the faith of the Christians explains the unparalleled severity of their persecution by the Romans, and it accounts for another development much more important for the history of political thought. Since the Christians were at first only groups of believers without racial or tribal institutions as a basis for the maintenance of their faith and worship, nothing in fact but scattered *collegia* or *sodalitates*, and for a long period illicit ones under the Roman law, "a separate society, which attacked the established religion of the Empire"; they were, as Gibbon says, "obliged to adopt some form of internal policy, and to appoint a sufficient number of ministers, intrusted *not only with the spiritual functions, but even the temporal direction, of the*

[1] *Decline and Fall*, chap. 16 (vol. ii, p. 74 of Bury's edition).

Christian commonwealth." [1] During the long period from the
first emergence of the Christians as a sect distinct from the nation
of the Jews, to the final establishment by law of their faith as the
official and exclusive faith of the Roman Empire, this development
of their ecclesiastical institutions went on in increasing volume,
with the result that when the faith was at length established, along
with that establishment arose a problem entirely new to politics,
practical or theoretical, something, in the words of the *Defensor
Pacis* in the fourteenth century, attributed to Marsiglio of Padua,
"which neither Aristotle nor any other philosopher of his time or
of an earlier time could possibly perceive." [2]

For the first time we have established by the state a religion
whose claims are exclusive, maintained by an association or society
hitherto not only separate in origin and development from the
state, but in some ways hostile to it, and forbidden by it, and one
whose internal organization had reached a high point of independent development before its recognition and establishment by law.

By ordinance of the state itself the peculiar laws and institutions
of this religious society are now made coextensive with the state
and every member of the Empire from the highest to the lowest
brought within the jurisdiction of the constituted authorities of
the Christian Church.

The Establishment of Christianity in Rome thus merged and
brought face to face two societies that up to that time had been
separate, each with its own traditions, laws, and institutions.   It
is true that the old antagonism between them was for the time at
an end, but it might reappear.   The peculiar problem of Church
and State had definitely emerged for the first time in history
though not yet in acute form, the most serious practical problem
in modern politics as a whole up to the Industrial Revolution, the
greatest perturbation which has ever drawn men's thoughts about
the state out of their proper political orbit, and for many ages the
most powerful stimulus to all political speculation.   For a thousand years after the establishment of Christianity in Rome political
writing of every sort was affected directly or indirectly by this
great question, and for the half-millennium between the eleventh
and the seventeenth century it is not too much to say that the bulk

[1] *Decline and Fall*, chap. 15 (vol. ii, p. 39 of Bury's edition).   The italics are mine.
These words in italics indicate one of the causes, probably the chief cause, of the later
appearance of the problem of Church and State.
[2] I, cap. 19, section 3, in the edition of Previté-Orton (1928), p. 101.

of all the writings which we may term political were directly and primarily concerned with the great controversy between the spiritual and the secular authority. For much of that long period politics became little more than an incidental adjunct to religious or ecclesiastical argument and it is only in comparatively recent times that a scientific spirit like Aristotle's seems to have made any marked headway against this tendency. The details of the first phases of the great conflict may probably be better treated as a part of the political thought of the middle ages.

Another problem, allied, but somewhat different, and far more difficult, was created for the historian of political ideas by the entrance of the Christian community into the political life of Rome, the question whether Christianity as such had developed any important political ideas of its own, and if so what was their origin and how great their affect upon subsequent thought. These are questions of importance, but in the present state of our knowledge, definite answers cannot be given to them.

The historical books of the Old Testament seem to indicate that the earlier Jewish political tradition was purely theocratic, with a later development in the direction of monarchy, but there are few evidences of conscious theorizing about forms of government or the nature of political relations. Nevertheless these historical books have been the armory from which almost all political controversialists from the fourth to the eighteenth century selected their weapons, all of them taking Jewish history as the inspired record of God's chosen people and therefore as a binding precedent for all Christian peoples and for all time, but each of course interpreting these divinely ordered events as a proof of his own political views. As such the early political history of the Jews is a subject of great importance for the history of political thought as a whole.

Turning to the New Testament, the Gospels trace the lineage of Christ back to King David. The gravamen of the charge of his enemies was that he claimed a kingly power inconsistent with the Emperor's sovereignty, and in the fourteenth century Papalist writers deduced from his position as earthly king a coercive power in his vicar, the Pope, over all secular rulers. Yet the Gospels had also repeated his words, "My kingdom is not of this world" and, "Render unto Caesar the things that are Caesar's"; and the well-known words of St. Paul in his Epistle to the Romans urging obedience to earthly rulers as a religious obligation because their power is ordained by God for the good of mankind is of the greater political significance since these rulers were heathen.   But the very use of such words as these of St. Paul seems to indicate the existence of a belief among some Christians, that for them political obligations do not bind, have ceased to bind, or are to be ignored in preparation for the new life soon to come.   There are thus indications in the New Testament of several cross currents of thought, political and social, in the early Christian Church, some almost anarchical or at least antinomian in tendency, others authoritarian; some communistic, others opposed to this.   On the question of slavery all the passages touching the subject seem to indicate a general belief in the Hellenistic view, regarding it merely as an established institution, but one affecting only the outward man, and in no sense "natural" as Aristotle considered it.   It is impossible to say that all Christians accepted any one of these conflicting views, equally impossible to prove that the Church had adopted it as an orthodox doctrine.   Furthermore, though most of these views are practically the same as the ones we have already traced back to the earlier Greek philosophers, it would be rash to conclude for that reason alone that Greece *must* have been their sole source.[1]   The scanty knowledge we have on these points scarcely warrants any positive conclusions.

The effects on subsequent thought of these views when combined with the views already current in the heathen Empire are perhaps somewhat easier to discover than their origin or their relative importance.   These effects are to be found mainly in the writings of the early fathers of the church which furnish the bulk of our materials for the earlier middle ages.

[1] For an excellent summary see Carlyle, *History of Mediaeval Political Theory*, vol. i, part iii, chap. viii.

CHAPTER V

THE EARLY MIDDLE AGES [1]

Long before the end of the Western Empire developments had begun which were in time to bring profound changes in the nature or the course of western political thought, such as the intrusion of the barbarians, the further decline of Roman culture including the knowledge of Roman Law, the gradual extension of a system of legal administration based upon the principle of the personality of law instead of its territoriality, the withdrawal of the emperors to the East, and the rift between the Western and the Eastern parts of the Church.

Some of the political results of these important developments were not long in coming, but their effects upon western political thought are not clearly apparent at once. In the early middle ages political thought as a whole seems to follow much the same general lines as under the later Empire, in the main an interpretation in the light of Hebrew and Christian tradition of political ideas long current in Rome.

There was little room in the West of the early middle ages for the older Greek idea that great men are a law unto themselves or that the discretion of a philosopher-king is higher than the fixity of rigid law. The Stoic or Roman ideas of the universality of law are always and everywhere assumed and it is in terms of law that human relations, including political relations, are invariably conceived. But Hebrew and Christian ideas had considerably changed men's views as to the origin of that law without in any way affecting their belief in its universal character. The early Christian fathers all expressly or tacitly identify the law of nature

[1] To two books especially, parts of the outline in this chapter owe more than can be adequately acknowledged by mere references to specific points. One is *Die Soziallehren der christlichen Kirchen und Gruppen*, by Ernst Troeltsch (3d ed., Tübingen, 1923, chaps. 1 and 2) (now available in English translation by Olive Wyon, *The Social Teaching of the Christian Churches*, two volumes, The Macmillan Company, New York, 1931), the other, *A History of Mediaeval Political Theory in the West*, by R. W. and A. J. Carlyle (vol. i, parts iii–iv, and vol. iii, New York, 1903–1916).

with the law of God.[1] This is an important and a characteristically Christian idea, but it is not unique. The Stoic view as expressed by Cicero was substantially the same.[2] Nevertheless the
uncompromising monotheism of Christianity and its view of God's
personal nature and his relation to his creation gave the idea a
definiteness and a practical effectiveness hitherto unknown. And
there was besides one element in this Christian idea of the law of
God of which there was no counterpart in pre-Christian Roman
thought — a portion of that law had been written by the finger
of God himself and that writing was still in existence.

What was the relation of this revealed law to the rest of God's
law inscribed only in the heart of man by his nature? It is the
law of nature, says one writer, in part reformed by Moses, in part
confirmed by his authority, which forbids sin and makes it known,[3]
but, St. Ambrose adds, if this natural law had fully served, the
law of Moses would never have taken its place.

It was sin then that first brought men under external coercive
law, God's as well as man's. This seems to be essentially the
same view as St. Paul's. It seems clear that in St. Paul's time
there were differences among Christians on the question whether
Christ came to destroy this law of Moses in whole or in part, or to
fulfil it, but more important for later political thought is the
unanimity of all patristic writers throughout the early middle ages
in accepting the view common to St. Paul, the later Greeks, and
the Romans generally, that there is one law written in the hearts
of all men by nature, inclining them to good and drawing them
away from evil. None followed Ulpian in making this a law common to men and the lower animals, but all agreed with him in
distinguishing sharply between the *jus naturale* and the *jus gentium*.

Nothing serves better to show the mingling of Christian and
pre-Christian political ideas at this time than the explanations
given of this distinction and of its historical origin. Seneca had
imagined a primitive state of innocence where men were free of all
external compulsion, and government, slavery, and property were
unknown,[4] and some of the classical jurists had ascribed the development of the institutions of the *jus gentium* to war and human
avarice.[5] Genesis now furnishes to the patristic writers the

[1] Carlyle, *op. cit.*, I, pp. 103–106, with references.   [2] *Ante*, pp. 111–113.
[3] "Ambrosiaster," Carlyle, *op. cit.*, vol. i, pp. 104–105.   [4] *Ante*, p. 119.
[5] *Ante*, pp. 119–120.

explanation of it all. The golden age of innocence is the period before the expulsion of Adam from the Garden.

The corruption of man began with the fall, and that corruption, the inheritance of all the children of Adam, created for the human race the necessity for coercive law and other like institutions. To supply the need God gave man the Mosaic law, and sanctioned human laws and institutions necessary to curb the evils arising from avarice, violence, and other forms of vice. Coercive law, above all the human portion of it common to all nations, is no part of man's original nature; it came as a corrective of conditions arising from man's fall from innocence. It is no branch of the law of nature, it may even be as the Roman jurist had said, *contra naturam*, occasioned by man's sin; but it is none the less provided by the ordinance or sanction of God as a partial remedy for the consequences of that sin, and to this extent has a divine origin and a divine character. Its precepts must therefore be obeyed as a religious obligation. "Wherefore ye must needs be in subjection, not only because of the wrath, but also for conscience' sake." [1]

This explanation applied not to law alone, but to many of the human conditions which make law necessary and to the human institutions requisite for its enforcement. In the state of innocence men were equal, it was sin alone which made inequality necessary. Sin it was, therefore, which occasioned, though it did not necessarily cause, all forms of subordination of one man to another, whether in the relation of master and slave, or in that of ruler and subject. Human government is one of God's remedies for man's corruption. "Let every soul be subject unto the higher powers (ἐξουσίαις ὑπερεχούσαις). For there is no power but of God: the powers that be are ordained of God. Whosoever therefore resisteth the power, resisteth the ordinance of God: and they that resist shall receive to themselves damnation." [2] Civil obedience is a religious duty, which implies — and this was sometimes expressly said — obedience even to evil rulers as well as to good, up to the point at least where it becomes one's higher duty to "obey God rather than man."

For evil rulers are God's penalty for the sins of their subjects and it is God's ordinance that they must be endured and even reverenced because their authority comes from Him. The true remedy of an oppressed people is to turn away from their own sins.

[1] *Romans*, xiii.   [2] *Ibid.*

The phrase "powers that be" (αἱ [ἐξουσίαι] . . . οὖσαι) adopted
from St. Paul by practically all writers of this period, itself seems
also to imply the view long accepted in Rome that civil government was a human convention; ordained indeed by God, but
originating in human action for men's needs though not necessarily in any definite or formal compact.   This view seems to have
been the one generally held though not always distinctly expressed.
These "powers that be" may include, and to St. Paul no doubt
did include, all lawful magistrates from the lowest to the highest,
a fact seen and made effective use of by the opponents of monarchical power in the sixteenth century.   To the writers of the early
middle ages the phrase probably had the same meaning, but little
use was made of any part of it except the authority of a king or
emperor.   In this period monarchy is generally accepted as the
normal form of the state and there is as yet no marked tendency
either to question it as an institution or to put limits to its authority.   It is not a period of scientific political investigation in which
the varied forms of human government are compared on their
merits.   Such political ideas as we may gather must be taken
from incidental statements in letters and polemics written more
for religious than for political purposes.   As Professor Ferguson
says, "During the two millenniums and a quarter that intervene
between the rise of the Macedonians and the downfall of the
Romanoffs, Hapsburgs, and Hohenzollerns, monarchy in some
form or other has been the normal form of political life." [1]   This
is especially true of the middle ages and early modern times, but
in the middle ages at least it seems to have been felt that the
allegiance that subjects should render was due, by God's ordinance,
rather to the monarch's sacred office than to his person.

Distinct statements of the last of these principles are seldom to
be found in contemporary writers and a few may seem to imply
an opposite theory.   Possibly the distinction between the office
and its holder was not very clear in the minds of most, but the
interpretation here suggested seems to be the one applicable to the
greater number of their own statements with the least forcing of
their meaning.   St. Chrysostom in the fourth century leaves no
doubt as to his views.

"*For there is no power*, he [St. Paul] says, *but of God*.   What say
you? it may be said; is every ruler then elected by God?   This

[1] *Cambridge Ancient History*, vol. vii, pp. 8-9.

I do not say, he answers. Nor am I now speaking about individual rulers, but about the thing in itself. . . . Hence he does not say, *for there is no* ruler *but of God;* but it is the thing he speaks of, and says, *there is no power but of God. And the powers that be, are ordained of God.*" [1]

St. Chrysostom's interpretation of St. Paul was unquestionably that of the later medieval writers almost without exception. It was the form of monarchical theory accepted generally in the later middle ages. As, for example, Peter Abelard says in the twelfth century, their power rulers received from God, their evil purpose they have of themselves. "It is one thing to resist the tyranny of an evil ruler, it is another to resist his just power which he has received from God." And he adds significantly, that when a ruler does an act of violence beyond his authority if we resist him in this we are opposing his tyranny rather than his power, we are withstanding man rather than God because he has usurped the power by his own act unauthorized by God. But when we stand out against him in the things for which he was lawfully ordained, then we are resisting his power.[2] This distinction, always important theoretically throughout the middle ages, became of vital practical importance in the middle of the sixteenth century. But whether reverence were due to the office or to the person of a king or emperor, none denied that God's ordinance required it to be paid to him as to God's lieutenant. "The King is adored on earth as the vicar of God." [3]

"Above the Emperor is none but God alone who made him Emperor" declared St. Optatus.[4] Some of the utterances of St. Gregory the Great seem in some ways to go even further, and these statements were later to play a great part in support of monarchy against both popes and people. Occasionally it is said that the king is *legibus solutus,* but oftener he is urged to follow the law in his judgments, advice which may or may not necessarily imply a right to disregard it. Strong as most of these statements are, however, they differ greatly from the definite claims of divine personal right made for kings in the seventeenth century. They constitute

---

[1] *Homily XXIII on the Epistle of St. Paul to the Romans, The Homilies of S. John Chrysostom (Library of the Fathers of the Holy Catholic Church),* vol. vii, p. 393 (Oxford, 1841).
[2] *Petri Abaelardi Commentariorum super S. Pauli Epistolam ad Romanos Libri Quinque,* Lib. IV, cap. xiii, Migne, *Patrologia, Series Latina,* vol. 178, column 946.
[3] Quoted by Carlyle, *op. cit.,* I, p. 149, note 2.
[4] Quoted by Carlyle, *op. cit.,* I, p. 149.

a theory of the divine right of kingship, rather than of kings. For this strongly monarchical doctrine Dr. Carlyle assigns three main causes, opposition to certain anarchical tendencies in the primitive Church, the relations existing between the Church and the Emperor after the conversion of Constantine, and the influence of the Old Testament conception of the King of Israel.[1]

No doubt one reason for the height of power thus attributed to kingship was the greatness of the end for which God was believed to have ordained it and the vast coercive power necessary to achieve that end. God's purpose in establishing kingship, and all subordinate magistracies as well, is to secure and enforce justice among fallen men. The end of all secular government is justice, and without it no political authority can ever be legitimate. Such is the theory of all writers of this period and the later middle ages, as it was of Cicero and the Roman jurists.

To this last statement, however, one striking exception is usually made. The greatest of all the political writers of this time, St. Augustine, it is said, did not believe that justice was necessary to the being of a state.

In the *City of God* he quotes Cicero's famous definition — "A people is not an assemblage of men brought together in *any* fashion, but an assemblage of a multitude associated by consent to law and community of interest."

But, says the late Dr. Figgis in the last thing he ever wrote on politics, St. Augustine quotes this definition only to reject it as untenable.

"So far indeed is Augustine from saying that injustice destroys the being of a commonwealth, that he uses the admitted injustice and corruption of Rome in the later days of the Republic as a *reductio ad absurdum* of Scipio's definition. . . . His sense of reality led him to prefer a definition which would include all existing and historical communities, and hamper him as little as possible by an abstract ideal. . . . He saw that a State, reduced to its lowest terms, might be a people whose 'manners are none and their customs beastly' — associated for bad ends, yet still a State, because keeping internal peace. . . . So far is St. Augustine from giving a clericalist definition of the State, that he definitely discards it, and shows us that he does so with intention, and gives his grounds. It is contrary to the facts of life."[2] This is an

---

[1] *Op. cit.*, I, p. 157.   [2] *The Political Aspects of St. Augustine's 'City of God,'* chap. iii.

anticipation of Machiavelli indeed — if true; and Dr. Carlyle seems to agree, for he says, "It would appear, then, that the political theory of St. Augustine is materially different in several respects from that of St. Ambrose and other Fathers, who represent the ancient tradition that justice is the essential quality, as it is also the end, of the State." [1]

As the statements of the greatest political thinker of the early middle ages on this important subject are unique before the sixteenth century if correctly interpreted in these extracts, it seems worth while to test the interpretation by a comparison with St. Augustine's own words.

We may start with his famous question, *Remota justitia, quid sunt regna nisi magna latrocinia?* "Without justice what are realms but great robber-bands?" But he goes on to ask — and this is often omitted from the quotation — *quia et latrocinia quid sunt, nisi parva regna?* "Since robber-bands themselves, what are they but little kingdoms?" He then goes on to explain further his meaning, "A company, and a robber-band itself, is composed of men; it is ruled by command of a chief; it is bound together by a compact of association (*pactum societatis*); and spoils of war are divided by the law of consent (*placiti lege*). This evil thing if it grow by the accession of abandoned men to such a pitch that permanent boundaries are established, that cities are occupied, that peoples are subjugated, assumes the more high-sounding title of a kingdom (*regnum*); but it is not the laying aside of cupidity that openly effects this, it is only the addition of impunity." [2] The heading of the brief chapter which includes this passage is, *Quam similia sint latrociniis regna absque justitia,* "Kingdoms without justice, how like they are to robber-bands."

It is clear, then, that to St. Augustine, a kingdom (*regnum*) may exist without justice. But does he really believe that this more "high-sounding title" (*evidentius nomen*) without justice can transform a band of robbers into a true *res publica*? In short is there no essential difference to him between a *regnum* and a *res*

---

[1] *Mediaeval Political Theory*, I (1903), p. 170. More mature reflection on this point apparently led Dr. Carlyle later to modify somewhat the view expressed here. "I am myself, therefore, not at all certain whether St. Augustine did deliberately attempt to change the conception of the State." *The Social and Political Ideas of Some Great Mediaeval Thinkers*, p. 51 (1923); but he seems to have returned to his original view that for St. Augustine justice was non-essential to a true commonwealth. *Mediaeval Political Theory*, vol. v (1928), p. 405.

[2] *De Civitate Dei*, Bk. IV, chap. 4.

publica? This is the crux of the whole matter, of which both Dr. Figgis and Dr. Carlyle seem to admit no doubt.

In Book XV, chapter 8, of the *City of God*, St. Augustine defines a city in practically the same terms as used of a realm. "A city (*civitas*) is nothing else than multitude of men bound together by *some* bond of association" (*hominum multitudo aliquo societatis vinculo colligata*). In this fashion a robber-band might grow into a city, with no bond of association higher than a common agreement for the division of plunder. Is such a city the same to St. Augustine as a *res publica?* Or, to put the question otherwise, does all this prove that he thought a true *res publica* could exist without justice? Any bond whatever (*aliquod vinculum*), for a good purpose or an evil, provided it amounts to a *pactum societatis*, any aggregation of a rational multitude, as he puts it in Book XIX, chapter 24, if only they are associated in common agreement upon the objects they pursue, any kind of *koinonia*, we are tempted to add, may be properly called a realm or a city, if it has a territory and sufficient size and strength. But can this be the *political koinonia* if it seeks only mere life, not the good life; is such a realm or city a true *res publica* or commonwealth if the bond of association is *any* bond and not the bond of justice and law (*vinculum juris*) which Cicero required? The care with which St. Augustine confines these statements of his to *civitates* and *regna* seems to me to indicate that he means to exclude *res publicae;* at least it gives no warrant for citing these passages as affirmative proof of a view that justice is non-essential to the being of a true commonwealth.

But the strongest statements tending to prove the interpretation of Dr. Figgis have not yet been noticed. They are in Book XIX of the *City of God*. In chapter 21, St. Augustine repeats the definition of Cicero and says that if it is a true definition, then pagan Rome never was a true *res publica* or *res populi*, because there was no *populus;* no *populus* because no justice; no justice because no rendering to each of his due; and no such rendering, where the rites — which are the "rights" — of the true God were neglected for sacrifices to impure demons.

But on the other hand, if a *populus* is defined in another way, "as if it were said (*velut si dicatur*), 'A people is an assemblage of a rational multitude associated by concordant communion in the things which it cherishes,'" then it would not be absurd to call this multitude a people, whether it unites in furthering a good end or a bad. And according to this definition the ancient Romans without doubt were a *populus* and the Roman state a *res publica*. Notwithstanding its wars and civil commotions, St. Augustine says in effect, I should not on this basis venture to assert that Rome was no *res publica*, so long as there remained any kind of assemblage of a rational multitude held together in pursuit of a common end; and I should also be taken as saying and thinking the same of the states of the Athenians, of the rest of the Greeks, of the Egyptians, of Babylon, and of all races whatsoever. "Generally, of course, a city of impious men, where God does not rule over a people obedient to him so that sacrifice is not made except to him alone, and where as a consequence the soul does not rule rightly and faithfully over the body nor reason over the appetites, that state is devoid of the truth of justice." [1]

This passage, in which the old sophistic view is repeated as an alternative to Cicero's, is taken as conclusive proof that it expresses the personal opinion of St. Augustine himself in condemnation of the latter. Its phraseology and its context alike make me more than doubtful of this. It is worth remembering that it is not justice of which St. Augustine is here directly in search as Plato was in the *Republic*. He is primarily concerned, not in finding justice, but in defending Christianity against paganism, and he wishes to show that his arguments against the latter must hold good no matter which of the two possible views of the nature of the state one may adopt. According to one of these views, justice is necessary to the being of a state; but in a heathen state there can be no such justice, therefore no state. This *is a reductio ad absurdum* indeed, but it is the absurdity of heathenism not of Cicero's definition which St. Augustine means to prove.

But, it might be said, this line of argument could prove nothing in favor of Christianity unless one were to accept Cicero's definition. Suppose, then, says St. Augustine, we were not to accept it. Suppose the alternative definition were taken instead, if you will (*velut si dicatur*, etc.). Let it be assumed that justice is unnecessary to a state. Even so, it still remains true that there can be no real virtue where the true God is not worshipped, for then the soul can have no real dominion over the body nor over the passions.

[1] *De Civitate Dei*, XIX, chap. 24.

In this general line of argument, which I have tried not to distort in the summary, and in St. Augustine's use of such expressions as "velut si dicatur" to introduce the anti-Ciceronian view, I can see little ground for assuming that when the author sets forth a conception of the state "according to the definition of Cicero" and then follows it with another of contrary character, it must be taken as proved that his own personal preferences must be against the first and in favor of the second. And yet this seems to be all the proof adducible for the confident assertion that St. Augustine practically alone of all medieval thinkers dispensed with the need of justice in a commonwealth.

But if St. Augustine did not thus discard justice, what was his real belief on this important subject? The conclusions to be culled from the general argument of the *City of God* I should summarize thus: Justice and justice alone is the only possible bond which can unite men as a true *populus* in a real *res publica*. The great states before Christianity were *regna* but they were not true commonwealths because there was no recognition in them of what was due to the one true God, and without such recognition there could be no real justice, for justice is to render to *each* his due. They were, however, *regna* and their undoubted merits in many ways entitle them to great admiration and respect.

In the time before the introduction of the new law by Christ, as St. Paul said, "When the Gentiles, which have not the law, do by nature the things contained in the law, these, having not the law, are a law unto themselves" (*Rom.* ii, 14); "And the times of this ignorance God winked at" (*Acts*, xvii, 30). But since the coming of Christ and the new law — *i.e.* in St. Augustine's own day — no true justice can exist without the rendering to everyone his due, and "what justice of man is it which takes man himself away from the true God and makes him subject to unclean demons?"[1] Thus the great pagan empires may have been *regna*, and Athens truly enough a *civitas*, for each was bound together by some *pactum societatis*, and a community is a *regnum* or a *civitas* if bound together *aliquo societatis vinculo*, by *any* bond of association; but none of them, admirable as some were in other respects, could ever be a true *populus*, its association and its

[1] "It is the part of law to direct human actions according to the order of justice, but in this the new law bulks larger than the old." *St. Thomas Aquinas. Summa Theologica*, Prima Secundae Partis, Quaestio XCI, art. v.

government could never rise to the height of a real *res populi* or *res publica;* for a *populus,* in Cicero's phrase, means "not *every* assemblage of a multitude but an assemblage united in consent to law and in community of interest." It must be united *consensu juris,* by consent to law, and that law must include the law of God as well as the law of man. Such law and such justice there cannot be in any state in which the just claims of the one true God are denied. No heathen state can ever rise quite to the height of a true commonwealth.

St. Augustine's *City of God* probably had a greater influence on subsequent medieval political thought than any other book written in the early middle ages. Yet, as Dr. Carlyle says, no later writer believed a true commonwealth could exist without justice. This was not, as Dr. Figgis intimates, because the political writers of the middle ages either disregarded or rejected the views of St. Augustine on this important point : it was because their interpretation of St. Augustine was not in accordance with that of Dr. Figgis. For example, James of Viterbo, an Augustinian and a writer strongly under the influence of St. Augustine, at the opening of the fourteenth century cites these passages from the *City of God* in defence of the *Donation of Constantine* against those who based a denial of its validity on the ground that it was made in a state devoid of justice; but it is valid, he says, not because justice is non-essential to a commonwealth, but because justice was not entirely lacking in the pagan Roman Empire. "In the Roman realm," he says, "especially after it began to increase, there was a justice of a certain kind, though indeed not that justice which has been formed through the faith of Christ which alone is called true justice; and so the Roman realm was not a *latrocinium for that time*.[1] Yet it was not just in the highest sense, since in that sense there can be no just realm where the faith of Christ is wanting." [2]

Many other similar statements might easily be added, for this is the unvarying medieval interpretation of Augustine's words. No conception of the middle ages was more deeply woven into the political thought of the whole period than St. Augustine's idea

[1] The *italics* are not in the original.
[2] *De Regimine Christiano,* edited by H. X. Arquillière, part ii, chap. x, p. 305. For another similar interpretation, see Egidius Romanus, *De Ecclesiastica Potestate,* edited by Boffito and Oxilia, part ii, chap. vii, p. 60; part iii, chap. xi, p. 161. Mr. Woolf's treatment of this whole subject is admirable, *Bartolus of Sassoferrato,* pp. 64–67.

that justice is incomplete if it is not based upon Christian law as well as the law of nature. No one can read the impassioned writings of Gregory VII without being impressed with the fact that the spring of all his thought, and of his immense activity, is the Augustinian idea of a justice which must have the law of the Christian God as its chief basis. For Gregory it was a necessary inference from this that the duty of securing this divine justice upon earth must ultimately rest on none but the vicar of Christ upon earth. It was but a step from this to Innocent IV's claim that the Pope is the *judex ordinarius* of all men and to the whole later struggle of "Church and State." The jest of Voltaire that the Holy Roman Empire was neither holy nor Roman nor an Empire may be true for later history. As to the conception of the Empire up to the fourteenth century, it is utterly false. That Empire must be Christian as well as Roman, *the politia Christiana;* and for a long time it was only with difficulty that men could think that any other polity could be Christian in the same sense, for the unity of one polity was as necessary for earthly justice as ecclesiastical unity was for salvation. Not till the rise of the nation states, and the period of the Renaissance and Reformation were these ideas entirely dislodged, if then. The debt of medieval political thought to St. Augustine is incalculable and no effort is wasted that may lead to a better understanding of his true meaning.

In the period under consideration, as always in the middle ages, there was a tendency to look at the institutions of government, servitude, and property all in much the same way, and as it was the fall of man that furnished the explanation of government's origin, by men of the early middle ages the same general explanation was extended to slavery and to man's control over external things. In the state of innocence men were equal and they were free, there was no domination of any kind by one over another. But the fall of man altered all this. "The prime cause of servitude is sin," says St. Augustine.[1] But, as in the case of government, this must not be taken as proving that human slavery necessarily meets with God's disapproval. It is only another of the institutions ordained by God to cope with man's wickedness. As such, however, it must be considered only as an outward status and must never obstruct the effects of God's grace;

[1] *De Civitate Dei*, XIX, chap. xv.

it does not deprive the slave of the character of a man nor reduce him to the level of an "animate instrument" as Aristotle thought. Masters and slaves are fellow men and by the Grace of God may become brothers in Christ, equal before God though necessarily unequal under human law while sojourners in this "earthly city."

Such in brief was the general belief of this time regarding the instutution of slavery, and it is easy to see how much it owes to Stoic ideas and the doctrines of Roman law, though greatly colored by Christian tradition and the new theology.

On the prevailing conceptions regarding property the effect of Christianity was relatively greater and the contribution of Roman law, though very important, apparently considerably less than in the case of slavery. Some of the survivals in Roman law may indicate an early period when property was held in common, but the earliest legal sources we have give clear proof of the existence of private ownership. It was a settled principle deeply imbedded in the Roman legal system. This principle is not repudiated by the Church writers of the early middle ages, but it arose, they hold, out of the *jus gentium*, not from the *jus naturale*, and hence became a part of the *jus civile*, by virtue of which alone it is binding upon men. It is purely conventional, not natural. As for government and servitude, they offer an explanation of its origin which comes in part from Christian tradition, in part from heathen philosophy. As with servitude, its prime cause is sin, in this case the particular sin of avarice. But in the case of property they go further than this and introduce ideas which can scarcely have originated anywhere but in the Christian community or in traditions which go back beyond it. These were ideas not merely of the *origin* of property — concerning that the Romans had held views not unlike, but with slight effect on the practical rules of their law — they were very distinctive ideas as to man's proper *use* of it, and they had a very definite influence on Christian ethics in this respect and on practical life.

Roman law does not go beyond the maxim, "Make such use of your own as not to harm another's," [1] which implies private ownership and puts only negative limitations upon use. Christian writers went far beyond that.

---

[1] *Sic utere tuo ut alienum non laedas.* So far as I know this maxim does not occur among the sources of Roman law, but it expresses the general principle of the law.

The following summary of their ideas on the subject is taken from Dr. A. J. Carlyle's paper on *The Theory of Property in Mediaeval Theology*.[1]

"This view is the opposite of that of Locke, that private property is an institution of natural law, and arises out of labour. To the Fathers the only natural condition is that of common ownership and individual use. The world was made for the common benefit of mankind, that all should receive from it what they require. They admit, however, that human nature being what it is, avaricious and vicious, it is impossible for men to live normally under the condition of common ownership. This represents the more perfect way of life, and this principle was represented in the organization of the monastic life, as it gradually took shape. For mankind in general, some organization of ownership became necessary, and this was provided by the State and its laws, which have decided the conditions and limitations of ownership. Private property is therefore practically the creation of the State, and is defined, limited, and changed by the State.

"While, however, the Fathers recognize the legal right of private property, as a suitable and necessary concession to human infirmity, a necessary check upon human vice, they are also clear that from the religious and moral standpoint the position of private property is somewhat different. The conventional organization of life is legitimate, but the natural law is not only primitive, but also remains in some sense supreme. Whatever conventional organization may be found necessary for the practical adjustment of human affairs, the ultimate nature of things still holds good. Private property is allowed, but only in order to avoid the danger of violence and confusion; and the institution cannot override the natural right of a man to obtain what he needs from the abundance of that which the earth brings forth. This is what the Fathers mean when they call the maintenance of the needy an act of justice, not of mercy: for it is justice to give to a man that which is his own, and the needy have a moral right to what they require."[2]

"When, therefore, the Fathers say that almsgiving is an act

---

[1] *Property, Its Duties and Rights*, Second Edition, pp. 117–132. Another paper in the same collection is also valuable for this subject. *The Biblical and Early Christian Idea of Property*, by The Rev. Vernon Bartlet, D.D. (pp. 83–116). See also Ernst Troeltsch, *Die Soziallehren der christlichen Kirchen und Gruppen* (*Gesammelte Schriften*, vol. i, 3d ed., Tübingen, 1923) chap. i.

[2] Pp. 125–126.

of justice, there is little doubt that they mean that the man who is in need has a legitimate right to claim for his need that which is to another man a superfluity." [1]

All property is the gift of God and it was His will that the earth which He created should be the common possession of all men and satisfy the needs of all; it was avarice which created rights or private property.

"It is therefore *just* that the man who claims for his private ownership that which was given to the human race in common, should at least distribute some of this to the poor." [2]

At most it is only the use of property that any man can rightly have, and this use should be restricted to his proper needs and limited by the needs of others. Among the principles constituting the law of nature, according to St. Isidore of Seville in the seventh century, one is *communis omnium possessio*.[3]

There remains to be briefly discussed one more topic important for his period alone, but more important as the beginning of later controversies, the question of the relations of "Church and State."

To understand the views held in the early middle ages of the relation of Church and State one must first of all know the institutions and practices of the Church as they were at the stage in their development reached in the period immediately following the toleration and later establishment of Christianity by the Roman state and before the changes produced in those views by the break-up of the western Empire and the establishment of the new kingdoms. Toleration and establishment were concessions made by the state and sanctioned by secular law, but these concessions were granted to a large body of the Emperor's subjects who already formed a community, united not only in a common faith, but by a comprehensive ecclesiastical organization with extensive disciplinary powers and definite institutions of independent growth and long standing. The establishment of Christianity meant not only the full submission by Christians to the Emperor's sovereignty; it also involved the recognition by the state of this organization and its spiritual authority. Churchmen never questioned the Emperor's sovereignty or the binding character of his decrees,

[1] *Ibid.*, p. 124.

[2] A. J. Carlyle in *Property, Its Duties and Rights*, p. 123, summarizing St. Ambrose.

[3] *Etymologies*, Bk. V, chap. iv. For a commentary on this very ambiguous phrase, see Carlyle, *History of Mediaeval Political Theory*, I, pp. 142-144.

but they were at times confronted by cases in which obedience to these decrees seemed inconsistent with the spiritual claims and authority of their Church, and it is not surprising to find among them differences in the answers given to the puzzling and novel questions raised by such cases.   In the latter half of the fourth century St. Optatus reminded the Donatists who rejected the Emperor's decision against them that the Church was in the state, not the state in the Church, and that there was none above the Emperor but God alone who made him emperor,[1] and such statements probably do not go beyond the generally accepted view. But at other times, when the Emperor's acts were not so acceptable to the orthodox, their emphasis was very different.   It is also in the late fourth century that St. Ambrose wrote to the Emperor Valentinian II to remind him that in matters of faith it belongs to the bishops to judge Christian emperors, not to emperors to judge bishops.   "The Emperor is within the Church, not above it. . . .   The things that are divine are not subject to imperial power."   He withheld the Eucharist even from Theodosius the Great, and on one occasion when the surrender of a church was demanded in the name of the Emperor he refused with the words, "The palaces belong to the Emperor, the churches to the priesthood."[2]

In causes of God it befits rulers to learn rather than to teach (*discere potius quam docere*), declared Pope Felix II.[3]

In the last years of the fifth century the most sweeping and most comprehensive statement of these matters in this period is found in the letters and tractates of Pope Gelasius I.   The Emperor, he says, is the son of the Church, not its director.   In matters of religion it is his to learn and not to teach.   He has the privileges of his power which he has obtained by the will of God for the sake of public administration.   But God willed that dispositions for the Church should belong to the clergy, not to the secular powers, which, if they are Christians, He willed should be subject to his Church and to the clergy.   Not by public laws, not by the powers of the world, but by the bishops and the clergy, did the omnipotent God will that the lords and priests of the Christian religion should be ordained, removed, or restored when renouncing their error.   Christian emperors ought to entrust the administration to the heads of the Church, not to exercise it.

---

[1] Carlyle, *op. cit.*, I, pp. 148–149.   [2] *Ibid.*, pp. 180–184.   [3] *Ibid.*, p. 186.

Therefore no sentence is certain, nor can that stand which the Emperor has taken upon himself, if the Church by its own laws and by its own competent officers has never discussed the case nor restored the culprit to communion.

Before the time of Christ, he says, some did have the offices of both king and priest, and in heathen times the devil copied this and the pagan emperors held the office of Pontifex Maximus. But Christ who was both king and priest never entrusted both powers to the same hands, but separated the two offices and the functions and dignities proper to each, and therefore, as Christian emperors stand in need of priests for eternal life, so the priests for the course of temporal things employ (*uterentur*) the directions of emperors.

"There are two authorities by which principally this world is ruled, the sacred authority of the bishops, and the royal power, and the obligation of the bishops is the heavier of the two in proportion as they shall render account to God for the kings of men themselves." [1]

There is here a clear statement of the principle "that the Church has its own laws and principles, its own administrative authority, which is not at all to be regarded as dependent upon the state, but as something which stands beside it and is independent of it; that the relations between the Church and the State are those of two independent though closely related powers." [2] But it is at the same time admitted that in Christian society, "the spiritual and the temporal powers are intrusted to two different orders, each drawing its authority from God, each supreme in its own sphere, and independent, within its own sphere, of the other"; and the fact is distinctly recognized that "while these two authorities are each independent of the other, and supreme in their own spheres, they are also dependent upon each other, and cannot avoid relations with each other; so that while each is supreme in its own sphere, each is also subordinate in relation to the other sphere. The king is subject to the bishop in spiritual matters, the bishop to the king in temporal matters. Gelasius is conscious of the fact that no division between the two powers can be complete; . . . and, more than this, we may say that Gelasius perhaps feels that the question which is the greater of the two cannot be wholly avoided." [3] Dr. Carlyle seems warranted in feeling that these

---

[1] Carlyle, *op. cit.*, I, pp. 187-191.   [2] *Ibid.*, I, pp. 175-176.   [3] *Ibid.*, I, p. 192.

statements go far "to establish a theory of a strict dualism in society, and they are not therefore in accord with the tendency of those mediaeval thinkers who thought of society as organized under the terms of a complete unity." [1] The latter conception prevailed over the former in the eleventh and twelfth centuries, and the higher power was the spiritual; [2] by the late sixteenth century the dualistic view had revived and was generally held by both ecclesiastics and *politiques*, and though often contested it has never since been wholly absent from the history of the state, notwithstanding the fact that the balance has in general swung over toward the temporal power in modern times.

In the statements of the early middle ages we may see appearing in their earliest indistinct form some of the concrete points that have divided Church and State ever since, the immunity of the clergy, the mutual limits of spiritual and temporal jurisdiction, the obligations of Church property, and even obscurely the question of Supremacy; and a study of these statements discloses a steady advance in the consciousness of its distinctive character and peculiar rights by the Church, which to be thoroughly understood must be studied in closest connection with the history of the successive changes in its actual relations with the Roman government throughout this period.

The progress of this spirit of independence moved side by side with a growing consciousness within the Church of its unity — in fact with two closely related tendencies, one toward unity, the other toward the conception of the Church as a definite visible institution outside of which there is no salvation; and both ideas were developed in the contests with heathenism without and heresy within.

As early as the third century St. Cyprian likens the Church to the sun with many rays but one light, to a tree whose many branches draw their strength from one root, or to a spring from which many rivulets flow. But a branch torn away from the tree cannot grow, and a rivulet dries up if not fed by its spring. So whoever is separated from the Church is separated from the things promised to the Church. He shall not enter into the rewards of Christ, who leaves the Church of Christ. He is a stranger, a

[1] Carlyle, *op. cit.*, I, pp. 184–185.
[2] See Gierke, *Political Theories of the Middle Age* (Maitland's translation), p. 9 ff. for the statement of later views on this subject.

profane man, an enemy. "He cannot have God for his father who does not have the Church for his mother." "Whoever does not hold to this unity, has not the law of God, has not the faith of Father and Son, has neither life nor salvation." [1] As long as the Church was a society unrecognized by law the enforcement of these strict views could go no further than excommunication, but with the establishment of Christianity these questions assume a political importance, and ultimately the penalties against breaches of this unity were inflicted by the state. Thus religious uniformity enforced by secular authority was becoming the rule and this uniformity included adherence to a visible, external, exclusive institution. It is true that St. Augustine defines the Church as the community of all believers and that his "City of God" is not the exact counterpart of the visible Church on earth.[2] Yet the weight of his great authority was always thrown on the side of unity and orthodoxy, and the influence of other sides of his many-sided mind clearly appears only centuries after his death.

There is no part of the history of the age-long struggle between Church and State more essential to a thorough mastery of it all or to an impartial estimate of the conflicting claims, than this period of its beginnings in the early middle ages.

Fortunately the complicated question of the causes of the "Decline and Fall" of the western Empire may be left to the general historian. The chronicler of the growth of political thought is concerned only with the changes in men's conception of the state produced by the new political conditions that accompanied and followed this decline. These changes were gradual but they were fundamental, and the two aspects of them probably most important here are their effects upon the relations of the secular and the ecclesiastical authorities, and the infusion of habits of thought concerning law and government derived from the tribal conditions of the barbarians who swarmed into the Roman Empire, and ultimately found themselves its heirs. It seems best to take the second of these first, and within it the early Germanic conceptions of law.

Roughly speaking we may trace three principal phases in the development of these conceptions between the fifth and the tenth

[1] *De Unitate Ecclesiae*, chaps. 5–6.
[2] For a discriminating discussion of the varying modern views on these points see Figgis, *The Political Aspects of St. Augustine's 'City of God,'* chap. iv, with the notes at the end of the volume.

century, first the period without discoverable beginnings during
which the primitive idea of tribal law was little affected by new
conditions or by "international" questions, a period when the
custom of the tribe was exclusive in its scope and racial rather
than territorial in its character.[1] A second phase, which should
be considered a development in this primitive idea rather than a
breach of it, was inevitably brought about by the irruption of the
barbarians into the western provinces of the Empire, coming as
they did increasingly by whole tribes, and in competition with
each other, or in succession one to another. This is the phase
most prominent from the sixth to the ninth century, characterized
by the phrase "the personality of law." It has been held that
the peculiar conditions implied by this phrase were inherent in
the early Germanic conception of law itself, but Brunner and
others have pointed out certain facts that seem inconsistent with
such a theory. The texts of the Salic law, one of the earliest surviving records of Germanic customary law, seem to recognize no
such distinction between a Frank and "a barbarian" who lives
under Salic law,[2] and there is evidence of its non-existence even
in the ninth century in England.[3] So far as surviving documents
go, the principle of personality seems to appear first in the Lex
Ribuaria, of later date than the Lex Salica.[4] "This is no ancient
Germanic principle." "Its development was the result of the
exigencies of the time," and of the attempt of certain tribes "to
extend the enjoyment of their tribal law into the scattered districts
over which they had spread." [5] Under this principle a racial
group within a state was not brought under the tribal law of the
state but permitted to employ its own customary rules, and before
a particular case could be determined it was necessary to ascertain
which law should apply, usually through the "profession" of the
defendant. In parts of the country over which successive waves
of migration had passed each leaving a sediment of population as

[1] For the best modern account of customary law see Siegfried Brie, *Die Lehre vom Gewohn-
heitsrecht*, vol. i, Breslau, 1899 (all published) especially sections 27–32 (*Das deutsche Recht
im Mittelalter*).
[2] Brunner, *Deutsche Rechtsgeschichte*, I (2d ed.), p. 384; Geffcken, *Lex Salica*, pp. 40,
161. Schröder seems to regard the matter as still "disputable." *Lehrbuch der deutschen
Rechtsgeschichte* (5th ed.), p. 242, note 12.
[3] In the treaty between Alfred and Guthrum, Liebermann, *Die Gesetze der Angelsachsen*,
I, p. 126.
[4] *Lex Ribuaria*, edited by R. Sohm (*Monumenta Germaniae Historica*), 31, 3; 61, 2;
Brunner, *op. cit.*, p. 384.
[5] Brunner, *loc. cit.*

it moved onward, the number of these law-groups became considerable and the administration of law very complex. This diversity
of laws was so great, as Bishop Agobard of Lyons quaintly says
in the first half of the ninth century, that it was to be found "not
only in particular districts or cities, but even in many houses."
"For it often happened that five men were present or sitting together, and not one of them had a law the same as another." [1]
The application of the principle sometimes resulted in the promulgation of two sets of laws, one for the Roman, the other for the
Germanic subjects of the King, as in the Visigothic and Burgundian
kingdoms.

The importance of this phase of European legal history in the
development of political ideas is incalculable. Under such a system of personal laws it was possible for Roman law to survive the
invasions of barbarism, if the Roman population was large enough
for its law later to form a part of the local law of the district, after
the peoples had become stabilized and their laws had become
territorial. But for this principle of personality it is hard to see
how Roman law could ever have thus persisted as local custom, as
it did in places, and had it not so persisted it seems probable that
the renaissance of Roman law might never have come, at least
when it did, and as it did, in the eleventh and twelfth centuries.
For in this darkest period of the law's history it was certainly as
local custom chiefly that the Roman rules of the law lived on; it
was not in the form of a scientific jurisprudence if we may judge
from the few slight, scattered, and exceedingly crude epitomes
that have been thought to date from this period.[2] For these
reasons the obscure period of the personality of law must be considered one of the most critical in the whole history of political
thought, for if the continuity of Roman law had been broken at
this time it is safe to say that the entire subsequent development
of political thought in the West would have been far other than
it has been. And that continuity was in the greatest danger of

---

[1] *Adversus legem Gundobadi*, c. 4 (*M. G. H.*, *Leg.*, III, 504), quoted by Brunner, *op. cit.*,
I, p. 383.

[2] The fullest account of these sources is Max Conrat's *Geschichte der Quellen und Literatur
des römischen Rechts im früheren Mittelalter*, Leipzig, 1891. A few are printed in H. Fitting's
Juristische Schriften des früheren Mittelalters, Halle, 1876. For the argument that these
writings come from the dark period between Justinian and Irnerius, see Fitting, *Die
Anfänge der Rechtsschule zu Bologna*, Berlin, 1888. Flach, on the contrary, holds that they
date either from the time of Justinian or after the establishment of the law school at Bologna,
not between. *Études critiques sur l'histoire du droit romain au moyen âge*, Paris, 1890,
Étude I°.

being broken. Our knowledge of the full text of Justinian's *Digest* hangs by a single thread, the precious manuscript of it preserved at Florence. But for the effects of the principle of personality, there might well have been no Irnerius, no Bartolus, no Cujas, no Bodin.

But as changing conditions had thus brought about the prevalence of personality, so further changes ultimately put an end to it and made the law territorial. By the ninth century this change is all but complete. The wandering peoples have almost ceased to move, their territories have for the most part become fixed and permanent, and the various racial elements within these territories have gradually become fused into true local communities. In like manner their tribal customs have become *local* customs, they are "the law of the land," with few exceptions binding upon all within it, and binding upon them because of their domicile, not their race.

As a whole this is a period of customary law, of the gradual fusion of older and newer elements in political thought, of the slow assimilation of Roman ideas by the barbarians, and the "barbarizing" of these ideas in this process of assimilation. It is necessary therefore to consider something of the nature and extent of the new ideas about the state, of Germanic or at least non-Roman origin, which in this way became a part of the heritage of modern times from the political thought of the middle ages.

The description of the Germanic invaders given by Caesar and Tacitus and the later and fuller evidence in the fragmentary written compilations of their own customary tribal law disclose habits of thought about law, government, servitude, and property far different in many respects from those of the provincials who had inherited the traditions of imperial Rome. To the Germans, law remains primarily the immemorial custom of the tribe, as much its unique possession as the tribal religion, and if a part of this customary law happens to be put in writing, through contact with Roman ideas of written law and increasingly complex relations with other racial groups and laws, this in no way changes men's habitual conception of the essential nature of law itself, of its origin, or of the basis of its authority over them. The primary fact is that, notwithstanding all the so-called written "codes," custom continued to comprise the bulk of the actual law of the invading hordes, and that it was as immemorial custom alone that any of these laws, whether written or not, were held to be binding. The writing and formal promulgation were incidental, not essential, to the character of law. Even the smaller, written, part of that law, as Professor Jenks well says, was "not legislation, but record." [1] "The law was not made, it was only proved." [2]

It is scarcely necessary to say that this idea was not new. It is found at a corresponding stage in the cultural development of most races, and it was as characteristic of primitive Romans centuries before, as it was of the Germanic peoples in the early middle ages. But in the latter period Roman law was developed, Germanic law still primitive, and some of its primitive characteristics were retained through the whole period of the personality of law to become a part of the territorial law that succeeded it in the period we call feudal. Possibly the most significant of these characteristics for the history of political ideas is the prominence of custom. In 319 A.D. the Emperor Constantine had declared that the authority of custom and ancient usage was not to be ignored, unless it ran counter to reason or *lex*.[3] In the twelfth century the author of the second book of the *Libri Feudorum* turns this statement completely around : the authority of the Roman laws is not to be disregarded but it does not extend so far as to overcome *usum aut mores*.[4] Explain this difference as we may, and many explanations have been offered, the great fact stands out that the Germans have brought to the political thinking of Western Europe a new and permanent contribution of great significance, a conception of law different from that of imperial Rome. They have brought, or they have restored, a new, or possibly we may say, an old, emphasis. They habitually think of law primarily as the immemorial custom of the tribe, not as the legislative enactment of any supreme authority in the state.

What St. Isidore of Seville says on the subject seems a little obscure, but it is certainly not exactly what a Roman jurist of the classical period would have said. "*Jus* is a general term, *lex* is a species of *jus*. *Jus* is so-called because it is just. Moreover all *jus* stands firm through *leges* and *mores*. *Lex* is a written enactment. *Mos* is custom approved by its antiquity, or unwritten *lex*. For *lex* is so called from *legendo*, since it is written. *Mos* on the

---

[1] *Law and Politics in the Middle Ages*, pp. 7–8.
[2] R. Schröder, *Lehrbuch der deutschen Rechtsgeschichte* (5th ed.), p. 238.
[3] C. 8, 52, 2.
[4] Lehmann, *Das langobardische Lehnrecht*, p. 115.

other hand is custom long used and drawn only from usages. Moreover custom (*consuetudo*) is a kind of *jus* instituted by usages, accepted in place of *lex* where *lex* is lacking. And it is immaterial whether it is established by a writing or by reason, since it is reason also which commends *lex*. Besides, if *lex* stands firm through reason, *lex* will be everything which is established by reason, provided it be consistent with religion, that it accord with discipline, and that it conduce to salvation. Moreover it is called custom because it is in common use." [1]

"*Lex*, therefore, will be honest, just, possible, according to nature, *according to the custom of the country*, suitable to the place and time, necessary and useful; clear also, lest it contain through the obscurity of its wording something furthering a private interest, but written rather for the common utility of the citizens." [2]

The interesting thing about the first passage is the assimilation of *lex* and *consuetudo*. They are in essence the same. The same point was made centuries later for England in the law book of the twelfth century ascribed to Glanvill.

It is unnecessary to repeat in detail the well-known description of Germanic institutions by Tacitus in proof of the fact that the same tribal ideas affect the principal institutions of central government, as well as law. In a régime of customary law there is little place for legislative authority and Tacitus naturally has nothing to say of any among the primitive Germans. But even in absence of legislation there are other decisive questions of tribal policy to be determined, questions of war, peace, and alliances, and these the Germans did not entrust to their kings when they had kings — Tacitus implies that sometimes they had not — but agreed upon in the assembly of the warriors of the tribe. Nor was this all which Germanic kings lacked, and Roman emperors had. The trial of offenders was not entrusted to them, and not even the carrying out of judicial sentences. Furthermore they were passed over in time of war for military leaders (*duces*) of more vigor and greater influence. Kingship is only an incident in early Germanic tribal institutions and ideas. By the time of the establishment of the Frankish kingdom this had greatly changed. The long period of movement and inter-tribal war between the second century and the ninth necessarily strengthened the authority of kingship, but

---

[1] *Etymologies*, Bk. V, chap. iii.
[2] *Ibid.*, Bk. V, chap. xxi. The italics are mine.

the new kings were not the old aristocratic kings of Tacitus, but successors of the *duces* whose ability in war had raised them to the position of permanent head of the tribe. Kingship had become stronger, but it still remained tribal, and its ultimate basis was service to the tribe and originally the only kind of merit worth much at such a time, eminence in war.

"Kings are such by ruling" (*Reges a regendo*), says St. Isidore of Seville; "for just as a priest is such by his sanctification, so a king is king through his ruling, and he does not rule who does not correct. Therefore the title of king is held by proper administration, by wrong-doing it is lost. Wherefore it was a proverb among the ancients 'You shall be king if you rule rightly, if you do not, you shall not be.'" [1] *Duces*, he says in the same chapter, may even be called kings, and in time of war it is greater to be called *dux* than king. Such statements of the seventh century no doubt reflect the influences of "the ancients" of Greece and Rome, but one suspects the existence of other and much later ones also.

It is in the relation of the king to the law that these newer influences appear in their most important form. Princes, St. Isidore says, should be bound by "their" laws,[2] but the laws of this time even when promulgated in the names of such princes were not so much "their" law as the law of the tribe as a whole.[3] The so-called "Edict" of Rothar, king of the Lombards, in the seventh century, is one of the most striking examples. Even in pleas of the crown, with rare exceptions, the penalty must be "according to ancient custom," [4] and the whole edict, the King declares at the end, "we have established by inquiring into and recalling to mind (*rememorantes*) the ancient laws of our ancestors which had not been written." This has been accomplished by "subtle inquisition" concerning the ancient laws of the Lombards, not only on the king's part "but by ancient men" and it is confirmed by the assembly (*gaerethinx*) "according to the rule of our nation," to stand for all future time "for the common good of all men of our nation." [5] In

---

[1] *Etymologies*, Bk. IX, chap. iii. The same ideas and others are to be found in his *Sentences*, Bk. III, chaps. 47–51.

[2] *Sentences*, III, cap. 51.

[3] See, for early examples, *Lex Alamannorum*, 36, 1; *Lex Ribuaria*, 88, Hoc autem consensu et consilio seu paterna tradicione et legis consuetudinem super omnia iubemus. . . . Brie, *op. cit.*, p. 225 ff.

[4] *Edictus Rothari*, edited by Bluhme (*M. H. G.*), cap. 369.

[5] *Edictum Rothari*, edited by Bluhme, p. 386.

731 King Liutprand would abolish trial by battle to which he objects, but, he says, "On account of the custom of our nation of the Lombards, we are not able to forbid it." [1] The preambles of the same king to additions made at several times during his reign, are very interesting in the same way. These additions to the law it is said in one year, are made by the King "along with all the *judices* of Austria Neustria and Tuscany and all his *fideles* of Lombardy, "the whole people being present," and by "common consent." [2] In another year further additions were made to clear up existing doubts, some holding that certain points should be determined *per arbitrium*, others, that they should be decided "according to custom"; and this process of definition was carried through by an assembly which debated the matters and "ordained and defined them along with" the king. [3]

Almost all the writers of the period repeat the aphorism of St. Augustine "It is not for judges to judge of the law but according to the law," and they apply it to kings. A king is no king if he does not rule, and he can rule only in accordance with law. He promises so to do in an oath at his coronation. He is truly a king only on these conditions. Many references to this oath and to these conditions are found in this period in both official and non-official sources, and in germ they go back far into the history of the Germanic tribes. The texts of the Salic law employ the term *pactum* or agreement, and this term is repeated in Beneventum and in many later enactments elsewhere. The substance of the coronation oath is found in many places in the Frankish sources, and an early English form of it is to be found in a pontifical, probably of the eighth century. Alcuin seems to summarize the oath in one of his letters. Hincmar of Rheims even reminds the king that he and his episcopal colleagues have chosen him to the government of the realm under condition of preserving the laws. But it is unnecessary to multiply further such instances. [4] The general principle is unmistakable.

---

[1] *Liutprandi Leges, Anni XIX*, cap. 118 (edited by Bluhme).

[2] *Anno primo.*

[3] *Anno, XIV,* "Preamble."

[4] For a fuller discussion and more contemporary expressions of the same ideas both official and non-official, see Carlyle, *History of Mediaeval Political Theory*, I, chaps. 18–19, from whom some of these instances are taken. The former come chiefly from the capitularies of the Frankish kings. The preamble of Charlemagne's *Capitulare Aquisgranense* is typical. *Karolus etc., cum episcopis, abbatibus, comitibus, ducibus, omnibusque fidelibus Christianae ecclesiae* CUM CONSENSU CONSILIOQUE *constituit* EX LEGE SALICA, ROMANA ATQUE GOMBATA *capitula ista in palatio Aquis etc.* The principle of consent is here prominent, also the reën-

As time went on there was an undoubted strengthening of kingship, but even the high-sounding titles borrowed by the Frankish monarchs from the Roman emperors fail to conceal the fact that their authority is far from the same. In form and expression the capitularies of the Frankish kings are modeled on the imperial constitutions, but their content is totally different. Some were mere administrative orders, which had scarcely the sanctity of true "law" and possibly not its permanence. Promulgations of "law" still remained in reality affirmations of ancient tribal custom, notwithstanding the pompous titles of the king.

There are many disputed points in regard to the Frankish capitularies and their relation to existing customary law,[1] but there can be no doubt of the general fact that they still reflect the ancient Germanic idea of a tribal law, immemorial in character, and binding upon king and people alike, and a kingship based primarily upon service to the nation. These are all ideas of the greatest consequence in the history of thought, for they survived the Frankish monarchy to form the basis of the feudal régime, when the tribe had become a local community, and after kingship had been all but dissipated.

In this period the same general ideas of slavery expressed by the earlier patristic writers are repeated, but their application must have been considerably changed by Germanic institutions. In strict theory the early Germanic law apparently regarded one's slave in much the same way as his ox, but as early as the time of Tacitus it was remarked that the actual condition of slaves among the Germans was more like that of a Roman *colonus* than of a *servus*. Furthermore, actual enjoyment of free status under developed Germanic legal procedure gave the advantage in proof to the one so enjoying freedom over anyone who disputed it, just as actual dependence created a corresponding disadvantage. Enjoyment of freedom thus in a sense raised a presumption of the right to it, and this undoubtedly operated in time, in combina-

actment of earlier law. In this particular case the inclusion of Roman and Burgundian law in the enactment is an indication of the importance of the capitularies in the development from personal law to territorial.

For a very judicious modern statement, see Émile Chénon, *Histoire générale du droit français public et privé*, 1926, vol. i, pp. 174–179.

[1] For an interesting modern statement and proposed solution of these problems and a review of the varying theories, see J. Pétrau-Gay, *La notion de "lex" dans la Coutume Salienne et ses transformations dans les capitulaires* (doctoral thesis), Grenoble, 1920. On the subject of the duties and functions of the medieval king, see especially G. von Below, *Der deutsche Staat des Mittelalters*, vol. i, part ii, chap. v (1st ed., Leipzig, 1914).

tion with other factors, to make the proportion of true slaves much smaller than in Rome. The bulk of the agricultural class in this way at length became serfs rather than real slaves, bound to the soil and dependent upon lords, but with rights of freemen against all but these lords, and not completely rightless even in relation to them. The word "unfree" indicates better the status of the later *villanus* than the word "slave," and some of the conditions that made this so lie in earlier Germanic institutions. Contemporary evidence does not warrant us in saying that these institutions made any significant change in the general political view of slavery, but when combined with the influence of the Church they tended greatly to restrict the scope and extent of the institution itself, a matter in the long run at least as important.

Germanic ideas of property, especially the important subject of property in land, to the end retained the influence of a primitive period, when the use and enjoyment of land were protected rather than "ownership." Interests in land were much like personal status in that both had more the character of rights *in personam* than of rights *in rem*. Decisions in favor of the right of one claimant and against another were no bar to the claim of a third person, they decided only the question as to which of the two disputing parties had *the better* claim (*majus jus*); they implied no exclusive right in anyone against the world, as Roman ownership did. There were in Roman law, of course, *jura in re aliena*, "rights in a thing 'owned' by another," but that very phrase is a confession of the great theoretical superiority of the owner's right over all these other rights subtracted from it.

Germanic "seisin" (*gewere*), no matter which of the varying modern views of it we may adopt, implied no such marked superiority of an "owner's" rights over other interests. Many different rights in the land might in fact subsist side by side, each protected by remedies against the particular person infringing it.

Thus Germanic ideas of land-holding fostered, or at least permitted, the growth of many different rights and interests in the same piece of land from that of the "lord paramount" at the top to that of the "tenant paravail" at the bottom, as we sometimes find them later in the language of the feudal land-law. The subject is too intricate to follow into its details here,[1] but it serves

---

[1] A good bibliography of this difficult but important subject is given in Brunner, *Grundzüge der deutschen Rechtsgeschichte*, Bk. I, part ii, par. 46. One of the best accounts of it is

in part to explain the close connection of government and ownership of land which colors and controls all feudal ideas of government; and its beginnings are for that reason significant not for
legal history alone, but in the development of thought that we
style "political." But for such a mingling in the middle ages of
the ideas of proprietary right and governmental authority, which
the Romans had so carefully distinguished, and the corresponding
fusion of public and private law which they had kept separate,
feudal institutions and feudal conceptions of government could
never have become what they were in the later middle ages.
Without some understanding of the factors which led to these
changes, the political ideas of the feudal period are inexplicable.
For example, the peculiar but important conception shared by
Richard Fitzralph and Wycliffe, of the nature of all human relations, expressed by the word *dominium*, is a conception largely
"feudal" in character, and it arises in part out of institutions
whose beginnings were influenced by Germanic ideas of land-
holding in the period now under discussion. A whole library has
been written on the difficult and disputed subject of early Germanic land-holding, and it cannot be adequately treated in an
outline, even for political thought, but its significance in the
evolution of ideas few will deny who know anything of either law
or politics.

Aside from these important institutional developments and
their effects, the conceptions of the duties and rights incident to
property seemed to remain, in this period, much as they were in
the writings of the earlier Church fathers. St. Isidore of Seville
makes one or two significant statements that may show some
later influence. He enumerates as one part of the law of nature,
communis omnium possessio, and in his chapter on divine and
human law makes some interesting additions which may help to
interpret the former: "All *leges* are either divine or human, the
divine based on nature, the human on customs. And so the
latter vary, since some satisfy one people, some another. *Fas* is
divine *lex*, *jus* is human *lex*. *To cross the field belonging to another
is* FAS; *it is not* JUS." [1]

In the nature of things the unstable relations between the

available in English, *A History of Germanic Private Law*, translated from the German of
Rudolf Huebner, by Francis L. Philbrick, Boston, 1918. (*The Continental Legal History
Series*), Bk. II, chaps. v–vi.

[1] *Etymologies*, Bk. V, chaps. 4 and 2.

authorities in Church and State could not remain unaffected by the decline and final extinction of the authority of the Emperor in the western provinces and the rapid rise to power of the various Germanic nations which were crowding one after another into this territory.

No part of the long history of the relations of Church and State is more important or more critical than the two centuries immediately following the reign of the Emperor Leo the Isaurian in the eighth century. In this period powers were assumed by the Church and decisions taken whose effects we still feel at this day, and a more than superficial knowledge of them is indispensable for an understanding of all the later phases of the great controversy. Yet the reaction of these great events upon political thought itself does not appear clearly before the eleventh century nor fully before the fourteenth. Then men on both sides turned back to this critical period for the decisive precedents on which to base their conflicting claims of supremacy in the Pope or the Emperor.

They read the history of this period in the light of the controversies of their own day, and each side forced a meaning upon every transaction between Frankish King and Roman Pontiff which would serve the purpose of its own argument. In this way every step by which the authority of the Church had been advanced was later represented as part of a preconceived plan on the part of the Roman Pontiffs, to lay the foundation for the sweeping claims of a Boniface VIII or a John XXII. Gregory II, it was assumed, had the same ends in view and was actuated by precisely the same motives as Gregory VII. This mode of reasoning was followed equally by the defenders and the antagonists of the Papacy, and the acts of the kings were interpreted by both in the same fashion. Supporters and opponents of the Emperor alike attributed to Pepin and his successors a determination to check the "encroachment" of Popes, as conscious, and as much the result of premeditation, as were those encroachments themselves. Like assumptions are sometimes made by modern historians, even by some very great historians, both Catholic and Protestant.

But as a matter of fact in this particular period from the eighth to the tenth century, political speculation does not seem to have been particularly prominent. It was a period of action rather than of theorizing. The speculative results were to come later.

It seems very doubtful whether either Kings or Pontiffs looked very far into the future or anticipated the momentous results of their acts. Each was fighting a desperate battle of which the outcome was by no means certain, one against a powerful nation, the other against heresy in addition, and each welcomed all the help the other could give. Each was anxious more to ensure the success of their common enterprise, — or at least of his own part in it — than to protect himself at every possible point against the other. Thus only could so many important questions have been left open for later debate. "Anyone who studies the papal correspondence and the 'Liber Pontificalis' in the eighth century will, we think, feel that the leadership of the Roman *res publica* in the West was forced upon them [the Popes] rather than deliberately sought."[1]

Strictly contemporary speculation in this period seems to concern itself little with the supremacy of either Pope or King. It appears to make no significant advance beyond the theoretical views already laid down in the fifth century by Pope Gelasius I, under which the spheres of bishop and king were regarded as distinct and separate, but very closely related, in that spiritual authority extended over all laymen, even kings, and secular authority over churchmen as well as laymen. Year by year things were happening which made it harder for each of the two powers actually to keep within the field thus assigned it, and the struggle between them for supremacy over both fields was becoming more and more imminent and possibly more obvious to the leaders on both sides; but in this period these great events seem to belong as yet more properly to the general historian than to the chronicler of opinion.

No aspect of the Frankish period is more important in the growth of political ideas than the change from the personality to the territoriality of law. The course of the change is obscure, but the fact is obvious. By the ninth century the old question "under what law do you live?", if it had still been asked, would have been answered in most cases by the place, not the race, of the party. Law is the same for the whole district. But it retains,

[1] Carlyle, *History of Political Theory*, I, p. 289. A convenient translation of part of the *Liber Pontificalis* is now available in *The Records of Civilization*, by Louise Ropes Loomis (Columbia University Press). For the original text see L'Abbé L. Duchesne, *Le Liber Pontificalis*, 2 vols., Paris, 1886–1892; for an account of it, his *Étude sur le Liber Pontificalis*, Paris, 1877.

otherwise, the character it has always had. It still remains immemorial custom, handed down by one's ancestors, but now as the custom of the district. The tribe or the clan has become a local community and its customary law is the law of that community. We bring up some very ancient ideas when we speak, as we still properly do, of a local district as a "community." The custom of this community was still "proved" as before in the period of personality, but it was proved by local neighbors, and it applied to all.

This process of development from personality to territoriality was not complete when another began of no less importance, the disintegration of the short-lived centralized authority of the Frankish monarchy. Thus there arose in time a great number of legal or jurisdictional units, often very small in extent, each with its own body of local custom proved and enforced in its own courts, and without any effective central authority above it. These are the chief external characteristics of the administration of law in the period of feudalism.

"Feudalism" is the word we use to characterize the sum of the conditions, social, political, and economic, which prevailed in western Europe in the period, varying from place to place, between the stabilizing geographically of the Germanic tribes in their conquered territory and the emergence among them of centralized administrative systems "national" in scope, character, and extent. It is a term descriptive of the later transitional form in the development of European institutions out of those of the tribe into those of the national state. Almost everywhere those institutions arose out of earlier conditions much alike, everywhere their development followed the same general course, and everywhere that development tended to culminate in the same general way. But this is all. The development of some or of all "feudal" institutions was retarded in some parts of Europe, accelerated in others. Centuries might separate the appearance or the disappearance of particular feudal institutions in different places, and even at the time when most of them are found extended most widely — roughly, from the ninth to the eleventh century — we also find innumerable local points of difference in their form and operation. Feudalism, then, is properly nothing more than a general name for the common features of many diverse local institutions.

The term feudalism itself comes from "fief" (*feodum*), and the fief may probably be considered the most common of all its features. "The proper meaning of the Latin word *feodum*," says Brussel, "is *mouvance*," [1] and the nearest English word to that is probably "tenure." It is something which moves from one person to another, something held by one person of another. That something might be a right or interest in land, but by no means always. It might be an office, a dignity, or a chattel, a sum of money, or even a mere immunity or franchise. Everything of value was brought under the conception of the fief, one's land, one's personal status, one's office. One had an "estate" in them all, a proprietary interest that "moved" from some one, that was held of some one. Many of these rights or interests of whatever kind might be ancient, without known beginnings, yet the theory developed that everything had moved from some one, was held of some one, had at some time been granted by some one. And it continued to be held of him. His interest in the thing granted did not cease with the grant. If he had granted land as lord to a vassal, his rights over the land remained, except for the particular interest he had parted with. A new interest or right in the land had been carved out of the original one without extinguishing it, and that new interest involved a new continuing personal relationship, reciprocal in character, between the grantor and the grantee, whose character was determined by the nature of the tenure indicated in the grant.[2] Nor is this all. Tenure also

---

[1] *Nouvel examen de l'usage général des fiefs*, vol. i, p. 2.

[2] Under Roman law ownership was indivisible and therefore not partible between owner and tenant, but in the middle ages after vassalage had become an actual fact, the Romanists and canonists attempted to fit the new conditions into the older law, on the analogy of the original Roman distinction of actions as *actiones directae* and *actiones utiles*. The interest of the original lord, or grantor, was termed *dominium directum*, that of the vassal, *dominium utile*, and the latter came to be regarded by most as no mere usufruct but a true proprietary interest though subordinate to that of the grantor. Opinions were for long not unanimous, however. Hostiensis declared that dominion remained with the chief lord exclusively, and that the grant transferred no *proprietas* but *usufructus* merely. "In contrario videtur quod non habeat (vassalus) aliquod dominium, sed penes dominum remaneat. Nam cum dominus facit investituram alicuius beneficii, proprietas remanet penes eum et usufructus transit ad investitum et ad ejus heredes." *Summa decretalium, tit. de feudis*, Lyon, 1517, folio 271. Out of this distinction grew the common one between the *dominus directus, seigneur direct*, and the *dominus utilis, seigneur utile* and between the *dominium directum, seigneurie directe, domaine direct* — later *domaine éminent* — and *dominium utile, seigneurie* or *domaine utile*.

The Frankish grantors, as Loyseau says, reserved a right over a private seignory, unknown to the Romans, "which we have called *seigneurie* directe." *Traité des seigneuries*, chap. 1, par. 62, *Les Oeuvres de Maistre Charles Loyseau*, Paris, 1678. See in general A. Esmein, *Cours élémentaire d'histoire du droit français*, 11th ed., pp. 241–242, from which the above quotation from Hostiensis is taken; Ragueau, *Glossaire du droit françois, s. v. Seigneur, Seigneurie;* J. Declareuil, *Histoire générale du droit français* (1925), pp. 272–275; and above all the valuable paper of E. Meynial, *Notes sur la formation de la théorie du domaine divise*, in

affected the personal status of a grantee, it made him a peer of his co-vassals of the same fief, a fellow-member with them in the lord's court and entitled to a judgment of these "peers" before he could be lawfully punished for a wrong or deprived of a right. It determined, in other words, much of his social, economic, and governmental position and relations. The grantor was now his lord with definite rights over him and definite obligations to him of a continuing character, and he as vassal had reciprocal duties and rights in relation to the lord. If this relation were created *de novo* it was by contract, by ceremony of homage and with oath of fealty.

Even this inadequate summary is enough to show some things important for political thought. The line between public and private law is obscured, almost obliterated. One's governmental duties and rights are to a large extent both created and measured by a contract not unlike a modern private contract. The relation of lord to vassal confers on the lord some powers and duties over his vassal which for the Romans and for us seem to belong properly only to a sovereign over subjects. Every lord is a "sovereign" lord — the word properly means only superiority, but already carries with it somewhat more. The feudal relation is created by a solemn reciprocal engagement confirmed by an oath on one side and considered equally binding on both — it is contractual; but the rights so created on both sides are legal rights, they can be judicially interpreted only by the whole body of the peers of the fief, not by the lord. Theoretically there never was a period when rights were more insisted upon, but in the tangle of cross relationships existing, there were so many points open to dispute, and though no one, not even the lord, could be judge in his own case, the sanction of the law was so weak, that it is not altogether strange that some should see in feudalism nothing but a régime of unrestrained force. Yet throughout this period of decentralization, of legalized private war and actual violence, the old idea that a political community is one associated by a bond of law and of common interest is never wholly lost, and there were some feudal institutions which tended to strengthen rather than to weaken it.

Mélanges Fitting (Montpellier, 1908), vol. ii, pp. 409–461, where many extracts from the jurists from the twelfth to the fourteenth century are given. There is a brief but admirable account of these developments in von Schwerin, *Deutsche Rechtsgeschichte*, Leipzig, 1915, pp. 76–77; another by Gierke, in Holtzendorff's, *Encyklopädie der Rechtswissenschaft*, 6th ed. vol. i, pp. 488–490.

The whole period which we call feudal is a period of transition, rapid transition in fact, and our danger is over-simplification. The formula of decentralization is often applied to it without discrimination, and this era of decentralization is represented as ending sharply with the beginning of national states. The facts do not support so extreme a view. Throughout the period of greatest decentralization, factors of an opposite character never ceased to operate. National governments did destroy feudalism in the long run, but they did it in large part not by discarding existing institutions *in toto* or by a frontal attack on them all, but largely by turning to their own advantage certain institutions which had been in constant use throughout the whole period. This is especially true in the earlier part of the growth of national states. The institutions of the "feudal" period are too complex to be brought under a single formula, least of all the formula of complete decentralization. There was *in fact*, for a century or two, a decentralization that was all but complete, in certain parts of Europe, but even in this period there were theoretical elements derived from earlier sovereign power and susceptible of use in restoring it again.

The theory of the nature of the feudal bond now most widely accepted regards the oath of fealty as a remnant of the oath of a subject to a ruler; in its commonest form, at least after the tenth century, it usually contained reservations of the rights of superior lords over lower ones; and it was often taken by men whose obligations were not connected with a territorial fief at all. In 1176 Henry II of England instructed his justices to exact such an oath "even from rustics." These were not his "men" in a feudal sense; they were his *subjects*, and this is not exceptional for England, nor anything new, except in the thoroughness of its application. The complete decentralization of feudalism was more a fact than a theory. These are considerations important for the political thought of the time. They seem to indicate a greater continuity of older political ideas than is sometimes thought possible in this period, and they explain in part the undoubted fact that nationality was not so completely opposed to "feudal" principles that its beginnings could not exist in the very midst of the period that was most "feudal." In truth the period is marked by the interworking of many different factors which we are too ready to assume to be incompatible, some of which we even call anti-feudal. It would probably be truer to call them all feudal, at least in the sense that they all coexisted in this period, and any other sense is likely to be one arbitrarily imposed by ourselves in flat contradiction of some of the facts. Some of these factors, it is true, had a tendency to turn the general development of institutions in one direction, others in another, and some finally did supersede the others in the later establishment of national systems of administration; but many of these differing tendencies coexisted side by side throughout the whole feudal period, and it is scarcely safe or sound to deny to one the "feudal" character we ascribe to another. These considerations make necessary great discrimination in drawing political conclusions from the contemporary sources. Most of these sources come from the later period when the national tendencies have become strongly developed, others contain elements of Roman law of late introduction; and such elements must always be accounted for if we wish to find in these writings true indications of the political conceptions of the period called "feudal" *par excellence*.

The sources are of different kinds and of varying value for the history of political ideas. We find for the earlier period a large number of specific grants but no collections of customary law; that law was still transmitted orally in the different districts. Later we begin to find written summaries of local custom in many places, often the work of private and usually unknown persons; more rarely in the form of an official redaction. Lastly we have the more systematic treatises, not always clearly distinguishable especially in the earliest of them from the class of documents just mentioned except in their greater elaboration and more systematic form. They come generally however at a later period and are usually written much more under the influence of ideas derived from the new national governments, from Roman law, or from both.

The reason why the later of these books may be used to illustrate institutions of a period so much earlier, is not the one usually given — that the middle ages are a period of stagnation. The truth is the very opposite: it was a period of development, relatively of exceedingly rapid development. The reason is that these are books on *law*, and that the prevailing conception of law as immemorial custom kept them closer to older modes of thought than other historical sources of their own age. This persistence of an older conception of law as immemorial custom throughout a period of rapid and almost revolutionary change may seem a paradox, but it alone can account for the actual developments in the legal history of western Europe in the late middle ages. It is no more difficult to accept and to understand than the theoretical permanence of the XII Tables at Rome during the whole period in which Roman social relations were completely revolutionized, or the American doctrine that notwithstanding the enormous development of the nineteenth and twentieth centuries, the federal constitution of 1789 is still the basis of the constitutional law of the United States.

As early as the eleventh century some of the customs of local districts were finding their way into writing, as in the *Usatici Barchinone Patrie* in Barcelona.[1] Later these begin to appear in many places, and after the thirteenth century they are found in great numbers.

Some of the important earlier ones are, the *Libri Feudorum;*[2] the so-called *Tres-ancien Coutumier de Normandie*, probably of the early thirteenth century; *Le Grand Coutumier*, or *Summa de Legibus* as it was known in its Latin version, probably about a half century later, also for Normandy;[3] the *Leges Henrici Primi*, written in England between 1109 and 1118, but much influenced by outside sources;[4] the *Sachsenspiegel* in Saxony in the thirteenth century;[5] the *Assizes of Jerusalem;*[6] and many more. The treatises include Bracton, *De Legibus et Consuetudinibus Angliae*,[7] the most important law-book of medieval England, but not written till the middle of the thirteenth century, and requiring still further caution in its use on account of additions made in the manuscripts by later hands and the admixture of royal and Roman law; the *Coutumes de Beauvaisis* of Philippe de Beaumanoir,[8] of

---

[1] Printed by Ch. Giraud, *Essai sur l'histoire du droit français au moyen age*, vol. ii, p. 465 ff.

[2] Text in *Das Langobardische Lehnrecht*, edited by Karl Lehmann.

[3] *Coutumiers de Normandie*, edited by E. J. Tardif.

[4] Liebermann, *Gesetze der Angelsachsen*, I, p. 544 ff.

[5] Edited by C. G. Homeyer.

[6] Edited by Count Beugnot. For a good modern account and estimate see Maurice Grandclaude, *Étude critique sur les livres des Assises de Jérusalem* (doctoral thesis), Paris, 1923.

[7] The only satisfactory edition is edited by George E. Woodbine (New Haven, 1915-) but it is not yet completed. An older complete edition with English translation, but very unsatisfactory, is edited by Sir Travers Twiss.

[8] Edited by Am. Salmon, Paris, 1899-1900. A comprehensive account of some other French law books not specifically mentioned here is given by Paul Viollet, *Histoire du droit*

almost equal value for thirteenth century France but also much influenced by Roman law; and a number of others of great interest but probably somewhat less important than these two.

The general conception of law disclosed in all such sources is the familiar one of immemorial custom, but custom now definitely territorial in character, though the latest of the sources also give frequent indications of the presence of Roman ideas which had begun to come in by the twelfth century.   Before that time outside the Church few traces can be seen of anything regarded as true "law" which was not customary law, even in the south where some Roman principles persisted in the form of local customary rules; and even after the renaissance of Roman law, the older conception remained dominant for many generations.   From a general survey of these sources it seems true to say that in its strictly "feudal" connotation, "law," in the highest sense of that term, was nothing but the immemorial custom of a community defined territorially.   Many illustrations of this are to be found, only a few are given here.

One of the most interesting is a statement of the *Summa de Legibus* or *Grand Coutumier de Normandie* in the thirteenth century.   "*Consuetudines* are customs held from ancient times, approved by princes and preserved by the people, determining whose anything is, or to whom it pertains.   Moreover *leges* are institutions made by princes and preserved by the people in a province, by which particular cases are decided; for *leges* are, as it were, instruments in law for the declaration of the truth of the contentions.   Furthermore customs attend upon *leges*, for customs are the modes in which we ought to employ *leges*.   For example, it is *consuetudo* that the widow should have the third part of a fief of which her husband was seised at the time of their marriage.   But if a contention should arise concerning any fief of which he was not seised at that time, it is the practice that by the process of inquest (*per legem inquisitionis*) the widow shall demand her dower in the same, and that a contention of this kind shall be ended.   Moreover customs are the modes in which a procedure (*lex*) of this kind is conducted, as by twelve persons of esteem under oath who have first had view of the

civil français, Bk. I, chap. 3–4, and by A. Tardif, *Histoire des sources du droit français*, Bk. VI, chap. iii.   For English ones see P. H. Winfield, *The Chief Sources of English Legal History* (Cambridge, Mass., 1925), chap. ix.

fief. These (*leges*) approve possessions so that they introduce rights, for when they are changed, rights are changed, when they are varied rights are varied, when they are made rights are made." [1]

This passage is very remarkable, even unusual, but its general tenor is typical of feudal ideas, and the *Summa de Legibus* is one of the least Roman of all the greater law-books of the thirteenth century, much less so, for example, than its contemporary, the *De Legibus* of Bracton, or the work of Beaumanoir; which means that it reflects a more archaic conception of law and is, on the whole, probably a truer index of the legal ideas of the centuries preceding. The author of this book thinks of the enactments of the princes only as "instruments" for determining particular cases. They are administrative orders, in reality only a part of the *droit administratif*. The term *lex* itself means procedure, it does not mean the substantive principles of law. Those principles can be found only in custom "held" (*habiti*) from ancient times, "approved" (*approbati* — not "made") by princes and preserved (*conservati*) by the people, while the *leges* are "made" (*factae*) by princes and preserved by the people. Many instances may be found in the twelfth century treatise on English law attributed to Glanvill in which *lex* is used in the same way to indicate mere procedure instead of the substantive principles of the law, and other instances are frequent.

The Norman ecclesiastical author of the early twelfth century treatise on English law which passed under the misleading title *Leges Henrici Primi*, in his enumeration of the pleas of the Crown — an enumeration which includes no "common pleas" — concludes his list with "unjust judgment," "defect of justice," and "*prevaricacio legis regiae*"; [2] and such a "royal *lex*," in such a context, can scarcely mean anything but some such administrative order determining judicial procedure, of which we have note-

---

[1] *De Consuetudine.* The French version is also interesting as well as the gloss added later by Guillaume le Rouillé. The only modern critical text of both the Latin and the French version is given by Tardif, but the gloss is to be found only in the earlier editions, one of which was published at Rouen in 1539. The chapter *De Consuetudine*, from which the above extract is taken is the tenth in Bk. I, in Tardif's edition, in the sixteenth century editions it is the eleventh.

[2] *Leges Henrici Primi* (c. 1109–1118), X, i, Liebermann, *Gesetze der Angelsachsen*, I, p. 556. Cf. XII, 4, where the same offense is apparently referred to as that of one *qui legem apostatabit, Op. cit.*, I, p. 558; and XXXIV, 8, in which occurs the phrase *prevaricator vel eversor conscripte legis, Op. cit.*, I, p. 566. Many other passages in this treatise illustrate the same point.

worthy later instances in the assizes of Clarendon and Northampton of the reign of Henry II, or in the provisions for the grand assize and the assize of *novel disseisin* which no longer survive. Egidius Romanus uses the same phrases, and apparently with the same meaning, when he urges subjects to strive "not to transgress" (*ne prevaricentur*) the king's "laws and precepts" (*leges et precepta*); "for it is the worst of all for a realm to forsake royal ordinances (*leges regias*) and lawful precepts (*precepta legalia*) and not to be ruled by the king." [1] *Lex* "made" by the prince to determine particular cases, it appears, is not "law" in the highest sense, the latter can be found only in ancient custom. This remained the normal view long after the great advances of monarchy in the eleventh and twelfth centuries; it was surely no less so in the period before. It is still considered the king's duty, in the words of St. Augustine, "not to judge of the law but to judge according to the law." "Law," the only law in the highest sense, is something that none can "make," not even a king. He should approve it, and men may find, and preserve or maintain it, but it comes solely from ancient custom. These *consuetudines* or ancient customs are maintained or preserved by usage of the people (*more utentium*) and the king approves them either tacitly or by making provisions to ensure their enforcement. The latter may be *assisae, provisiones, ordinationes, ordonnances, stabilimenta,* or *établissements,* even *statuta;* they are *leges,* but they are not yet "law."

As late as the sixteenth century this view has an echo in France. "The Kings," says du Tillet, "abolish the *coutumes* if they will, as to their contracts, not as to those of their subjects, in destroying their right. For the *coutumes* are accorded by those subjects, not ordained by those Kings." [2] "We have two kinds of laws," declared de Harlay, President of the Parliament of Paris, to the King in 1586, "the ordinances of the Kings which may be changed with the change of time and circumstances," and "the ordinances of the realm which are unchangeable, under which you have ascended the royal throne"; [3] and the same idea lies behind the important limit which Bodin puts to sovereign power in the sixteenth century, as Bartolus had done in the fourteenth, in refus-

[1] *De Regimine Principum* (written in 1285 or before), Bk. III, part ii, chap. xxxiv.
[2] *Recueil des roys de France,* ed. of 1580, pp. 173–174.
[3] Du Vair, *Œuvres* (1617), p. 170, quoted by Declareuil, *Histoire générale du droit français,* p. 391.

ing to include within it a right to interfere with the property rights of subjects.[1]

In England the same distinction clearly appears in the difference recognized in the fourteenth century between a statute and an ordinance,[2] it underlies Fortescue's well-known contrast between England and France,[3] and it was the fundamental basis of the whole contention of English parliamentarians in the seventeenth century and of Pitt and Camden and the American colonists in the eighteenth, that there should be no taking of property by government without the subjects' consent, though Parliament itself, the recognized "sovereign" after the Revolution of 1688, had abandoned this theory for its opposite in its dealings with these subjects in "British possessions" beyond the realm.

Royal ordinances are thus not "law" in the highest sense. "Their competence was circumscribed by their object," [4] and their object was neither the creation nor the abrogation of law, but its maintenance. They had their origin in the king's *bannum* and are connected therefore with the formal promulgation or publication of law and with its enforcement; they have nothing to do with its creation. Law is perpetual in its nature, the decree of a king is temporary "because it is only a governmental act." The Roman magistrate had his *jus edicendi*, the Frankish king, his *bannum*. The essence of both is "a publication or communication," made in execution of the law, conforming to its prescriptions, and designed to secure its observance. In the Frankish period — and afterward — it was by the *bannum* of the king that law was put in execution. As Flach aptly says, a Frankish Papinian might well have said of it, as of the edict of a Roman magistrate, that it existed to aid, or to supplement, or to correct the *jus civile*, for the public utility. "The execution of the law, under the form of a royal order, such was the fundamental *raison d'être* of the *bannum*," [5] and it was nothing more.

The essential function, duty, and right of the king "is not to make law, but to promulgate it"; the basis of his sacred character

---

[1] In his distinction between "royal" and "seignorial" monarchy, *De Republica*, Bk. II, chap. iii.

[2] On this point see my paper on *Magna Carta and Common Law*, in *Magna Carta Commemoration Essays*, London, 1917.

[3] *The Governance of England*, edited by Charles Plummer, Oxford, 1885. See *post*, p. 354 ff.

[4] Jacques Flach, *Les origines de l'ancienne France*, vol. iii, p. 331.

[5] Flach, *op. cit.*, III, p. 342. I have taken several of the statements above from this illuminating discussion. See especially pp. 329–364.

"is his judicial power." If this power extends to the touching of the rights of the king's subjects, it is only by way of jurisdiction, "for the sake of protection" because protection of the subjects' right is one of the chief obligations of a medieval king: it implies neither the proprietary right to their lands or goods nor the control over the nexus of personal "rights" incident to these in the feudal period.[1]

"The king, in the middle ages, concerned himself with the government alone, and not with the private law."[2] It pertains to the magistracy or to judges, says Egidius Romanus in the thirteenth century, "to judge well according to laws *found (inventas) by the counsellors and guarded (custoditas) by the prince.*"[3]

Such a survival of medieval ideas concerning unwritten custom in the sixteenth century or the eighteenth might be regarded not unreasonably as an anachronism, but in the later middle ages these views were normal and natural and the ones generally held.

"The customary law is a guaranty; it is in its way a contract, imperfect it is true, tacit, imposed by history, but it is the first

---

[1] Of great significance in this connection is the interpretation in the medieval glosses of an incidental phrase of Justinian contained in a constitution of the year 531 (*Code*, VII, 37, 3, *De Quadriennii Praescriptione*), *cum omnia principis intellegantur*, "since everything should be considered as belonging to the prince." In the *glossa ordinaria* to this passage it is said that Martinus advised the Emperor Frederick Barbarossa at Roncaglia, "whether through love or fear," that this meant that he as prince was proprietor of all the possessions of his subjects. This Bulgarus denied and contended that the prince's authority extended only *ad protectionem vel jurisdictionem*, the interpretation adopted by Accursius himself. "My book," says the latter, "belongs to me, not to the prince"; a *vindicatio rei* to recover it would be granted to me, not to the prince. Azo was of the same opinion: "Do not conclude that the property of any private person is his [the prince's] except as to protection" (*nisi quo ad protectionem*). (Commentary on the *Code*, VII, 37, 3.) The discussion of this general question by Francis Hotman in the sixteenth century is remarkably acute and his conclusions are in accord with the interpretation of *Code* VII, 37, 3 made by Azo and Accursius though he does not refer to that passage. *Fr. Hotomani Quaestionum Illustrium Liber* (1576), "Quaestio 1, An Regibus ius sit regna & ditiones suas arbitratu suo deminuere." For a valuable treatment of the question with references to contemporary sources and some modern discussions, see Gierke, *Johannes Althusius*, p. 268 (3d ed.), Breslau, 1913. There is also a valuable discussion of the difference between Martinus and Bulgarus in Georg Meyer, *Das Recht der Expropriation*, Leipzig, 1868, pp. 86–94. This is followed by an account of the views on the same subject of the Canonists (pp. 94–97), the Post-Glossators (pp. 97–115), and a few of the great jurists of the sixteenth century (pp. 115–119).

Sir Thomas Craig, the celebrated Scottish feudist, gives an admirable account of the various views on this moot question of the proprietary right of the vassal in his fief. He wonders how one could think that Rollo as Duke of Normandy had nothing more than a mere right of usufruct, or in his own day the Duke of Saxony, the Margrave of Brandenburg, or the Count Palatine; and he sums up his conclusions in saying, "If we were not to admit a transfer of the *dominium utile* to the vassal, innumerable difficulties would arise in our own practice." *Jus Feudale*, Lib. I, Tit. IX, §§ vii–x (Lipsiae, 1716, pp. 77–80; written probably in 1603).

[2] Olivier Martin, *La Coutume de Paris*, 1925, p. 7.

[3] *De Regimine Principum*, Bk. III, part ii, chap. i.

form of the social compact which was to intervene between governors and governed." [1]

In the fourteenth century Bartolus, following earlier commentators, says that those peoples who refuse to be bound by authority of the Empire are exempted "because they are *not worthy* of being bound by the laws," [2] and this general idea was in existence long before and applicable to other laws than the Roman. "There could be no more curious or interesting example of the difference between our conception of law and that of the Middle Ages. To them law was the 'gift and invention of God,' and was therefore something too good for the 'vile' and the 'unworthy'; while to us, who have brought law down from Heaven, and put it, as a command, into the mouth of a 'sovereign,' the notion of law as too good for its subjects, the notion of a 'sovereign' voluntarily abdicating his claims over a part of his subjects, 'ne leges sintapud eos ludibrio' is almost incomprehensible." [3] This just observation of Mr. Woolf must be kept in mind if we are ever to understand the medieval conception of law. We may note in addition that by the thirteenth century some had certainly come to regard unwritten custom as not quite the same in substance as the written *lex* which St. Isidore had made it in the seventh century. [4]

As early as the capitularies of the Frankish kings at least, the latter seems to be in a certain sense a secondary or subordinate form of enactment, and in the twelfth and thirteenth centuries these *leges* have come to be regarded by some as procedural rules, while all men without exception seem to hold that *consuetudo* has really changed places with the old Roman *lex* and become "law," the only law in its true meaning, as the *Libri Feudorum* indicates. [5]

When Roman law was revived and men again studied Justinian's books, they found this contradiction staring them in the face, but the strength of customary law was too great to be denied. The words in the Prologue to Glanvill are very interesting in this connection. ". . . each decision is governed by the Laws of the Realm, and by those Customs which, founded on reason in their introduction, have for a long time prevailed." "For the English Laws, although not written, may as it should seem, and that

---

[1] Imbart de la Tour, *L'évolution des idées sociales du XIe au XIIIe siècle, Questions d'histoire sociale et religieuse* (1907), p. 170.

[2] In his commentary on the Code of Justinian (I. 1. 1.) quoted by Woolf, *Bartolus of Sassoferrato*, p. 41.

[3] Woolf, *op. cit.*, pp. 42–43.   [4] *Ante*, pp. 171–172.   [5] *Ante*, p. 171.

without any absurdity, be termed Laws (*leges*), (since this itself
is a Law (*lex*) — that which pleases the Prince has the force of
law) I mean, those Laws which it is evident were promulgated
by the advice of the Nobles and the authority of the Prince, concerning doubts to be settled in their Assembly. For, if from the
mere want of writing only, they should not be considered as Laws,
then, unquestionably, writing would seem to confer more authority upon Laws themselves, than either the Equity of the persons
constituting, or the reason of those framing them. But, to reduce
in every instance the Laws (*leges*) and rights (*jura*) [Beames here
has "Constitutions"] of the Realm into writing, would be, in our
times, absolutely impossible, as well on account of the ignorance
of writers, as of the confused multiplicity of the Laws." [1]

The distinction between *lex* as a mere administrative order and
consuetudo or law in the true sense, is fundamental, but it was not
always expressed as clearly as in the *Grand Coutumier*. Bracton,
for example, was possibly too much influenced by Roman terminology to do so, but he is no whit behind in his insistence upon the
importance and validity of custom. He repeats Glanvill's approximation of Roman *lex* and English custom and adds with a curious
insular misconception of foreign law, "While, however, they use
leges and a written law in almost all lands, in England alone there
has been used within its boundaries an unwritten law and custom.
In England legal right is based on an unwritten law which usage
has approved. . . . For the English hold many things by customary law which they do not hold by *lex*." [2] But England,
Bracton's assertion notwithstanding, was no exception in this,
for such statements are to be found all over the feudal world. [3]

The most interesting aspect politically of this general régime of
custom was the view men took of the nature and consequence of
its formal promulgation, and of the respective parts taken in this
by princes, the learned in the law, the magnates, and the people.

---

[1] *Tractatus de Legibus et Consuetudinibus Regni Angliae*, edited by John Rayner, London,
1780, English translation by John Beames, Washington, 1900, pp. xxxvii–xxxix. The
glosses to title 8 of Bk. I of the *Liber Pauperum* of Vacarius, which seem to come from the
same general period as Glanvill, furnish further evidence of the most interesting kind, of
the deep interest men had in the problem of reconciling the English customary laws with the
rediscovered texts of Justinian. These glosses are now accessible in the valuable edition
of Vacarius edited by Professor de Zulueta for the Selden Society, London, 1927, pp. 13–19.

[2] Folio 1 A.

[3] For a judicious selection of passages illustrating this point drawn mainly from the
Assises of Jerusalem and Beaumanoir, see Carlyle, *History of Mediaeval Political Theory*,
III, pp. 42–57.

Consuetudo, or law in its true sense, could not be made, but even if it were to be "found" only, questions must arise as to who was qualified to "find" it, by whose authority such a finding should become binding upon all when it was formally promulgated, and to whom it belonged to determine finally its true meaning. These are important matters which throw much light upon contemporary political ideas.

There is an interesting story told by the twelfth century author of an English book known since the seventeenth century as the *Laws of Edward the Confessor,* and the ideas it discloses are significant even though the story itself may be apochryphal or nothing but a confused account of the Domesday Inquest. "After the acquisition of England, King William, in the fourth year of his reign, with the counsel of his barons, caused to be summoned throughout all the counties of England, English nobles wise and learned in their law, in order to learn from them their *leges* and rights and customary laws.

"Twelve men, therefore, chosen from each of the counties of the whole land, in presence of the King, took an oath first of all to make known the provisions of their *leges* and *consuetudines,* so far as they were able, in a straight path, turning neither to the right nor the left, passing over nothing, adding nothing, changing nothing by walking crookedly." [1] A similar story was told of the drawing up of Assizes of Jerusalem,[2] and both are based on legal conceptions held generally at this time and on the methods prevailing everywhere for the proof of customary rules in the courts, great and small, through the *enquête par turbe* (*turba,* multitude, the *vulgus* of the later English coronation oath).[3] Law is made by the custom of those who use it (*more utentium*) and it can therefore be proved only on their testimony. Thus knights alone were used in the English grand assize, probably the earliest form of the jury in civil cases, because they alone knew enough to answer questions about land titles; but when a custom was in doubt which affected the common people, they or their represent-

---

[1] Liebermann, *Gesetze der Angelsachsen,* I, p. 627.

[2] Carlyle, *op. cit.,* III, p. 43.

[3] An ordinance of St. Louis in 1270 prescribing the methods to be followed shows the general procedure, but indicates some changes introduced by the increased use of writing. It is printed by Langlois, *Textes relatifs à l'histoire du Parlement,* p. 79. The best account of the general methods of proof in use is by H. Pissard, *Essai sur la connaissance et la preuve des coutumes* (doctoral thesis), Paris, 1910. See also H. Brunner, *Die Entstehung der Schwurgerichte,* Berlin, 1872, a classic.

atives alone could supply the necessary information. When it was so supplied the king's authority gave binding effect to the finding through a judgment of his court, if in a particular case, through an ordinance in his Council, if general in character. The laws are the king's, but they are his because it is a king's chief function to "approve" and maintain them, not because he can either make or break them. He can do neither. For these reasons enactments of law should be made by kings with the "counsel" (*consilium*) of the magnates or others who know it. It is misleading to inject the later idea of sovereignty into this "counsel" and think of it as exactly the same "consent" often required under modern constitutions. What was requisite in medieval "counsel" was knowledge rather than authority. In *consensus*, the word generally used, the emphasis fell on the unanimity or agreement of witnesses to the existence of custom, as members of an inquest or jury, not on their legal *indispensability* as in the modern meaning of the term. In these facts we have the explanation of many important statements scattered through the medieval law books, such as Bracton's, when he says, that in England it is not exactly "what has pleased the prince" that has the force of law, but "whatever shall have been justly defined and approved (*definitum et approbatum*) with counsel and agreement (*consensu*) of the magnates, and the common guaranty (*sponsio*) of the republic, the authority of a king or prince going before." [1]

Though the king may make new *establissemens*, says Beaumanoir, he should take care that they are made "for reasonable cause, for the common profit, and *par grant conseil*." [2]

English *leges* and *consuetudines*, according to Bracton, command, forbid, or punish, through the authority of kings, and these, "since they have been approved by consent of those using them and confirmed by the oath of kings, can neither be altered nor destroyed without the common consent of all those by whose counsel and consent they have been promulgated." [3]

This general conception of law, common in the feudal period, is the key to the theory of the nature and the limits of kingship held at the same time.

Kings are still called vicars of God but by evil rule they become vicars of the Devil, for he who does the Devil's work is the Devil's minister. A king is truly king "by ruling well, not by reign-

[1] Folio 1.   [2] Chap. 49, § 1515, edited by Salmon.   [3] Folio 1.

ing," and ruling well meant to men of the middle ages, the defence of the Church, the preservation of the peace, the enforcement of the just rights of subjects, the tempering of justice with mercy, and the maintenance of the ancient laws "which the common people have chosen." Kings must not judge of laws but according to them. The king is under the law, and he must rule justly and "for the common profit of all the realm." If he fails to do so he is no king but a tyrant. It is evident that in this period there are no kings by divine right, though the office of kingship makes its holder the vicar of God and confers upon him the highest authority on earth in temporal matters. The unction at the coronation gives him a character apart from others, but his oath imposes on him duties heavier than any other man's.

He stands above all his subjects, and can have no peer upon earth, much less a superior, "especially in the justice of his actions." This is the gist of a passage in Bracton remarkable in more ways than one. It continues thus:

"For as a king is the minister and vicar of God he can do nothing on earth which is not according to law, nor is this contrary to the saying 'what pleases the prince has the force of law,' since there follows at the end of the law 'In conjunction with the *lex regia* which has been passed concerning his *imperium*' (*cum lege regia quae de imperio eius lata est*); and this is presumed to be not every rash expression of the king's will, but what shall have been duly defined with the counsel of his great men, the king warranting its authority after deliberation and consultation upon it." [1] Now this is a complete distortion of the meaning of Justinian's *Institutes* that could scarcely have been unwitting, and it has puzzled historians ever since the days of John Selden, who read it "not without amazement." The original words are these:

"What has pleased the prince has the force of law, inasmuch as by a *lex regia* which has been enacted concerning his *imperium* the people grants to and bestows upon him all its *imperium* and *potestas*" (*utpote cum lege regia quae de imperio eius lata est, populus ei et in eum omne suum imperium et potestatem conferat*). How possibly could a good Latinist like Bracton, knowing this text of the *Institutes* as presumably he did, twist a *cum* introducing a causal clause into a preposition, and then deliberately omit all the

[1] Folio, 107.

words following? And if he knew what he was doing why did he do it?[1] Was it because he had to bring these words into accord with the ideas and facts of his own time?

If England had a *lex regia* then, it was the coronation oath, but that certainly conferred on the king no such *imperium* or *potestas* as the Emperors exercised. It did, however, contain certain limitations, and in the form used a little later, it concluded with a promise to give effect to the laws "which the common people have chosen" (*quas vulgus elegerit*)[2] and had no way to choose but by immemorial custom (*more utentium*).

When, then, Bracton says that the king's will has the force of law, only "in conjunction with the law passed concerning his imperium," if he is referring to an English coronation oath which includes a promise to maintain the ancient customary law, he is giving a not inaccurate statement of English medieval principles, however far it may be from the words and spirit of his Roman sources. In one place he goes even further than this if the words of the text are his own: "The king has a superior, namely God. Likewise the law through which he was made king. Likewise his *curia*, that is the earls and barons, since earls (*comites*) are so called for being as it were associates of the king, and he who has an associate has a master. And so if the king should be without a bridle, that is without law, they ought to put a bridle on him, lest they themselves, along with him, be without a bridle."[3]

It is impossible to say positively, on account of the peculiar

[1] There is considerable difference of opinion among modern scholars in regard to Bracton's knowledge and understanding of the texts of Roman law, Maitland holding it in low esteem, while Vinogradoff rates it much more highly. Even Vinogradoff, however, believes, contrary to the view of Selden, that Bracton's knowledge of Justinian's law books was only second-hand, derived from late epitomes such as the *Liber Pauperum* of Vacarius. It does not seem to me, however, that any of these things furnishes an adequate explanation of the startling alteration that Bracton made in the text just quoted, an alteration that Selden regarded "not without amazement."

See Selden, *Ad Fletam Dessertatio*, edited by David Ogg, Cambridge, 1925, III, ii; F. W. Maitland, *Bracton and Azo* (Selden Society), p. xvii, *et seq.*; Sir Paul Vinogradoff, *The Roman Elements in Bracton's Treatise* (1923), *The Collected Papers of Paul Vinogradoff*, Oxford, 1928, vol. i, p. 237, *et seq.*; C. H. McIlwain, *The High Court of Parliament*, New Haven, 1910, pp. 101–103.

[2] The interpretation of the clause *quas vulgus elegerit* adopted here is the one insisted on by Robert Brady in the seventeenth century against the parliamentary view expressed by Prynne, who held that *elegerit* meant "shall have chosen" not "have chosen" and must therefore refer to future legislation and not to past custom. For discussions of this controversy and references, see Arthur Taylor, *The Glory of Regality*, London, 1820, p. 329 ff., and the documents in the appendix to Bk. III, p. 383 ff.; Stubbs, *Constitutional History of England*, vol. ii (4th ed.), pp. 109, 331 ff.

[3] Folio 34. See also folio 171.

character of the Bracton manuscripts, whether these remarkable words are Bracton's own or not, but the probability is strongly against them, as they seem to contradict some other authentic statements of his. Nevertheless they were repeated in their full force by the author of another English book as early as the reign of Edward I,[1] and may be considered therefore an expression, though certainly an extreme expression, of a theory of monarchy held by sor.e in England in the late thirteenth century.

Our evidence seems to warrant the statement that this famous passage so often quoted with effect in later struggles against absolutism expresses a particular view held, but apparently not held generally, in England in the latter half of the thirteenth century, and probably before that time held nowhere, with the possible exception of the kingdoms in the Spanish peninsula. It is the theory of the framers of the Provisions of Oxford and of the author of the Song of Lewes, but probably of a minority only of the statesmen and theorists of the time.

If one were tempted to apply the word "medieval" to anything reactionary, as thoughtless people usually do today, it might be well to ponder some of these passages. Political absolutism is an achievement of modern times. The middle ages would have none of it.

But with medieval monarchy, as with feudal relations, the prevailing theory was one thing, the actual facts were often quite another. A nobler conception of kingship — a higher conception of government even — has seldom been expressed than that of the middle ages. Yet injustice was rife and private war almost constant, and lords and kings alike often ruled arbitrarily and oppressively. The main political defect of the time was not a lack of principles, but an almost total absence of any effective sanction for them, and this is undoubtedly one of the chief reasons for the later acquiescence in royal absolutism. One tyrant was preferable to a thousand.

Though the king was under the law in theory, there was little effective machinery in existence to make this theory a practical reality.

---

[1] *Fleta*, Bk I, chap. 17. The author was an able man and no mere copyist though he does draw very largely from Bracton. The main reason why his book cannot be taken as proof of the prevalence of his extreme political views is the fact that it was apparently not much circulated or copied. Only one manuscript of it has survived to modern times, while many are found of some of the other legal treatises of the period.

In a feudal age when the tenure of land fixed the whole status of men, determined their rights and secured their liberties, the land-law and the "law of the land" were almost equivalent terms and included most of the provisions protecting the personal as well as the proprietary rights of the subject. It was this immemorial custom which English kings of the latter middle ages had to swear to preserve, it was this which Du Tillet and De Harlay said, even in the sixteenth century, that a King of France could not alter, it was this that Sir Edward Coke included among the "fundamental" things of the English common law. But on the other hand the indefiniteness of these feudal rights, the tendency in some quarters toward a fusion of *imperium* and *dominium*, and the failure of the middle ages clearly to distinguish between the king and the Crown or between the official and the private revenues of the king, all tended often to defeat these rights and to imperil the "liberties of the subject." The king was without doubt supreme landlord even though this did not exclude the proprietary rights of his subjects. Was he in the Roman law sense the proprietor as well as the ruler of his kingdom, or was he ruler solely, and were his subjects the only proprietors? Could he, therefore, or could he not, take contributions without his subjects' consent?

It is little wonder, when medieval ideas of tenure gave way before the returning "antique-modern" view of Roman law that ownership is indivisible, that some later writers should, on the medieval precedents, make the king the sole proprietor of his whole kingdom and assert that the king may levy a subsidy on his subjects without the consent of their representatives, as James I and Dr. Cowell do; that the only "fundamental law" is the Law of the Crown (*jus coronae*), not the Law of the land; and that this fundamental law does not include "the matters which are to be established for the Estate of our Lord the King and of his Heirs, *and* for the Estate of the Realm and of the People, but only those "concerning the Royal Power of our Lord the King or of his Heirs." [1] Nor is it strange that others, on the same precedents, should at the same time deny the king all proprietary rights whatsoever, and insist on the "fundamental" character of all such matters and on the voluntary character of

---

[1] The phrases of the *Statute of York*, 15, Edward II (1322), *Statutes of the Realm*, I, 189.

all parliamentary grants. Medieval instances seemed in fact to give some color to both these claims. There were some apparent precedents in the middle ages for both "royal" and "seigneurial" monarchy as Bodin distinguished them in the sixteenth century, for a medieval king was at once *rex* and *dominus*, and as *rex* he was both "absolute" and "limited." [1]

In strictly feudal law, of course, any lord could in theory be compelled to respect the rights of his vassals, but exactly how far a king was thus liable in the earlier period it would be difficult to say. At a later time, after all the courts had been effectively centralized under royal control, no coercive remedy was available against him for any infringement of a subject's right.

The quaint and erratic author of the *Mirror of Justices*, written in the reign of Edward I, thought that an English freeman, if denied his rights under Magna Carta, ought to recover damages by an assize of novel disseisin,[2] but unfortunately, as Bracton said, "No writ runs against the King." [3] The complainant has at most only an opportunity to petition for royal grace. As yet there was no doctrine that "the King can do no wrong," but neither was there any effective check on his doing it, or legal redress for it when done.[4] The chief political advance of modern times has been the gradual and painful process, often accompanied by violence and bloodshed, by which men have stumbled upon the means to make "constitutional limitations" more practical and effective, but the final goal is still far away. "To live with freedome in a regular way, a thing generally affected, hath beene very hard hitherto in any state to bee lighted upon : such as fixed on monarchy have beene much troubled how to find a means to

---

[1] This indefiniteness in the conception of "property," inherited perhaps — he gives no references — through his predecessors from the wider conception of medieval tenure, takes away some of the one-sidedness of Locke's insistence upon the protection of property rights in the seventeenth century. He seems to include in "property" not external goods only as we do, but "life, health, liberty or possessions" (*Second Treatise on Government*, chap. ii, § 6), and he says distinctly that "every man has a 'property' in his own 'person.' (*Ibid.*, chap. v, § 27.) He has "property" in his own person and in "that which made up the great part of what he applied to the support or comfort of his being, when invention and arts had improved the conveniences of life." (*Ibid.*, chap. v, § 44.) This is not strikingly different from the tenure under which the middle ages restricted the arbitrary rule of rulers over subjects.
[2] P. 176 (Selden Society).
[3] Folio 5.
[4] For a valuable study of the history of remedies against the Crown in England see the paper of Ludwik Ehrlich in *Oxford Studies in Social and Legal History*, edited by Sir Paul Vinogradoff, vol. vi. Maitland gives a short but brilliant summary in Pollock and Maitland's *History of English Law*, 2d ed., vol. i, pp. 511–526.

limit it." [1] "The world, now above 5,500 years old, hath found means to limit kings, but never yet any republique." [2]

If we have been able to improve on the middle ages in political matters it is rather through the availability of more effective means; not the existence of nobler ends.

[1] Sir Roger Twysden, *Certayne Considerations upon the Government of England* (Camden Society), p. 91.

[2] *Ibid.*, p. 10.

CHAPTER VI

THE LATER MIDDLE AGES

The present tendency in historical writing is to emphasize the continuity of cultural development and minimize the breaks in that continuity: it is regarded as an evolutionary process; and this view is a sound one if not pressed too far. And yet an evolutionary process need not be and in fact seldom is a process of development entirely even and uninterrupted. There are periods in it of relative quiescence and periods of more rapid change, and neither is ever wholly unaffected by influences from without. In the development of thought and institutions we may discard the word "renaissance" but we must still recognize phases in their history when ideas which have long lain dormant seem to spring into sudden life and activity, though it is seldom easy to say how far these transformations come from within and how far they may be said to be a reaction to the environment without.

In the realm of political ideas and institutions such a transformation occurred in western Europe between the eleventh century and the fourteenth, to which historians have sometimes applied the term, "the Renaissance of the twelfth century." There are few important developments in this epoch of which the germs cannot be plainly seen in the centuries before, but in this period these germs seem to burst into flower with an apparent suddenness which is the amazement and despair of historians. These centuries seem to mark the transition from the early to the later middle ages, between which there are differences no less profound than those always recognized as existing between medieval and modern times. In this period, for example, Roman law, though never entirely unknown before in some parts of western Europe, was regained in something like its completeness for the first time since the break-up of the Empire of the West. In the thirteenth century Europe had its first direct contact with the ethical and political writings of Aristotle. By the eleventh century the

counter claims of Empire and Papacy had become distinct enough
to bring on the first of the great contests between them, the
struggle of Pope Gregory VII and the Emperor Henry IV.   The
period is also marked by the formation of the *Corpus Juris Canonici,* the growth of a system of common law in England and its
beginnings in France, and by the development of medieval estates
and of representative institutions and ideas almost everywhere in
Europe from Scandinavia to the Spanish Peninsula.   In the
extent and rapidity of the growth of political institutions and
ideas few periods in European history can compare with the centuries to which we apply the term, "the Renaissance of the twelfth
century." [1]

One of the first great illustrations of the working of these new
forces in the political thought of the West is to be seen in the
unprecedented outburst of polemical writings which accompanied
the struggles between the Emperors Henry IV and Henry V and
Popes Gregory VII, Urban II, and Paschal II.   Within a period
of little more than half a century, from 1052 to 1112, it has been
estimated that no fewer than one hundred and fifteen separate
writings appeared in defence of the papal and the imperial pre-
tensions, fifty of them on the imperial side, sixty-five on the
papal, written by sixty-five different authors; and that more
than half the whole number came within the twenty-seven years
between 1085 and 1112. [2]   To us this may not seem strange, but
so far as is known nothing just like it had ever occurred before.
In number, in bitterness, and in the manner of political argument,
these pamphlets of the eleventh century mark the first definite
appearance of a type of political writing which was destined

---

[1] See, in general, C. H. Haskins, *The Renaissance of the Twelfth Century,* Cambridge,
Mass., 1927.

[2] Carl Mirbt, *Die Publizistik im Zeitalter Gregors VII* (1894), pp. 81–83, 92–95.   This is
the standard account of this great controversy.   See also Imbart de la Tour, *La polémique
religieuse et les publicistes à l'époque de Grégoire VII (Questions d'histoire sociale et religieuse)*
(1907), pp. 225–266, for a valuable summary, based largely on Mirbt; also Carlyle, *op. cit.,*
vol. iii, part ii; vol. iv, parts i-iii, a detailed and judicious account of the whole struggle;
Augustin Fliche, *La Réforme grégorienne,* Louvain, 1924–1925; *Études sur la polémique
religieuse à l'époque de Grégoire VII,* Paris, 1916; Ernst Bernheim, *Mittelalterliche Zeitan-
schauungen in ihrem Einfluss auf Politik und Geschichtsschreibung,* Tübingen, 1918, part iii,
Die Anschauungen über das Verhältnis von Regnum und Sacerdotium, pp. 110–233, especially
pp. 195–233, a valuable discussion in which the author emphasizes the influence of the
ideas of St. Augustine; Élie Voosen, *Papauté et Pouvoir Civil à l'époque de Grégoire VII,*
Gembloux, 1927, a dissertation of the University of Louvain, dealing in a comprehensive
and masterly fashion with the legal and political basis of all the principal arguments on both
sides.   It includes a valuable list of modern books and articles dealing with the investiture
controversy.

almost to monopolize the field for five or six centuries to come. The controversy marks an era not only in the relations of Church and State but in the history of political literature. "This ecclesiastical literature is none the less a popular literature, and in this lies its great originality. It was not written solely for the monasteries or the schools: it aimed to make its appeal to opinion; and to sway opinion striking cases were necessary, and forms of expression, clear, simple and such as the people could understand or at least retain." [1]

It is unnecessary here to recount in detail the struggle itself.[2] Its remoter causes run back to the very establishment of the Church in the Empire, but some of the more immediate ones are to be found in the nature of feudal institutions. Though it is usually spoken of merely as the "Investiture Controversy," in the course of it the controversialists on one side or the other managed to touch on the most fundamental questions of the origin, the nature, the extent, and the sanction of all forms of authority both spiritual and secular, and in some cases to anticipate theories of the state that we are prone to think of only as "modern."

Behind the specific issues raised concerning the election and the form of royal investiture of bishops, and whether the latter was to take place before or only after their consecration, lay a deeper question created by the institutions of feudalism itself and by the two-fold character imposed by these institutions upon practically all the higher secular clergy. They were the ordained of the Church to whom were committed the administration of its sacraments (*ordo*) and its management and the cure of souls. But they were also administrators of vast properties including lands held by regular feudal tenure on which rested the usual feudal obligations to the overlord of military service, of counsel, and of *auxilium* or aid. Must a royal overlord stand helplessly aside and let a hostile clergy impose upon him without his consent or even in defiance of his protests a vassal who thus became a peer of his court and a sharer in his counsels? But how otherwise could the Church prevent the abuses that must and did result from the intrusion into its sacred offices of unworthy hirelings often of

---

[1] Imbart de la Tour, *La polémique religieuse*, p. 236.

[2] For a very satisfactory account and bibliography see *Gregory VII and the First Contest between Empire and Papacy*, by Z. N. Brooke, *Cambridge Medieval History*, vol. v, chap. ii, pp. 51-111, 850-854, Cambridge, 1926.

vicious life on the mere nomination of a prince who might be indifferent to the Church's spiritual aims, or even the avowed opponent of its rightful claims? "Freedom of election" was essential to the Church, but equally essential to the King was the royal supervision of it and the King's acceptance of the bishop elect; and the question whether the latter must do homage for his lands before he could be ordained was one of vital importance to both Church and King. But the real question behind all these was whether the King could freely choose and control his own feudal vassals without clerical interference, and whether at the same time the Church could exclude from its sacred offices those whom it considered unworthy. Could one be at the same time a true bishop and a faithful feudal vassal? Was it possible in the tangle of feudal and ecclesiastical relations any longer to separate or to harmonize the different spheres of the *regnum* and the *sacerdotium* which Pope Gelasius II had distinguished in the fifth century; and if not, in case of a collision of the two powers, to which must supremacy be conceded? It is easy to see why this difficulty must draw into controversy, as it did, the whole question of the relations of "Church and State" and the basis of the authority of each.

But this was not the only root of the difficulty. The clergy were the only ones in an age of general illiteracy who were equipped by their training to handle the growing administration of the courts and chancelleries in the rising kingdoms of western Europe, and even of those belonging to inferior lords. No doubt there often were outstanding ecclesiastics, of purity of life and consecration to the welfare of the Church, holding the office of Chancellor or Treasurer or Chief Justiciar, but it was not always so, and the gravity of the issues raised by the reforms of Gregory VII is amply proved by innumerable references in the contemporary chronicles. Simony was a great and growing evil, but hitherto the power and emoluments of high secular office had proved a temptation stronger than the attempts of the Church to combat it.

For the development of political thought it is not these particular issues that give the Investiture Controversy its importance, so much as the far-reaching arguments by which the rival contentions were supported. For a clear understanding of the latter it is necessary first of all to have in mind the points on which the contestants all agreed.

In the matter of investiture the clerical party was not disposed to deny some right of royal interposition, for which there were long-standing precedents, nor could the adherents of the King ignore the fact that the election of bishops rightfully belonged to the clergy and the people, not to the prince. Even on the deeper question of the sanctions of royal and episcopal authority the two parties were in substantial agreement on some of the most fundamental points. The contest was not for either party a struggle between "Church and State" in our modern sense, for neither of them could conceive of a society that was not at the same time both Church and State. The *civitas Dei* and the *civitas terrena* were only two aspects of the life of man on earth which must remain mingled together till death or the day of judgment, as St. Augustine had said. Society was but one, and the State and the Church alike were only different aspects of this oneness. The contest for supremacy was not between two rival institutions, a State and a Church, it was between two sides of human life, two elements in the constitution of man, two powers that claimed his obedience, the *regnum* and the *sacerdotium*. "Theocracy or imperialism, the contrary solutions, came back to the same single idea, unity." [1] "Therefore in all centuries of the Middle Age Christendom, which in destiny is identical with Mankind, is set before us as a single, universal Community, founded and governed by God Himself. Mankind is one 'mystical body'; it is one single and internally connected 'people' or 'folk'; it is an all embracing corporation (*universitas*), which constitutes that Universal Realm, spiritual and temporal, which may be called the Universal Church (*ecclesia universalis*), or, with equal propriety, the Commonwealth of the Human Race (*respublica generis humani*). Therefore that it may attain its one purpose, it needs One Law (*lex*) and One Government (*unicus principatus*). Then however, along with this idea of a single Community comprehensive of Mankind, the severance of this Community between two organized Orders of Life, the spiritual and the temporal, is accepted by the Middle Age as an eternal counsel of God." [2]

It was only the growth of the nation-states that ultimately weakened this medieval insistence on unity, and as usual, the

[1] Imbart de la Tour, *La polémique religieuse*, p. 244.
[2] In the translation by F. W. Maitland from *Das deutsche Genossenschaftsrecht* of Otto von Gierke under the title *Political Theories of the Middle Age*, Cambridge, 1900, p. 10. The whole section from which this is taken is valuable, pp. 9-21, 101-129.

earlier ideal lingered on for ages after the emergence of conditions which were at length to destroy it. In the eleventh century there was no one yet prepared to deny the solidarity of Christendom, though on the clerical side some asserted that this single society was primarily a Church and only secondarily a State. For them the State was in the Church, not the Church in the State, as St. Optatus had said,[1] and the *sacerdotium* therefore superior to the *regnum*.

But even these who thus upheld the supremacy of the spiritual power did not in so doing necessarily deny the legitimacy of the temporal: without exception they admitted that the latter was necessary and most of them even held the view that it was ordained or at least permitted by God as a corrective of the sin and weakness of mankind. It was in anger that God granted the prayer of the Jews to be ruled by kings instead of priests, but it was God who granted it. On the other side the supporters of the Emperor while trying to limit the extent of episcopal authority never ventured to deny its divine origin and character.

No doubt it was in part these ideas held in common by both parties which kept the hope of compromise from ever being wholly illusory; but on the other hand the claim made by each party, and admitted by the other, of the divine character of its head, tended in some ways to make the struggle between them more bitter and irreconcilable in character and more far-reaching in its results.

The contest of the eleventh century, like many another in history, was in appearance a struggle between two powers each seeking no more than independence of the other, and the antagonists themselves usually thought of it as such. But under the peculiar conditions of the time what each party regarded as essential to their own independence was considered by the other party as fatal to theirs, and therefore neither antagonist could feel really secure until the duel had resulted in his own supremacy. In such a contest the initial advantage lay with the papalist party, for their opponents with very few exceptions were not ready to deny that the spiritual authority was in some sense higher than the temporal. In the eleventh century the opponents of papal power were not yet prepared to cut the knot, as Marsiglio of Padua did in the fourteenth, by repudiating utterly every form of coercive authority in the clergy, spiritual as well as temporal, direct

[1] Carlyle, *op. cit.*, I, 148; *ante*, p. 164.

and indirect; and until this was done, the imperialist party was forced in the main to take a negative and defensive position in the war of words, which weakened its appeal and contributed to its defeat. "Not venturing to formulate the idea of independence, of the separation of the spiritual and the temporal, they continued to take refuge in discussions concerning forms, in attacks upon persons, in cavils regarding procedure; and they had no alternative but to withdraw from the Papacy or to obey it." [1]

Among the opponents of royal authority at this time few were more extreme than Gregory VII himself. After quoting from the Gospel of St. Matthew Christ's famous words addressed to St. Peter, "Whatsoever thou shalt bind on earth shall be bound in heaven; and whatsoever thou shalt loose on earth shall be loosed in heaven," he asks why kings should be excepted. "Are they not of the sheep which the son of God entrusted to the blessed Peter? Who, I ask, considers himself exempted from the power of Peter in this universal concession of binding and loosing, who indeed but the miserable wretch, unwilling to bear the yoke of the Lord, who submits to the yoke of the Devil, and refuses to be numbered with the sheep of Christ? . . ." "Who does not know that kings and rulers had their beginning in men inspired by the Devil, the prince of the world, to turn away from God and presume in the blindness of their lust and their intolerable arrogance to bear rule over men, their equals, through pride, violence, fraud, bloodshed, and almost every known crime? . . ." "Far better that any good Christians, rather than evil princes, should be considered kings. For the former keep strict rule over themselves for the glory of God, while the latter, seeking their own good and not God's, are enemies even of themselves and tyrannical oppressors of others. These are the body of Christ the true King, those, verily the body of the Devil. These govern themselves to the end that they may rule forever, together with the highest ruler, the power of the others tends to this, that they fall into eternal damnation along with the prince of darkness, who is king over all the sons of pride." [2]

[1] Imbart de la Tour, *La polémique religieuse*, pp. 261–262.

[2] Letter of Gregory to Hermann, Bishop of Metz, 1081 A.D., *Registrum* of Gregory VII, no. 21 (P. Jaffé, *Bibliotheca Rerum Germanicarum*, vol. ii, pp. 454, 457, 460); printed also in *Das Register Gregors VII*, ed. by Erich Caspar (*Monumenta Germaniae Historica, Epistolae Selectae*), Berlin, 1920–1923, pp. 548, 553, 557. The older edition has now been practically supplanted by this one, which incorporates the results of some, and has itself been the inspiration of other valuable studies on the *Register* of Gregory VII, made in recent years.

These are extreme words and bitter words, and their bitterness
has led some modern historians to conclude that the Pope is here
flatly denying the divine character of all secular rule and attributing its origin solely to the Devil.   But this is not the only interpretation of which these remarkable statements are susceptible,
and Gregory himself in other places expresses a view not consistent
with it.   The warning of Dr. Carlyle is in point: "We must not
make the mistake of reading back the extremest papalist theories
of the thirteenth and fourteenth centuries, or the systematic
thinking of the thirteenth century, into the eleventh."   There is
ample evidence that Gregory VII adopted a "new policy" and
"a new attitude of the Papacy towards the Temporal Powers,"
but there is no like evidence of his adopting a new theory of either
Church or State: nothing to prove a "conscious intention to
establish the power of the Papacy as supreme over the Temporal
Power." [1]   Secular government is necessary and it is not in itself
evil, but by nature the authority of the bishop is above it just as
the spiritual part of man is superior to the carnal; it is divine in
a higher sense than royal power because it is the direct instrument
of God to fulfill his will, while man's wickedness was the occasion
of the creation of all temporal rule though its cause might be
God's ordinance.   This did not mean that the Pope was above
the king in secular matters; it did not imply that the Pope had
any strictly secular authority whatever.   The Pope, in Gregory's
view, was not temporal lord of the world, not even of the Christian
world.   He was *pastor of the flock of Christ*.   But as such it was
his duty to see that the flock received no harm, and he must take
any measures necessary for its defence and welfare.   For such an
end he might if necessary even depose a king or emperor and sanction the election of another, and he had authority to release all
subjects from their oaths and obligations.   In practice, then, the
power exercised by Gregory VII and claimed for him as of right
by most of his adherents may have been little less in actual extent
than that demanded for the Pope by his supporters of the fourteenth century, such as Egidius Romanus or Alvarus Pelagius,

[1] Carlyle, *op. cit.*, vol. iv, pp. 211, 172.   To the same effect, Voosen, *Papauté et pouvoir
civil à l'époque de Grégoire VII*, p. 158 ff.   The charge that Gregory made the Devil the real
author of the state was almost made in his own time by Hugh of Fleury, *Tractatus de Regia
Potestate et Sacerdotali Dignitate* (*Libelli de Lite*, *M. H. G.*, vol. ii, p. 467): "I am acquainted
with certain persons of our own time who assert that kings had their beginning not from
God but from those without God."   Cited by Voosen, *op. cit.*, p. 158.

but its basis seems very different from theirs; and, even though not yet clearly understood, it was much more akin to the "indirect power" of Cardinal Bellarmine, who is on the whole a truer interpreter of early Papal development than they.[1]

If temporal rule was occasioned by the weakness or wickedness of men, as the papalist writers insisted, the natural inference was that it was also introduced by men under the providence of God for their own betterment and hence must be under their control. "By a singular contradiction, the theorists of the papal monarchy are those of popular sovereignty." [2] This aspect of the papalist theory of the state was emphasized by Manegold of Lautenbach in one of the most interesting and able of the writings in the investiture controversy.

"As royal dignity and power excel all mundane powers, so no person of wicked or scandalous life should be instituted to exercise them, but one who surpasses the rest in wisdom, justice and piety as well as in place and dignity. It is necessary therefore that one who bears the burden of the care of all, and the government over all, should stand above all in splendor of virtue, and should strive to administer the power entrusted to him with the most impartial fairness. For no people raises him above themselves to give him an opportunity to act the tyrant over them, but to prevent the tyranny and wrong-doing of others. And when he who is chosen to defend the good and to hold the evil in check, himself begins to cherish wickedness, to stand out against good men, to exercise most cruelly over his subjects the tyranny which he was bound to combat; is it not clear that he justly forfeits the dignity conceded to him and that the people stand free of his rule and subjection, since it is evident that he was the

---

[1] There is one papalist writer of the twelfth century, Honorius Augustodunensis, who seems definitely to anticipate some of the extremer doctrines of the fourteenth century, but as Dr. Carlyle truly says (*op. cit.*, vol. iv, p. 288), his view was "entirely new, and even contradictory to the normal tradition." The *Libelli* of Honorius are printed in *Libelli de Lite*, vol. iii, pp. 29–80. The views of the basis of Gregory's claim set forth above in the text seem inconsistent with those expressed by Gierke, who seems to me not to have distinguished sufficiently the views accepted before and after Pope Innocent IV (*Political Theories of the Middle Age*, note 13, pp. 107–108). For other interpretations differing from or contrary to Gierke's, see especially Bernheim, *Mittelalterliche Zeitanschauung*, p. 203 ff., *passim*; L'Abbé H. X. Arquillière, *Sur la formation de la 'théocratie' pontificale*, *Mélanges d'histoire du moyen âge offerts à M. Ferdinand Lot* (Paris, 1925), pp. 1–24; Voosen, *Papauté et pouvoir civil*, pp. 235–257, *passim*. Dr. Voosen's recent admirable thesis has been doubly welcome to me in confirming some views that I have long felt to be more consistent with contemporary statements than those of a few of the most eminent modern historians of the thought of this period.

[2] Imbart de la Tour, *op. cit.*, pp. 247–248.

first to violate the compact (*pactum*) on account of which he was made ruler? Nor could anyone with justice or reason charge them with perfidy, for it is clear that he was the first to break faith. To take an example from humbler things: if one were to entrust to another the herding of his swine for a proper wage, and afterwards found the swine-herd stealing, slaughtering and driving away the swine instead of feeding them, would not the employer withhold the promised wage and dismiss him in disgrace from his service? If, I say, it is the rule in the humblest matters that none should even be called a swine-herd if he scattered the swine instead of feeding them; then in proportion as the condition of men is above the swine's, it is the more fitting in justice and reason, that one who fails to rule over men but strives to drive them into error should be deprived of the power and dignity which he has received over them. . . . It is one thing to rule, another to act the tyrant in a realm. For as faith and reverence ought to be rendered to emperors and kings for the sake of the safeguarding of the administration of the realm, so surely, in reason, if these rulers break out into acts of tyranny, it is no breach of faith or piety that no fealty or reverence be paid them." [1]

These vigorous sentences speak for themselves and are a remarkable anticipation of the discussions of tyranny and resistance of the sixteenth century, as well as of its theories of the origin of the state in the compact between the ruler and the ruled.

With few exceptions [2] one looks in vain for the same assertiveness and vigor among the writers on the opposing side, though they are often violent enough. Most of them rely on history more than on theory, and the majority are content to protest against an unprecedented extension of papal authority instead of questioning its basis. Many, for example, admit the Pope's power to excommunicate a king but deny the authority to remove him or to absolve his subjects of their oaths. Two writers, however, may be worthy of particular notice here on account of peculiarities. The *Defence of King Henry* by Peter

---

[1] *Manegoldi ad Gebhardum Liber*, edited by Kuno Francke, *Libelli de Lite* (*M. G. H.*) vol. i, p. 365.

[2] Among these one of the most notable is the *Tractatus de Regia Potestate et Sacerdotale Dignitate* of Hugh of Fleury, printed in *Libelli de Lite*, II, pp. 465-494. There is a good summary of its main conclusions in Carlyle, *op. cit.*, IV, pp. 266-273. Another is the *Liber de Unitate Ecclesiae Conservanda*, *Libelli de Lite*, II, pp. 173-284; summary in Carlyle, *op. cit.*, IV, pp. 242-249.

Crassus [1] does not greatly impress the reader by the general strength of its reasoning, but it employs arguments not found elsewhere and it is unique as being the work of a layman and in the fact that its author is one of the very first to cite as his authority the lawbooks of Justinian, some of which he clearly knew. "The treatise announces the entry of Roman Law into medieval political thought." [2] His argument further differs from the usual ones in placing its greatest emphasis on the Pope's alleged violation of Henry's personal hereditary right to the throne. Far more striking in content than this is the series of remarkable tracts, some of them apparently written in support of King Henry I of England against Archbishop Anselm, now known as the *Tractatus Eboracenses*.[3]

Their author, unlike most of his fellows, disputes the very basis of the papal claims and anticipates some of the most radical antipapal positions taken in the fourteenth century and even in the sixteenth. He denies two of the most fundamental and most essential points of the papal argument, the superiority of a bishop over a king and the superiority of the Pope over a bishop. In so doing he makes nothing of the king's personal right, as Peter Crassus does, but bases all his positive claims on the divine character of the royal office. On the words of Christ he comments thus: "Render unto Caesar," he says, "the things that are Caesar's, not to Tiberius the things that are Tiberius's. Render to the power, not to the person. For the person is evil, but the power is just. Tiberius is wicked, but Caesar good." [4] But one of the papal arguments was that kings and emperors obtained this royal office and power only through consecration by the clergy, who must therefore be superior to those whom they ordain; another argument was that the ordination of bishops was different in character and effect from that of kings. Both these assertions

[1] In *Libelli de Lite*, I, pp. 432–453. For the importance of the citations of Roman Law by Peter Crassus as an indication of the extent of the acquaintance with the texts of Justinian as early as the eleventh century at Ravenna, see Ficker, *Forschungen zur Reichs- und Rechtsgeschichte Italiens*, III, p. 112; Fitting, *Die Anfänge der Rechtsschule zu Bologna*, p. 40.

[2] Woolf, *Bartolus of Sassoferrato*, p. 70.

[3] *Monumenta Germaniae Historica, Libelli de Lite*, III, pp. 642–687, edited by Heinrich Boehmer, especially those numbered IV, V, and VI: *De Consecratione Pontificium et Regum, De Romano Pontifice*, and *De Obediendo Romano Pontifici*. Boehmer gives the fullest account of these tracts in his *Kirche und Staat in England und in der Normandie im XI und XII Jahrhundert* (Leipzig, 1899), pp. 177–266. A brief but excellent summary with extracts is given by Carlyle, *op. cit.*, IV, pp. 273–282.

[4] *Libelli de Lite*, III, p. 671.

this author strenuously denies and on the denial bases some far-reaching conclusions. If the clergy are superior to the king because they consecrate him, then the cardinals must be superior to the Pope, for they consecrate him, — a very telling rejoinder; but in truth consecration never implies any superiority in those who officiate, for their office is merely ministerial, and God alone is the author and source of the efficacy of consecration. Nor is the effect of consecration different upon kings and priests. In both cases a divine character and authority are conferred. If a difference exists, it is only in the nature of this character, not in the mode or effect of consecration. And a difference does exist. The sacred office of the king is the higher. "And the angel said unto Mary, 'The Lord God shall give unto him the throne of his father David.' He did not say, 'He shall give unto him the throne of his father Aaron.' He said, 'The Lord shall give unto him the seat of David and he shall sit upon the throne and rule over the kingdom of David.' By these words it is manifest that there is one throne and one seat and one kingdom of Christ and of David. And therefore in the spirit there is one Christ and David and one power, one glory, one dignity, of Christ and David. Therefore also the seat of David, his throne and kingdom and power and glory and dignity are above all and greater than all and holier than all. So likewise the Lord gave to him the power and the rule over all, even over the priests of God. The Lord, I say, gave it, who does nothing unjustly but everything justly. Therefore it was just that the king should have the power and rule over the priests." [1]

The author then turns from the Old to the New Testament. Both kings and priests, he says, "are one with God and with His Christ, they are very Gods and Christs through the spirit of adoption, and in them speaks Christ and the Holy Spirit, in them He fulfils his office and performs it, in them He hallows and reigns over and rules His people. Therefore also each of them is in the spirit both Christ and God, and in his office is the figure and image of Christ and of God, the priest the image of Him as priest, the king the image of Him as king, the priest the image of an inferior office and nature, that is His humanity, the king the image of a superior, that is His divinity. For Christ, God and man, is the true and highest king and priest. He is king, but from the eternity of the Godhead, not made, not created, not lower than the

[1] *Libelli de Lite*, III, p. 666.

Father or different from Him, but equal and one with the Father. He is priest from the assumption of his humanity, made according to the order of Melchisedech and created, and so lower than the Father. As king He created all things, He rules all, He governs and saves both men and angels, as priest He merely redeems men to make them reign with Him. For this is the sole intent for which He was made priest, and offered Himself as a sacrifice, that He might make men sharers in His kingdom and royal power. For everywhere in the scriptures it is the kingdom of Heaven that He promises to the faithful, never the priesthood. Hence it appears that the royal power in Christ is greater and higher than his sacerdotal power in the proportion that his divinity is greater and higher than his humanity. Therefore some venture to think that among men likewise the royal power is greater and higher than the sacerdotal and the king greater and higher than the priest, as being the imitation or ideal of the better and more exalted nature of Christ. And so they say that it is not against the justice of God if the priestly dignity is instituted by the regal or made subject to it, for with Christ it so happened that He was made priest through his own royal power and through his priesthood was made subject to the Father with whom in royal power He was the equal." [1] Though attributing to kings such supernal power as this, the author is careful to point out the difference between a king and a tyrant. What is said above, he says, is true of kings in general, but is not true of those who do not rule through the grace of God, for these are not kings, but have become tyrants ruling in the spirit of evil and opposing virtue.[2]

Still more startling than this denial of papal supremacy over kings even in spiritual matters, are the author's statements concerning the authority of the Pope over the clergy and the laity. The Roman pontiff, he says, "is recognized as apostolic because he is believed to do the work and fulfil the office of the apostles, and if he fulfils it truly then he is called apostle, who, if he is a true apostle of Christ, has been sent by Christ, for 'apostle' means one who is sent. But if he has been sent by Christ he ought to make known Christ's commands, to seek Christ's glory, to do Christ's will, that he may be a true apostle of Christ. For if he should issue commands of his own, or seek his own glory, or do his own will and not Christ's, who then would dare confess that he

---

[1] *Libelli de Lite*, III, p. 667.　　　　[2] *Ibid.*, p. 666.

was the true apostle of Christ ?   If he should make known Christ's commands, and seek out and do his will, he must be received by us as Christ's apostle in all reverence and honor on account of the authority of Him who sent him; but otherwise no obligation rests upon us to receive him as an apostle." [1]

"In the Roman state are many churches, and we are bound to obey either all equally or particular ones only.   But no one would say we are bound to obey all equally, for all have not equal dignity. If then we owe obedience to particular ones, we owe it to more than one of them or to one alone; but not to more than one, since they are not equal in dignity.   Wherefore we are bound to obey one church only, the one namely which is in the Lateran, in which is the seat of the apostles.   But we must ask whether we owe this obedience to stones and buildings or to men.   It is absurd to say we owe it to stones and buildings.   But if to men, then it is either due equally to good men and bad, to those who are the members of Christ and those who are members of the Devil, or else it is due to good men only and such as are the members of Christ. But far from it that we should be obedient to evil men and to those who are the Devil's members.   If then it is right that we should obey only the good and the members of Christ, it is right to obey either one of these or more than one.   But since they are not all equal in dignity we are not bound to obey them equally, but that one alone who is apostolic.   And so it follows that we are bound to obey not a church but a person.   But in what are we bound to obey him ?   For we owe him obedience either because he is a man or because he is apostolic, that is, because he has been sent by Christ.   But it is not because he is a man.   Such obedience should not be rendered to a man.   If it were it would be due to every man.   Wherefore, obedience must be rendered him because he is apostolic.   For if he has been sent by another than Christ no duty rests on us to render him this obedience.   But if he has been sent by Christ, for what was he sent ?   To this end was he sent, either to bring to us the commands of Christ and teach us, or for an end we know not of, one which seems to have little to do with the Commands of Christ, and one on which we are not even bound to hear him.   If then he has been sent to bring to us the commands of God, and to teach us, this has become superfluous since we have the prophetic writings and the apostolic

[1] *Libelli de Lite*, III, p. 680.

gospels in which all the commands of God are contained, and of these we have a fuller knowledge than he, we have it in truer form, and we practice it more frequently. Let him go to the nations which have never had the faith of Christ or a knowledge of his commands, and let him preach to them and teach them, that through that preaching and teaching they may receive the faith and doctrine of Christ and the knowledge of him, just as did Peter and the other apostles, who were sent by Christ to 'go into all the world and preach the gospel to every creature and to teach all nations, baptizing them in the name of the Father and of the Son and of the Holy Ghost.' Let him do these things, I say, if he would have his mission a saving mission and profitable, and unless he is willing to depart from the footsteps of Peter and from the headship of the apostles."

"We must consider whether the Roman church is the more worthy because it is Roman or because it is a church, and to me it seems so because it is a church. For by virtue of this it is the spouse of Christ, the dove of Christ, the close and dear friend of Christ, his elect, glorious and immaculate, 'not having spot, or wrinkle or any such thing,' but wholly beautiful. It is not thus because it is Roman, but it holds a few elect sons of God, and many reprobate sons of the Devil who are like chaff on the thresh-ing-floor of God covering up the grains of wheat, that is over-whelming the elect. These we may indeed call the church of Satan not of Christ. For only the elect and sons of God may we truly call the church of Christ, because they are members of the body of Christ, because they are his temple which is holy 'and in them dwells the holy spirit of Christ.' But the reprobate and sons of the Devil, of whom the number is greater, are not members of the body of Christ, they are not his temple, nor does his spirit dwell in them; and so they belong to the church of Satan, not of Christ. Thus there are two Roman churches, one of Satan, the other of Christ. But under no conditions should the church of Christ be subject to the church of Satan. Yet we should show reverence to the few elect and holy sons of God who are in Rome, but such reverence as our Father in Heaven commands and wills — that we show it to our brothers in charity, not as an exaction; on account of God, not on account of the pride of the world." [1]

---

[1] *Libelli de Lite*, III, pp. 686–687. In much of this, of course, there was nothing new. See, for example, the valuable summary of the views of Claudius of Turin and Agobard of

These long extracts are not inserted here as an illustration of views generally accepted at the opening of the twelfth century. They are more extreme in thought and statement than any other surviving writing on either side in the controversy of the time. They do indicate a theory of church and state which is on the whole consistent, and one which in many ways is distinctly "medieval" in character, but it is doubtful whether even their author clearly saw the implications of his words, and scarcely likely that he would have accepted them all if he had. For the logical outcome of the *York Tractates* is not merely a rejection of papal supremacy in state and church; it implies a virtual denial of the whole sacramental view of the church, and is an early, indistinct, expression of the doctrine of the essential "priesthood of the Christian man" which is the core of later "Protestantism." These writings prove the soundness of the view of M. Imbart de la Tour that for the supporters of the Emperor there could really be no middle ground between their submission to the papal jurisdiction and the renouncement of it altogether. For when this author asserts the right to judge a bishop by the character of his acts as one might judge the administration of a king, and when he distinguishes the church of Christ from the church of Satan at Rome, he can ultimately mean nothing less than a right to judge, existing in the individual Christian, whether he be ecclesiastic or layman.

These statements make clear the fact that in certain quarters, at least, the opposition to papal claims began far earlier than some would admit, and they must come with something of a shock to those who are accustomed to think of the middle ages only as a period when all thought had sunk to a dead level of uniformity. It is true that the usual argument employed then was the argument from authority, but when we find writers on every side using their authorities with such freedom of interpretation, it is idle to argue that the result must have been nothing but uniformity and stagnation.

"The traditional Protestant view of Church history, which made of the thousand years between the 'Early Church' and the Reformation a thick darkness of superstition and priestcraft,

Lyons in R. L. Poole's *Illustrations of the History of Medieval Thought and Learning*, chap. i (2d ed. London, 1920). But statements like these seem in some ways far more startling to us coming from the twelfth century than from the ninth, or before.

illumined only by a few morning stars like Wyclif and Huss and the nameless heretics of the Italian valleys — this has been for some time discredited. . . . There are few Puritans and Evangelicals who have claimed their inheritance in the Middle Ages: there are perhaps fewer Catholics who have admitted the claim. It is still too commonly assumed that the modern Catholic movement contains the whole tradition of the undivided Latin Church, and that puritanical living with evangelical doctrine is a new thing in earth. Yet neither of these opinions will bear examination, for neither has more to recommend it than the loud and unanimous assertions of all the controversialists. . . . The romantic and 'Catholic' elements in the medieval Church no one today is likely to forget, but it is not superfluous to recall its evangelical and its puritan qualities, its sanity, its commonsense, and its rationalism; to emphasize the fact that not only one half of modern Christianity but the whole has its roots in medieval religion. . . . The battle with rigid Protestantism and the final discomfiture of the enlightened rationalists a hundred years ago were necessary preliminaries to the rediscovery of the Middle Ages, but the memory of these historic struggles does not justify the appropriation of medieval religion by any modern party or the repudiation of it by any other. For the medieval Church is the mother of us all." [1]

Among the contentions of Gregory VII none is more important for the history of political thought than his statements concerning his relation as Pope to the existing law of the church, and none, probably, has been the occasion of more misunderstanding in modern times. It has been thought that Gregory was demanding for himself nothing less than an authority free of the law, to change the law of the church, a "legislative" power, which would be "sovereign" in the full modern meaning of the term. But such a contention would have stultified the Pope's whole claim, and his words and those of his adherents may be and should be interpreted in a sense entirely different. They do indeed insist upon his exclusive right "to establish new provisions for the needs of the time" (pro temporis necessitate *novas leges condere*),[2] but to read into this a demand for "legislative" authority is to ignore

---

[1] *The People's Faith in the Time of Wyclif*, by Bernard Lord Manning, Cambridge, 1919, pp. 184–188.

[2] *Dictatus Papae*, in *Registrum* of Gregory VII, II, 55 a (P. Jaffé, *Bibliotheca Rerum Germanicarum*, vol. ii, p. 174; edited by Caspar, p. 202).

the usual medieval distinction between *leges* as mere administrative provisions, and fundamental principles, in this case principles founded on Scripture and the tradition of the Church, on which Gregory based his whole claim to superiority over bishops and kings alike. These traditions, as he and his supporters declared, authorized him when the necessity of the case demanded "to mitigate the rigor of canons or decrees." [1] But this seems to extend no further than to administrative decrees somewhat like those recognized in the secular law by the author of the *Summa de Legibus* of Normandy,[2] or to the right of dispensing with the law in its administration where justice requires it in a particular case. But as Mirbt pertinently asks, what if the ancient law actually declares the opposite of the new? Has the Pope the right to abolish existing canons, or is he bound by them? Is he the master of the canons or their subject? The consensus, even of the papal writers, seems to support the view that the Pope was so bound, except for his "dispensing power" and the right to issue "administrative laws." What, then, if a Pope should abuse these discretionary powers, as King James II of England did in the seventeenth century, and make the exception the rule? Here, as usual, was the crux of the practical difficulty, the same difficulty which so often nullified all theoretical limitations on secular rulers in the middle ages and even in modern times. A discretionary power, as such, is illimitable in its exercise. A pope or a king *should* dispense only in particular cases, but what is to prevent his turning dispensation into actual legislation by dispensing in many or in all cases? The Pope is "judge of the canons" (*judex canonum*) even though he may not be master of them. He may be bound theoretically, as St. Augustine said, to judge "according to the law" not to judge of the law, but for his judgment nevertheless he is answerable to God alone. Although his decrees may be against law, and amount even to heresy, yet no power on earth may judge him, not even a General Council.[3] Such was the claim of some of the more extreme of the papal party. To concede it was, it is true, to make the Pope potential dictator over the Church, and might conceivably result in a suspension of her laws, but it

---

[1] Bernold *De incontinentia sacerdotum*, cap. v (*Libelli de Lite*, vol. ii, p. 21), cited by Mirbt, *op. cit.*, p. 555.

[2] *Ante*, pp. 186–187.

[3] *Dictatus Papae, Registrum* of Gregory VII, II, 55 a (Jaffé *op. cit.*, p. 175; edited by Caspar, p. 206).

was not for that reason a claim to a right of legislative "sovereignty," as has sometimes been maintained.

"If Gregory was an innovator, it was less on account of his ideas than of the consequences of the vigorous return to some of the principles which the feudal régime had effaced little by little from the Christian conscience." [1]

"Gregory VII made no innovation, but he was determined to enforce respect for the decisions of the Church, to surmount difficulties apparently insurmountable, and to impose his reforms upon bishops and clergy as well as upon temporal princes." [2]

He "was not so much an innovator . . . as a logician." [3] Fliche regards Peter Damian as probably the most important single inspirer of his policies. There is here as always no warrant for reading modern conceptions into medieval statements, and ideas of law in the middle ages were much the same in the Church as in the state. The chief practical problem of politics was also the same for both; it arose out of the great gulf between the obligation of law and the lack of effective sanctions for its observance.

A reading of the more important tracts — especially those of the Gregorians, whose arguments are the more positive and therefore usually of greater significance for the development of thought — leaves on my mind certain more or less definite impressions. First, that the vital question at the centre of the whole controversy and the point most important for the general history of political thought was whether the papal authority over princes is really "direct" or "indirect," or, in the language of the day, whether the Pope could of right control the temporal as well as the spiritual sword. Second, that all ideas concerning this question were necessarily far more indistinct in the twelfth century than they had become by the sixteenth through the political break-up of Christendom, the consequent weakening of the conception of its unity, and the universal recognition of the independent existence of a number of strong nation-states — differences which made the "indirect" power of Cardinal Bellarmine a much more clean-cut one than that of the earlier writings on which he relied as precedent or authority, and a greater departure from it than he him-

---

[1] Imbart de la Tour, *La polémique religieuse*, p. 264.
[2] A. Fliche, *Études sur la polémique religieuse à l'époque de Grégoire VII*, p. 288.
[3] F. Rocquain, *La papauté au moyen âge*, p. 108.

self was probably aware of. Third, that notwithstanding this indistinctness and lack of precise formulation in either thought or word at this time, the supremacy claimed for the Pope by the Gregorians as his of right was a supremacy not based on a new conception of the *sacerdotium* or the *regnum*, either in fact or in the minds of the writers themselves, but based rather upon claims long made and now merely carried to their logical conclusion and defined in somewhat more clear-cut terms; in other words, that Gregory was in reality "standing upon the ancient ways" and can be truly called an innovator only in the practical application of his principles, not in the underlying principles themselves. Fourth, that this supremacy which he claimed and exercised was in fact a spiritual one only, and if in practice it involved — as actually it did — far-reaching acts of interference in secular government, that this interference was never thought of by Gregory or by his supporters as implying any direct temporal authority ordinarily resting in his hands. It was in reality an "indirect power" only and never properly exercised except when employed for a spiritual end. In the eyes of all these writers the Pope was not king over the world, not even over Christendom, but he was pastor of the whole flock of Christ with authority over all his sheep, which meant over all Christendom, and this authority inevitably entailed the heavy responsibility for ensuring in this world God's peace, justice, and order, necessary for the flock's eternal welfare; but great as this authority was, and superior to that of all kings and princes on earth, it included no claim to the direct rule over the world or even over Christendom in matters strictly secular. Lastly, that this spiritual supremacy, while it conferred upon the bishop of Rome supreme power over all the clergy and the whole laity, not even excluding emperors and kings, and while it made him "judge of the canons" (Bernold of Constance applies to him the term *judex canonum* and even *auctor canonum* [1]), thus giving him a power limited only by his own discretion, for whose exercise he was answerable to none but God alone in the pronouncing of judgments, in dispensing with the canons in particular cases, and in the enactment of new canons where circumstances required it, and canons which might even be a revocation of old ones; yet, in spite of all this, his power, so uncontrollable in practice, was founded on the unchangeable law

[1] Quoted in Voosen, *op. cit.*, p. 131, note 44.

of God whose precepts not even a Pope could alter or detract from, though in giving them effect he might create new canons and dispense from old or even abrogate them. For the canons were held to be really of two kinds, those affirming the immutable divine law, which are subject to neither change nor dispensation, and those contingent upon the changing needs of God's flock, to be made or unmade by the Pope as its needs require. The latter it is not only his right but his duty to make or unmake at need, of this need he alone can be the judge, and for any judgment he may make he can be held accountable to none but God.

The view that Gregory VII was consciously aiming at a "sovereign" law-making power over the Church and a temporal supremacy over the Empire is largely owing to a failure to distinguish between the Pope's power of dispensing on the one hand, a power incidental to his authority as *judex canonum,* an essentially judicial authority based on the canons themselves and not inconsistent with them; and on the other, an unlimited authority to make or unmake laws of every kind totally without regard to any existing law. The misconception also arises in part from a disregard of the distinction commonly made in the middle ages between the fixity of law in its highest sense and the mutability of the subsidiary provisions that temporary necessity might require for its enforcement.

This distinction, it is true, like the one between legislation and dispensation, was never very precise, and its indefiniteness perhaps furnished the chief material for controversy between the two parties, the one restricting the fundamental laws of the Church narrowly to the word of God and undoubted ancient tradition, the other including within it all preceding ecclesiastical enactment, with which, it was charged, Gregory had broken. But however the two contending parties might differ as to the content of this immutable law, they were in substantial agreement in admitting its existence and in attributing to it a different and a higher character than that possessed by mere administrative provisions made necessary by new contingencies.

These great controversies of the eleventh and twelfth centuries are of the highest importance in the history of political thought, both as a cause and a proof of the growing political self-consciousness of western Europe. They stimulated a new type of political literature, and they developed arguments, some of them for the

first time, which remained a part of the common stock of controversialists on the great question of Church and State for centuries
to come.

Not many in this period accepted the view that a king ruled by
a right inherent in his person instead of his office, but Peter
Crassus asserted it, though it was a right based on Roman
rather than divine law; still fewer, if any, had ever yet adopted
or even clearly formulated the doctrine of the Pope's supremacy
in matters distinctly temporal, but Honorius Augustodunensis
implies very nearly that when he says that Christ instituted the
priesthood, but not the kingship, to govern his Church, which, of
course, means all Christendom;[1] and it is likely that the idea of
the state's originating in compact had occurred to few or none
at the time beyond Manegold of Lautenbach, although he himself
gives a perfectly clear exposition of it.

On the whole the period is one of intense intellectual activity,
of rapid development of political thought, disclosing many diver-
gent views; but there is, except in a few scattered instances, no
distinct breach with the political ideas of the past.

In the preface to a book written at the order of Louis XIV,[2]
its author, Le Vayer de Boutigny, describes the Church as follows:
"The Church may be considered in two ways; either as a body
politic, or as a body mystical and holy. It is considered as a
body politic in reference to the state of which it is a member. It
is considered as a mystical body in reference to the Son of God
whose spouse it is, in the words of the Fathers. As a body politic it is a congregation of people joined together by the same
laws and subject to the same temporal ruler, that they may together contribute to the preservation of the state and of the
public peace. As a body mystical and holy it is a congregation
of the faithful joined together by the same faith and subject to a
spiritual ruler, that they may work together for the glory of
God and each for his own salvation." Whether this Gallican
statement be true or false is no question for the historian; its
significance lies in the sharpness of the definition of one of the
two opposing views of the Church which were beginning to compete for mastery in men's minds during the critical period in the

---

[1] *Summa Gloria*, cap. 15, *Libelli Honorii Augustodunensis*, in *Libelli de Lite*, vol. iii, p. 71.

[2] *Dissertations sur l'Autorité légitime des Rois, En matière de Regale*, par M. L. V. M. D. R.,
Cologne, 1682. In the edition published at Amsterdam in 1700 it is wrongly attributed to
Talon, *Avocat général* of the Parliament of Paris.

intellectual development of Christendom following the investiture struggle, and it may be taken as a pretty faithful statement of the position held by the anti-clerical party generally from the end of the first third of the fourteenth century onward, with the one very important reservation, that the older medieval idea of the solidarity of Christendom is entirely abandoned.

Under this theory the powers of a bishop and even of the supreme pontiff, considered merely as an organ of the universal Church, were practically restricted to the spheres of preaching and administering the sacraments; they included the *potestas ordinis* only, not the *potestas jurisdictionis;* all jurisdiction and all coercive power were entrusted by divine ordinance directly and immediately to the King to be delegated by him to his ministers; the unity of the Church universal became a communion in faith and sacraments only, a mystical body (*corpus mysticum*), but in no sense a body politic (*corpus politicum*); the only bodies politic were the Empire and the *regna*. It is a dualistic theory of government and of human life. The spiritual and the temporal are sharply distinguished so far as the actual enforcement of law upon earth is concerned, and it professes to go back for its justification to the famous separation of the spheres of the king and the bishop defined in the letters and tractates of Pope Gelasius I in the fifth century. Its opponents saw in it even more than this and openly charged its adherents with the heresy of the Manichaeans.

But the tendency of the human mind to strive for a single synthesis of all things is unavoidable. It resulted in this period in the development of a counter theory under which, since all things in heaven and earth are under the government of God, all on earth must be subject to the control of the Pope, his vicar, whether they are "spiritual" or "temporal," whether a part of the *potestas ordinis*, or of the *potestas jurisdictionis;* for the Pope has PLENI-TUDO *potestatis*, and may either exercise it directly or entrust a part to kings and princes as his agents to be enforced only under his supreme direction (*ad nutum*).

Such were the two rival theories of the state which faced each other in the first half of the fourteenth century and they were irreconcilable. Each had a long history lying behind their first dramatic collision in the struggle between Pope Boniface VIII and Philip the Fair, King of France.

Under the earliest Christian emperors of Rome, as we have

seen, the *jus sacrum* was a part of the *jus publicum* and under the
Emperor's control, but almost the last vestiges of this control
disappeared in the period of decentralization which followed,
especially after the break-up of the Frankish monarchy, and coercive power thus naturally fell by force of circumstances more and
more into the hands of the only agents who remained capable of
exercising it, the bishops, a power necessarily ill defined. The
revival of centralized secular governments in the Empire and in
nation-states such as England and France brought with it a
challenge to this authority exercised by the officials of the Church,
but at first the conflicts of the two powers which resulted belong
more to the realm of fact than of theory. The ultimate rise of
two rival theories to justify these conflicting claims came no
doubt as a part of the general intellectual awakening of western
Europe, which might be considered partly a cause, partly a result
of the great controversy between the *regnum* and the *sacerdotium;*
but two important factors in that intellectual revival may be
singled out especially, on account of their unmistakable influence
in shaping the course of the opposing theories and in determining
their final outcome. These are the revival of Roman law as a
science, and the direct contact with the ethical and political
works of Aristotle. Most of the earlier distinct formulations of the
extreme papal claims seem to have been made by the Canonists
in their glosses on the decretals, especially Pope Innocent IV and
the Cardinal of Ostia (Hostiensis), and the first flat denial of them
came from the civil lawyers at the court of Philip the Fair, Peter
Flotte and William of Nogaret. In a sense the contest was one between the canon law and the *jus civile* of Rome, and little wonder.

It was natural that the civil law should furnish the strongest
basis for the royal claims, for in all the texts of Justinian's books
in which powers are given to the clergy these powers are distinctly treated as concessions made by the sovereign Emperor.
The *jus publicum* embraced the whole of the *jus sacrum*. But
the decretals, true and false, that later found their way into the
corpus of the law of the Church which was assuming its definite
form from the twelfth to the fourteenth century, attributed to
the Church and to its head, powers over all its members lay and
clerical, which were scarcely less extensive than those of the
Roman Emperors over their subjects. The *jus sacrum* tended to
swallow up the *jus publicum*. Thus the canon law became in

time the most dangerous competitor of the *jus civile*, but both alike received their first stimulus from the legal conceptions of imperial Rome. As a result of these Roman conceptions, after the revival of Roman law at Bologna and elsewhere, men were coming more and more to think of the Church as well as the state in terms of law; to look upon the functions of its officers as rights; to fix their minds on its jurisdiction rather than its sacramental character. Neither the Church nor the *regnum* may have been definitely conceived of as a corporation, but men had gone a long way in the direction of that conception when it had become their habit to regard the Church's normal activities as the exercise of legal rights inhering in it as a community. Roman legalism had made of it something more than a mere *corpus mysticum*. It was thought of as an *institution*, established and maintained by God, with at least a quasi corporate character; and its head, as exercising powers usually designated by writers of the time as regal and not merely episcopal. On its theoretical side this was largely a result of the renaissance of Roman law.

But the view of the nature of the ecclesiastical community received further elaboration from the ethical and political theories of Aristotle which became the common property of the learned after the recovery of the manuscripts of Aristotle's ethical and political works, and their translation into Latin in the latter part of the thirteenth century. Thus the idea returned that the state — now a theocratic state embracing all Christendom — was according to nature, and it became a *societas perfecta*, the culmination of all social and political relationships, designed by God to ensure for man on earth the nearest possible approximation to the *summum bonum*. The blending of these philosophic views with the institutional conceptions of the canonists appears in all the more general treatises of the time, and in the greatest of them it is marked by a profundity and an acuteness seldom exceeded in the whole course of political thought.

The net result of it all was that the Church was no longer believed to be in the state, as St. Optatus had declared. Christendom had rather become one great church, and now that church in the eyes of its defenders was assuming the character and power of one great universal state, with the Pope as its head. Another effect of the growing legalism and institutionalism was a sharper distinction between clergy and laity. If the *ecclesia* has rights, they are more and more thought of as rights of the clergy, to be defended by canon law against the infringement of the secular powers. "In the Middle Ages Church and State in the sense of two competing societies did not exist; you have instead the two official hierarchies, the two departments if you will: the Court and the *Curia*, the kings' officials and the popes'." [1] Notwithstanding the struggle for unity the tendency toward dualism was ineradicable, and one form it was taking was a widening of the actual gap that lay between the clergy, in whom the institutional rights of the Church were becoming more and more concentrated, and the great body of laymen for whose spiritual good these rights in theory chiefly existed. Contrary to the doctrine of all the philosophers of the Church, the facts, and even the canonists themselves, were beginning to sap the foundations of the universal theocratic state and preparing the way for its break-up into the two societies of Church and State, and for their altered relations to each other under which the struggle between the spiritual and the temporal power was resumed or continued at the end of the middle ages. Dr. Figgis would find the beginnings of these great changes in the "habit of reasoning about political societies" which came in with St. Thomas Aquinas, and their chief cause in the influence of the political ideas of Aristotle.[2] With greater justice, Mr. Woolf would push back these beginnings to the eleventh century and assign as their chief cause "the entry of Roman Law, not of Aristotle, into political thought." [3]

It remains, first, to trace briefly these changing conceptions in the period of their growth after the Investiture struggle, and second, to summarize the nature and results for political thought of the dramatic duel between Boniface VIII and Philip the Fair in which the irreconcilable elements in these concepts are brought to a direct issue.[4] Gregory VII himself was probably less con-

[1] J. N. Figgis, *Respublica Christiana* (Appendix I to his *Churches in the Modern State*, London, 1913), p. 190.

[2] *Op. cit.*, p. 215.

[3] *Bartolus of Sassoferrato*, by C. S. N. Woolf, Cambridge, 1913, p. 105.

[4] The outline given here of the first of these subjects is based directly on some of the more important contemporary sources and on four modern accounts chiefly, Carlyle, *A History of Mediaeval Political Theory in the West*, vol. iv (1922), part iv, vol. v (1928), part i, chap. 10, part ii, chaps. 1–7; Jean Rivière, *Le problème de l'église et de l'état au temps de Philippe le Bel*, Louvain and Paris, 1926, *Introduction;* Albert Hauck, *Der Gedanke der päpstlichen Weltherrschaft bis auf Bonifaz VIII*, Leipzig, 1904; and *Political Theories of the Middle Age* by Dr. Otto Gierke, translated by Frederic William Maitland, Cambridge, 1900.

General acknowledgment is here made of the great debt to these admirable treatments of this subject. Dr. Hauck's paper is chiefly valuable for the earlier part of the develop-

cerned with the institutional rights of the Church as such than with the obstacles placed by princes in the way of his great reforms. If he could be said to have any very definite theory on the relation of the two powers, it seems to have been the theory of his great predecessors rather than the more legalistic conception which became current later. He was primarily a man of action rather than of theory, unflinching in the face of difficulty and opposition, determined at any cost to bring about the reformation of the Church which he believed necessary for the accomplishment of its great mission. It was this rather than any institutional theory that actuated him, yet the very boldness of his acts and the great extent of the authority he enforced in practice make the years of his incumbency one of the great stages in the development of the theory of the Papacy. If in the writings of his own time and immediately after statements are to be found here and there among his adherents which seem to anticipate the views which became definite later, they are seldom carried to their logical conclusion. But in the years ensuing, the plenitude of Hildebrand's actual power became the basis of a theory justifying that power, which was developing rapidly both as to its comprehensiveness and its definiteness, and the changing political conditions of this time all tended to hasten the process.

It is in England in this particular period that the influence of these conditions may probably be first seen most clearly, because in England, largely as a result of the Conquest, the administration of government and law became more concentrated in the Crown, and the royal administration further extended at the expense of the competing jurisdiction of the courts Christian, than can be found elsewhere at so early a date. The great struggle between Henry II and Becket was a dramatic trial by combat between the champions of two rival institutional systems each of which could expand only at the expense of the other, and it was a struggle for the *potestas jurisdictionis;* it had less to do with sacramental matters. Two powers, expanding rapidly and becoming more and more conscious of their "rights," stood face to face, each

---

ment, the other accounts cover it all, that in Carlyle in considerable detail and including valuable extracts from contemporary sources. A useful selection of extracts chiefly from official documents is contained in Carl Mirbt, *Quellen zur Geschichte des Papsttums und des römischen Katholizismus*, 4th edition, Tübingen, 1924; a still fuller one, especially for Imperial documents, is to be found in Karl Zeumer, *Quellensammlung zur Geschichte der deutschen Reichsverfassung.*

demanding its share of a government which was more temporal than spiritual. The effects of such a contest on the development of the institutional theory of the Church are incalculable, but they must have been very great, and they were heightened by the frightful circumstances of Becket's brutal murder in 1170, by the wave of horror unparalleled in medieval history that swept over western Europe as a result of it, and by the withdrawal of some of Henry II's most important claims which followed. But Milman does Becket scant justice in designating him "the martyr of the clergy, not of the Church; of sacerdotal power, not of Christianity; of a caste, not of mankind." [1] It is true that the distinct claims for which he died were more institutional than truly spiritual, more immediately affecting the clergy than the Church as a whole; and in this lies the great influence of Becket's martyrdom on the further development of the Church's institutional theory. But it is exaggeration and injustice to intimate that he himself clearly distinguished between the clergy and the Church and laid down his life only for the former. He was no more a theorist than Hildebrand. "I have loved justice and hated iniquity, and therefore I die in exile." These were the dying words of the great Pope, and they are not far different either in their meaning or in their deep and sincere conviction from the words of Becket just before he was struck down: "I am ready to die, choosing the assertion of justice, the liberty of the Church, instead of life." [2]

In these circumstances it is not surprising to find in England and in the midst of the controversy between Becket and Henry II, or near it, some of the most distinct evidences of the growth of ecclesiastical theory in this general period. For example, Becket, while in exile, wrote in 1166 to the English king, reminding him that kings "receive their power from the Church while the Church receives hers not from kings but from Christ." [3]

One of the most distinct assertions of the growing conception of ecclesiastical and papal authority in this period comes from one of Becket's closest friends, his companion almost to the moment of

---

[1] History of Latin Christianity, vol. iv, Bk. VIII, chap. viii.
[2] Radulfi de Diceto . . . Opera Historica (Rolls Series), vol. I, p. 343.
[3] Materials for the History of Thomas Becket, edited by J. C. Robertson (Rolls Series), vol. v, p. 281. See also Ibid., pp. 485–486.
A generation before, Ivo of Chartres, one of the staunchest but most moderate defenders of clerical rights, had warned Henry's grandfather, Henry I, to bear in mind that he was "the servant of the servants of God, not the master; the protector, not the possessor," Ivonis Episcopi Carnotensis Epistolae, Paris, 1585, No. 51, folio 53.

his martyrdom, the famous John of Salisbury, probably the most accomplished man of his day in western Europe; an assertion so clear and definite that some consider it the first explicit claim of a direct power in temporal things existing in the Pope.[1] It runs as follows: "This sword, then [coercive jurisdiction in temporal matters], the prince receives from the hand of the Church, although she herself in no sense holds the sword of blood. She nevertheless possesses this sword, but she uses it by the hand of the prince on whom she confers the coercive power over the body, reserving the authority over spiritual things for herself in the pontiffs. The prince, therefore, is in a sense the minister of the priestly office, and one who performs that part of the sacred functions which seems unworthy of the hands of the priesthood. For every office concerned with the sacred laws is religious and holy, yet this is a lower office because it consists in the punishment of crimes, and seems to bear something of the character of the executioner." [2]

It was the fashion in John of Salisbury's day to use the figure of the sword in referring to the administration of law of any kind. The sword had a symbolic sense, like the crown, the throne, and the sceptre,[3] and its use can be found in the great argument concerning the two powers as far back as the time of the Emperor Henry IV; but the terms "spiritual sword" and "temporal sword" had been gaining a more definite meaning in the twelfth century and they were playing a constantly greater and greater part in the contest between the two powers. If we may trust the citations of the time, this was in large part the result of some famous words of St. Bernard of Clairvaux addressed to Pope Eugenius III. "You are urging me to feed serpents and scorpions, not sheep," St. Bernard represents the Pope as saying in answer to his own fervid appeals, to which Bernard replies, "All the greater reason, I say, to go to them, but with the word not the sword. Why should you try to draw again the sword, which you have once been ordered to put back in the sheath? And yet if any one denies the sword to be yours he seems to me not to have noted the word of the Lord when he said, 'Put up your sword in the sheath.' Therefore the sword is yours, and to be unsheathed, perhaps, at

---

[1] For example, Gosselin *Pouvoir du Pape au moyen Age*, English translation (London, 1853), vol. ii, p. 360.
[2] John of Salisbury, *Policraticus*, edited by C. C. J. Webb, Oxford, 1909, Bk. IV, chap. iii.
[3] Jacob Grimm, *Deutsche Rechtsalterthümer*, 3d ed. pp. 165-170; *Von der Poesie im Recht* (*Zeitschrift für geschichtliche Rechtswissenschaft*, vol. ii, part 1, p. 25 ff., 1815).

your command though not by your own hand. For were it not
to belong to you in some way, when the Apostles said, 'Behold,
here are two swords,' the Lord would not have replied, 'It is enough,'
but, 'It is too much.' So therefore to the Church belong both
swords, the spiritual and the material, but the temporal is to be
drawn indeed for the church, the spiritual in truth also by the
Church; the spiritual by the hand of the priest, the temporal by
the hand of the knight, but truly at the will (*ad nutum*) of the priest
and by order of the Emperor." [1]

There may seem little room for doubt as to the meaning of
John of Salisbury's calm incisive statement, quoted above. It
appears to be a clean-cut claim for the Church to the supreme
authority not only in spiritual matters, but in temporal; and in
the latter, kings and princes are nothing but the deputies of the
bishop. But it is seldom possible to point to the exact time when
the changing meaning of any symbol like that of the two swords
first reaches its final definition, or to indicate with any certainty
the first man who uses it with full consciousness of all its later
implications. To say with confidence that John of Salisbury was
the first to do so would seem unwarrantable; yet his does seem to
be a more distinct formulation of these papal claims than any earlier
statement of them surviving to modern times. In cool precision
it is in contrast to the earlier rhetorical passage from St. Bernard's
De Consideratione. It seems by no means clear from his words
that St. Bernard believed that kings were merely the Pope's
agents in the administration of their realms, as the words of John
of Salisbury might seem to mean.

It is possible that he may have held no very definite view on the
subject at all, since his mind was of a mystical rather than a legal
cast; but of one thing we may be certain. These words of his
were taken up and interpreted in such a way within the next
hundred years or so, that they must be considered one of the chief
literary sources of the extreme views of papal supremacy expressed
by the supporters of Boniface VIII in the early fourteenth century.

By the middle of the twelfth century it is evident that views
somewhat like John of Salisbury's have spread widely among the
clergy. In 1157 the Emperor Frederic Barbarossa felt it necessary to declare that anyone saying that the Emperor had received
the imperial crown as a gift of the Pope was "an opposer of the

[1] *Sancti Bernardi abbatis primi Claraevallensis, De Consideratione*, Lib. iv, cap. iii, 7.

institution and doctrine of Peter and guilty of falsehood." [1]
The idea was greatly strengthened and extended by the dramatic
and forceful exercise of papal authority by Innocent III in the
earlier part of the thirteenth century, the period of the Papacy's
greatest actual power, though the Pope himself, as was usually
the case, made his contribution through his vigorous enforcement
of papal "rights," rather than by any new or more advanced
theory of his own in support of them. Lack of space makes it
impossible to set forth here in any detail his pronouncements.
Over the Empire he asserted a power that was practically without
limit, especially in the matters of election and coronation,[2] but as
his interference in these cases was in part based on historical matters such as the Donation of Constantine and the "translation of
the Empire," they furnish less definite illustrations of his general
ecclesiastical theory perhaps than his relations with France and
England. It is noteworthy that even in England, which King
John had surrendered to the Pope as feudal overlord, Innocent
III's annulment of *Magna Carta* in 1215 was not based on feudal
grounds. "It is upon his ecclesiastical rights that Innocent
founded his action and upon them alone." [3] It is probably in
his famous decretal *Per venerabilem* of 1202, and in his claim of the
right to dictate terms of peace to France and England, that the
clearest indications of his general ecclesiastical theory are to be
found. "It is not alone in the patrimony of the Church where
we have full power in temporal things," he says, "but even in
other territories, that we exercise a temporal jurisdiction incidentally (*casualiter*) and on investigation of certain cases (*certis causis
inspectis*); not that we wish to prejudice another's right or to
usurp a power not due us." "Three kinds of jurisdiction are to
be distinguished," he says, in interpretation of the words in Deuteronomy, chapter seventeen, "first, *inter sanguinem et sanguinem*,
and therefore called criminal and civil [*civile, i.e.* belonging primarily to secular jurisdiction]; lastly, *inter lepram et lepram*,
and therefore known as criminal and ecclesiastical [*ecclesiasticum*,
as distinguished from *civile*]; and intermediate, *inter causam et*

---

[1] Mirbt, *Quellen*, p. 169.

[2] For example, in his decretal *Venerabilem fratrem* of 1202, Mirbt, *op. cit.*, pp. 174–175.
There is a masterly review of this subject in Carlyle, *op. cit.*, vol. v, part ii, chap. ii.

[3] George Burton Adams, *Innocent III and the Great Charter* (*Magna Carta Commemoration Essays*), 1917, p. 40. Professor Adams' paper is an admirable treatment of this phase
of the subject. Innocent's bull annulling the charter is printed by Bémont, *Chartes des
libertés anglaises*, pp. 41–44.

causam, which belongs to either, ecclesiastical or civil; and when anything difficult or ambiguous arises in these [*i.e.* in things falling within the jurisdiction concurrently "civil" and "ecclesiastical"] recourse must be had to the judgment of the apostolic throne, and one who in his pride disdains to submit to its sentence, is ordered to die and to receive the plague of Israel, that is, by the sentence of excommunication to be separated from the communion of the faithful as one dead." [1]

In demanding jurisdiction in the quarrel between the kings of England and France Innocent protests that he intends no infringement or diminution of the jurisdiction or power of the King of France. "Why should we wish to usurp another's jurisdiction when we are not able to exhaust our own?" In this case it is not of the fief that the Pope proposes to pass judgment, but to determine a matter of sin (*decernere de peccato*) "and of this without doubt the judgment belongs to us and we can and ought to pass it on any one whomsoever." "For we depend on no human constitution but rather on divine law, for our power is not from man but from God, and there is no one of sound mind but knows that it pertains to our office to correct mortal sin of whatever sort and to inflict an ecclesiastical penalty on any Christian whomsoever if he refuses to submit to correction." [2]

In one of his sermons, Innocent says the Church has conferred on him both a plenitude of power over spiritual things (*spiritu-*

---

[1] Decretal *Per venerabilem* (1202), Mirbt, *op. cit.*, pp. 176–177. If this interpretation of this important passage is the correct one the Pope is here claiming a right to determine on final appeal only those matters which are in the first instance concurrently within the jurisdiction of both temporal and spiritual courts. He is not yet making quite the sweeping claim set up later by Innocent IV that the Pope is the *judex ordinarius* of every man. If the words "in these" (as I have translated *in quibus* in the clause *in quibus cum aliquid fuerit difficile vel ambiguum*) refer back to all three kinds of jurisdiction, then the interpretation above is wrong, and Innocent IV later added practically nothing to the claim of his predecessor.

That the true antecedent of *quibus* in this sentence is the jurisdiction *inter causam et causam* alone, and not all three jurisdictions, seems to me probable, mainly from the fact that Innocent III has altered the order of the text of Deuteronomy to place the "intermediate" jurisdiction in the last place and immediately before the words *in quibus*. Why he should thus have changed the original order, it is hard to imagine, if not for the purpose of bringing antecedent and consequent as close together as possible. On the other hand, the canonist Alanus, whose *apparatus* is thought to date from the pontificate of Innocent III, refers very definitely to a different doctrine: the Pope "iudex ordinarius est et quoad spiritualia et quoad temporalia" (F. Schulte, *Literaturgeschichte der Compilationes antiquae, Sitzungsberichte der K. Akademie der Wissenschaften*, Philosophisch-historische Klasse, vol. 66, pp. 89–90); and if such a doctrine were already accepted by canonists it would not be strange if a skilled canonist like Innocent III should give official expression of it. It is, however, generally true that official statements of the Pope's *potestas* fall short of contemporary claims made by the canonists with reference to its scope and extent.

[2] Mirbt, *op. cit.*, p. 177.

alium plenitudinem) and a *latitude* in temporal things (*latitudinem temporalium*).[1]

From these and from other writings of his it seems clear that the jurisdiction claimed by Innocent III was almost illimitable and his exercise of it without parallel either in extent or effectiveness. Yet it was a jurisdiction in its nature primarily spiritual, and temporal only incidentally (*casualiter*), a power grounded on the Pope's duty as Vicar of God to judge of the sins (*de peccato*) of all Christians, not on his right as a temporal ruler to administer law for his subjects. Innocent then in his official utterances appears to have made no explicit claim to a direct power in temporal matters, but it remains none the less true, as Dr. Carlyle has pointed out, that "it is in the Decretal letters of Innocent III that we must look for the ultimate sources of the extreme view of the papal authority in temporal matters which was developed in the second half of the thirteenth century." [2]

From the death of Innocent III, in 1216, to the end of the century, the chief struggle lay between the Papacy and the Empire and the period of its greatest intensity was the reign of the Emperor Frederick II. In this period the claims of the Empire remained much as before, defensive rather than offensive, negative not positive; they did not go, officially at least, beyond a demand for the recognition of the independence of the Emperor in the administration of his Empire, and of the direct concession of his authority by God himself without the mediation of the Pope; they admitted the jurisdiction of the Pope in spiritual matters, even the supreme jurisdiction in matters of sin, but they denied that it extended to temporal things.

It is probably in the answer to these imperial claims made by Pope Innocent IV that we find the first definite official adoption and elaboration of the words of John of Salisbury, the doctrine that the Pope has by divine ordinance a jurisdiction over all temporal matters directly and of course, which he may delegate to princes as his subordinates to be exercised at his will and if need be under his direction, and that princes have no lawful authority which has not been thus delegated. So, Innocent declared, in a sentence involved but significant, ". . . the Lord Jesus Christ,

---

[1] Migne, *Patrologia*, Series Latina, tom. 217, col. 665, quoted by Carlyle, *op. cit.*, vol. v, p. 153.

[2] *Op. cit.*, vol. v, p. 318.

the son of God, as very man and very God, so remaining true king and true priest according to the order of Melchisedech, just as He makes clearly manifest the dignity of the pontificate in the eyes of the Father now by employing before men the honor of royal majesty, now by executing it before them; has established in the apostolic throne not only a pontifical but a regal monarchy, committing to the blessed Peter and his successors the government of both an earthly and a celestial empire, which is duly signified by the plurality of the keys; in order to make known by the one key which we have received applicable over the earth in things temporal and by the other over the heavens in things spiritual, that the vicar of Christ has received the power of judgment." [1]

If this and other official statements of Innocent IV seemed to lack somewhat in clear definition of the vast powers he was claiming, this lack was supplied in the cooler and more explicit words of his glosses on the Decretals, for he was a great canonist as well as Pope. For example, he says, "We believe that the Pope who is the vicar of Jesus Christ, has power not only over Christians, but also over all infidels." "For all, the faithful and infidels alike, are the sheep of Christ through the creation, though they may not be of the flock of the Church. And so from this it appears that the Pope has jurisdiction over all and a power of right, even if not in fact. Wherefore by the power which the Pope has, I believe that if a gentile who has not the law, except of nature, if he acts contrary to the law of nature, may be rightly punished by the Pope." [2] He also claimed the same right over Jews. The Pope was in fact nothing less than the normal judge over all men (judex ordinarius omnium).[3]

In the latter half of the thirteenth century, proofs increase that this was becoming the view of many of the supporters of the Papacy in its contests with the secular rulers. In one tract, written in support of the Pope against the Emperor, certainly before the year 1298 and probably about 1281, under the title, Determinatio Compendiosa de Jurisdictione Imperii, the doctrine of Innocent IV is applied in terms free enough from ambiguity.[4] Its modern editor attributes it to Tholommeo of Lucca, the probable continua-

---

[1] Mirbt, op. cit., pp. 197-198.
[2] Quoted by Carlyle, op. cit., vol. v, p. 323.   [3] Ibid., p. 320.
[4] Edited by Marius Krammer, Hanover and Leipsic, 1909 (Fontes Juris Germanici Antiqui . . . ex Monumentis Germaniae Historicis separatim editi). In the preface the editor sets forth the evidence, mostly internal, indicating its date and authorship.

tor of the treatise *De Regimine Principum* begun by St. Thomas
Aquinas. By arguments drawn chiefly from history and scripture,
the author sets about to disprove the claims of the Emperor and
to prove that the Imperial authority is derived from the Pope,
but some of his statements are of a more general character, fore-
shadow the universal claims of the papal party in the next century,
and employ some of the same arguments in their support. In
many ways it may be shown, says the author, that the supreme
pontiff "in his authority, whether spiritual or temporal, excels
the power or domination of any one whomsoever." [1]

"While in temporal matters the Emperor has no superior in
the person of any temporal lord, yet the validity of his jurisdiction comes from the Pope's jurisdiction as from a fountain of
authority, from which as in the place of God all jurisdiction
arises." [2] Such statements are further explained and amplified
by chapters 10 and 19 of the third book of the *De Regimine Principum* which deal with the Pope's *plenitudo potestatis*. This plenitude, its opponents say, does not extend beyond the spiritual
power, "but this cannot be, for the corporeal and temporal ever
depends on the spiritual, as the movement of the body depends
on the power of the mind." [3]

The views of St. Thomas Aquinas himself on this important
question are not given at length in that part of the *De Regimine
Principum* generally attributed to him. In others of his voluminous writings however he deals more than once with this subject,
but in such a way that it is not easy to say precisely whether he
accepted outright the whole of Innocent IV's doctrine or not.
No detailed examination of these passages is possible here, but a
comparison of them has led to the conclusion that on the whole,
St. Thomas, while he concurs in advocating a *plenitudo potestatis*
as sweeping in its supremacy as that of Innocent IV, probably
does not mean to include within it any direct power in matters
strictly temporal. Possibly his most distinct utterance on this
point occurs in his commentary on the Sentences of Peter Lombard
in which he says that both spiritual and secular power have a
common divine origin and it is necessary in strictly civil matters
to obey the secular rather than the spiritual authority (*In his*

---

[1] *Op. cit.*, cap. v, p. 12.
[2] *Ibid.*, cap. xv, p. 33.
[3] *De Regimine Principum*, Bk. III, chap. 10, *S. Thomae Aquinatis Opuscula Selecta*, vol.
iii, p. 342, Paris, 1881.

autem quae ad bonum civile pertinent est magis obediendum potestati saeculari quam spirituali).   But he hastens to make one exception : — "unless perchance the secular power is joined with the spiritual, as in the Pope who stands at the top of both," (*qui utriusque potestatis apicem tenet*) as both priest and king.   Probably no keener analysis of this passage has ever been made than by Cardinal Bellarmine, and he concludes that this "conjunction" of the two powers is either in the states of the Church, where it proves nothing, or that it can be explained as including only an indirect power.[1]   St. Thomas's "normal and mature judgment was that the Pope had an indirect rather than a direct authority in temporal matters."[2]

The contrary theory that papal power should directly control all temporal administration, was mainly a logical development of the institutional conception of the Church rooted in Roman legal ideas, and one naturally fostered and elaborated by canonists rather than by pure theologians.   As one might expect, therefore, it is in the glosses of the canonists rather than the works of a great theologian like St. Thomas, that we find the most exact definition of the Pope's *plenitudo potestatis* and the clearest assertions that it rightly extends over the whole field of human law.   The canonists are the chief authors of the theory of the direct power of the Pope in temporal matters, and in this period it developed rapidly under their hands.   They are the ones, Dante declares, who strive against the truth, "known as 'Decretalists,' ignorant and devoid

---

[1] *De Romano Pontifice,* Lib. v, cap. v.   In the same chapter he argues against St. Thomas's authorship of Bk. III of the *De Regimine Principum.*   See Rivière, *Le problème de l'église et de l'état,* pp. 48–50, where this passage of St. Thomas is quoted and the commentary of Bellarmine briefly referred to.   Extracts from the same passage are given by Carlyle, *op. cit.,* vol. v, p. 352.

[2] Carlyle, *op. cit.,* vol. v, p. 354.   This view seems not inconsistent with St. Thomas' statement in the Summa Theologica.

"The secular power is subject to the spiritual as the body to the mind . . . and therefore it is not a usurpation of jurisdiction if a spiritual official interfere in temporal matters to the extent of those in which the secular power is subject to him or those which have been surrendered to him by the secular power."   Secunda Secundae Partis, Quaestio LX, art. vi.

This also seems to have been the general position taken by another great churchman of the thirteenth century, Robert Grosseteste, Bishop of Lincoln.   His courageous defiance of Innocent IV, "filially and obediently I refuse obedience, I resist, I rebel" has sometimes created the impression that he repudiated the papal claims.   Other passages in his letters show conclusively that he accepted them in their fullest extent, — but apparently as a spiritual rather than a material *plenitudo potestatis.*   For example, *Roberti Grosseteste Epistolae,* Ed. Luard (*Rolls Series*), pp. 90–94, 348–349, 436–437.   On Grosseteste, see Francis Seymour Stevenson, *Robert Grosseteste,* London, 1899, especially pp. 179–182, 306–318; also A. L. Smith, *Church and State in the Middle Ages,* Oxford, 1913, Lecture III.   This author sees such a discrepancy between the other letters of Grosseteste and his famous defiance that he is inclined to regard the latter as a fabrication by Matthew Paris.   Pp. 101–111.

THE LATER MIDDLE AGES

of theology and philosophy alike." [1] Meanwhile, he says, "your Gregory lies covered with spiders' webs, Ambrose is hidden away in forgotten closets of the clergy, Augustine is ignored, Dionysius, Damascene and Bede rejected, and they prate of a certain *Speculum*, and Innocent, and Hostiensis. And why? Those were seekers after God as the end and the supreme good, it is gifts and benefices that these are pursuing." [2]

The glossed editions of Gratian's *Decretum* show a tendency on the part of the canonists of the earlier thirteenth century still to adhere to the older and less ambitious view that papal power extends directly only over spiritual matters,[3] but in the second half of the century this rapidly gives way. The views of Innocent IV as canonist have been briefly noted already.[4] The complete and final exposition of these newer views in their most developed form is to be found in the famous *Summa super Titulis Decretalium*, popularly known as the *Summa Aurea*, of Henricus de Segusia, Cardinal of Ostia (Hostiensis) who died in 1271, one of the most famous of all the glosses on the canons, of which some eleven editions appeared after the invention of printing;[5] and in the *Speculum Juris* equally important, of Willelmus Durandus, the "Speculator" (died 1296), of which no less than thirty-nine editions were printed.[6] In Hostiensis, as Rivière truly says, we find the germ of the theories so fully elaborated a half century later by Egidius Romanus.[7] So, Hostiensis declares, although the two jurisdictions are distinct as to their administration, "yet the Emperor holds his imperium by the Roman Church and may be termed its official or vicar." "For the enactment of the Emperor can have no binding force except over those bound by the laws of the Romans and the authority of the Catholic Church." As to superiority, there is but one head, namely the Pope. "And we ought to have but one head, the lord of things spiritual and temporal, since the earth is his and the fulness thereof." Not without

---

[1] *De Monarchia* III, 3, cited by Rivière, p. 53.
[2] *Epistola Cardinalibus Italicis, Tutte le opere di Dante Alighieri*, edited by E. Moore, Oxford, 1904, p. 412.
[3] See Rivière, *op. cit.*, pp. 53–56, where some extracts are given.
[4] *Ante*, pp. 233–234.
[5] A. Tardif, *Histoire des sources du droit canonique*, p. 323. The edition used here was published at Lyon in 1542. Carlyle prints the most important of the glosses with valuable commentary, vol. v, pp. 325–332, also extracts from the *Speculum* of Durandus. *Ibid.*, pp. 335–337. See also Rivière, *op. cit.*, pp. 56–59.
[6] A. Tardif, *op. cit.*, p. 325.
[7] *Op. cit.*, p. 57.

reason, did the Lord of Lords say to Peter, "'I will give you the keys of the kingdom of Heaven.' He did not say 'key' but 'keys,' namely *two* keys, one which shall close and open, bind and loose as to spiritual things, the other which he shall use as to temporal things."

"The spiritual power is prior to the earthly in three ways, in dignity or rank : . . in institution . . . and it is prior also in power or authority, for it belongs to the spiritual power to call the earthly into existence and to judge whether it be good." [1] As Rivière remarks,[2] the canonists go further than the theologians. To them the extension of the Pope's *plenitudo potestatis* over the temporal is no longer a debatable question, it is asserted without reservation, hesitation, or even discussion, as a matter of fact. In the canonists of the later thirteenth century, papal authority reaches a height beyond which it is difficult to go; but, adds the same author, at the very hour of that triumphant expansion, its decline begins. We must turn, in the next place, to the dramatic struggle of Boniface VIII and Philip the Fair, in which that decline was most marked and most sudden.

It is unnecessary here to recount at length the steps in the controversy between Boniface VIII and Philip the Fair. They are given in all the histories of the period, long or short.[3] We shall confine ourselves to the reaction of these quarrels on the great problem of Church and State and their influence in defining and amplifying the political doctrines of each. Roughly the controversy is divisible into three parts, first the years 1296 and 1297 when the main question at issue turned on the temporalities of the clergy and whether contributions should be made from these to King or to Pope; a later struggle, from 1301 to 1303, just before the Pope's death, when wider issues came in to add to the bitterness of the

---

[1] Carlyle, *op. cit.*, vol. v, pp. 328–329.

[2] *Op. cit.*, pp. 58–59.

[3] An excellent account is given by Langlois in Lavisse's *Histoire de France*, vol. iii, part ii, Bk. II, chap. ii, pp. 127–173. The older treatment of this subject by Milman in his *History of Latin Christianity*, vol. vi, Bk. xi, chaps. 8–10, is still valuable, especially for the author's summaries of the documents that issued from both sides. The fullest collection of these documents still remains the great mass of *preuves* added to Pierre Dupuy's *Histoire du différend d'entre le Pape Boniface VIII et Philippe le Bel Roy de France*, Paris, 1655. Some additional ones are given in Adrien Baillet's *Histoire des démeslez du Pape Boniface VIII avec Philippe le Bel Roy de France*, Paris, 1718; and in *Les Registres de Boniface VIII*, edited by Digard, Faucon and Thomas, Paris 1884. See also, Carlyle, *History of Mediaeval Political Theory in the West*, vol. v, part ii, chap. viii; Jean Rivière, *Le problème de l'église et de l'état au temps de Philippe le Bel*, chap. i; and Richard Scholz, *Die Publizistik zur Zeit Philipps des Schönen und Bonifaz VIII*, Einleitung (pp. 1–31).

conflict, and thirdly the continuance of these quarrels after the death of Boniface, in the early part of the period of the residence of the Popes at Avignon.[1]

In earlier medieval struggles between the supreme pontiff and the secular rulers ecclesiastical property had always been a contributing cause of great importance, but hitherto the specific cause of trouble had mainly lain in the conflict between the feudal obligations devolving upon the clerical tenants of such property, on the one hand, and on the other the legitimate needs of the Church itself. By the end of the thirteenth century the steady accumulation and the vast extent of this church property had become a source of great uneasiness to most of the secular rulers in western Europe; and in addition, in those realms in which the consolidation of royal authority had gone furthest, notably in England and France, the old problem was rapidly assuming a changed form with every step in the advance of royal power and with each stage in the decline of the economic and political importance of feudal institutions. It was no longer merely the proprietary rights of a feudal overlord in the Church's property with which the prelates had to contend; these were gradually becoming demands of the king as head of a nation for the financial contributions of subjects, both clerical and lay, toward the support of a national government which exacted these contributions as the price of the protection afforded by its laws, its courts, its administrators, and its armed forces. The Papacy at the centre of the ecclesiastical system, which had now become thoroughly institutionalized on the principles of monarchy, therefore now found itself face to face with a new competitor, the national monarch, and one of the newer questions at issue between them was whether the property, within a kingdom but devoted to pious uses, must or must not be exempt from a levy made by the king with "the common assent of all the realm and for the common profit thereof." The answer of Boniface VIII to this question was unqualified.[2] Such property must in every case be wholly exempt, unless the Pope himself should order otherwise, an answer that applied to England as well as to France, and one that received much the same reply and had much the same practical conse-

---

[1] Scholz, *op. cit.*, pp. 2–3.
[2] In the famous bull *Clericis laicos* (1296), printed in many places, see, *e.g.* Mirbt, *Quellen*, p. 208.

quences in both kingdoms.   In France, however, the royal replies
to this contention of the Pope were somewhat more general in
character, probably because prompted by civilians and based so
largely on Roman law principles, and this gives them an exceptional importance in the development of political ideas.

"Before there were any clerics," Philip the Fair declared in his
answer to Boniface, "the King of France had the custody of his
realm" and was able to enact statutes for its defence against
enemies, and he has now enacted therefore that no horses, arms,
or moveable property of any sort shall be withdrawn from his
kingdom without his own special license, and this property includes
the goods of the clergy.   The Church, the document goes on to
say, does not consist of clergy only, it was not for them alone that
Christ died, and it is an abuse that laymen should be excluded from
the liberty that Christ by his grace conferred on his Church.   It
is true that there are special liberties of the clergy necessary for
the edification of the people contained in statutes of the Popes
conceded by the grace or at least by the permission of secular
princes, and having once conceded these, princes cannot destroy
them.   But neither can they destroy those things adjudged
necessary and expedient for government and defence by the mature
counsel of good and prudent men.   The clergy who may not fight
need special protection from others, and no one will fight for
others at his own charges.   If the clergy will not contribute with
the rest for the protection of all they become "a useless and as it
were a paralyzed member" of the State.   It is a right and not an
abuse therefore to demand a subsidy from the clergy.   It is an
abuse in the clergy to refuse it, especially when they are wasting
their substance on feasting and gay clothing and the like, while
they neglect the poor.   It is in fact nothing less than the crime
of *Lése-Majesté* and as such we intend that it shall be punished.[1]

Boniface was warned by the French clergy that he had gone too
far and he hastened to explain that he was not questioning Philip's
rights as king or feudal overlord but aiming only at the notorious
abuses and extortions of the king's agents.

But a far-reaching question had been opened, in the remarkable
document summarized above, and some momentous assertions
made which were destined to have decisive results.   Most impor-

[1] Dupuy, *Histoire du différend, Preuves*, pp. 21–23.   There is no evidence that this document, preserved among the French archives, was ever actually delivered to the Pope.

tant of all these assertions perhaps is the announcement that there are in the kingdom of France certain things adjudged requisite for the government and defence of the realm which even the king may not destroy, an early and indistinct reference to "the fundamental laws of the French monarchy"; and that these include rights exercisable over the clergy, the basis of later Gallicanism. It is interesting, too, to note that the sanction, threatened in this document, for these rights is the penalty in the *Quaestio laesae majestatis* of Roman law. In determining what those things are that should be rendered unto Caesar, the law in France is to be the law of the Roman Emperor, not merely the canons of the Roman pontiff. This is one of the first definite instances of the employment of the Roman civil law against the canon law in the defence of any secular ruler except the Emperor, and as such it marks an epoch in the history of the controversy between the two powers. This particular document was probably the work of Peter Flotte, a layman, a doctor of the civil law, and a man apparently in no way connected with the feudal nobility, one of the first in the long line of eminent men to rise to the highest station in France by virtue of legal ability and legal services alone. Their rise is one of the important political by-products of the renewed study of the civil law of Rome in France.

We have already noticed the chief reason for the availability of Roman law as a weapon in the hands of the temporal prince against the Pope; its principles had been originally formulated in a state in which the *jus sacrum* was no more than a part of the *jus publicum* and the whole *jus publicum* subject to the Emperor's exclusive control. But on the same reasoning, if Roman law exempted the King of France from the Pope's authority in secular matters, why did it not at the same time make him subject to the authority of the reigning Emperor, who in theory had succeeded to all the rights as well as the laws of Justinian? The chief results of this embarrassing dilemma came only in the second phase of the controversy between the Pope and the King, after the turn of the century, and can best be treated as a part of it, but Philip apparently foresaw the difficulty and attempted to meet it in his firm declaration made in 1296 that "the control over the temporalities of his realm belongs to the King alone and to no one else, that he recognizes no one as his superior in it, and that in things pertaining to the temporal administration of the realm he is not bound, nor does he propose, to subordinate or subject himself in any manner whatsoever, to any living man." [1]

The first phase of the controversy had closed with the advantage evidently on the King's side; Boniface had so explained his earlier demands as almost to rob them of practical effect so far as the realm of France was concerned. But before the fighting died away it had called out at least one important writing in defence of the King's position, the *Disputatio inter Clericum et Militem*, as it is usually entitled,[2] a brief and very interesting discussion in dialogue form between an ecclesiastic and a knight, in which the knight has, and is obviously intended to have, somewhat the better of the argument. This short writing is apparently the first of its kind and it is clearly based on the document summarized above at page 240, beginning "Antequam essent cleri" (Before there were any ecclesiastics). The times are out of joint, groans the cleric, in the beginning of the dialogue. In these days justice is buried, laws are overturned, rights are trampled underfoot. Big words, answers the knight and I only a layman of little learning. If you wish to have talk with me, Reverend Sir, you must adopt a plainer style. I can remember, explains the cleric, when the Church was held in high honor by princes and all others, but now she is utterly wretched, with her rights torn from her and her liberties broken through. I can hardly believe it, the knight answers. What do you call right (*jus*)? Why, the decrees of the Fathers and the statutes of Roman pontiffs, of course. What they ordain, if for temporal matters, may be "rights" for you, but they are not for us, says the knight. No one can make ordinances affecting things over which he has no dominion. The King of the French can't do it for the Empire, nor the Emperor

---

[1] Dupuy, *Preuves*, p. 28; also reprinted in Isambert, *Recueil général des anciennes lois françaises*, II, p. 705.

[2] Text in Goldast, *Monarchia* (Frankfort, 1668), vol. I, pp. 13–18; Schard, *De Jurisdictione Autoritate et Praeeminentia Imperiali ac Potestate Ecclesiastica* (Basel, 1566), pp. 677–687. For discussions as to date, authorship, and contents, see S. Riezler, *Die Literarischen Widersacher der Päpste*, Leipzig, 1874, pp. 145–148, who attributes it to Pierre Dubois; R. Scholz, *op. cit.*, pp. 333–352, the fullest account; J. Rivière, *op. cit.*, pp. 128–132; Carlyle, *op. cit.*, vol. v, pp. 379–382, who gives extended extracts. The book was popular and appeared in a number of editions. In at least one of the Mss. it is attributed to Occam, and Goldast attributes it to him. Schard says it is by an "undetermined author," and that is the view of Scholz, Rivière, Carlyle, and most scholars. An English translation was printed in the sixteenth century by Berthelet, of which there is a copy in the British Museum — *A Dialogue betwene a knyght and a clerke, concernynge the power spiritual and temporall*. Langlois places the book in 1296 (*op. cit.*, p. 133), Scholz probably in 1296 or 1297 and certainly not after 1300, Rivière, probably in 1302. The earlier date seems preferable.

for France. And if princes are not able to make enactments for
your spiritualities, over which they have never received any power,
neither can you make them for their temporalities, over which you
have no authority. What you have enacted about temporals is
worthless, for you have received no power from God to do it.
So it lately seemed utterly ridiculous to me when I heard that it
had been enacted by "Lord Boniface VIII" that "he is and ought
to be placed over all principalities and realms" and can so easily
obtain for himself a right over anything whatsoever. For all he
needs to do is to write, since everything will be his when he has
written; and so everything will be yours, and to ordain will be
nothing else than to will to hold for oneself. So then to have a
right will be nothing else than to wish it, and if he should wish to
possess himself of my castle, or town, or field, or money and treasure, he would have nothing more to do than to write "I will that
this be the law (*jus*)."

The knight then goes on to prove that all of the power of Peter
and his successors came from Christ's human character only, and
therefore cannot extend to temporal matters. But, Sir Knight,
you won't deny that the Church has jurisdiction over sin, will you?
By no means, for that would be to reject penitence and confession.
Well then, if to act unjustly is sin, one who has jurisdiction over sin
has it over matters of justice and injustice. And if the just and unjust belong to temporal things, then it follows that he ought to judge
in temporal causes.[1] It may be so in some cases, objects the knight,
but this jurisdiction never extends to crimes or to property. And,
he says, when you contend that the Pope is superior in everything
you become utterly absurd. If when he was created Pope he
was made lord over everything, then in like fashion to create a
bishop would be to make him lord of his diocese, and my priest
would be the lord of my castle and lord over me; for each of these
will have the same power in the district subject to him which the
Pope has in all. So stop talking this nonsense which is the laugh-
ing-stock of everybody and is refuted by reason as well as
Scripture.[2] The knight then enlarges upon the debt the clergy
owe to princes in return for protection, and declares, almost in the
words of the document quoted above,[3] "But if kings and princes
at their own cost and risk are bound to defend you and expose
themselves to death without recompense, while you lie in the

---

[1] Goldast, *op. cit.*, I, p. 14.   [2] *Ibid.*, p. 15.   [3] *Ante*, p. 240.

shade, dine sumptuously" etc., "then you are truly the only lords, while kings and princes are indeed your slaves." [1] Concessions, it is true, have been made to the clergy, but if they become dangerous to the state the prince may withdraw them, for he may change the law to meet changing circumstances. Yes, replies the Clerk, good Emperors may in some cases change the law, but not kings. That answer is blasphemy, declares the knight, the result perhaps of ignorance but more likely of envy. History proves that the kingdom of France is an independent subdivision of the old Frankish monarchy and a coequal sharer with the Empire in its sovereignty. "Therefore, just as all things within the boundaries of the Empire are acknowledged to be subject to the Empire, so those within the boundaries of the Realm are to the Realm." [2]

The second phase of the controversy between Boniface and Philip was more bitter than the first, it ranged over a wider field, and brought to light many more written defences of the position of both King and Pope. These defences also go further in their claims than ever before, and on the papal side they reach a height never exceeded afterward. [3] A long series of difficulties between King and Pope culminated at the end of 1301 in the issuance of the bull *Ausculta fili*, in which papal authority was asserted in very high terms, but no definite claim of a direct control in secular matters was included. In France a false bull appeared which made a distinct claim to direct secular authority, and early in 1302 the Estates were called together by the King, to a meeting from which the French clergy issued a letter to the Pope, and the nobility to the college of cardinals. From these letters it is clear that both the French clergy and the French nobility interpreted the combined acts and utterances of Boniface as a demand for a direct temporal authority in France, and that both estates emphatically refused the demand. In both the letters referred to this is first and foremost among the complaints — that the Pope is claiming over France a direct authority in temporal matters in which it is known to the whole world that the King and the people of the Realm have always been considered to be subject to God alone, [4] a claim "wonderful, novel, and unheard of" for a

---

[1] Goldast, *op. cit.*, I, p. 16.   [2] *Ibid.*, p. 17.

[3] The best authorities for this part of the struggle are as before, Scholz, Rivière, and Carlyle, to which one more must be added, Heinrich Finke, *Aus den Tagen Bonifaz VIII*, Münster i. W., 1902. The chief sources are as before.

[4] Letter of the nobility to the Cardinals, Dupuy, *Preuves*, p. 60.

century among the people of France, in the significant words of
the clergy themselves.[1] Both the Cardinals and the Pope hastened
to make answer to these assertions. The answer of the Cardinals
addressed to the communes of France denies absolutely that the
Pope had ever written making the claim that the realm of France
was subject to him temporally, or that it was held of him, or making any other claim in violation of the rights, liberties, and honor,
of the king and the realm,[2] and the denial is equally explicit in
their reply to the nobility.[3] The statements of the Pope himself
are not quite so definite. He places the blame for the whole
trouble upon "that Devil" Peter Flotte, who had deceived the
King and the Estates and made them think his demands included
the recognition of his authority in temporal matters. "For forty
years now we have been trained in law, and we know that there
are two powers ordained by God. Who then ought to believe
or can believe that such fatuity, such folly ever entered our head.
We declare that in nothing are we wishing to usurp the jurisdiction of the King, and so our Brother of Porto has declared.[4] The
King cannot deny, nor any other of the faithful whosoever he is,
that he is subject to us on the ground of sin." [5] But he ends on a
somewhat different note. Preceding popes have deposed three
kings of France. We might depose this king who has committed
all the offences they have, and more, as we would dismiss a water-
carrier.[6]

All these explanations are of great value for the historian, but
their value consists chiefly in the light they throw on the meaning
of the bull which issued soon afterward, on November 18, 1302,
the famous *Unam sanctam*,[7] which concludes, "Moreover we
declare, we affirm, we define, and pronounce that for every human
creature it is absolutely necessary for salvation to be subject to
the Roman Pontiff." It is one of the most important documents
of the middle ages.

[1] Letter of the French clergy to Boniface VIII, Dupuy, *Preuves*, p. 68.
[2] Dupuy, *Preuves*, p. 71.   [3] *Ibid.*, p. 63.
[4] This is a reference to a sermon in the same consistory delivered by Matthew of Aquas-
parta, Cardinal of Porto. In it he explained that the Pope really has a temporal jurisdiction
for he has power to judge in all temporal matters on the ground of sin (*ratione peccati*), and
this is a temporal jurisdiction. It is his *de jure*, but its exercise does not belong to him.
In the sense of *use* therefore, this jurisdiction belongs to the Emperor and to other kings.
Boniface's reference to the Cardinal does not prove that their theoretical views are identical.
Dupuy, *Preuves*, p. 76.
[5] *Ibid.*, p. 77.   [6] *Ibid.*, p. 79.
[7] In Mirbt, *Quellen*, pp. 210–211, and many other places.

Before turning to the next subdivision of our subject, the more important books whose appearance was occasioned by the duel between Pope and King, it may be worth while briefly to note certain impressions arising from a study of the bull *Unam sanctam* and its antecedents.   In the first place, it is clear, that not a single assertion or claim made in the bull is new, and some of them are very old; even the oft-quoted statement about the two swords is no more than a rearranged quotation from the *De Consideratione* of St. Bernard with scarcely a change in the wording.   In the second place, however sweeping its demands, there is in the bull no explicit claim to a direct power in temporal matters.   This is very significant, but no one can doubt it who reads the whole bull with attention.

In the third place, if Boniface's claim to forty years' experience in the canon law was true — and it was — he well knew that the canonists insisted on a papal power far stronger than the one he put forth in the bull.   Did he, therefore, agree with the canonists? Was he actually trying to exercise direct powers in France as the French clergy thought?   And if so, why did he see fit to make a formal claim that fell so far short of this?   Was it wholly misrepresentation which led the French clergy to interpret the Pope's words *and actions* as an assertion of a direct power?   In short, may not the false bull, though a forgery, have indicated pretty accurately what Boniface was actually setting out to do before the extent of the opposition forced him to draw back?   May it not have been an appreciation of this accuracy which accounts in part for the Pope's evident excitement whenever he refers to this forgery?   It is obvious enough that he had not officially *said* that he possessed a direct power, and he does not say so afterward in the bull *Unam sanctam*.   But had he been acting on a different principle, as a canonist did he hold a different principle, which the French clergy had reason to fear and distrust?   It is certainly not without significance that the Cardinals in their answers to the French nobility and communes are very careful to protest only that the Pope "never *wrote*" (*numquam scripsit*) that he had a direct power,[1] and Boniface's own admission that there are two powers ordained by God[2] is in itself no distinct disavowal of the canonist doctrine which completely subordinates one of these powers to the other, even in temporal matters.

[1] Dupuy, *Preuves*, p. 71.   [2] *Ante*, p. 245.

It is obvious that at this time probably most of the leading canonists were holding a very advanced view of the institutional character of the Church and of the unlimited power of its head. It is equally obvious that many ecclesiastics did not share this view, that some were violently opposed to it, and that there were many of the latter among the clergy of France. It would be natural to suppose that a well-known canon lawyer like Boniface would share the views of his fellow canonists, yet his official utterances as Pope set forth a view considerably short of these. Was this moderation due to conviction or to motives of expediency? The answers to these questions cannot be safely given until we have considered some of the views expressed in the writings which appeared in defence of the papal claims just before and just after the issuance of the bull *Unam sanctam*. That famous definition of the Church's power does not expressly or necessarily go beyond Innocent III's decretal *Per venerabilem*, which grounds it upon the Pope's jurisdiction *ratione peccati*, a position which, as we have seen, the canonists had left far behind in the latter half of the thirteenth century. But we can only appreciate the bearing and the importance of matters like this for the development of political thought as a whole when we can look at them in connection, not only with the earlier expressions of churchmen and legists, but with the treatises and pamphlets strictly contemporaneous with, or closely following the struggle. To these we must now turn.[1]

The first of these pamphlets to be noted is one written in defence of the Pope in 1301 by Henry of Cremona, with the title *De Potestate Papae*, and first published in 1903 by Richard Scholz in the appendix to his book.[2] It is a very high statement of papal authority, supported by many of the usual arguments, and proving that the Pope has an undoubted direct power in temporal matters. The book seems to have attracted some attention at the time, but it does not impress a modern reader as an exceptionally able argument. The author's reply to the civilians, whom he refers to significantly as *juriste*, is characteristic. One of their arguments was that if the Church exercised an authority after Constantine

[1] Scholz, in the book already referred to, is the primary authority for the facts connected with this literature. It is an admirable treatment. Rivière, on the basis of these facts, is more concerned with the interpretation of them. His interpretation is candid and thorough, a most important contribution. Carlyle's treatment of the subject is, as usual, searching and wholly unbiassed. Finke gives important discussions of certain points.

[2] Scholz, *op. cit.*, pp. 459-471. See further, Scholz, *op. cit.*, pp. 152-165; Rivière, *op. cit.*, pp. 138-141; Carlyle, *op. cit.*, v, pp. 398-402.

which it did not exercise before, this authority must have come from the Emperor. Yes, the author admits, the Church did things after Constantine which it had not done before, "but it was not defect of right but defect of power, which led the Church to refrain from doing these things before."[1] In like fashion he dismisses the historical argument that the Pope has never actually exercised both powers. "It is not because the power is lacking but arises from the Pope's dignity and the meanness of temporal jurisdiction." It was for this reason that the Lord said to Peter, "Put up the sword in its sheath."[2]

Apparently before the end of the same year, 1301, two much more important books appeared, which are now generally conceded to be the two most influential statements on the Pope's side in this controversy and among the most noteworthy defences ever written of the extremest papal claims : the *De Ecclesiastica Potestate* of Egidius Colonna, referred to usually as "Romanus," and the *De Regimine Christiano* of James of Viterbo (Giacomo Capocci ?). It is very curious that neither of these two important books was ever printed before the beginning of the twentieth century.

Egidius Romanus was one of the most eminent men of his day, a doctor of both laws, Archbishop of Bourges, the former tutor of Philip the Fair himself, head of the Augustinian Order, and author of many well-known books in theology and philosophy, including one of the ablest and most interesting political treatises of the whole middle ages, the *De Regimine Principum*, written before the death of Philip III in 1285, for the instruction of Philip the Fair, translated into many languages and printed several times, the last edition appearing as late as the seventeenth century.[3]

The contribution of Egidius to the controversy between Boniface and Philip was his book *De Ecclesiastica Potestate* which appeared in 1301.[4] There is abundant evidence of the importance of this book

---

[1] Scholz, *op. cit.*, p. 467.   [2] *Ibid.*, p. 469.
[3] For the life and works of Egidius, see Scholz, *op. cit.*, pp. 32–45.
[4] The first complete edition of this important book was published at Florence in 1908, *Un Trattato Inedito di Egidio Colonna*, edited by Giuseppe Boffito and Gius. Ugo Oxilia. The passages given here were originally taken from this edition, but it cannot be called a critical one as it is based on a single manuscript and is marred by a number of obvious misprints. In 1929 a much better edition appeared, based upon four of the manuscripts, — *Aegidius Romanus De Ecclesiastica Potestate* herausgegeben von Richard Scholz, Weimar. The translations and paraphrases have been compared with this edition and corrected where necessary. For discussions of the book see especially the introduction of Oxilia to the edition of Boffito and Oxilia ; R. Scholz, *Die Publizistik zur Zeit Philipps des Schönen und Bonifaz VIII*, pp. 46–129 ; and the shorter ones in Carlyle, *op. cit.*, V, 402–409, and Rivière, *op. cit.*, chap. v.

at the time of its appearance and in the later phases of the controversy.[1] Egidius, says his admirer, Durand the younger, deals with his subject "with profundity and sublimity," and no candid modern inquirer trying to put this book in its proper place in the development of political thought can deny its truly "profound" character. The book is not always pleasant reading. It is marred by frequent repetitions, by many long arguments that carry little weight according to present-day standards, and by a dogmatism that sometimes tries to overwhelm opposition by mere weight of repeated assertion. Its lengthy discussions are occasionally irritating and frequently tiresome to a modern reader, and the book on the whole is far less agreeable than the *De Regimine Principum* of the same author. Notwithstanding all this, it is an epoch-making book, original in conception and powerful in treatment. It is certainly "copious" as well. Every argument, every text of Scripture, every analogy employed at any time in preceding controversies, is again pressed into service and carried to its furthest logical conclusion, and these conclusions are of the extremest kind. In short, we have in this book the completest and the most thoroughgoing of all the theological and philosophical defences of the furthest doctrines of the canonists, that the Pope is supreme lord in his own right over all the world and in all matters temporal as well as spiritual, and that all princes are his mere subordinates even in the secular administration of their own realms. This position is here explained and defended from every point of view and for the first time completely and exhaustively. The later treatment of the same subject by Agostino Trionfo and Alvaro Pelayo may have proved to be more popular, but they went no further in the exaltation of the political authority of the Papacy, for further it could not go. With Egidius this authority reached its highest point and apparently for the first time. This makes this book one of the first importance in the history of political thought. An examination of it would also show that its central theme is profound, and, though its roots run far back into the past, original in the truest sense.

[1] For example, Gulielmus Durandus, the younger, in his famous *Tractatus de Modo Generalis Concilii Celebrandi*, written probably about 1310, omits all discussion of the important questions concerning the authority of princes over the temporalities of the clergy and the authority of the Church over temporal princes, because "brother Egidius" has dealt with them "copiously and usefully" in a treatment in which "profundity and sublimity vie with knowledge." Part iii, titles 3 and 26 (Paris, 1545, pp. 167, 188).

Unfortunately no such examination in any way commensurate with its importance can be attempted here. The entire discussion in the book, and the whole of the political thought of Egidius, turn about one great central principle, the idea of *dominium;* and for Egidius *dominium* has a meaning no less comprehensive than for Fitzralph, Archbishop of Armagh, and John Wycliffe, who probably borrowed this conception from him later in the century. In the compact phrase of Wycliffe, it is *habitudo nature racionalis secundum quam denominatur suo prefici servienti,*[1] or, in the apt paraphrase of Professor Dunning, "The abstract relation of the being that is served to the being that serves."[2] All created things are related to each other in a certain order established by their Creator under which some are placed above others and in virtue of this superiority must be served by them according to the measure of their superiority. This preordained relation of superior to inferior is *dominium,* and if it is that of a person to a person it is government or authority, whether in the state or on a smaller scale in a household; if it is that of a person to a thing it is *proprietas* or property. Anyone may be actually exercising some power over another as a matter of fact, but if this exercise is not *of right,* then it is not a true authority, it is not *dominium;* nor is mere control over a physical object or thing *proprietas;* if it is not accompanied by right, it falls short of true *dominium.* This *dominium* God possesses over his whole creation animate and inanimate, therefore such men only can be truly said to have either legitimate authority or true *proprietas* as have received it from God through his grace, and all these have it in a measure which exactly corresponds to their place in the hierarchy of created things as established by God himself. These seem to be the essential points in the famous and profound conception of dominion founded in grace which controls the whole of the political thought of Egidius, and was taken up later by Wycliffe as the basis for conclusions widely different. In the *De Potestate Ecclesiastica* Egidius sets forth in detail the relative position of the Church with the Pope as its head and the secular rulers of the world, as parts of this divine plan. In the elaboration of it one suspects that the order is the converse of the original one in Egidius's mind; that

---

[1] *Johannis Wycliffe De Dominio Divino Libri Tres,* edited by R. L. Poole, London, 1890, p. 4.

[2] *A History of Political Theories, Ancient and Mediaeval,* pp. 260–261.

in the latter the doctrine of papal omnipotence was the *terminus a quo*, not the *terminus ad quem* as in the book, but this in no way lessens the power or the importance of the discussion. All political thought of the period and for long afterward had the same characteristic: in the middle ages it was usually only a by-product of ecclesiastical theory.

In chapter VII of Book II of his treatise Egidius sets about to prove that there can be no true dominion (*dominium cum iusticia*) either over temporal things or over lay persons, except one held subject to the Church and instituted by it.[1] He explains it thus: Reason and authority both prove that no man is fit justly to have dominion over any other man or to possess anything, by virtue alone of the fact that he has been begotten (*generatus*) by his father; he must be begotten again, "born again," regenerated (*regeneratus*) spiritually by the Church. Without such regeneration he cannot justly succeed to his inheritance nor obtain any true *dominium* by succession. As one begotten of his father, he has only the first and lowest qualification (*initium*) to inherit, the completion and perfection of his capacity to do so only comes from his being regenerated by the Church. If on feudal principles the father has the *dominium* over the inheritance in conjunction with the son and has it more fully than the son, so the Church has dominion over every inheritance and over all things and has it in a fuller and a higher sense than any of its members themselves can have. Succession to an inheritance on account of birth is only the beginning of justice, succession because of regeneration is its perfection and consummation; this perfect and complete justice is richer and wider, and if it is wanting there is no justice at all. No son can justly succeed to his father's inheritance unless he is born again spiritually through the Church.[2] If then there is no just dominion of any kind, whether it is a mere *dominium utile*, or the higher dominion that implies jurisdiction (later *dominium eminens*), if it is not held subject to God — which is possible only through the sacraments of the Church — then you are lord over your holding and over everything that you have more because you are the spiritual son of the Church than because you are the son of a father in the flesh. You must therefore derive your title to your inheritance, to your whole *dominium*, to everything you possess, from

---

[1] Edition of Boffito and Oxilia, p. 57; Scholz, p. 70.
[2] *De Potestate Ecclesiastica*, Bk. II, chap. vii, Boffito and Oxilia, pp. 57–58, Scholz, 70–71.

the Church, through the Church, and from being a son of the Church, rather than from your earthly father, or through him, or because you are his son. For if your father, during his own life, is lord of your inheritance in a higher sense than you, so the Church, which does not die, is more lord of your possessions than you are yourself. But it should be noted that when we say that the Church is the mother and has the lordship over all possessions and all temporal things, by so saying we are not taking from men their dominion or possessions, for the Church has dominion of this kind and the faithful have the same; but the Church has such dominion as the universal and superior dominion, its members have it only as the particular and inferior. We do then render unto Caesar that which is Caesar's and unto God that which is God's, when we concede to the Church the universal and superior *dominium* over temporal things and bestow on the faithful the particular and inferior *dominium*.[1]

This explanation is ingenious and profound, and it furnishes a solid basis for all the later deductions as to the Pope's plenitude of power. In it can be seen directly or by implication practically the whole of Egidius's doctrine concerning the two powers and his entire political philosophy.

So the author in applying his general doctrine to government, one of the two main divisions of *dominium*, goes on to say, "So you see clearly that kings are more worthy possessors of their realms, princes of their principalities, and all the faithful of their possessions, through their mother the Church by which they are regenerated spiritually, than through their fathers and hereditary succession, for from those earthly fathers and through them they are born in original sin, not subject to God but estranged from Him. If, then, a prince or any *fidelis* says he has any inheritance, whether it is a principality or any other kind, from his father by whom he was begotten in the flesh, he ought rather to say that he has a principality of this kind and an inheritance from his mother the Church by whom he has been regenerated spiritually and absolved sacramentally; since one so regenerated and absolved begins to be worthy of his inheritance and possession, who was unworthy of it before, and from that time begins justly to possess that of which before he could justly be deprived." [2]

---

[1] *De Potestate Ecclesiastica*, Bk. II, chap. vii, Boffito and Oxilia, p. 61, Scholz, p. 75.
[2] *Ibid.*, Bk. II, chap. viii, Boffito and Oxilia, p. 64, Scholz, p. 79.

The deductions which Egidius makes from this general principle regarding the effects of excommunication are interesting for themselves and for the way by which he reaches them. He wishes to show that if the Church through her power of binding and loosing should excommunicate one of her members, such a person could have nothing which he could justly call his own. It should be understood, he says, that in the beginning the rightful possession of this thing or that which enabled one to say, "This is mine," came only from a convention or agreement which men had with each other, and that this agreement or pact dealt merely with the distribution and division of land, so that the sons of Adam in this way had appropriated certain possessions and held them as their own in proportion as they had parcelled out the lands, and according to conventions and compact had agreed that this thing should belong to one and that to another. But in course of time some men began to dominate and to be made kings, and also laws were desired securing the observance of these voluntary compacts and agreements under which men could say "this is mine, this is yours." So laws were added beyond the conventions and pact. Therefore these laws and "rights" were the only ground on which one might say "this is mine," for they included the agreements and the rules by which one is adjudged the just possessor of property. It was from this perhaps that the maxim was derived, that if the laws were destroyed no one could say "this is mine, this is yours." But when the foundation is overthrown, the whole building falls. The foundation of all these is the communication of man with man, from this arose partitions, and then grants, transfers, and purchases. If men had no communication with each other, but each lived to himself, laws to distinguish the just from the unjust would be entirely unnecessary. For if there were no communication between man and man, there would be no partitions, no buying and selling, nor anything of the kind. So then if the Church is able to shut one out from the communion of men, it can take from him the foundation upon which all those things rest. Thus to one so deprived, partitions, sales, grants and the like, and laws of every kind are of no benefit. An excommunicate in being deprived of the communion of the faithful is deprived of all the goods he possesses as a member of the Church and in relation to other members. And if one were a non-Christian and in the midst of other infidels he would be deprived all the more, because infidels

are unworthy of all possession and all *dominium*. There is therefore nothing in the nature of either authority or property which
an excommunicate or an infidel can ever rightly call his own.[1]

At the end of his book Egidius applies the conclusions about
dominium to the burning problem of the day, whether the Church,
that is the Pope, has any immediate authority over matters strictly
temporal. The Church, as Church, he says, has a superior and
primary *dominium* in temporal things but not immediate jurisdiction and execution. The secular ruler holds the temporal sword.
Nevertheless, the spiritual sword is over the temporal, since the
dominium of the Church is superior and primary while that of the
prince is inferior and secondary. Therefore the prince has a
large right in temporal things, as a right of use (*i.e.* in revenues
and returns) it is larger than the Church's, though as a right of
lordship or control (*dominativum ius*) it is less. The prince even
has a right of authority and control in addition to this right of
use (*ius utile et dominium utile*) over his cities, castles, and lands,
in the jurisdiction in matters of blood (*iustitiam et iudicium
sanguinis*), — [where the penalty is loss of life or limb]. But
this *dominium* of the prince, whether it is of use (*utile*), or directive
(*potestativum*), in no case destroys the *dominium* of the Church
which is superior and primary. This *dominium* of the Church
then is a *dominium* more controlling and higher even in temporal
things than that of the prince or of any temporal lord, since it is
superior and primary, and the Church by virtue of it receives
from the faithful and their possessions a *census* or tribute,[2] from
the faithful, oblations, and from their possessions, tithes. From
this it follows that the Church has the rights of lordship over all
and claims the powers of lord and master.

Therefore we do not claim that Caesar has no *dominium utile*
in temporal matters, but we do claim that the Church's is higher
and that Caesar's right ought to be disposed according to the
right of the Church. We do not even say that Caesar has no
directive power or jurisdiction over the persons of men or their
temporal goods. We do say that the Church's directive power
is far higher than Caesar's since she has the power to judge of the
person of Caesar and of his temporal goods and can even reach his

---

[1] *De Potestate Ecclesiastica*, Bk. II, chap. xii, *passim*, Boffito and Oxilia, pp. 83-86,
Scholz, pp. 103-106.
[2] For the *Census Ecclesiae Romanae* see Ducange's Glossary, *s.v. census*.

person by ecclesiastical censures, and can hand over his goods to the *dominium* of another. The directive *dominium* or jurisdiction of Caesar, and even the material sword which he uses, must be exercised through the Church and at her will, for though the Church does not herself employ the material sword she does punish others by the material sword in that this sword though not wielded *by* the Church is wielded *for* the Church and at the Church's nod. There can be nothing temporal under the control of Caesar which is not under the control of the Church,[1] and every lawful administrative act of the prince is in reality "by commission" of the Church his superior.[2]

In chapters seven and eight of book three Egidius comments at length and in a most interesting way on Innocent III's decretal *Per venerabilem*, showing that the papal jurisdiction claimed in it is no less because *casualiter*, but in fact far greater than if it were ordinary and regular, and indicating to what cases the jurisdiction in this way extends. Nothing could show more clearly than this discussion how long a step had been taken in the development of the theory of papal omnipotence in the century between Innocent III and Boniface VIII.

All these great powers are claimed as powers of the *Church*. The only remaining link therefore in the chain of Egidius's reasoning is the establishment of the principle that what belongs to the Church, belongs of necessity also to the Pope. This argument occupies a considerable portion of the book, and is enforced by the usual appeals to Scripture, history, and analogy, and it goes without saying that the conclusion reached is one which denies to the Pope no power to which the Church itself may lay rightful claim.

In the supreme pontiff is a plenitude of power, not any power whatever, but whatever power rests in the Church itself, for the whole of the power of the Church is embodied in the supreme pontiff.[3] This part of the discussion, though second to none in practical importance, is perhaps less original and certainly less distinctive than the arguments noted above, and must be passed over entirely here, except for a single but very significant point, the question whether the Pope as head of the Church is or is not a

[1] *De Potestate Ecclesiastica*, Bk. III, chap. xi, Boffito and Oxilia, pp. 162–164, Scholz, pp. 202–205.
[2] *Ibid.*, Bk. II, chap. xiv, Boffito and Oxilia, p. 107, Scholz, p. 133.
[3] *Ibid.*, Bk. III, chap. ix, Boffito and Oxilia, p. 155, Scholz, 193.

monarch *legibus solutus*, free of the law. This was a question on which there was much dispute, and many of the clergy, even some who conceded the most extensive powers to the Pope over temporal princes, in matters which were strictly ecclesiastical, regarded him as a constitutional monarch rather than an absolute one, bound in matters of legislation and administration, including dispensation, by "the common law" of the Church.[1] This was not distinctly a question of Church and State, it was one concerning the true constitution of the Church, the old problem as to the true extent of the Pope's power as *judex canonum;*[2] yet it was related very closely to the former question, and in France particularly, the two were never separated. Egidius, as might be anticipated, goes as far as anyone of his time in the direction of absolutism, but he does not go quite the whole way. He admits as a general principle that the Pope's *plenitudo potestatis* is to be exercised "according to the common law,"[3] but in special cases he may "go beyond" that law *in temporal matters.*[4] It is true that judges are bound to judge "according to law," not to judge of the law itself, but to the maker (*conditor*) of laws this restriction does not in all cases apply.[5] So in dealing *casualiter* with temporal matters the Pope may go beyond the law. Thus these matters are brought within the Church's power, not as a power without bound or limits, but as a power regulated by certain rules. "For though the supreme priest is an animal without halter and bridle and is a man above the positive laws, yet he ought to put a halter and a bridle on himself and live according to the laws established, and unless necessity requires and particular cases demand it, he ought to obey those laws."[6] But just as God in certain cases may go beyond the laws of nature by a miracle, so his vicar, in imitation of Him may do likewise in special cases, and rarely, when it is necessary for the government of the Church, as for example in the Pope's appointment of a bishop, whose election ordinarily belongs by the common law of the Church, not to the Pope but to the chapter.[7] If it was true that the Pope could exercise every power belonging to the Church, this

---

[1] For example, Gulielmus Durandus the younger, in his book, *Tractatus de Modo Generalis Concilii Celebrandi*, part i, title iii.

[2] See *ante*, pp. 217–219.

[3] *De Potestate Ecclesiastica*, Bk. III, chap. ii, Boffito and Oxilia, p. 122, Scholz, p. 152.

[4] *Ibid.*, Bk. III, chap. iv, Boffito and Oxilia, pp. 133–134, Scholz, p. 166.

[5] *Ibid.*, Bk. III, chap. viii, Boffito and Oxilia, pp. 151–152, Scholz, pp. 189–190.

[6] *Ibid.*, Bk. III, chap. viii, Boffito and Oxilia, p. 152, Scholz, p. 190.

[7] *Ibid.*, Bk. III, chap. ix, *passim*, Boffito and Oxilia, pp. 153–156, Scholz, pp. 190–195.

deduction of practical absolutism — practical rather than theoretical — from it was natural if not inevitable. Yet there were many among the clergy who refused to accept it, and the outcome of their opposition was the constitutional theory of the councils of Constance and Basel.

This remarkable book of Egidius Romanus raises some interesting historical questions on which modern historians are not always in agreement. We may ask, for example, to what extent these extreme papal powers asserted by Egidius are merely elaborations and explanations of a doctrine already held by the canonists, and how far they are new. Dr. Carlyle points out the difference between Innocent IV's view that infidels may justly hold property and jurisdiction, and the doctrine of Egidius that they can have no legitimate claim to anything, and this is important; but if instead of comparing Egidius with Innocent IV, we were to compare him with later canonists like Hostiensis and Durandus, the contrast would not be so sharp. Some of the brief but definite statements of the latter, and even a few of Innocent IV himself, seem to fall very little short, if short at all, of the *plenitudo potestatis* which Egidius expounds and defends afterward at so much greater length. We may easily agree with Dr. Carlyle that "Egidius is setting out a new theory, not only of government but of property"[1] and regard this as his chief claim to a high place in the history of thought, but a reading of Hostiensis and Durandus makes it hard to believe it equally true that he is setting out a new doctrine of the *plenitudo potestatis* of the Pope.

In another place Dr. Carlyle speaks of the way in which the doctrine of Egidius's treatise "runs counter to his earlier doctrine" as expressed in his *De Regimine Principum*,[2] and Scholz notes the same conflict, which he explains by the exasperation caused by Philip IV's treatment of the clergy after he became king;[3] but Rivière, on the other hand, is able to see between Egidius's views of 1301 and those of the *De Regimine* a great difference perhaps, but nothing that could be called a real inconsistency.[4] He finds in this difference no evidence whatever of any fundamental change in the author's views on the central question of the relation of the two powers. The view of Rivière is strengthened somewhat by a comparison of Egidius's *De Regimine Principum* with the other

[1] *Op. cit.*, v, p. 406.
[2] *Ibid.*, p. 405.
[3] *Die Publizistik*, pp. 40, 118–119.
[4] *Op. cit.*, p. 226.

De Regimine Principum most of which was written probably nearly twenty years later. The former of these two books was finished by Egidius before the death of King Philip III of France, which occurred in 1285, the other was a continuation written, as its references seem to indicate, between 1301 and 1303,[1] of a book begun by St. Thomas Aquinas, who died in 1274; and this continuation is thought to be by Tholommeo of Lucca. The two books are alike in object, somewhat alike in manner of treatment, and they have something in common in their arrangement. It is interesting that they both end with a detailed discussion of the military arrangements of a realm. But there is one singular and significant contrast. Tholommeo in his third book, as we have seen above,[2] has an important discussion of the relation of the two powers in which he asserts very definitely the Pope's direct jurisdiction in temporal matters. Though the book of Egidius is longer and more comprehensive, there is not to be found in the corresponding place nor in any other place, any treatment whatever of the relations of the two powers. Egidius may have had very definite views on this subject; but there were excellent reasons for omitting them from a book written at Philip III's order for his son's instruction. The undoubted secular tone of the treatise is noticeable not on account of any denial of the rights of the Church, for there is none; but in the entire absence of any discussion of them. The impression one gets is that this omission was no accident; the views of Egidius if expressed would not have been acceptable, but there was no need to express them. It is entirely possible to think with Rivière that Egidius may have held the same general views of papal power then as later; but he was dealing here only with the actual administration of a realm, which to the end he held to be within the province of the prince; it was not necessary in this particular treatise, and it might even be embarrassing, to include a discussion of the higher authority on whose will (*ad nutum*) he believed this administration ultimately to depend.[3]

Another question that arises in connection with the book of Egidius is its possible relation to the famous bull *Unam sanctam,*

---

[1] For the date of the continuation of the *De Regimine,* see *Die Annalen des Tholomeus von Lucca* edited by Bernhard Schmeidler (*Monumenta Germaniae Historica,* Scriptores, N. S., vol. viii, Berlin, 1930), "Preface," p. xxxi, note 2.

[2] *Ante,* p. 235.

[3] The edition of the *De Regimine Principum* of Egidius used here is the one published at Rome in 1482.

and on this too, the well-matured views of Rivière seem to furnish a very probable explanation. He holds that the book was written before the appearance of the bull, and that it had much to do with some of the most important statements of the latter, but that there is no sufficient evidence for the belief sometimes held that Egidius was its real author.[1] In connection with this, however, the important fact should be noted in addition — whatever its explanation may be — that Egidius believed and had expressed without equivocation the doctrine of a direct papal authority in temporal matters, while the bull certainly does not in words contain it.

When all is said, it must appear that Egidius Colonna is one of the greatest names in the history of political thought in the later middle ages. He was author of one of the closest and most comprehensive if not the earliest medieval adaptation of Aristotle's political ideas, in his *De Regimine Principum;* a quarter century later he combined these same ideas with the extreme canonist views of papal omnicompetence in what appears to be the first comprehensive defence of the *plenitudo potestatis* of the Pope on a philosophic basis; and in the theory of dominion set forth in his *De Potestate Ecclesiastica* at that time he made a further combination of these two sets of ideas with a third, the feudal conception of tenure and its parcelling of proprietary rights among lords and vassals. As long as feudalism retained its vitality, this synthesis of human rights and powers kept its hold upon the minds of men. That it was one of the most vital principles of the political thought of the fourteenth century none who reads the political literature of that time can doubt; that Egidius was its first formulator cannot be equally certain, for its roots run far back toward the beginnings of western political thought; but the theory of *dominium* in its complete form implies a combination of ideas which could not have occurred much before his time, and he seems to have been the first of whom we have any knowledge to see and to take full advantage of all its implications as an argument for papal claims.[2]

---

[1] See Rivière, *op. cit.,* "Appendice II," pp. 394–404, *Gilles de Rome et la bulle "Unam sanctam."* See also Finke, *Aus den Tagen Bonifaz VIII,* chap. iv; J. Berchtold, *Die Bulle Unam sanctam,* München, 1887.

[2] St. Thomas Aquinas in his *Summa Theologica* had set forth some of these conceptions in less complete form. "God," he says, "has the principal dominion over all things, He in his providence ordained certain things for the bodily sustenance of man, and through this man has a natural dominion over things (*naturale rerum dominium*) to the extent of the power

The book of James of Viterbo [1] is in some ways much like the *De Potestate Ecclesiastica* of Egidius; its main conclusions are fully as extreme and the papal authority is no less exalted and complete. But the whole plan of the book is different; both books are deductive, but this one is a deduction of the relations between spiritual and temporal powers drawn from a central principle differing entirely from the *dominium* of Egidius, though the conclusions are in all essential respects the same and reached by many of the same particular arguments and illustrations. This book is also much the shorter and more compact of the two and the absence of repetitions and digressions gives it the effect of greater coherence, and makes it on the whole more readable. In detail it also leaves the impression of being somewhat less dogmatic in tone, and on some particular points less extreme but more subtle in treatment. For example, Egidius will not admit that the Church is not prior to the state, even in time as well as in essence and thought, while James on the other hand accepts the priority of the state to the Church *in time*, but ingeniously makes this itself one ground for holding the latter prior and superior in essence, by applying to Church and State Aristotle's conception of the relation of the *polis* to the village or household; and thus making the Church the *societas perfecta* of which the state is only an earlier, partial, and undeveloped approximation.

Instead of developing his philosophy of Church and State from *dominium* as its underlying principle, as Egidius does, James of Viterbo starts with the central conception of the world as one single universal *regnum* or realm, and that realm he identifies completely with the Church. By divine ordinance the Church is a true *regnum*, in the highest sense the *one* and only true *regnum*, and the government of it is regal. His whole theory of Church and State is drawn out of this great principle.

to use them." Apparently, too, there were gradations in this right, for, as he says, "the imperfect exist for the sake of the perfect." Secunda Secundae Partis, Quaestio LXVI, art. 1.

For the significant contribution of Tholommeo of Lucca to the development of the theory of dominion, which may have preceded that of Egidius, see *post*, pp. 336–338.

The theory was much influenced by Aristotle's four-fold classification of government, (*Politics*, I, 1), William of Moerbeka's translation of it, and St. Thomas' commentary. See Appendix II.

[1] This book was first printed at Rome in 1914 under the editorship of G. L. Perugi, but in an uncritical edition based on a single manuscript. The edition used here is the far superior one edited by H. X. Arquillière, Paris, 1926, *Le plus ancien traité de l'église, Jacques de Viterbe, De Regimine Christiano (1301–1302)*, Étude des sources et édition critique.

For commentary see Arquillière, as above, pp. 13–81; Scholz, *op. cit.*, pp. 129–152; Carlyle, *op. cit.*, V, pp. 409–417; Rivière, *op. cit.*, chap. vi.

The book of James like that of Egidius is dedicated to Boniface VIII, and consists of two main divisions. In the first part the author treats of the nature of the Church as a whole, "the most ancient treatise on the Church," as its editor terms it. In the second and much longer portion of the book, the primacy of the Pope in the Church is considered, and his *plenitudo potestatis* established, as a result of the conclusions reached in Part I. In Part I James shows that the Church is a realm or *regnum*, and that it is orthodox, one, Catholic, holy, and apostolic. It is "most rightly, most truly, and most properly called a *regnum*, for it is a community, since it is a congregation or union of many of the faithful." [1] Here the influence of Augustine and of Cicero is clear. James was an Augustinian and the influence of Augustine as well as of St. Thomas and Aristotle is prominent throughout his whole treatise. Thus he completely identifies the *civitas Dei* of Augustine with the visible Church, and most of his conclusions follow from this identification. But the Church, though a *regnum*, is different from and superior to all other *regna* in that it is no mere community "of nature," but a community "of grace." [2] Like all true communities, however, it is one, and in the chapter dealing with its unity, James seems almost to define it as a corporation. He appears to come closer to the corporate idea of the state — for the Church is a true state — than any other writer of this time.[3]

The Church is a *regnum*, and in it, as in every *regnum*, there are two powers, the regal and the sacerdotal. These powers are distinct and they may be entrusted to different persons or both conferred upon one. There have been three forms of the priestly power, first that existing by natural reason among almost all peoples, but imperfect and incomplete, second the one established by the law of Moses, and third the priesthood proceeding from grace, under the new law. The last priesthood exists not through the destruction of the two earlier forms but as the consummation of them — an interesting application of an Aristotelian conception. This final form, however, has completely replaced the earlier and less developed ones, and it is perfect, divine, and perpetual. This priestly function is sacramental in character and equivalent to the *potestas ordinis*.

[1] *De Regimine Christiano*, p. 89.
[2] *Ibid.*, p. 94.
[3] *Ibid*, p. 106. Ostendum est autem primo, quod regnum ecclesie est unum. Quod ex hoc patet: *nam omnis multitudo participat aliqualiter uno.*

Regal power like the sacerdotal is either of a lower kind created by human law alone, or the higher spiritual kingship, created by God, which is the perfection and consummation of the other and necessarily superior to it.   This divine kingship, therefore, includes a priestly power, but it is also a truly royal or judicial power, for it contains the power of binding and loosing.   Under the régime of the old law this spiritual kingship (*potestas regia spiritualis*) was entrusted to priests, under the new it is given to Peter and his successors alone.   In sacramental power all priests are equal, in royal or jurisdictional power they are unequal and the Pope is above them all as he is above all kings.   Thus it is clear "that the pastors of the Church are true kings, and among them the highest, the successor of Peter, is king of kings both secular and spiritual" as well as king of all the faithful.   "Like Christ, whose vicar he is, he is called chief of the kings of the earth, which means those who are upon the earth." [1]

There is a short but very interesting tract written probably about 1308 by Augustinus Triumphus [2] in which the influence of some of these ideas of James's may probably be seen.   In this tract there is the same emphasis on the Pope's regal power and the fullest account to be found anywhere at this time of the difference between the *potestas ordinis* and the *potestas jurisdictionis*.   The latter power the clergy have only through the Pope, whose jurisdiction is complete over all laymen and all princes; to deny it is to fall into the heresy of the Manichaeans.   In the Pope as king rests the power over both spiritual and temporal things, but the immediate execution of this power in temporal matters he entrusts to secular kings and princes, "who ought to be his organs and instruments in obeying his commands in everything, and in administering the temporal power at his order." [3]

The answers to the extreme pro-papal arguments of Egidius and James roughly fall into two classes, those made by the civilian lawyers, who rely almost entirely on history and the texts of Justinian for their arguments, and a small number of tracts written by ecclesiastics, in which the range is wider and the political importance greater.   The latter are all characterized by a moderation lacking in the lawyers and lacking in their chief opponents

---

[1] *De Regimine Christiano*, part. ii, chap. iii, p. 182.
[2] *Tractatus Brevis de Duplici Potestate Prelatorum et Laicorum*.   First printed by Scholz, *op. cit.*, pp. 486–501.   See also pp. 172–175, 184–187.
[3] Augustinus Triumphus, *De Duplici Potestate*, Scholz, *op. cit.*, p. 500.

such as Egidius or James. Like all defences of temporal authority
which preceded them, these arguments in favor of Philip IV are
not aggressively anti-papal; they admit to the full the spiritual
authority of the Pope and even an authority in temporal matters
casualiter; all they insist upon is the absolute independence of
temporal princes in the regular administration of their realms.
In short they insist on the complete or almost complete separation
of the spheres of the temporal and the spiritual and deny the subordination of the former to the latter, holding that kings as well
as bishops have a direct and independent mandate from God.

At least three of these defences of royal authority appeared
within a few months after the issuance of the books of Egidius and
James and in answer to them, the so-called *Quaestio Disputata in
utramque Partem pro et contra Pontificiam Potestatem,* printed by
Goldast and attributed by him without any evidence to Egidius
Romanus. It is a short and not very significant anonymous tract
which Egidius could not possibly have written.[1] Another tract,
somewhat longer and more important, is printed at the end of
Dupuy's *Preuves,* beginning with the words *Rex Pacificus.*[2] All
the arguments contained in these two tracts, and many more, are
to be found in the longest and much the ablest of all the writings
which issued at this time on the king's side, the *Tractatus de Potestate Regia et Papali* of John of Paris.[3] The position of the apolo-
gists for secular monarchy will be illustrated here from this important book alone. John of Paris wrote as a philosopher and theologian and his political philosophy is largely based on Aristotle,
and St. Thomas's interpretation of Aristotle. Even a superficial
examination of his book would also show that it is a direct answer
to James of Viterbo and Egidius Romanus.

He begins with a short preface in which he sets forth clearly
two extreme doctrines, that of the Waldenses under which the
clergy can have no property nor anything whatever to do with
temporal things, and the other which turns the Pope into an
earthly king — the error of Herod — and makes all other prelates

---

[1] Goldast, *Monarchia,* vol. ii, pp. 95–107. For commentary see Scholz, *op. cit.,* pp. 224–251,
Rivière, *op. cit.,* pp. 274–281.

[2] Dupuy, *Histoire du Différend, Preuves,* pp. 663–683. Commentary in Scholz, *op. cit.,*
pp. 252–275; Rivière, *op. cit.,* pp. 262–271.

[3] Goldast, *Monarchia,* vol. ii, pp. 108–147; Schard, *De Jurisdictione,* pp. 142–224.
Scholz analyzes this work and gives all the known facts about its author, *op. cit.,* pp. 275–
333. For other excellent accounts see Rivière, *op. cit.,* pp. 281–300; Carlyle, *op. cit.,* vol. v,
pp. 422–437.

and all princes no more than deputies and servants entirely subject
to his will.[1] I think the truth lies between these extremes, he
says. The clergy and the Pope at their head do have a true dominion in temporal matters, but they have it not as vicars of Christ
or successors of Peter but from the grant or concession of princes.[2]
He proceeds to prove this point, first by defining his two main terms,
the *regnum* and the *sacerdotium*. "A *regnum* is a government over
a perfect multitude ordained by one for the common good," as distinguished from the less perfect household whose end and aim is less
than the whole of life. This is according to nature, for man is a political and social animal; but it also grows out of the *jus gentium*.[3]
John has discarded the belief of Seneca, the jurists, and the Fathers,
in a primitive golden age and a decline from it into the later
conventional state occasioned by violence or vice, for Aristotle's
doctrine of a progressive natural development with the state as its
consummation. The view of James of Viterbo is similar, except
that the consummation is in the spiritual monarchy of the Pope
alone. In this evolution, the growth of a *jus gentium* is a normal
stage, not a departure from nature, and it marks the gradual
development out of the primitive association of men as gregarious
beasts into a political association under laws and government.
Monarchy is the highest and most developed form of such an
association. The temporal monarchy, in short, is the natural
consummation of man's earthly life. The *sacerdotium* on the
other hand, "is the spiritual power of the Church, conferred by
Christ on its ministers for the administering of the sacraments to
the faithful." In chapter four the author asks which of these two,
the *regnum* or the *sacerdotium*, is prior in time, and he answers,
like James of Viterbo and unlike Egidius, that the state is older
than the true priesthood of the new law. In the next chapter
he asks which is the higher of the two powers in dignity, and concludes that the dignity of the priest is the higher. What is prior
in time is less perfect in nature in all organic developments. But
at this point John introduces an important distinction. Granted
that the priestly power is higher than the royal in dignity, yet it
does not follow that it is higher in everything, nor is the royal
power for that reason necessarily derived from the priestly. The
lower of two powers is sometimes derived from the higher, as the
proconsul's power is derived from the Emperor; but not always.

[1] Goldast, II, p. 108.   [2] *Ibid.*, p. 109.   [3] *Ibid.*, p. 110.

The power of a *pater familias*, for example, is lower in dignity than that of the *magister militum*, but it is certainly not derived from it. Both are derived independently of each other from a power higher than either. So the secular power, though lower in dignity than the spiritual, is superior to it in temporal matters, for it is not derived from the spiritual: both powers are derived immediately from the supreme divine power. It is as unreasonable to argue the contrary as it would be to say that because a tutor rules the members of a household for a nobler end in teaching them virtue, than a physician does in looking only to their bodily health, therefore the physician should be subject to the tutor's control in the prescribing of medicine. As a matter of fact the *pater familias* has installed them both in the household and has not made the physician subject to the tutor in this matter.[1]

"So the priest in spiritual matters is greater than the prince, in temporal matters the prince is greater than the priest, while in general the priest is the greater of the two in proportion as the spiritual is greater than the temporal."

From this the author passes to the point treated at such length by Egidius, the power of the Pope over the property of the clergy and the laity. Over the property of the Church the Pope has no *dominium;* he has the right and the duty only to administer it; he is *dispensator universalis* in regard to all the Church's goods, he has no proprietary right in any.[2] Over the goods of laymen, on the other hand, the Pope is not even *dispensator*, much less lord or owner. He has no rights of any kind with respect to such goods, beyond the exceptional one arising out of the extreme necessities of the Church, in which case he is acting not as an administrator but as a definer of right. The goods of laymen have never been granted to the community as the goods of the Church have been granted to the Church. They belong to the individuals who have acquired them by their labor and industry. These individuals have the only right to such goods, the only power over them, and the sole *dominium* in them, they alone may treat them as their own, no one else has even the power of a *dispensator* over them.

Therefore "*neither princes*" nor popes have dominion or administration of such goods. Even in the cases where the prince may interfere for the preservation of the peace, he does it not as an administrator of the property but as a judge determining what is

---

[1] Goldast, II, p. 113.   [2] *Ibid.*, II, pp. 114–115.

just and unjust either in case of necessity or for the common good. And the Pope likewise, as "general instructor in faith and morals," may interfere in matters concerning the goods of the faithful in cases of necessity and for the common faith, for example in demanding a tithe for defence against an attack of the heathen and prescribing its payment in due proportion. But even in so doing he is only declaring what the law is; he is no administrator.

It is clear then that to have jurisdiction over external goods, to have authority of determining what is just or unjust with reference to them, is not the same as having *dominium* in them. Princes have the former right over the goods of their subjects, but have no *dominium* in them. The Pope has no such *dominium* either; but has he *jurisdiction* as the prince has? Some say so, but it is untrue. He cannot have it from Christ, for Christ as man did not have it himself, and granting that He had it, He never committed it to Peter. Christ had the character of God and therefore king over all created things, but this character He conferred on none, not even Peter. He was also "king of men" in making them sharers in the kingdom of Heaven and by virtue of this his anointed may administer the sacraments. But that Christ as man was king of a temporal realm with royal jurisdiction over temporal goods, that "is absolutely false." [1]

But granted though not admitted, that Christ had a temporal jurisdiction, did He endow Peter and his successors with it ? As man He conferred temporal power directly upon the prince, as man He conferred spiritual power on the priest, and there were some spiritual powers which as man He might have conferred on Peter but did not, such as the power to create a new sacrament. But if it is to be proved that Peter's successor has a temporal jurisdiction an express grant of it must be shown. There is such an express grant of the spiritual power to the priest and of the temporal power to the prince, but none of the temporal power to the priest.

All bishops have spiritual power and the Pope for the sake of unity is supreme in it, but none of them have any authority and dominion over the temporal goods of the laity. The temporal and spiritual powers are distinct, so that neither can be reduced to the other; both come immediately from God. The Pope does not hold his sword of the Emperor, nor the Emperor his of

[1] Goldast, II, p. 117.

the Pope. The Pope does not have both swords, nor a jurisdiction in temporal things, unless it is granted by the prince out of devotion." [1]

John dismisses the papal arguments based on the relation of sun and moon and the scriptural texts concerning the two swords, as merely mystical and allegorical "on which no argument can be based." [2] It is a very able and interesting argument, and in many respects may be considered the first definite statement of the chief principles of later Gallicanism. Its actual influence on Gerson and other Gallican leaders is proved by their own citations.

Before the second phase of this historic controversy was over another issue had been clearly defined which was to have a considerable influence on all subsequent political speculation especially in France, the concrete question of France's political relation to the Empire, involving the more general theoretical question as to the relation of all *regna* to the Empire, and to the Pope through his connection with the Empire.

Innocent III in his decretal *Per venerabilem* took note of the *fact* that the King of France refused to recognize any superior in temporal matters; Boniface VIII also recognized the fact, but denied that it had any basis in *right*. In his confirmation of Albert of Austria as King of the Romans, Boniface claimed the superior right of the Pope but recognized a lower right in the Emperor "temporal and imperial, to rule the whole world" as "Emperor and Monarch over all kings and princes of the earth." Nor is this affected by "Gallic arrogance which declares that it recognizes no superior. They lie, for *de jure* they are and ought to be under the Roman King and Emperor." [3]

All the writers on the side of Philip the Fair took more or less notice of this claim,[4] and tried to refute it, usually by historical arguments including a denial of the validity of the Donation of Constantine, or an explanation of it which excluded the kingdom of France from its operation. But it required more than mere matters of fact to answer the claim of right made by the Emperor over France or by the Pope through the Emperor. Thus a counter

---

[1] Goldast, II, p. 120.

[2] *Ibid.*, pp. 128, 135. The author of the *Rex Pacificus* does the same. Dupuy, *Preuves*, pp. 676–677.

[3] De Marca, *De Concordia Sacerdotii et Imperii*, Paris, 1704, p. 110.

[4] References to these and to earlier expressions of the idea, running as far back as 1280, are given by Rivière, *op. cit.*, "Appendice IV."

theory to that of imperial omnicompetence gradually grew up,
and ultimately became one of the central principles of French
public law, the principle that "the King is Emperor within his own
realm"—*Rex est imperator in regno suo*—a principle that obviously
has a significance not for France alone and its law but for all *regna*
and for the whole development of political thought in the West.
Richard II of England invoked this principle at the end of the
fourteenth century, and Henry VIII made a famous statement of it
in the Statute of Appeals in 1534.[1] "It was this phrase alone" —
Rex est imperator in regno suo — "which could sever the connection between the Empire and Imperial Law, and which could make
arguments adduced for an Emperor applicable to other secular
powers." [2]   Under cover of it, by a theory of prescription or otherwise, independence *de facto* was ultimately translated into a
sovereignty *de jure*.   The importance of the maxim in the history
of western political thought it would be difficult indeed to overrate.
Even at the end of the first third of the seventeenth century Lebret
still considered these Imperial claims based on Roman law sufficiently menacing to French independence to require an elaborate
refutation, and all the forms of the modern doctrine of the equality
of states in international law show distinct marks of the influence
of the theory that a king is an emperor in his own kingdom, and
may be considered in large part an outgrowth of it.

   In an attempt to indicate generally the main currents of political
thought and their course, it is unnecessary to dwell on the controversy between the Papacy and the French kingdom after the
death of Boniface VIII.   The main issues were already clearly
defined.   Probably the things of chief importance in this period
for the history of political thought and institutions were the gradual
definition of the rival jurisdictions of the courts Christian and secular in the various kingdoms of the West,[3] the discussions of the

---

[1] There is an excellent account of the development of this idea in France in Declareuil,
Histoire générale du droit français (1925), pp. 427–441, with references to contemporary
statements and modern discussions.   One of the most important thirteenth century statements of the principle occurs in the so-called *Établissements* of Saint Louis: "car li rois ne
tient de nului fors de Dieu et de lui." — *Les Établissements de Saint Louis*, Liv. I, lxxxiii,
edited by Paul Viollet, vol. ii, p. 135; vol. iv, pp. 22–23.   For the influence of the idea more
generally, see especially C. S. N. Woolf, *Bartolus of Sassoferrato*, chap. iii.   As early as
1208 or before, the canonist Alanus declared "Unusquisque enim tantum iuris habet in
regno suo quantum imperator in imperio."   Rivière, *Le problème de l'église et de l'état*,
"Appendice IV."

[2] Woolf, *Bartolus of Sassoferrato*, p. 379.

[3] See particularly E. Friedberg, *De Finium in Ecclesiam et Civitatem Regundorum Iudicio
Quid Medii Aevi Doctores et Leges Statuerint*, Leipzig, 1861; Olivier Martin, *L'Assemblée de*

Pope's true relation to the rest of the clergy, and the disputes concerning the question of apostolic poverty.[1]

One additional writer of this period probably merits a short notice even in a brief sketch, though his contemporary importance was apparently slight, Pierre Dubois, author of the treatise *De Recuperatione Terre Sancte.* Pierre Dubois is mainly a discovery of the nineteenth century. His personality and his advanced views, economic, social, educational, and political, are of great interest to the modern historian of medieval intellectual history, but on his own contemporaries there is no evidence that his radical opinions had any marked influence. The *De Recuperatione* belongs to the last phase of the great controversy, written between the election of Clement V in 1305 and the death of Edward I of England, to whom the book was dedicated. The author was a civilian and a determined enemy of the papal claims, and his practical proposals were the most radical of his time. He proposed among other things the destruction of the temporal power of the Pope, the secularization of ecclesiastical property, the substitution of schools for convents, the formation of a league of the states of Europe under the leadership of France for the recovery of the Holy Land, and a codification of the civil and the canon law. His book is a remarkable one and a most interesting disproof of the prevailing belief in medieval uniformity, but it had little influence on the actual course or development of political ideas in his own day, the principal subject we are trying to make clearer here.[2]

As a whole the historic struggle between Boniface VIII and

Vincennes de 1329, Rennes, 1908; Paul Fournier, *Les officialités au moyen âge,* Paris, 1880, part ii, chaps. 1 and 2; Leona C. Gabel, *Benefit of Clergy in England in the Later Middle Ages (Smith College Studies in History,* vol. xiv, nos. 1–4) Northampton, Mass.

[1] This question came up at the Council of Vienne, and was afterward debated more than once in the presence of the Popes at Avignon. In 1357 Richard Fitzralph, Archbishop of Armagh, delivered there a famous sermon against apostolic poverty which is reprinted in Goldast's *Monarchia* under the title *Defensio Curatorum* (vol. ii, p. 1391 *et seq.,* edition of 1668). Its principles are developed at greater length in his book *De Pauperie Salvatoris* (of which the first four books are printed as an appendix to Wycliffe's *De Dominio Divino,* edited by R. L. Poole for the Wyclif Society, London, 1890, in which the general theory of dominion as set forth by Egidius Romanus is adopted and expounded at length. From Fitzralph, apparently, it was in turn taken over by Wycliffe himself and made the central point of his philosophic system. For Fitzralph, see the article in the *Dictionary of National Biography* by Reginald L. Poole.

[2] *De Recuperatione Terre Sancte, Traité de politique générale,* edited by Ch. V. Langlois, Paris, 1891. The editor gives most of the known facts about Dubois and his book in the introduction. An interesting estimate is also given by Professor F. M. Powicke, in *Pierre Dubois, a Mediaeval Radical, Historical Essays* edited by T. F. Tout and James Tait, Manchester, 1907, pp. 169–191; another by Eileen E. Power, in *The Social and Political Ideas of Some Great Mediaeval Thinkers,* New York, 1923, pp. 139–166.

Philip the Fair stands out as one of the most significant in all the middle age. In it we find the first important reaction on men's thoughts about political relations — particularly the relations of the *regnum* and the *sacerdotium* — of the new national states whose further development accounts for the greatest difference between medieval and modern history.

The struggle between Pope Boniface and Philippe le Bel had brought to direct issue the opposing claims of Church and State in their most general and most comprehensive form, stripped, for the most part, of considerations drawn from earlier history or from the supposed necessity for a political unification of all Christendom. But the particular problem of the Empire and the Papacy, though narrower in scope, was far older, and the conditions of the early fourteenth century brought on a renewed contest between these two powers as bitter as any of the preceding ones and productive of theories and writings — on the Imperial side especially — which went far beyond anything ever heard of before in the middle ages.

Fully to appreciate the importance of this struggle in its influence upon political thought as a whole it is necessary to bear in mind the more general claims of *regnum* and *sacerdotium* which had appeared already, and also to have some understanding of the peculiar problems which earlier events and theories had added to these in the case of the one *regnum* which was also an *Imperium*. These problems are concerned mainly with the so-called Donation of Constantine and with what was known in the later middle ages as the *translatio Imperii* or transfer of the Empire from the East to the West, a phrase whose various meanings will perhaps become clearer after we have traced some of the controversies which centred about it.

The Donation of Constantine purported to be a document by which the Emperor, in prospect of the removal of his capital from Rome to Constantinople, delivered and relinquished to Pope Silvester "and to all his successors who shall sit upon the seat of the blessed Peter to the end of the world" complete power and jurisdiction over the Lateran and over the *provinciae, loca*, and *civitates* of the city of Rome and all those of Italy "*seu occidentalium regionum.*" [1]   The genuineness of this document

---

[1] Text in Mirbt, *Quellen zur Geschichte des Papsttums*, 4th ed., pp. 107–112; Galante, *Fontes Juris Canonici Selecti*, pp. 89–96. In some of the later texts of the document the particle "or" (*seu*) which connects the phrase covering the territory of the city and of Italy

was seldom impugned during the middle ages, though the papal interpretation of it, the territories included, and even its validity, were often questioned by anti-papal controversialists; but since the critical examination and rejection of it as spurious by Lorenzo Valla in 1439 [1] it has been suspect, and is now regarded practically universally as a fabrication, probably of the eighth century. Nevertheless its importance in the controversy between Papacy and Empire is very great. The pro-papal interpretation of this document was progressive. In the beginning, apparently, it was held to apply no further than to the Exarchate of Ravenna and the other Italian portions of the Byzantine Empire,[2] but during and after the Investiture Controversy not only were these narrow territorial limits vastly extended, but the essential character of the grant itself received a new explanation menacing to the independence of all secular powers in the West, regal and imperial alike. In short, the territories included were held to comprise the whole of the Empire of the West, and it was asserted further that in "relinquishing" them Constantine had made no grant but had merely recognized a dominion which had been in existence before. If the Pope had not in fact exercised authority in this vast territory before the time of Constantine, it was on account of no defect of his right to do so, but only for lack of power, and Alvarus Pelagius and Augustinus Triumphus go even further. The former regards Constantine's surrender of authority to the Pope as an admission on the Emperor's part that he had never had this authority legitimately, because it had not been conferred upon him by the Church.[3] Augustinus says the Donation must be considered not as a gift but a restitution of powers "unjustly and tyrannically" wrested from the clergy.[4]

These far-reaching claims were countered in differing ways by supporters both of the Emperor and the King of France. Sometimes the prior right of the Papacy was denied, as by John of Paris, who attributed all the Pope's secular authority to the concession

with "the regions of the West," is replaced by "and." See, for example, Döllinger's *Die Papst-Fabeln des Mittelalters* (English translation, *Fables Respecting the Popes in the Middle Ages*, New York, 1872, pp. 125–127).

[1] *De falso credita et ementita Constantini donatione.* It follows the text of Lupold von Bebenburg's *Tractatus de Iuribus Regni et Imperii* (pp. 265–378) in the 2d ed. of the latter published at Basel (1562), and includes an introduction, by Ulric von Hutten (pp. 250–264). Both are reprinted in Schard, *De Jurisdictione Imperiali* (1565), p. 734 *et seq.*
[2] Carlyle, *op. cit.*, vol. i, pp. 288–289.
[3] *De Planctu Ecclesiae*, Lib. I, art. xiii.
[4] *Summa de Ecclesiastica Potestate, Questio* I, art. i.

of princes alone.   At other times, the territorial extent of the grant
was narrowed, John of Paris, for example, refusing to admit its
extension to France, others to Germany.   And some even went so
far as to reject the donation as altogether invalid, because it was
beyond the legal competence of any Emperor to dismember the
Empire, though, as has been said, the authenticity of the document
itself was seldom if ever brought in question.

These conflicting claims may possibly be best illustrated here
first by contrasting briefly two writings of the late thirteenth
century, on the papal side the *Determinatio Compendiosa de Jurisdictione Imperii* attributed by its editor to Tholommeo of Lucca,
a noteworthy ecclesiastic, and historian, and the probable continuator of St. Thomas's *De Regimine Principum;* [1] on the imperial
side, the *Tractatus de Prerogativa Romani Imperii* of Jordan of
Osnabrück.[2]   It is interesting to note that they seem to have
appeared at almost the same time and possibly not entirely accidentally.[3]   The views of the *Determinatio* on the Donation are
summed up in the statement that while Constantine did relinquish
the *imperium* to Silvester, it was "not in the nature of a gratuity
but of a surrender to the vicar of the true and proper lord." [4]
Jordan on the other hand is not concerned with the Donation at
all, but he is very much concerned with proving that the *translatio
Imperii* was a transfer to the Germans and not to the "French,"
and that this German *imperium* must be preserved if Christendom
itself is to be saved from destruction.   The Jews, he or his collab-
orator declares, in their madness would have no king but Caesar,
"but I have feared and I now fear that when the Roman Church
shall come to that state where it can say 'we will have no king but
the Pope,' then tribulation will come upon the clergy like that we
know came upon the Jews." [5]   For Jordan and for others who
wrote on the same side at this time, as Mr. Woolf points out, "the
'State' does not really exist.   Mankind or Christendom forms a

---

[1] Edited by Marius Krammer, Hanover and Leipzig, 1909 (*Fontes Juris Germanici Antiqui in usum scholarum ex Monumentis Germaniae Historicis Separatim Editi*).

[2] *Des Jordanus von Osnabrück Buch über das Römische Reich*, herausgegeben von G.
Waitz.   Göttingen, 1868.

[3] The *Determinatio* is placed by Krammer "about 1280 or a little later " ("Praefatio,"
p. ix).   The conclusions of Dr. Wilhelm Schraub would seem to place the *Tractatus* in 1281 or
a little before.   *Jordan von Osnabrück und Alexander von Roes*, Heidelberg, 1910 (*Heidel-
berger Abhandlungen zur mittlerin und neueren Geschichte*, No. 26), pp. 50–62.   It is impossible here to touch on the many doubtful questions connected with this tract.   See Schraub;
and Woolf, *Bartolus of Sassoferrato*, pp. 227 ff.

[4] *Determinatio Compendiosa*, cap. xxvi.   [5] Page 41, edited by Waitz.

single Church, a Christian Republic or People, within which are different nations and kingdoms. Therefore the *Imperium*, for the maintenance of which in German hands they plead so earnestly, is not a universal 'State,' but the 'Gelasian' *Imperium* — a ruling power within the Church. Their thought was unaffected alike by the political theories of the Roman lawyers, as by political theories still newer." [1]

This tract of Jordan of Osnabrück is a good example of what Mr. Woolf aptly calls "the German answer" to the "problem of the Empire," and it is true that for Jordan no Empire but a German one could possibly be the political centre of the *Respublica Christiana*, yet it would be a misinterpretation of Jordan's thought to find in him nothing more than a champion of German "nationality." One cannot read his short treatise without being struck by his deep and disinterested piety and by the fact that it is not for Germany's sake that he pleads for a German *imperium;* it is because God has chosen the German nation to be the champion and savior of the whole Christian world, the only power that can avert or postpone the coming of Antichrist. His outlook may not have been cosmopolitan, but neither was it narrowly nationalistic. The boundaries of his political thought are to be found in the *Respublica Christiana*.

In this respect his tract, and some other defences of the Empire of the same period, fall short of the breadth of view that marks the political writings of St. Thomas and his followers, owing to their acceptance of Aristotelian conceptions, universally applicable even if not cosmopolitan in their original form. There is little if any trace of St. Thomas or of Aristotle in Jordan's political ideas, though it is probable that he wrote after St. Thomas's death in 1274. But by the turn of the century the acceptance of these newer ideas seems to be all but complete. We have already remarked the prominence of Aristotelianism by the side of an older Augustinianism in the powerful defences of papal authority written by Egidius Colonna and James of Viterbo. It is equally prominent in most of the writings on the Imperial side in the early years of the fourteenth century. One of the most important of these is by Engelbert, Abbot of Admont.[2]

[1] *Bartolus of Sassoferrato*, p. 266.
[2] *Engelberti Abbatis Admontensis . . . de Ortu et Fine Rom. Imperii*, printed in Goldast's *Politica Imperialia*, Francofurti, 1614, pp. 754–773. Mr. Woolf gives an excellent summary of the tract in *Bartolus of Sassoferrato*, pp. 278–302.

The immediate occasion of his treatise, Engelbert tells us in the prefatory chapter, was a conversation he had had with some of his friends, "prudent and mature men," in which some of them contended that the Empire was now a complete failure and ought to come to an end, while others thought that the various realms and governments and nations should make war upon it until it was totally destroyed, because from the very beginning its power had been based on injustice and wrong in the subjugation of the various nations and peoples by mere force of arms.   It is interesting that "prudent and mature men" could be found arguing in this fashion in the first quarter of the fourteenth century, and the character and moderation of the answer the author gives to their arguments are no less interesting.

He holds that the Roman Imperium is both necessary and just, and he essays to show this by much the same historical evidence as used by Dante to prove its independence of the Papacy.   His position is very like that of Jordan of Osnabrück, though his exposition of it is more secular, and is influenced profoundly by the thought of Aristotle as well as by that of St. Augustine.   The Empire was not built on injustice, and it is essential to the peace and justice of this world and to the defence of the Church, but there must be harmony and coöperation between Papacy and Empire if the reign of Antichrist is to be averted.   This is the general theme of the treatise.   It assumes the unity of Christendom and the helplessness of the Church without the Empire to defend it, but "outside the Church there can be no *imperium*." [1] The author is no opponent of papal claims, not even an avowed defender of Imperial independence, as Dante was; he is an earnest apologist for the Empire who thinks of Empire and Papacy not as competitors but as collaborators.   It is an important tract; but another more important still in some respects, though not in all, and the most famous of all, is the *De Monarchia* of Dante.[2]

Though Dante was a layman, the political world for whose peace he pleads in the *De Monarchia* as in all his writings, was no less a "Christian Republic" than it was for Jordan of Osnabrück. The fundamental thought of the two men is essentially the same,

---

[1] Cap. xxiii, p. 772.

[2] *Tutte le opere*, edited by E. Moore, Oxford, 1904, pp. 341–376; or the same separately published with an introduction by H. W. V. Reade, Oxford, 1916.   There are several translations and many modern commentaries; among the former the translation of Philip H. Wicksteed in the *Temple Classics* has been found very satisfactory.

as well as the remedy proposed for existing ills, though Dante's Emperor is more the successor of Caesar, Jordan's the successor of Charlemagne, and though the logic and metaphysics of Aristotle mark the way by which one reaches the common goal, reached by the other by a different path. Thus Dante's answer to the "problem of the Empire," which is the problem of Christendom, might in a sense be called "the Italian answer," as Jordan's was the German, but a narrow nationalistic ideal was as foreign to his real thought as it was to Jordan's. It was not Italy of which he dreamed and for which he argues, though Italy was its earthly centre and the successor of Caesar its rightful head; Augustine's magnificent conception of "the City of God" is still the core of Dante's political thought as it is of the thought of most of his great contemporaries. The similarity of his thoughts of Italy to Machiavelli's has often been noted and with justice, but between the two, nevertheless, was "a great gulf fixed." Dante loved Italy as fervently as Machiavelli, but he thought of her as the institutional and spiritual centre of a greater commonwealth of God which had for Machiavelli become meaningless or negligible. His ideal may have been of the past, it may have been, as has been hinted, only a splendid anachronism, but splendid it certainly was, and it might even be questioned whether the acuteness of Machiavelli's cynical observations — if we could only search out the hidden thoughts of men — have really had more practical results in the world of thought and life than the moral grandeur of the glorious dream of Dante.

In the last chapter of the *De Monarchia*, Dante sums up his arguments concerning the burning question of "Church and State" and it may be best to give them in his own words : [1]

"And now already methinks I have sufficiently reached the mark I set before myself. For the truth of that question has been searched out in which was asked whether the office of monarch were necessary to the well-being of the world, and of that in which was asked whether the Roman people acquired empire for itself by right, and also of that last question in which was asked whether the monarch's authority depended from God, or immediately from some other. The truth concerning which last question is not to be received in such narrow sense as that the Roman prince is

[1] Bk. III, cap. xvi, the translation is by Philip H. Wicksteed. The italics are not in the original.

subordinate in naught to the Roman pontiff; inasmuch as mortal felicity is in a certain sense ordained with reference to immortal felicity. Let Caesar, therefore, observe that reverence to Peter which a first-born son should observe to a father, so that illuminated by the light of paternal grace he may with greater power irradiate the world, *over which he is set by him alone who is ruler of all things spiritual and temporal.*"

The age-long duel between *Imperium* and *Sacerdotium* came to a head soon after the close of the similar contest between the *Sacerdotium* and the *regnum* of France in the persons of Boniface VIII and Philip the Fair, in the bitter contest between Pope John XXII and the Emperor Lewis of Bavaria, "the last great struggle between the medieval Empire and the Papacy," [1] in which "for the last time before the Reformation Emperor and Pope engaged in violent conflict with each other." [2]   In it were several new factors which contributed to make it one of the most acrimonious and the most far-reaching of all the phases of this long combat.   One of the chief of these new factors was "the Babylonish captivity" of the Popes of Avignon which dates from the defeat of the Pope at the hands of the King of France.   From that time till the beginning of the last quarter of the fourteenth century the Popes and the papal *curia* were mainly French, largely under the control of the French king, and located in a territory near enough to France to be dominated by her influence. These things could not but add new complications to the relations between Pope and Emperor already strained almost to the breaking point. Another special cause of discord was the question of "apostolic poverty," which split the Franciscan order and forced the Pope to take sides, and thus to drive the *Fraticelli* or Spiritual Franciscans into violent opposition and even into a defensive alliance with the Emperor against him. Added to these were the violent political quarrels in Germany itself, and the vagueness and uncertainty of the constitutional provisions of the Empire concerning the election of an Emperor, which gave an opening for the assertion by the Pope of his disputed claim to render the final decision in case of a division, an opportunity of which he was not slow in availing himself.

It is unnecessary here to retrace the history of the struggle

---

[1] Richard Scholz, *Unbekannte kirchenpolitische Streitschriften*, vol. i, p. 211.

[2] C. Müller, *Der Kampf Ludwigs des Baiern mit der römischen Curie*, Tübingen, 1879–1880, I, p. vii.

between John XXII and Lewis;[1] or to set forth the particular claims of each, of which there were none that had not been asserted many times over. The specific claim of the Empire is well summed up in the famous enactment *Licet iuris*, promulgated by Lewis of Bavaria in 1338: "We declare that the Imperial dignity and power is held immediately of God alone, and that it is approved by right and by the custom of the Empire from of old that after anyone is elected Emperor or King by the Electors of the Empire, unanimously or by a majority of the same, immediately and by virtue of the election alone he is to be treated and styled as true King and Emperor of the Romans, that obedience is due him from all subjects of the Empire, and that he has full power of administering the property and rights of the Empire and of doing the other things which pertain to a true Emperor; and that he requires no approbation, confirmation, authority or consent of Pope, Apostolic See, or anyone else."[2] We shall turn at once to the contemporary writings which furnish evidence of the influence of this phase of the conflict between "Church and State" on the further development of the political thought that underlies it.[3]

Among the earliest of the writings on the papal side was one of the most important, the *Summa de Potestate Ecclesiastica* of the

[1] The fullest account of it is by Carl Müller, *op. cit.*

[2] Text in Mirbt, *Quellen zur Geschichte des Papsttums*, pp. 223–224; Zeumer, *Quellensammlung zur Geschichte der deutschen Reichsverfassung*, pp. 156–157.

[3] The most important of these writings on the Imperial side are to be found in volumes I and II of Goldast's *Monarchia*. Several, coming from both sides, were printed for the first time in Richard Scholz's *Unbekannte kirchenpolitische Streitschriften aus der Zeit Ludwigs des Bayern (1327–1354)*, 2 vols., Rome, 1911–1914, accompanied by a valuable commentary. The chief defences of the Papacy, by Augustinus Triumphus, Alvarus Pelagius, and others, were printed in the fifteenth and sixteenth centuries. The *Defensor Minor* of Marsiglio of Padua was first edited by C. Kenneth Brampton from a Ms. in the Bodleian (Birmingham, 1922), and the first critical text of the *Defensor Pacis* itself was published in 1928 (*The Defensor Pacis of Marsilius of Padua*, edited by C. W. Previté-Orton, Cambridge). Sigmund Riezler's *Die literarischen Widersacher der Päpste zur Zeit Ludwig des Baiers* probably remains the best general account of this polemical literature (Leipzig, 1874), though some of his minor conclusions have been somewhat modified by later research. A list of the major political writings of this period is given in Gierke, *Political Theories of the Middle Age*, translated by Maitland (Cambridge, 1900), pp. lxvii–lxx; and a much fuller one, of great value, by Scholz, *Unbekannte Streitschriften*, vol. II, pp. 576–585. Only a few of the most important books appearing in this list can be dealt with in this outline. Probably the most important of those omitted are the writings of Konrad von Megenberg which were first published in 1914 in Richard Scholz's *Unbekannte Streitschriften*, his *Planctus Ecclesiae in Germaniam* in poetic form (1338), *Streitschriften*, II, pp. 188–248; *De Translacione Romani Imperii* (1354), *op. cit.*, II, pp. 249–345; and *Tractatus contra Wilhelmum Occam* (1354), *op. cit.*, II, pp. 346–391. Konrad of Megenburg was a supporter of the Papacy, but a German and one fully cognizant of the abuses in the Curia. Scholz gives a very satisfactory account of him and his writings in *Unbekannte kirchenpolitische Streitschriften*, I, pp. 79–140.

Augustinian, Agostino Trionfo or Augustinus Triumphus, of Ancona, which was dedicated to John XXII between 1324 and 1328 as Scholz thinks, and printed two or three times before the sixteenth century.[1] There are few significant assertions in this book which had not already appeared in the glosses of the canonists or the writings of Egidius Romanus and James of Viterbo, and for that reason it may be passed here with a notice incommensurate with the popularity it undoubtedly enjoyed in its own day, a popularity probably owing in part to the fact that the book is thrown into the most rigorous scholastic form then prevailing, of determining specific points after an examination of the arguments pro and con. It may be said to be one of the half dozen most influential and important books ever written in which the papal claims are pushed to their furthest extreme. In fact it seems impossible to find any power ever claimed for the Pope which Augustinus does not assign to him in largest measure. His is a power held immediately of God,[2] and therefore a *potestas perfecta* which can lack nothing essential.[3] It is the highest of all powers in dignity, in causation, and in authority, and as a result of this supreme authority the laws or statutes of a king or Emperor can have force or validity only so far as they are confirmed and approved by the authority of the Pope.[4] Like his great predecessors Augustinus considers this jurisdictional authority of the Pope in nature a regal power, a power exercised by Christ and conferred by Him upon his vicar in more noble and excellent form than that of any earthly prince, because in him it extends to the confirming, deposing, and correcting of princes themselves, while they have no more than the administration of it. This, therefore, is no merely spiritual authority : it extends directly to things temporal, and the well-known words of Christ, "Render unto Caesar the things that are Caesar's," are no obstacle. They really mean that we are bound to render to each his due and no more. To the secular prince is due only "a certain legal justice" (*quaedam iusticia legalis*). This is his of right, but merely as the protector and minister of the Church and not otherwise.[5]

[1] The edition used here is the one published at Rome in 1479. A convenient and valuable collection of extracts from the book is to be found in Gieseler's *Compendium of Ecclesiastical History* (English translation), Edinburgh, 1853, vol. iv. pp. 31–34, 73–75, 76, 89.

[2] *De Potestate Ecclesiastica*, Questio I, art. i.

[3] *Op. cit.*, Questio I, art. ii.

[4] *Op. cit.*, Questio I, art. iii.

[5] *Op. cit.*, Questio I, art. vii.

In his discussion of the important question of the obedience due to the Pope, the author distinguishes between the obedience of a Christian, a pagan, and a Jew. Christians are, of course, not bound to obey the Pope if he commands anything contrary to the law of God or the law of nature, but it belongs to no subject to judge whether they are such or no, if not palpably against custom, or the command of God, or the plain precept of the law of nature. If the command of the Pope falls within the sphere of the positive law (*ius positivum*), though contrary to it, or to its usual interpretation, he must nevertheless be obeyed; for every positive law is derived from the Pope, either by his direct promulgation, as the canon law, or by confirmation and approbation, as the civil law. As it is his to establish (*condere*) all the precepts of the positive law, to confirm or to interpret them, so it belongs to him to abolish them all in any part of the world or in the whole of it;[1] and none are exempt from his dominion. Ecclesiastics are subject to it immediately, all laymen through the medium of the lay principality, which is subject to the spiritual superior in obedience, and as a minister.[2]

With pagans it is somewhat different. But they like Christians are subject to the power of the keys, for as Christ had a judicial power (*iudiciariam potestatem*) over every creature, no man may *de jure* withhold obedience to his vicar since none may rightly withhold it from God. Actually or potentially all rational creatures are the sheep of Christ. To say that pagans, because outside the Church, are beyond the Pope's control, is beside the point, for "Church" may mean more than one thing. To the Church in the sense of its judicial power, all belong, good and bad, faithful and infidel. They all have one God, and therefore must have one shepherd who rules in God's place.[3] The limitations which Augustinus finds in the Pope's relations to pagans do not affect his jurisdiction, they arise entirely from the nature of the law applicable to such persons, and his discussion of this point is very significant. Law is of three kinds, eternal, natural, and positive; the first two are created and not destroyed, the third is made and unmade. Of the eternal or divine law the Pope should be *imitator*, because all law, and justice for all, are derived through him; of the law of nature, he should be the *observator*: he cannot change it; of

---

[1] *De Potestate Ecclesiastica*, Questio XXII, art. i. [2] *Op. cit.*, Questio XXII, art. ii.
[3] *Op. cit.*, Questio XXIII, art. 1.

positive laws he should be both "maker and destroyer," according as the needs of the time may require (*lator et innitor pro temporum congruentia*); he may both make and unmake them. Thus as *observator* of the laws of nature he is able, and even bound, to compel pagans as well as Christians to obey it; but pagans, unlike Christians, may not be punished under the eternal or the positive law, "for they receive neither."[1] From such premises the author's conclusions upon the particular questions disputed in his day could not be a matter of much doubt. The only true authority of the Emperor is as defender and agent of the Church, acting under the orders of the Pope, its head. All other imperial authority exercised before the conversion of Constantine was usurped and illegitimate, and the Donation is an admission of the fact. Without papal confirmation, therefore, the Emperor has no authority, and over Imperial elections the Pope has practically unlimited control. The Pope is the supreme temporal lord of the whole world, and all secular rulers are his inferiors, his creatures, and his servants. He is the supreme interpreter and executor of all law and the supreme maker and destroyer of all positive law. And this is as true of the canon law as of the civil. To Augustinus the Church is a *regnum* and the Pope, its king, is an "absolute" monarch not a limited one, absolute in the highest and fullest sense of that word current before the beginning of modern times.

After the appearance of the *Summa* of Augustinus Triumphus the papal defenses apparently most read, and therefore most significant, were probably the *Tractatus de Causa Immediata Ecclesiasticae Potestatis* of the Dominican, Petrus de Palude, or Paludanus, Patriarch of Jerusalem, written about 1329 or 1330 and published at Paris in 1506; and, above all, the *De Planctu Ecclesiae* of the Portuguese Franciscan, Alvaro Pelayo, or Alvarus Pelagius, begun, as the author tells us,[2] in 1330 and finished in 1332, but revised in 1335 and again in 1340. The first part of this important book, which treats of "the nature of the Church, its foundation, jurisdiction, power, and sanctity, and those of the Lord Pope and of the other prelates,"[3] Gierke considers the most extreme of all the pro-papal writings; but the second part, and somewhat the longer of the two, dealing with "the sins of the corrupt members" of the Church,[4] is equally remarkable as a

---

[1] *Op. cit.*, Questio XXIII, art. iv.   [3] *Ibid.*, Lib. II, art. i.
[2] *De Planctu Ecclesiae*, folio cclxx.   [4] *Ibid.*

denunciation, almost as scathing even if not as rhetorical as Petrarch's, of the existing abuses among laity, and clergy both regular and secular, including the papal Curia itself; and it is noteworthy that both these parts could come from the same pen. All further illustrations of papal claims included here will be taken from this book.[1]

The Church is a true *regnum*, for it is community, an assemblage of many of the faithful;[2] it is the *Civitas Dei* which St. Augustine distinguished from the *Civitas terrena*,[3] a monarchy in which the successors of Peter rightfully hold the regal powers of Christ, as his vicars upon earth. As such the Pope is "universal monarch of the whole of the Christian people, and *de jure* monarch of the whole world"[4] (*universalis monarcha totius populi Christiani et de iure totius mundi*), with jurisdiction over it all, temporal as well as spiritual, though ordinarily the administration of the temporal sword is entrusted to the Emperor, the legitimate son of the Church, as its advocate and defender, and to other kings and princes of the world.[5] Alvarus does not agree with those papalists who derive the temporal power solely from the spiritual. They have distinct origins, and the former arises out of the natural inclination of men, and is to this extent derived directly from God, the creator of all. But like James of Viterbo he holds that all temporal power has its only perfection in a special act of God's grace, which does not destroy the work of nature but forms and completes it. Without this grace, all temporal power is unformed and incomplete, though it may be legitimate among the infidels who have no true faith and can have no real justice. For its perfection and completion the true faith is necessary, but not that alone. It requires the approbation and ratification of the spiritual power; for no secular power can be wholly true and perfect if it is not "ratified, approved, and confirmed" by the spiritual, as the unction of kings by the clergy clearly proves.[6] In reality, therefore, there is and there can be but "one principate of the Christian polity," and but one first prince. That first prince is the chief pontiff who is monarch in the ecclesiastical hierarchy.[7] Beneath that princedom, for ends that are incidental and unessential (*accidentaliter . . . ratione*

---

[1] The edition used is the one published by Johannes Clein, Lugduni, 1517.
[2] *De Planctu Ecclesiae*, Lib. I, art. lxi, folio liii a.
[3] Folio lv a.
[4] Lib. I, art. xxxvii, folio x a.
[5] Lib. I, art. xiii.
[6] Lib. I, art. lvi.
[7] Lib. I, art. xl.

extrinsicorum bonorum), there may be various princedoms, but they are subject to it and cannot rightly be separated from it. It cannot be true, therefore, that there is one principate which is spiritual and a distinct one which is corporeal and temporal, for no prince nor Christian subject can possess or acquire anything except in the service of the Christian princedom. Nor is it possible that there should be one prince at the head of the polity and others in control of its administration. In the Christian polity there must be one supreme prince ruling and moving or governing the whole polity. The supreme pontiff himself or through others, of his own authority institutes all who are connected with Christian politics in the administering of the sacraments by which the faithful are set apart and strengthened, and no excommunicate can justly serve in any office or place of authority in the Christian commonwealth. He who concedes that the supreme pontiff has a plenitude of power in spiritual, of necessity concedes the same in temporal and corporeal matters, for the whole of a Christian man is spiritual.

From these things it follows, then, that the ecclesiastical monarch, that is the supreme pontiff, is the first and highest prince, ruling the whole Christian commonwealth completely in respect to everything (*plene quoad omnia*), the spiritual immediately, because more worthy and of higher import, the temporal and outward, because of lesser worth and consequence, through *rectores* and temporal lords.[1] The spiritual power, and the Pope at its head, therefore, includes the temporal, it institutes it, it directs and controls it, and it may judge it. This means that all men and all things which are immediately subject to a temporal ruler are through him subject to the supreme pontiff, and that every power belonging to a temporal ruler belongs also to the Pope, if not in the same way, in a "yet more excellent" one.[2] It is, in fact, a sign of the higher power of the spiritual ruler not to perform these less worthy acts in person, but to entrust them to a subordinate to be carried out at his will — *ad nutum*. "For *nutus* is an indication of will: the spiritual power makes it known that it wishes a penalty to be inflicted upon malefactors; and that *nutus* is a kind of command."[3] But, though it is not customary for the spiritual power regularly to exercise this temporal jurisdiction

[1] *De Planctu Ecclesiae*, Lib. I, art. xl.
[2] *Op. cit.*, Lib. I, folio xliiii b.
[3] *Op. cit.*, Lib. I, folios xlix b–l a.

directly, yet in certain cases — *certis causis inspectis* — he may and he will do so, as Innocent III declared.[1] Alvarus derives the whole of this vast *plenitudo potestatis* from the necessary principle of unity. Christendom is the earthly kingdom of Christ and it must be one. Primarily it is the Church, only secondarily — "accidentally and for outward needs" — is it an Empire and may include *regna*. The Pope is necessarily the head of it all because he is by divine ordination *monarcha* ECCLESIASTICUS; the secular state is only a subordinate department of the Christian common-wealth (*politia Christiana*).

From such premises the deduction is inevitable that temporal rulers are no more than the deputies of the Pope, but a further deduction might be made, which may not be inevitable. The supreme pontiff by virtue of his ecclesiastical authority may appoint, control, judge, and remove all the temporal princes of Christendom. Is not, then, his authority as "arbitrary" over the Church and over Christendom, as it is "absolute" over Emperors and princes? Must it not follow, as Riezler insists, that he "is the source of all right and of all laws, that he can declare to be right whatsoever he wills, and can deprive anyone of his right if to him it seems good." [2] It might indeed seem so. For the Pope, Alvarus repeats, is rightful judge over all and can be judged by none, except for heresy, unless he voluntarily accepts the jurisdiction; and for no crime, not even for heresy, may he be lawfully deprived of the Papacy by a general council of the Church or by any lesser power upon earth. Though his decrees may be contradicted by the whole world, they must be obeyed, if not against the faith; for even the error of the prince creates right: the dignity or juris-diction or power cannot err though the man who holds it may.[3] In the promulgation of law the authority of the Pope is higher than that of the whole Council, and he has the power of a king to enforce what he ordains. He acts in the place of God upon the earth and has a plenitude of power; his will stands in place of reason; what pleases him has the force of law; he may dispense with law, and positive law he may abrogate entirely; he is *legibus solutus*. His judgments are from Heaven and on earth he has no superior.[4]

Yet a pope may be a heretic; only *positive* law is within his

[1] *Op. cit.*, Lib. I, folio xlv a.
[2] *Die literarischen Widersacher der Päpste*, p. 284.
[3] *De Planctu Ecclesiae*, Lib. I, art. iv, vi, viii, xlv.
[4] *Ibid.*, Lib. I, art. xlv.

power to destroy; and there are things entirely beyond his right to dispense. Some hold, Alvarus says, that he may dispense in all cases, even with a rule laid down by the Apostles, because the Pope as vicar of Christ is greater than any Apostle. He himself upholds this doctrine in one specific case on the ground that the power of Peter's successor must prevail against a prohibition of Paul, because Peter himself was greater than Paul; but he denies the power to dispense in another case where the prohibition was Christ's instead of Paul's. In general, he says, no Pope may dispense with the law of God clearly defined in either the Old or the New Testament, nor with the law of nature, and he cannot abrogate the decree of a General Council. It is not within his power so to act as to bring a stain upon the Church universal, and what the holy fathers and Roman pointiffs have decreed as the doctrine of the Church universal must remain unaltered.

If a Pope dispenses with the law without just cause, he commits sin and his dispensation is void in the sight of God, as for example a dispensation harmful to the Church. Alvarus closes his discussion of the dispensing power by quoting two rules laid down by Hostiensis; first, that no Pope may be accused or condemned by man of any crime but incorrigible heresy; and second, that the Pope may dispense in any case not contrary to the faith, provided it does not manifestly induce mortal sin, nor subversion of the faith, nor danger to souls. So against canon law dispensation may be made without distinction; against divine law, only where it is not prohibited, and where no sin is clearly involved.[1]

In our modern eyes, these considerable limitations are likely to seem contradictions of the claim made elsewhere of a *plenitudo potestatis;* and we are tempted to accept one of these to the exclusion of the other, as Riezler does. But to do so is to substitute modern conceptions of law and government for those which really dominate the thought of Alvarus and of all others in his age. We think of law primarily as a command, they did not. As a consequence we fix our main attention upon the penalty imposed by the maker of the law for a breach of it and this we term its "sanction." To the medieval mind, on the contrary, law is primarily reason, and its promulgation is less essential. In fact for most "laws" there was scarcely any definite "sanction" whatever, but they were none the less laws. If, for example, a feudal lord in-

[1] *De Planctu Ecclesiae*, Lib. I, art. xlvi.

fringed the "right" of his vassal, there was usually little remedy but a kind of feudal self-help — the vassal might "rightfully" renounce and disregard his obligations to that lord. There is little of the modern "sanction" in this, but in the vassal's mind there was none the less, a "right" which the lord had violated and that right rested upon principles or precedents which to him were no less than true law.

"If government as well as the individual was under a higher law it followed that governmental acts against the individual might well be illegal. In such case it would be obviously unfair to conclude the individual by the illegal decision of the government in its own favor, and since there was no other agency to judge between them, they were in the same position toward one another as independent states under modern international law."

"John of Salisbury does not seem to have conceived that the community, or *universitas*, could act except through the prince. If action was to be taken against him, it had therefore to be taken as private individual action. . . . The action . . . contemplated against the prince is public action; but public action not taken through the prince cannot be organized action; it can only be action by all or any, that is to say, action by separate individuals. This is the natural outcome of the patriarchal conception of society as an organized hierarchy. . . . Kings and governments and organized communities had no peculiar prerogative to know and enforce that [higher] law; it was binding upon them no less than upon private individuals, and knowledge of it was the result of grace and wisdom and not of official position. If this view was honestly and fully accepted there was nothing inherently objectionable in the idea that a private individual might enforce the law by private action; for its precepts were definite and uniform and were as accessible to private persons as to officials." [1] This admirable statement was no doubt made with secular law primarily in mind, but the same general conceptions were applied in the later middle ages to law of every kind whether it was the law of the State or the law of the Church. When these medieval ideas of law are applied to kingship we get the solution of many things that seem to us strange. For one, it is the explanation of medieval and even some modern ideas of tyranny and tyrannicide. Even

[1] *The Statesman's Book of John of Salisbury,* edited by John Dickinson, New York, 1927, "Introduction," pp. xxx, lxxvi, lxxviii.

such a respecter of law as John of Salisbury may admit, as no reputable modern writer could, that tyrannicide is necessary — on account of the lack of other sanctions and the absence of adequate machinery to enforce them.   All this means that to the medieval mind "government" is mainly an act of interpretation, and our so-called "executive" and "legislative" departments of it are subordinate to what we should term the "judicial."   For Bodin, and for almost all since his day the king is primarily a law-giver; for Alvarus and all of his time, every king is primarily a judge, and we have already seen that it is the kingship of the Pope and not his priesthood which accounts for the vast authority attributed to him in the Christian polity.

In Book I, chapter 10, of his *De Republica*, Bodin tells us that the *primum ac principium caput* of sovereignty is to be able to give (*dare*) law to citizens collectively and individually; in Book I, article 53, of his *De Planctu*, Alvarus says that "the first and highest act of royal power is to *judge*."   Judgment, he adds, "is the right determination of what is just, therefore to judge is to *declare* the law (*ius dicere*).   And since judgment ought to be according to the laws, it pertains to kings who judge to set those laws in order (*componere*) or to accept them as established by others, to promulgate them, and to secure their observance through admonition, fear of punishment, and promise of reward; and, *for this reason* they are called *legislatores*."   Legislation is incidental to adjudication, "the power of legislation depending upon the power of jurisdiction," in the phrase of Nicholas of Cusa a century later.[1]   Augustinus Triumphus is referring to the same current idea when he speaks of the power inhering *ex officio* in every public person to enact *leges* for the government of the multitude committed to his care.[2]   Nor was the conception a new one.   Among the many proprietary rights which the Emperor Frederick Barbarossa enumerated as *regalia*, at Roncaglia in 1158, occurs only one mention of power or authority, the "power to constitute magistrates for the administering of justice."[3]   It is the multitude, says St. Thomas Aquinas, which possesses the coercive power, or a public person to whom belongs the inflicting of penal-

---

[1] "Potestas statuendi dependens a potestate iurisdictionis."   *De Concordantia Catholica*, Lib. II, cap. xiii, Schard, *De Jurisdictione, Autoritate, et Praeeminentia Imperiali*, Basileae, 1566, p. 527.

[2] *Summa de Ecclesiastica Potestate*, Questio xliv, art. 1.

[3] Zeumer, *Quellensammlung zur Geschichte der deutschen Reichsverfassung*, p. 11.

ties, "and *therefore* (*et ideo*) it belongs to him alone to make laws." [1]

The Pope is the sole monarch in Christendom and his chief powers as king are those of a *judex canonum*. When we fully grasp all that this meant to a man of the fourteenth century and succeed in forgetting what it would naturally suggest to a man of today, the apparent contradiction in the statements of Alvarus disappears for us. The Pope is indeed supreme, he has no peer upon earth, his power is absolute, and all the princes of the earth are his mere subordinate officers. Yet his power and authority are based on the law of God, and his acts must conform to that law or they have no validity in the eye of God. "The laws which kings ordain should be such as make men good and virtuous, else they are not laws but corruptions of laws." [2] His authority, however, is divine, and the acts done under it must be accepted, even though wrong, — *error principis facit ius* — unless against the faith.[3] Shall not the judge of all the earth do right? To borrow once more a distinction from Bodin, it would seem that his conception of "royal" monarchy applies with equal force *mutatis mutandis* to the monarchy of the Pope as Alvarus thought of it: it was wholly "absolute," but not truly "arbitrary."

If this is an accurate account of the political ideas of Alvarus and his times, it will be seen at once that very few of these ideas were new. There is scarcely a claim made for the Pope by Augustinus Triumphus or Alvarus which Egidius Romanus, James of Viterbo, or some preceding canonist had not made already; yet these books are of the highest importance, because these older ideas are presented here in a more systematic and elaborate form than ever before and supported by a vast array of precedents and authorities. They are treatises on the constitution of the Church, but much more than that: they are "political" in the strictest sense, because the Church is an aspect of the State; there is and there can be in Christendom no state outside it. And possibly the very fact that the ideas of the generation before are so faithfully reproduced in these books may serve to explain the comparative

---

[1] *Summa Theologica*, Prima Secundae Partis, Quaestio xc, art. iii.

[2] *De Planctu Ecclesiae*, Lib. I, art. liii.

[3] "And yet in the iniquitous law itself insofar as it retains something of the similitude of law on account of the degree (*ordo*) of the authority of him who made the law, in this respect it is even derived from the law eternal. For all authority is from the Lord God as says Romans 13." St. Thomas Aquinas, *Summa Theologica*, Prima Secundae Partis, Quaestio xciii, art. iii.

neglect in after times of one or two remarkable writings of the early years of the century.

When we turn from the defenders of the Pope to the authors on the Imperial side we find among them representatives of several different groups, actuated by a common antagonism to John XXII and therefore favored by Lewis; constitutionalists like Lupold von Bebenburg, Spiritual Franciscans like William of Occam, and — harder to classify, but most radical and in some respects most important of all — the authors of the *Defensor Pacis*. All were employed more or less by the Emperor, and all made common cause with him against the Pope, but some were decidedly more anti-papal than pro-imperial. The last was not true, however, of the first of them to be noticed here, Lupold von Bebenburg, Bishop of Bamberg and former pupil of the celebrated canonist Johannes Andreae at Bologna, whose main motive in writing as he himself confesses was "fervent zeal for Germany his fatherland." [1] His book, *Tractatus de Iuribus Regni et Imperii Romani*, was finished probably in 1340.[2] Lupold contributed few if any new concrete arguments to the discussion of the great question of Church and State. His book is mainly historical in method, but it is a significant indication of the changing views as to the extent and character of the Empire and thus as to its relations with other powers. Like Dante, Lupold is under the impression that he is dealing with questions which his predecessors had never handled, but a comparison of his treatise with that of Jordan of Osnabrück shows that their general position is almost identical, though the later book alone is systematic and comprehensive. "Bebenburg is the first systematizer of German constitutional law, as John of Salisbury is of the law of the world." [3] On the question of Church and State, Lupold follows the general lines of all preceding writings on the Imperial side. He admits to the full the spiritual primacy of the

---

[1] *Tractatus de Iuribus Regni et Imperii Romani*, p. 208.

[2] Hermann Meyer, *Lupold von Bebenburg*, p. 1. The edition of the *Tractatus* used here, which Meyer believes to be the second, was published at Basel without date, but as Meyer thinks, in 1562 (*Lupold von Bebenburg*, p. 93). The first edition was printed in 1508, and the book was reprinted in Schard, *De Iurisdictione* (Basel, 1566, pp. 328–409, followed by another tract of Lupold's, *Libellus de Zelo Christianae Religionis Veterum Principum Germanorum*, pp. 410–465). Of modern commentaries, Meyer's (*Lupold von Bebenburg*, Freiburg im Breisgau, 1909) is the most elaborate. There is another in Riezler, *op. cit.*, pp. 180–192, and still another, short but valuable, in Hermann Rehm, *Geschichte der Staatsrechtswissenschaft*, pp. 182–185. Further discussion is to be found in C. Müller, *op. cit.*; and in Gierke, *Johannes Althusius*, and *Political Theories of the Middle Age*.

[3] Rehm, *op. cit.*, p. 182, note 3.

Pope and denies only his authority over the Emperor in matters strictly temporal. His book is a defence of the Empire, not an attack on the Papacy, but as such it is without an equal in clearness, cogency, and comprehensiveness.

The author begins with a consideration of the nature and effects of the *translatio Imperii*. The transfer of the imperial authority was effected through the coronation of Charles the Great by Pope Leo II in 800 A.D. "By this I believe that a transfer of the Imperium was made from the Greeks to the kings of the Franks, *and as a consequence to the Germans*." [1] But the results of it were little more than nominal. No actual authority was transferred because there was none to transfer. It had all been lost by the Eastern Emperor long before the time of Charles through the conquests of the Lombards and others, and therefore the *translatio* had no effect in exempting Charles from any real subjection and obedience to the Emperor at Constantinople. His own authority Charles obtained by right of succession or by his own conquests; he had it before his coronation as Emperor, and it extended to all the kingdoms or provinces which the kings or Emperors of the Romans now (in 1340) hold, besides others which they no longer possess. [2] Therefore all the Emperors following Charles held these lands by the same right as Charles, and as his successors, by virtue of election by the electoral princes. From this it follows that one chosen king or Emperor of the Romans by unanimous election of the prince electors or by a majority of them, "may immediately and by virtue of that election rightly assume the name of King and administer the rights and property of the Kingdom and Empire in Italy and in all the other provinces of the said realm and Empire"; [3] and that he has the same power there as an Emperor, [4] without any nomination or approbation of Pope or Roman Church. The name of Emperor and whatever right he may have beyond his right as King of the Romans, these and these alone follow upon the unction and imperial coronation; [5] and though they are received *after* and *through* unction and coronation, they come not by *virtue of it*, but by virtue of the translation of the Empire to Charles the Great. [6] Thus Lupold does not claim as some of the imperialists do that the *translatio*, in conferring the

[1] *Tractatus de Iuribus Regni et Imperii*, chap. iii, p. 52.
[2] *Op. cit.*, chap. iv, pp. 52–54.
[3] *Op. cit.*, chap. v, pp. 64–65; chap. vi, p. 78.   [5] *Op. cit.*, chap. viii, pp. 95–96.
[4] *Op. cit.*, chap. vii, pp. 82–83.   [6] *Op. cit.*, chap. xvi, pp. 195–196.

name of Emperor, added nothing but an absolutely empty title : he admits that there are some rights which are strictly imperial. But he does insist strongly on two important points : (a) that the King of the Franks — which now means the King of the Germans — as elected King of the Romans has complete sovereign authority over the whole western Empire merely as successor to Charles the Great and *before* he obtains the additional title and rights of Emperor; and (b) that the name of Emperor and the additional rights connected therewith, though added at the time of his coronation as Emperor by the Pope, are not added because of that coronation, but as a direct result of the original translation to Charles, the predecessor of the reigning King.

Several corollaries to this main conclusion have a direct practical bearing on the contemporary problem of Church and State, and some of them have an historical and theoretical importance which is even wider. In the first place, the Emperor has no superior and no partner in the secular administration; the power of the clergy is ordinarily confined to matters spiritual, and an election to the Kingship is to be finally determined by the prince electors, or by a majority of them, thus excluding the right claimed for the Papacy by some canonists, of deciding in case of every division among them; and this results from the constitution of the Empire based on ancient precedent. Even the kings of Christendom other than the King of the Romans, "who for the most part today do not recognize the Roman Emperor," have no superior in temporal matters except him, and do not hold their kingdoms, their jurisdictions, or their regalian rights, of the Church of Rome or of any other church.[1] The spiritual and the temporal jurisdiction are "distinct and divided," and the one does not depend upon the other.[2] Of the different views concerning the Donation of Constantine, Lupold gives almost the clearest contemporary account that I have seen,[3] but he himself will express no judgment in favor of any. "Which opinion among these is the best, I confess I do not know, but I have said that the decision of this doubtful point ought to be left to my betters." [4]

One of the most interesting portions of Lupold's whole discussion is his reasoning in support of the principle that a majority vote of

[1] *De Iuribus Regni et Imperii Romani*, chap. ix, p. 108.
[2] *Op. cit.*, chap. x, p. 113.
[3] *Op. cit.*, chap. xiii, pp. 164 *et seq.*
[4] *Op. cit.*, p. 169.

the prince electors shall be decisive. He bases this conclusion on the ground that the electors vote not as individuals, but as members of a body which represents the people as a corporate whole. "The *populus* of the Roman Empire may enact law today if the prince is absent or the Empire vacant, for the *populus* is higher than the Emperor and for just cause may depose him." He explains the passage of Justinian's *Code* which concedes the power of promulgating law to the Emperor alone as an exclusion of inferiors, not of the *populus* which is greater than the prince, and the *populus* — "taken not simply as the *populus* of the city of Rome but as the whole people subject to the Roman *imperium*" — this, he says, "I conceive of as including the electoral princes, as well as the other princes, counts and barons of the realm and Empire of the Romans." [1]

One last point may be added. Bebenburg admits that it was zeal for "the land of Germany" (*patria Germaniae*) which first led him to undertake his treatise. The subject matter of it is really the *right* of the German nation to control the Kingdom and Empire "of the Romans," and the chief basis of this "right" is for him, not the transfer of the Imperial title to a Frankish prince, but the *fact* that the Franks themselves had already gained and held the sovereignty of the West, and that this had become incorporated in the constitutional law of the Empire. The additional title of Emperor first came by the act of Leo III to a Frankish prince, rather than to any other, because the Franks were already masters of the Roman people; it did not make them so. And the true successors to the Franks by legitimate descent are the Germans alone. This is the gist of Lupold's historical argument, and one of its chief points of interest for the historian of political thought is the indication it affords of the growing influence of the new nation-states in the political thought of the West. Bebenburg seems to be the first political writer who frankly avows himself a champion of *German* rights, though his position is essentially the same as that of Jordan of Osnabrück. It may perhaps not be too much to add, as Meyer does, that he is "the first author of this time who saw clearly the fundamental distinction between the Empire in the narrow sense, and the government of the world." [2] But if so, it is necessary to note that in doing so Lupold did not

[1] *De Iuribus Regni et Imperii Romani*, chap. xii, p. 149; chap xvii, pp. 200–201.
[2] *Lupold von Bebenburg*, p. 134.

entirely renounce the rights of the German Emperors of his own time over any of the provinces formerly under the sovereignty of the Caesars. Yet on the basis of Lupold's own reasoning, if the Franks by their own efforts could seize and hold the sovereignty in Italy independent of the Emperor at Constantinople, why might not the Kings *of the French* in like manner legitimately secure and maintain in France their own independence of the Emperor at Munich? If the Emperor of the Roman people is and must be a German, what of those kings and peoples who "for the most part today do not recognize the Roman Empire"? The problem of the relations of Empire and *regna* could not be avoided, and Lupold shows that he saw it distinctly.

His own opinion seems to have been that the source of the Emperor's jurisdiction is the *populus Romanus* and that his authority extends *de jure* as far as the Roman people itself extends, and over the whole of it without exception. But *in fact* the King of the Romans is and must be a German actually deriving his authority from an election by the German nation; and Lupold was too much of a realist to blink altogether the other great *fact* in part resulting from this: there are kings and peoples *within* the "Roman people" "who do not recognize the Roman Emperor."

Such startling paradoxes between law and fact are not altogether unlike the modern political fiction under which the British Empire is assumed to be an "*Imperial* Commonwealth" — "of *autonomous nations!*" The modern as well as the medieval combination of fact and law is wholly illogical, both growing out of the juxtaposition of an older law too firmly rooted to be discarded, and a newer state of fact inconsistent with it, but too important to be ignored — the fact of nationality; and both are necessarily temporary in character: the older law must eventually give way when its utter unreality finally becomes too evident. Nevertheless one of these two fictions actually lingered on for centuries till its death in 1806, the other is still playing an important, and — to most minds — a useful part, in the modern political world. Both alike are natural incidents of the general conception of the state as an association held together by a bond of law (*vinculum juris*), and by consent to law (*juris consensu*), which, as we have seen, has been prevalent ever since Roman times. It required no small amount of penetration to see all this as clearly as Bebenburg saw it, so early as 1340.

The difficult question of the actual relations between *Imperium* and *regna* which resulted from the conditions just mentioned was one for practical jurists rather than theorists like Lupold von Bebenburg. The chief attempts to answer it were made by Lupold's great contemporary Bartolus, and — though in a sense widely different — the great lawyers in the service of the French King. The *fact* of French independence of the Empire had been noted more than a century before by Pope Innocent III; and a generation before Lupold another Pope, Boniface VIII, had denied its validity as a matter of law. Lupold himself recognized both positions though he made small effort to reconcile them, but even the recognition, in an avowed defender of the Empire writing before the middle of the fourteenth century, is much.

The obvious, or it might almost be said the inevitable, representative of the Fraticelli among the supporters of Lewis of Bavaria is the famous nominalist, the "invincible doctor," William of Occam or Ockham, so named from his birth-place, Ockham in Surrey. As might be expected of an English member of the Franciscan party condemned of heresy by John XXII, William's main motive in writing his polemics is not zeal for Germany as was Lupold of Bebenburg's, but rather hostility to what he regarded as the unlawful and tyrannical acts of the Papal Curia at Avignon, whether directed against members of his own order, the rest of the clergy, the Emperor, or the laity in general. Lupold was a canonist defending imperial claims, William, a theologian attacking papal abuses. His principal works of political interest are the short *Tractatus de Jurisdictione Imperatoris in Causis Matrimonialibus*,[1] the larger *Decisions upon Eight Questions concerning the Power of the Supreme Pontiff (Super Potestate Summi Pontificis Octo Quaestionum Decisiones)*,[2] the *Compendium Errorum Papae*,[3] the long *Work of Ninety Days (Opus Nonaginta Dierum contra Errores Johannis XXII Papae)*,[4] and longest and most important of all, the enormous *Dialogus*, which though incomplete covers between five and six hundred of Goldast's folio pages.[5] All these have long been known, but they are discouraging in their length and discursiveness. Recently, however, a short "compendium" by Occam of his views on Church and State has been made available

---

[1] In Goldast, *Monarchia*, vol. i, pp. 21–24.
[2] Goldast, *Monarchia*, vol. ii, pp. 313–393.
[3] Goldast, *Monarchia*, vol. ii, pp. 957–976.
[4] Goldast, *Monarchia*, vol. ii, pp. 993–1238.
[5] *Monarchia*, vol. ii, pp. 393–957.

for the first time in the *De Imperatorum et Pontificum Potestate*,[1] written apparently at the very close of his life when he was under the ban of the Pope, probably in 1346 or 1347. This tract gives in small compass the conclusions defended at such portentous length in his longer works, the *Dialogus* especially. It contains "the sum of Occam's political thought" expressed with evident care in clearer and more compact form than in any of his earlier writings,[2] and seems therefore the medium giving most promise of a clear and concise exposition of it here.

After a short introduction in which he makes a remarkable declaration of his intellectual independence — "Evident reason alone, or the authority of sacred Scripture reasonably understood shall weigh more with me than the assertion of the whole world of mortal men" — he plunges at once into the heart of his subject with the fundamental assertion, that Christ in setting up the blessed Peter as the head and chief of the whole body of the faithful, did not grant him such a plenitude of power in temporal and spiritual matters as would enable him to do *de jure* as a matter of course everything not forbidden by divine or natural law, but assigned certain bounds to his power which he might not exceed.[3] It follows, therefore, that papal authority by no means extends regularly to the rights and liberties of others so as to be capable of destroying or disturbing them, especially the rights and liberties of emperors, kings, princes, and other laymen, since rights and liberties of this kind, as in the case of most, are reckoned as among secular things to which papal authority in no wise extends as a matter of course. Thus the blessed Ambrose, commenting on the epistle to Titus says, "The Christian religion deprives none of his right." So the Pope cannot deprive any of their right, especially the right which they hold not from him, but from God or from nature, or from another man; and in like manner he is unable to deprive any of their liberties conceded to them by God and by nature.[4] As Christ did not come to take away from the world its goods and rights, Christ's vicar, who is less than he and in no wise his equal in power, has no power of depriving others of their goods

---

[1] This has been published twice from an apparently unique manuscript in the British Museum, by Richard Scholz, *Unbekannte kirchenpolitische Streitschriften*, vol. ii, Rome, 1914, pp. 453–480, with a brief introduction (*op. cit.*, vol. i, Rome, 1911, pp. 176–189); and by C. Kenneth Brampton, Oxford, 1927.

[2] Scholz, *Unbekannte kirchenpolitische Streitschriften*, vol. i, p. 187.

[3] *De Imperatorum et Pontificum Potestate*, cap. i.

[4] *Op. cit.*, cap. iv.

and rights.[1] If the Pope, by virtue of the power granted by Christ to him, were able, in those things which pertain to him, to make more burdensome for those subject to him the things which are easy, he could lay a heavier burden upon them than they would be bound to bear under the old law; and so the Pope could impose upon Christians a servitude heavier than that of the old law, which he says, "I think, ought to be adjudged to be heresy." [2] The principality of the Pope was instituted for the utility and advantage of its subjects, not for the honor, or glory, or utility, or temporal good of the prince, and so it should rightly be called a principality of service, not of power.[3] In so far as it exists by Christ's ordinance, it extends only to those things essential to salvation and to the government of the faithful, saving the rights and liberties of others, for Christ never entrusted to his apostles a despotic power over slaves, but the far higher power of ministering to free men.[4]

But it may be asked, what are those "rights and liberties of others" ordinarily exempt from the Pope's authority? William's answer is interesting. They include all the rights of non-Christians, which they justly and admittedly enjoyed before and after Christ's incarnation. Under the Christian law of liberty these could not be taken from Christians without making their status lower than that of infidels, and in the case of laymen in particular they include everything necessary to the disposing of temporal and secular affairs. The disposition of temporal things belongs to laymen.[5] To what, then, does the papal authority extend, if not to these? It extends, he says, to the reading, speaking, and preaching, of God's word, to divine worship, and to all the things necessary and proper to Christians for obtaining eternal life, which do not exist among the infidels. These belong to all bishops but in a special sense to the Pope who has a care over all churches. Moreover in case of necessity, or of utility which may amount to necessity, when all those fail to whom temporal matters belong, he might and should mingle in temporal affairs when the culpable and dangerous negligence of others makes it necessary, and this would be held to be a plenitude of power in which the Pope excels

[1] *De Imperatorum et Pontificum Potestate*, cap. iv.
[2] *Op. cit.*, cap. v.
[3] *Op. cit.*, cap. vi.
[4] *Op. cit.*, cap. vii.
[5] *Op. cit.*, cap. ix.

and shines forth, by which he can do *regulariter* or *casualiter* all things recognized to be necessary to the ordering of the faithful. But those things which are not necessary, in any particular case in which they remain not necessary, these the Pope has no power to command, even though they be spiritual matters, lest he should turn the evangelical law into a law of slavery; though he may be able to bring some about by persuasion.[1] The words of Christ to Peter, "Whatsoever ye shall bind," etc., ought to be understood with their exceptions, and that portion of the Pope's power which he derives from human law solely must be understood as extending only as far as the faithful have conceded it, no further. If a doubt arises as to how far that is, the decision must be left not to the Pope, but to him who granted the power or his successor; or else — and this is important — "to the prudence and counsel of a wise man of honest intent, whether he be a subject or a ruler." [2] Moreover the decree of the vicar of Christ need never be feared if it is against divine law or the law of nature, and if all these limitations apply even to a true vicar and pastor, how much the more must they apply to one who is reputed to be a true pastor but is not! [3]

Occam's own conclusions as to the actual extent and limits of ecclesiastical power are conservative enough and his ideal of the Papacy is a very high one; the part of his thought most unusual and most noteworthy is his reservation of the ultimate decision even on the deepest questions of faith and practice to the Gospel alone, and the Gospel interpreted not by the Pope or apparently even by the clergy alone, but by "the discretion and counsel of the wisest men sincerely zealous for justice without acceptance of persons, if such can be found, whether they be poor or rich, subjects or superiors." [4] In many parts of Occam's thought may be seen anticipations of the position of the conciliar party of the next century, in this part an anticipation of something much more radical: it is little less than the "private judgment" acted upon though disavowed afterward by the Protestant leaders of the sixteenth century. Occam's statement of it, however, is no more explicit than the remarkable words of the unknown author of the *York Tractates* nearly two centuries and a half before.[5]

---

[1] *De Imperatorum et Pontificum Potestate*, cap. x.
[2] *Op. cit.*, cap. xi.
[3] *Op. cit.*, cap. xiv.
[4] *Op. cit.*, cap. xiii.
[5] *Ante*, pp. 214–216.

Last, but not least in importance, among the books written on the Imperial side, and one of the earliest of them all, is the remarkable *Defensor Pacis*, which appeared in 1324.[1] The admirable coherence of the general argument running through the whole of this book has led a number of the chief modern commentators on it to the conclusion that it must be in everything but detail the work of a single mind, notwithstanding the well-known fact that two men were marked out for the papal censures and the imperial favors incident to its publication, Marsiglio of Padua and John of Jandun; and these critics therefore attribute the book generally to Marsiglio alone and reduce the collaboration of John of Jandun to proportions relatively insignificant. The evidence on which this conclusion is based is internal entirely, and from the same evidence other investigators have drawn inferences of a very different character. The question of the authorship of the *Defensor* is an open one, of considerable importance in estimating the character of the book as well as its place and importance in political thought, and it may not be entirely ignored. Is it practically the work of Marsiglio alone, or a joint production of his and John of Jandun's; and if the latter, for which parts of the book should we conclude that each author is ultimately responsible? Any answer given can be only personal and tentative in character. Dogmatically stated my own is briefly this: The *Defensor Pacis*, as we have it, Marsiglio constructed, by combining two separate treatises, one an interpretation by John of Jandun on Aristotelian principles, of political institutions in general, somewhat after the manner of the *De*

---

[1] Though a critical edition under the editorship of Richard Scholz has long been promised as a section of the *Monumenta Germaniae Historica*, the only one to appear thus far (1930) is that published at Cambridge in 1928, *The Defensor Pacis of Marsilius of Padua*, edited by C. W. Previté-Orton. All other complete or partial editions in print have now been superseded by this excellent edition based on the manuscripts, and need not be mentioned here. The book has been translated into English only once, by William Marshall in 1535, with the omission of a few chapters and passages for the obvious reason that they were thought to be inconsistent with the royal authority of Henry VIII, or with his title of "Supreme Head in Earth of the Church of England." The modern commentaries are numerous, and an excellent bibliography of them is appended to Felice Battaglia's *Marsilio da Padova e la filosofia politica del medio evo*, Firenze, 1928, pp. 263–270 (*Studi filosofici diretti da Giovanni Gentile*, Seconda Serie, IV). One other paper, omitted by Battaglia, might be added with profit: *The Authorship of the* DEFENSOR PACIS by Miss Marian J. Tooley (*Transactions of the Royal Historical Society*, Fourth Series, vol. ix, pp. 85–106), London, 1926. My indebtedness to many of the papers included in the bibliography just mentioned will be evident to every reader conversant with this subject, especially to the discussion of the question of authorship by M. Noël Valois; but it is possible to refer to them here for the most part only generally instead of specifically.

Regimine Principum of Egidio Colonna or St. Thomas Aquinas. This is the substance of *Dictio Prima,* or the first of the three books into which the *Defensor* is divided. The other treatise was a discussion of the question of Church and State, written by Marsiglio himself. It furnished the material of *Dictio Secunda* or Book II of the *Defensor.* In editing these, Marsiglio prefaced the whole with a short introduction, touched up the text of both treatises here and there by necessary omissions, additions, or changes, wrote a chapter, the last in *Dictio Prima,* to serve as a link connecting the two, and added the brief summary and conclusion which constitute *Dictio Tertia.*

The crux of the whole question really is as to who originally wrote *Dictio Prima.* Two main arguments tell against John of Jandun as its author, the numerous references in it to institutions which might seem to be exclusively Italian, and the complete unity in design and construction exhibited in all parts of the finished work.

On the other hand, one might point to the striking difference between Book I and Book II in manner of treatment, in *provenance,* and in language. On almost every page of Book I occur citations, repeated citations often, of Aristotle's ethical and political works which the writer professes to follow and even to reproduce, and invariably interprets with exceptional knowledge and keenness. Book II, almost three and one half times as long, contains, all told, about twenty direct references to Aristotle's works, only three of which are to the *Politics.* This great difference is, of course, accounted for, and possibly sufficiently, in Marsiglio's own statement that "Church and State" constitute a problem which Aristotle never considered.[1] But Book I is also full of some strange unidiomatic phrases corresponding exactly with those in William of Moerbeka's Latin translation of Aristotle's *Politics.*[2] These

---

[1] *Defensor Pacis,* I, i, 3; I, i, 7; I, xix, 3.

[2] The strangest as well as the commonest of these is the use of the Latin *conferens* as a mere adjective and even as a substantive, as for example "non debent communia conferentia impediri vel omitti" (I, xii, 5). Other political writers of the time occasionally show the same peculiarity, though usually less often. See, for example, Occam, *Dialogus* (Goldast, *Monarchia,* II, p. 794), where he speaks of the royal monarch as ruling "propter commune bonum, et non principaliter propter propriam voluntatem et conferens"; or Egidius Romanus, *De Regimine Principum,* Bk. III, Part i, chap. iv, in a passage proving that man is superior to the lower animals on account of speech by which "distincte significatur quid conferens, quid nocivum, quid iustum, quid iniustum." All these follow Aristotle in their thought and almost all knew him chiefly if not entirely through the medium of William of Moerbeka's translation, which is much more literal than literary. This particular expression and a few others apparently come from this source. In the translation of the *Politics,*

are almost totally lacking in Book II, but the statement of Marsiglio just mentioned might conceivably be accepted as adequate explanation of this fact also. Lastly, the supposed "Italianate" character of the institutions described in Book I, although there are undoubtedly some very close parallels in Italy, turns out on examination usually to differ in no very important way from the political institutions and ideas prevalent at the time in France or in any other of the more advanced parts of the West; and where differences do occur they seem more often to come from Aristotle than from Italy. Some of these points may receive incidental corroboration later.

Now John of Jandun was a Frenchman and he was also one of the most celebrated of Aristotelian scholars, whose various commentaries on Aristotle were in every one's hands then and are not entirely unknown even now; and he undoubtedly participated in the papal censures and the Emperor's approval. The Italian Marsiglio, on the other hand — to judge from his other surviving writings — was neither specially versed nor deeply interested in Aristotle, and his style is free from the peculiarities noted above.[1] It was Book II of the *Defensor*, the work of Marsiglio, whose conclusions against the Church alone directly touched the great controversy of the age, which naturally attracted the chief attention of contemporaries, and this in time may easily have given rise to the habit of referring to the entire work as Marsiglio's. But be this as it may, it in no sense explains away, rather it tends to accentuate the fact that both men while they lived were sharers in equal degree in the penalties and the rewards which directly resulted from the publication of this book.

To contemporaries *Dictio I* of the *Defensor* may have been arrest-

---

conferens simply stands for "συμφέρον." For example, "ὁ δὲ λόγος ἐπὶ τῷ δηλοῦν ἐστι το συμφέρον καὶ τὸ βλαβερόν " is rendered by William of Moerbeka "Sermo autem est in ostendendo conferens et nocivum." *Politics*, I, 2, 10, edited by Franz Susemihl, Lipsiae, 1872, p. 9.

[1] For example, in the *Defensor Minor*, written by Marsiglio some time after the appearance of the *Defensor Major*, there is not a single instance of the peculiar use of the word *conferens* just referred to, although a small portion of the work deals with the same subjects discussed in *Dictio I* of the larger treatise, where it occurs so frequently. There is but one reference in the *Defensor Minor* to any writing of "that famous philosopher called Aristotle" (*The Defensor Minor of Marsilius of Padua*, edited by C. Kenneth Brampton, Birmingham, 1922, p. 41) and this is a reference to the *Nicomachean Ethics*. Aside from the occurrence of specific peculiarities like the one mentioned above, style is a very uncertain criterion in matters of this kind, and yet I must record a distinct impression of a much closer resemblance in the *Defensor Minor* to the style of *Dictio Secunda* of the *Defensor Major*, than to that of *Dictio Prima*.

ing chiefly as a preliminary to the argument of the part following, but for us today it has a great added importance of its own as one of the most interesting of all medieval treatises on pure politics. After an account of the growth of political institutions which closely follows Aristotle, the author comes to his main theme, the analysis of political relations and a description of the human institutions by which they are controlled. Following Aristotle, the State is conceived of as a natural whole composed of elements — *partes* in the words of William of Moerbeka — whose functions combine for the attainment of their common end, the life and the good life of the whole; and these elements or *partes* are the same economic or social classes, six in number, as enumerated by Aristotle, agriculturists, artisans, warriors, fiscal officials, the priesthood, and last and most important, the *pars iudicialis seu principans et consiliativa*.[1] The material cause of these *partes* or functions (*officia*) in the state is to be found in the natural inclination of men for one pursuit or another, the formal cause lies in the precepts or commands of the moving cause which consists of "the minds and wills of men," and the immediate or efficient cause in almost all cases is, in the phrase of William of Moerbeka, the *legislator* or *legislator humanus*. This *legislator* creates, distinguishes, and separates these various classes or orders, by first forming or establishing the ruling class or *pars principans;* and then, through it as an instrument, moulding all the others, including the *sacerdotium* or priestly order.

The ruling part thus set up by the *legislator,* and referred to by the author under various names as *pars principans, principativa, iudicialis, consiliativa, principatuum,* or simply as *principatus,* may be either well tempered — ruling in the interest of the subjects, — of which there are three varieties, royal monarchy, aristocracy, and a Polity in which each citizen participates in his turn in government according to station, faculty, or condition; or it may be "vitiated," as in a tyranny, oligarchy, or democracy. Democracy is a form of rule in which the mob or the mass of the poor establishes a *principatus* and rules alone against the will and consent of the rest of the citizens and not for the common good in proper proportion.

Every form of government is therefore created by the ordinance of the *legislator*, whether that government be good or bad, monar-

[1] Compare Aristotle's *Politics*, III, i, i.

chical, aristocratic, or something else. But the author is thinking of his own time primarily and is therefore concerned almost wholly with monarchy, and monarchy as he conceives it truly to be, not a tyranny, nor even a *principatus despoticus*, but *regal* monarchy, a well-tempered form of government established by the *legislator* under forms of law framed for the common good of the subjects. The monarch is the administrator or ruler, but the establishment of both ruler and rule is the work of the *"legislator,"* who is also *"principatuum institutor."* Even hereditary monarchy, though inferior to elective, is an institution "chosen" by the *legislator* for particular reasons. In a "royal monarchy," as well as in other forms of government, the *pars principans* is the ruler or administrator created and chosen by the *legislator* "to regulate the political or civil acts of men," but in this most perfect of all human governments, to do so only according to the rule which is and ought to be "the form" of the ruling office. This rule or "form" the *legislator* alone can establish, and it is commonly called *law (lex)*, whether it consists of custom or statute, and in all perfect communities it is assumed to be self-evident. Nevertheless, in its most proper meaning, it is a coercive command proceeding from the *legislator* alone, and binding upon ruler and subjects alike, by which all judgments shall be determined if possible, instead of by the arbitrament of a judge.[1]

It thus appears that the source of all political authority, the ultimate *institutor* of all magistracies, "the effective cause of the laws," is what our author calls the *legislator*, or sometimes the *legislator humanus*. In chapter XII he tells us who this *legislator* is. "We declare, according to the truth and the opinion of Aristotle, Politics III, chapter 6, the *legislator*, or prime and proper effective cause of law, to be the *populus* or body of citizens, or the dominant portion thereof, through its choice or will expressed

---

[1] The exact contemporary meaning of such words as "tyrannical," "regal," "politic," and "despotic" must be kept clearly in mind if one is to understand the various distinctions drawn in the *Defensor Pacis* or in other political writings of its time. One distinction especially, drawn by them very sharply, between a "tyrant" and a "despot" has become so blurred as to be almost non-existent now.

This change is comparatively recent, apparently the result of the egalitarian principles of the period of the French Revolution. Before that time a "despot" could lawfully rule men as slaves, but he was no "tyrant" unless he abused them in his own interest instead of theirs. This depravation of the "despot" had apparently not become common even as late as Bodin's time though his definition is colored by the conceptions of feudal law. The Greeks in the period of their freedom commonly applied the word to the gods. In Appendix II I have printed a few extracts which illustrate these medieval distinctions more clearly than any modern commentary can do.

verbally in a general assembly of the citizens, commanding or determining that something be done or not done which concerns the civil actions of men, under a temporal punishment or penalty — I say 'the dominant portion' (*valentiorem partem*), having in mind the number and the quality of the persons in that community for which the law is enacted — whether the body of the citizens aforesaid or its dominant part does this directly and in its own person, or entrusts the doing of it to some other person or persons." In the latter case those persons to whom it is entrusted are not and cannot be the *legislator* properly speaking: they are such merely *ad hoc*, and subject to the authority of the original *legislator*.[1] In every case the establishment of the authority of human laws belongs solely to the body of citizens, or the dominant part of it which stands for (*repraesentat*) the whole, because it is seldom possible or convenient for the entire body to meet together. If one person or a few of the citizens by their own authority were to make a law for the whole body, they would be despots (*despotes*), and the government would be what Aristotle termed a despotism or servile dominion (*servile dominium*); it would not be a government of and for free men, and free men would obey it either grudgingly or not at all.[2] "The things that may touch the advantage and disadvantage of all ought to be known and heard by all in order that they may be able to secure the advantage and avoid the opposite."[3]

---

[1] *Defensor Pacis*, I, xii, 3.

[2] *Op. cit.*, I, xii, 6.

[3] *Defensor Pacis*, I, xii, 7. "Quae igitur omnium tangere possunt commodum et incommodum, ab omnibus sciri debent et audiri, ut commodum assequi et oppositum repellere possint." This should be compared with the phrase of Edward I of England in his writs for the Parliament of 1205 issued to the archbishops, "Sicut lex iustissima provida circumspectione sacrorum principum stabilita, hortatur et statuit ut quod omnes tangit ab omnibus approbetur, sic et innuit evidenter ut communibus periculis per remedia provisa communiter obvietur." (Palgrave, *Parliamentary Writs*, I, p. 30.) The "lex" referred to in these writs comes from Justinian's *Code*, 5, 59, 5 — "ut quod omnes similiter tangit, ab omnibus comprobetur," but it has no reference to political matters, merely directing that where "*co-tutores*" have been appointed under a will or otherwise their joint action is necessary. Boniface VIII in the concluding title to the *Sext*, *De Regulis Juris*, in *Regula* XXIX, quotes the same law — "Quod omnes tangit, debet ab omnibus approbari." The *Sext* was added to the corpus of canon law in 1298, three or four years after the issuance of Edward I's writs. It is interesting, and entirely characteristic of the late thirteenth century, to find this private law provision thus used in a new and a political sense. In the fifteenth century Nicholas of Cusa invokes it as an argument for the authority of a General Council of the Church. (*De Concordantia Catholica*, Lib. III, "Praefatio," Schard, *De Jurisdictione*, p. 603.) I cannot express too strongly my dissent from the view of the late Professor G. B. Adams, when he says, "No weight should be allowed . . . to the quotation of the maxim. . . . Some one who was writing writs in the reign of Edward had a love for proverbial and banal phrases and a very good opinion of his own

This Chapter XII of *Dictio Prima* is probably the most interesting and important in the whole book, and notwithstanding the very emphatic form of the author's statements, modern commentators have found in it a number of things to differ about. To take the easiest first, the author — usually assumed to be Marsiglio — has been hailed as an advocate of the modern political expedient of assuming, contrary to fact, that a majority of the members or units in a political body constitute the whole of that body — the "majority principle"; and the author's phrase, *"valentior pars,"* is therefore translated "the majority." Many things in the context make this improbable, and, in my opinion, the corrected text of Mr. Previté-Orton now shows it to be impossible. "I call it *'valentiorem partem,'"* says the author, "having in mind the number *and the quality* of the citizens." The additional words "and the quality" (*et qualitate*) were omitted in all the texts printed before 1928. We now know that they were included in most of the manuscripts, and in all of the best of them. I have, therefore, with little hesitation translated these words by the phrase "dominant" part instead of "major part," or "majority." In fact this is not a modern touch at all, it is strictly medieval in character and antique in origin, corresponding in its nature much more closely to the *maior* ET SANIOR *pars* of a cathedral chapter which took account of "quality as well as number," in determining the election of a medieval bishop, than to the mere numerical majority which enacts a law in the name of a modern legislative body.[1] This author is not thinking in terms of modern individualism to which the majority principle belongs, but has in mind the *populus* as a medieval *universitas*, in which quality is considered as well as number: he conceives of the *populus*, like Lupold of Bebenburg, "as including the electoral princes, as well as the

Latin style." *The Origin of the English Constitution*, p. 336. Mr. Adams himself gives English instances beginning as early as 1225 and others might easily be added. He seems to regard these frequent contemporary expressions of the idea as proof of its "banal" character! For an interesting instance of the use of the maxim in 1249, see note 1 below. There is another equally clear in the statutes of the English Benedictines in the year 1225. Dugdale, *Monasticon* (ed. of 1817), vol. i, l. See also Matthew Paris, *Chronica Majora* (*Rolls Series*), IV, p. 37 (1240).

[1] Compare the following passage from the statutes of the Benedictine order in England, dated 1249: "Moreover it has been provided that if any business shall arise in the realm which touches all the prelates of monasteries, when this comes to the notice of the heads, they shall call the prelates together if it can be done; but if not, they shall call those who, on account of the character of the business, they think ought to be called, so that what touches all should be done by all or by their *senior pars.*" (*Matthaei Parisiensis Chronica Majora* (*Rolls Series*), vol. vi. (*Additamenta*), p. 183.

other princes, counts and barons of the realm and Empire of the
Romans." [1] Thus the members of a general council, composed
of important men, as the *pars valentior* of the Christian *populus*,
may "represent," or act for the whole, just as the electoral princes
act for the Empire, or the Roman Senate in place of the whole
populus. The *pars valentior* is in fact in much closer correspondence with the anti-democratic ideas of Aristotle than with the
political conceptions of our modern time. The author of *Dictio
Prima* agrees with Aristotle in designating democracy as a "vitiated" form of government, and he does it for precisely the same
reason: the multitude of the poor rules the whole body of the
people "not according to the proper proportion" (*secundum pro-
portionem convenientem*).[2] Absolute, not proportional equality,
is the essential doctrine of modern democracy and it is implied in
the principle of majority rule. It was as abhorrent to the author
of *Dictio Prima* as to Aristotle himself; he has in mind *the quality*
as well as the number of the citizens. This *pars valentior* is no
mere numerical majority. But neither is it any one of the six
partes or classes, agricultural, artisan, etc., into which the state is
divided according to the dictum of Aristotle, although the author
uses the same word, *pars*, here as he did for them. The context
shows that *pars* is used here in a more general sense to mean a
definite portion of the *populus*, which by consent of all may act
for (*repraesentare*) it all, because it is difficult or impossible for
all to agree on anything. In this Mr. Previté-Orton sees a very
close parallel to some medieval Italian institutions, and so it is;
but the parallel to the relations between the Roman Senate and
Comitia Centuriata in the later Republic is even closer. Justinian's
Institutes tell us almost in this author's exact words, that *Senatus-
consulta* were allowed to have the force of law because of the incon-
venience of convoking the whole *populus*,[3] and we know from other
references that Roman constitutional history furnished many of

[1] *Ante*, pp. 290–291. Early in the fifteenth century Cardinal Zabarella makes use of the
phrase, *pars valentior*, in such a way as to leave no doubt that it means for him, as I think
it does for the author of Book I of the *Defensor*, "the representative part," which in a
general council of the Church is *pars potior*. *De Schismatibus authoritate Imperatoris
tollendis*, Schard, *De Jurisdictione*, p. 689. Such a "part" must not only be large but it
must be made up of "representative" men.

[2] *Defensor Pacis*, I, viii, 3.

[3] *Institutes*, I, 2, 5; *ante*, p. 128. The reason as given in the *Defensor* runs, "quoniam
non facile, aut non possibile, omnes personas in unam convenire sententiam." (I, xii, 5).
The reason as given in the *Institutes* is thus given: — "*ut difficile sit in unum eum* [*populum
Romanum*] *convocare legis sanciendae causa*."

the precedents for *Dictio Prima* and that Cicero was one of its writer's favorite authors.[1]

Even more disputed than the meaning of the *pars valentior*, and probably more important practically, is the exact sense in which we must take the term *legislator* which this author uses so frequently. From the whole context it is clear that "legislator" is a very bad translation of the Latin *legislator*. The *legislator* is *principatus institutor* [2] as well as *legis lator*, and the *lex* which proceeds from him has little in common with the annual output of a modern "legislature"; the author even speaks of it as *forma principantis*,[3] which might be translated without much forcing as "the frame of government." He clearly has in mind something very different from our conception of the routine output of a regular law-making organ of the state. It may be of some help to note that *legislator*, like so many other technical terms used in *Dictio Prima*, is a word regularly used by William of Moerbeka, and in this instance used always to translate Aristotle's νομο-θέτης. Now the Greek *nomothete* was not a "legislator." Aristotle sometimes applies the term νομο-θέτης to individual law-givers like Solon, Lycurgus, or Cleisthenes, and William calls them *legislatores*. Moses no doubt was one. The *legislator* is primarily the *institutor* of the government and the framer of the main rules under which it must be conducted. A clear-cut conception of such a "constituent" function, distinct from those of every-day government, was habitual among the Greeks as it is today in the United States or on the continent of Europe. Under the Roman constitution, however, the two functions were more or less fused as they are in the modern British constitution, and in post-Roman times the two ideas tended to coalesce as well. During the middle ages *consuetudines* tended to take the place of *leges* in the normal con-

[1] Rehm rejects the view of Bezold, Riezler, and Merkel which, like that of Previté-Orton, ascribes to Italian influence most of the departures from Aristotle found in the *Defensor*. He himself considers the constitution of the Church the chief source of these. *Geschichte der Staatsrechtswissenschaft*, pp. 190–191.

There can be no doubt that the author was primarily interested in the solution of the practical problems of his own day, or that his proposed solution of these specific problems was deeply influenced by existing ecclesiastical practice and institutions, such as the election of bishops by the *maior et sanior pars* of a cathedral chapter, or the convocation of a general council composed of or "representing" all the faithful, as proposed by Occam and other contemporaries; but for the ultimate origin of most of his chief political conceptions — insofar as these are a departure from Aristotle — the author's own statements would seem to me to point to the institutions of republican or imperial Rome rather than to the institutions of the Church or to any other source.

[2] *Defensor Pacis*, I, ix, 10.   [3] *Op. cit.*, I, x, 1.

ception of "law," and one effect of this no doubt was to push still further into the background the distinction we now draw so clearly between the framing of a constitution and the enactment of a statute. As we might expect, then, the general meaning of *legislator* in *Dictio Prima* is plain enough, and it is mainly Aristotelian in origin as the author declares, but in its application we frequently find some apparent uncertainty or obscurity which may be attributed to later and quite different habits of thought.

The *legislator* institutes the *pars principans*, and draws up the rules under which it in turn establishes the other *partes* in the state, and continues to rule them when so established.[1] The *pars principans* is thus the supreme ruler;[2] in a medieval kingdom it is the king. In the medieval king we have as a consequence, to all intents and purposes, the equivalent of Aristotle's *politeuma*, but a *politeuma* with a difference.[3] Aristotle thought of it in political terms, and this to him meant ethical, social, and economic terms chiefly. The author of *Dictio Prima* thinks of the *pars principans* only as an organ of the state performing a particular function. To Aristotle the *Politeuma* is the constitution, because the ruler or group of rulers moulds or shapes the whole state according to his own peculiar views or doctrines. In the *Defensor*, the supreme ruler moulds them also. He "institutes the rest of the offices or parts of the state," but he does so only "as an instrument," "by the authority of the *legislator* conceded to him," and "according to the form handed on to him" by the *legislator*, namely the law.[4] This is a considerable difference. Aristotle's *politeuma* is the master of the state, the *pars principans* of the *Defensor* is its "instrument," an organ of the *populus* established to perform a particular function or office (*officium*). In all well-ordered states Aristotle of course recognizes that the ruler will be guided by law, but it is law in the abstract. For this author, the supremacy in such a state is a supremacy determined and controlled by "the constitution." He is thinking in terms of law,

---

[1] *Defensor Pacis*, I, xv, 4.

[2] Its authority is the equivalent of Aristotle's τὸ περὶ τὰς ἀρχάς. See Rehm, *Geschichte der Staatsrechtswissenschaft*, p. 189.

[3] William of Occam makes a very clear identification of Aristotle's *politeuma*, which he calls *policernia*, with the *pars principans*. "Principans autem in civitate aliquando vocatur ab Aristotele *policernia*. *Policernia* autem secundum quosdam tres habet significationes. Primo autem significat impositionem ordinis politiae. Secundo impositorem ipsius. Tertio significat ipsum ordinem impositum, qui est politia, et ita *policernia* in una significatione idem est, quod Dominus et principans in civitate." *Dialogus*, Goldast, *Monarchia*, II, p. 794.

[4] *Defensor Pacis*, I, xv, 4.

not of politics merely. His conception of the state is legal and corporate where Aristotle's was natural and organic.[1]

The *pars principans* is therefore the instrument of the *legislator* instituted to perform a particular function. But what function? The function, says the author, of *regulating* "the political or civil acts of men." [2] What this means is further shown by the phrase, *iudicialis seu consiliativa*, used by him as equivalent to *principans*.[3]

It has been said that the *Defensor* anticipates our modern distinction between the legislative and the executive parts of government, and that the *pars principans* is the "executive." This is true only in a sense so different from our own that it is hardly true at all. The *officium* or function of the *pars principans* was not that of a modern "chief executive," it was, in a word, rather the imperfectly differentiated function of a medieval king. We have already seen something of what that function was, and it need not be repeated. The king is *pars principans*, and this is called *pars iudicialis seu consiliativa;* nowhere *pars executiva*.

Most of the mistakes made in interpreting this interesting political treatise are the result of reading into its words a modern meaning which was never there. There is nothing in it of democracy, nothing of majority rule, no "separation of powers"; but it is none the less interesting on account of their absence. It is a great deal to find at such a time so comprehensive a treatment of government, and one in which the king is so clearly the servant of the people, and this dependence of the prince upon the law and upon the people as the source of law, the author does not consider a mere academic matter as it was under the later Roman Empire. He recognizes that the power to regulate all the civil actions of the citizens carries with it the danger of an abuse of this great authority which may render the government a despotic one (*principatus despoticus*) or free from the restraint of law, and the life of the citizens therefore servile, or subject to arbitrary will. To prevent such an abuse of power, the *legislator* has authority always to correct and punish the *pars principans* or prince, even to the extent of removing him from office, either by its own direct act or through the agency of another whom the *legislator* appoints for this purpose; but such correction or punishment should be according to the gravity of the offence, and meted out if possible according to

---

[1] On this see Rehm, *op. cit.*, pp. 187–191.
[2] *Defensor Pacis*, I, x, 2.
[3] *Op. cit.*, I, v, 1.

a law already determined. If the latter is impossible, however, the punishment may always be at the discretion of the *legislator* (*secundum legislatoris sententiam*).

Though typically medieval in most respects, this provision shows our author to be the most modern of all theorists before the period of the Councils in one.

He seems to be almost the first writer who has clearly in mind, as a perfectly normal feature of monarchy, a preference for something like a modern "limited monarch," with another governmental organ independent of the prince clothed with authority to judge him, though it must be noted that the organ in this case is an extraordinary one called into existence only in exceptional circumstances and used even then merely to curb acts in excess of or abuse of authority, not to control legitimate acts within it.

It is clear from all this that the prince is the servant as well as the creature of the people. But he is a servant entrusted with enormous power, and while the great limitations just indicated affect the tenure of this power or a wrongful use of it; they put scarcely any limits to its legitimate extent. The prince is entrusted with the entire civil government of the state, and this clothes him with a lawful authority which, though he may not exceed it, reaches to every civil act of every man high or low, ecclesiastical or lay. Under this theory the clergy are as much one of the "other parts" of the state "instituted" and "regulated" by the king, as agriculturists or artisans. Their only legitimate function includes preaching, teaching, and the sacraments, with which the secular ruler is not concerned; and in all "civil and political" matters they are as much subject to the secular laws and the secular ruler as any of the other "parts" of the state; while in the making and the enforcing of these laws, they have as clergy, no part whatever. The Church is really a department of the State, the exact converse of the contemporary papalist view. It was this portion of the political construction of *Dictio Prima* which furnished the basis for the main argument of the part immediately following.

Three main fundamental assumptions underlie Marsiglio's argument in *Dictio Secunda*,[1] first, the normal political doctrine of his day, that the whole of Christendom is comprised in a single

---

[1] For a valuable summary of the whole argument of *Dictio Secunda*, see Ephraim Emerton, *The Defensor Pacis of Marsiglio of Padua*, Cambridge, Mass., 1920 (*Harvard Theological Studies VIII*), pp. 32–71. Nothing is possible here beyond a brief analysis.

Christian commonwealth which is at once an Empire and a Church. Therefore, "the body of Christian citizens" (*civium fidelium universitas*) which is the equivalent of "the people" (*populus*) in it, is the same body of citizens (*universitas civium*) or people which in *Dictio Prima* was regarded as the seat of final authority in any state; and thirdly, the political principles upon which that state is based in *Dictio Prima* are principles applicable to Christendom, as fully in its ecclesiastical as in its strictly secular aspect. We must, therefore, expect to find, in the principles laid down in Book I, the true constitution of both "State" and "Church," and the true basis for a proper solution of the problems of each.

The Church is often defined wrongly but in its true and original meaning it is nothing else than "the body of the faithful believing in and calling upon the name of Christ" (*universitas fidelium credentium et invocantium nomen Christi*).[1] Marsiglio recognizes as fully as James of Viterbo that this *Ecclesia* or Church is a true *regnum*, and that its government is monarchical and regal; he even admits that the Bishop of Rome is in a limited sense supreme within it in the matters within his lawful competence. It is a Christian commonwealth. But it is none the less a commonwealth, and in every commonwealth the only source of authority must be the "body of the citizens" (*universitas civium*); if this commonwealth happens to be one existing among Christians instead of infidels, this body will be the "body of Christian citizens" (*universitas civium fidelium*), and that is all: in every case the *populus* is the sole source of every law affecting the civil acts of men, and the prince is the supreme agent in its administration. Where, then, is there left any legitimate sphere for the *clergy*? Is there, after all, any real difference between clergy and laity? Marsiglio's answer to this is one of the most important parts of his book. The law under which any act must be judged is either divine or human, and law of either of these two kinds, as well as any particular judgment based upon law, may be regarded in one of two ways; first, as the "science or doctrine" determining "what is just or unjust, advantageous or injurious," or secondly, as "a command enforceable by penalty or reward."[2] All judgments based on an existing law must include a determination of what that law is, and this should follow the opinion of those skilled in the particular science or doctrine involved. In a matter concerning the metal

---

[1] *Defensor Pacis*, II, ii, 3.   [2] *Defensor Pacis*, I, x, 4.

of a vase, we should trust to the judgment of a smith, if it is a question whether one is a leper or not, we ought to leave the decision to a physician, if there were doubt as to the teaching of the Scriptures concerning lepers the determination of theologians might be necessary.   And so in any judgment based upon a law of God, if the provision of that law is uncertain, the determination of it belongs to the clergy as experts in that "science or doctrine"; the priest who is the "healer of souls" (*medicus animarum*) should diagnose the case as a physician diagnoses the ills of the body.[1] But this is all.   If the physician pronounces a man a leper, it does not follow that he can expel him from the community.[2]   He cannot compel men to observe the rules of health, but merely urge and warn them, by pointing out the danger of disease and death which must follow a failure to observe these rules.   And so likewise the priest, or "physician of souls," may determine, and may exhort men, in those things which affect the "eternal health of the soul," or everlasting death, or the punishments in this world that stand in the place of those in the world to come.[3]   But as no physician is competent to expel a leper and no one has authority to do so except the body of the citizens or their deputy, so no power of pronouncing a coercive judgment based on the law of God belongs to any priest or to any body of priests whatsoever, although the decision ought to be based on their special knowledge of that law.[4]   Even a judgment of heresy, and all penalties inflicted for it if any exist by human law, belong solely to the prince by authority of the people, and not to any priest or bishop whatsoever.[5]   The clergy have no coercive authority of any kind, divine or human, temporal or spiritual.   They have the *potestas ordinis*, but no *potestas jurisdictionis*.   If it is the Divine Law alone which has been broken, then there is but one judge, "and this is Christ alone, no other."[6]   "Christ has always remained the head of the

---

[1] *Op. cit.*, II, x, 9.
[2] *Op. cit.* II, vi, 12; II, vii, 4.
[3] *Defensor Pacis*, II, vii, 4.
[4] *Op. cit.*, II, vi, 12.
[5] *Op. cit.*, II, x, 8.   Marsiglio no doubt draws conclusions far different from those of St. Thomas Aquinas, but the distinction on which they are based is much the same as St. Thomas's, when he says, that a pronouncement of the truth carries with it no compulsion : one is free to receive or reject it as he wills; while a judgment implies coercive authority. *Summa Theologica*, Secunda Secundae Partis, Quaestio LX, art. vi.   The sentence of a judge, he says, is analogous to a particular law applying to a particular fact, and like a general law it ought to have coercive force, but this coercive force in human affairs no one can lawfully have but one who exercises public authority (*qui fungitur publica potestate*). *Ibid.*, Quaestio LXVII, art. i.
[6] *Op. cit.*, II, ix, 1; II, ix, 3.

Church."[1] For an offence against the Law of God alone, no penalty may be inflicted by man in this world. If human law has added a temporal penalty for offences against God's law, as it may, then the judgment and its enforcement under this human law belong to the prince alone by authority of the people. And if all this be true of divine law, it goes without saying that in the case of law purely human, the clergy have no coercive jurisdiction, and not even a right of determination. The former belongs to the prince alone, the latter is the province of secular jurists. "Neither the Roman bishop called Pope, nor any other priest or bishop or spiritual minister," whether acting individually or collectively, has or ought to have "any coercive jurisdiction whatsoever, real or personal, over any priest, bishop, or deacon whatsoever, or college of the same; and much less has he, or any of them, collectively or individually, such jurisdiction over any prince or government, community, college, or individual layman whatsoever, whatever his or their condition may be; except only where that jurisdiction shall have been conferred upon a priest, or some bishop, or a college of these by the human legislator in the province."[2]

Marsiglio discusses at great length and with remarkable skill the application of this fundamental dictum to the practical questions of the day, such as the temporalities of the clergy, the duty of apostolic poverty, clerical immunity from state taxation or the state's jurisdiction, and the historical question of the Pope's authority over the Emperor and his right to determine imperial elections, etc., and his discussion of these points is of great importance and interest; but on the general principles with which he starts, his answers to all these specific questions may easily be anticipated and are never in doubt. It is enough for our purpose to note that the sum of it all is the rigid restriction of the sphere of the clergy in the Church, to the preaching and teaching of God's word, and the administration of the sacraments of the Church; they have the cure of souls and nothing more. As to the *plenitudo potestatis* of the Pope, this is a mere presidency over the rest of the clergy, never ordained by Christ and without any divine sanction whatever, but introduced in after times for convenience and better administration only, and by ordinance or custom which is purely human: the vast structure erected by the canonists is based on false and dishonest interpretation of Scripture and history. It is

---

[1] *Op. cit.*, II, xxviii, 27.   [2] *Op. cit.*, II, i, 4; II, iv, 1; II, v, 9.

this fictitious plenitude of power, false in theory and unsupported by history, which has been allowed to creep into every land through the craft of priests, the ignorance and superstition of the laity, and the weak compliance of princes; and everywhere it has bred the pestilence of division, war, and confusion. The chief disturber of the peace of Christendom is the *plenitudo potestas* of the bishop of Rome "called Pope." But this power rests on no divine sanction, it has been created by man, and by man it may be and should be destroyed; and until it is destroyed there can be no true peace. The real earthly authority in Christendom is not the Pope nor even the clergy, it is the body of all the faithful. This body and this alone, in a general council may restore and should restore the Church to its primitive purity by removing these false and dangerous human additions which are destroying the peace of the world.

This is the general burden of Book II of the *Defensor*, but we are concerned only with its political aspects. Historically considered these are two-fold mainly: its relation to the old contest between *sacerdotium* and *regnum* as to the true boundary between their respective jurisdictions, which had been the central political problem of western Europe since the eleventh century; and secondly, its connection with the great issue to be fought out in the great councils of the next century concerning the constitution of the Church and the true relation of its parts to each other.

To the first of these two questions the contribution of the *Defensor Pacis* is second to none in importance. Papal claims, as we have seen, had really reached their extreme logical limit in the struggle between Boniface VIII and Philip IV. The papal plenitude of power could go no further, though it might be more systematically set forth. And up to 1324 the papal supporters had never lost the strategic advantage of being the aggressive party; there was no defence of secular authority written before that time which did not admit that in some sense the spiritual power was higher in jurisdiction than the temporal, thus leaving a fatal breach through which the papal doctrine of direct or indirect power might enter. As long as the adherents of the secular prince admitted the legitimacy of the Pope's spiritual jurisdiction, they were powerless against interpretations which might and did extend it with flawless logic over every department of human government. As we have seen, this long contest from its beginning in the eleventh century was ostensibly a struggle on each side for its liberty of action, but from the nature of the case and the fact that Christendom was one commonwealth of Christians, the "liberty" claimed by the clergy could never be secured in a commonwealth in which the secular government was not reduced to the inferior position of a department of the Church. Alvarus Pelagius did not over-state the case when he said that the Pope's supreme power over princes was his power as *monarcha ecclesiasticus.* For centuries the central problem of politics had been whether the one commonwealth of Christendom was primarily a Church or primarily a secular polity; though the arguments might be negative, though it was only freedom that was openly claimed, supremacy alone could secure what was demanded in the name of liberty on either side. In this respect the position of the Empire was the same as that of the *Sacerdotium.* What it considered its rightful independence was really impossible unless the jurisdiction of the clergy were under the superintendence of the state.

The clergy saw all this first. For a generation before 1324, if not much more, what they demanded in the name of liberty was really mastery. But before the appearance of the *Defensor Pacis* all defenders of secular government had been content to take a merely defensive position, which was logically untenable in the face of a clerical attack which claimed that Christendom was a *regnum,* in which the *plenitudo potestatis* of the Pope as "ecclesiastical monarch" was the ultimate and supreme authority over all.

The great significance of the *Defensor Pacis* is the fact that in it for the first time the secular state claims a practical equality which can be obtained only by a theoretical superiority. By the extremer papalists the state for some time had been treated as a subordinate department of the Church. The *Defensor* is the first book wh.ch reverses the process and regards the Church as a department of the State in all matters of earthly concern. It is the first book in the whole long controversy which denies to the clergy coercive authority of any kind whatsoever, spiritual or temporal, direct or indirect. It must therefore be regarded as one of the real landmarks not alone in the history of the struggle between Church and State, but in the development of political thought as a whole. So far as content alone is considered, the two really epoch-making political books appearing between 1300 and 1500 seem to be the *De Potestate Ecclesiastica* of Egidio Colonna and the *Defensor Pacis* of Marsiglio of Padua and John of Jandun.

It is no part of the historian's task to decide between the two positions which were thus brought face to face in the latter centuries of the middle ages. He may properly define the issues, trace the development of the controversies over them, and note their result, but no more. By the middle of the fourteenth century the long controversy had at last succeeded in untangling the fundamental issue between *Regnum* and *Sacerdotium* from a mass of incidental questions, and the arguments of both sides had been carried to their extreme logical conclusion. The issue is really this : Assuming that the government of the world is under divine control, was this government entrusted by God to a single authority empowered to guide and control the affairs of men in this life preparatory to the life to come. If so, the Commonwealth of Christians is in reality a Church and the head of the Church is the ultimate earthly seat of all authority and over all.

If, on the other hand, God entrusted the guidance of the world to two separate and distinct authorities instead of to one, then one of these should be spiritual exclusively and the other must be supreme in all temporal matters. The defenders of secular government insisted that the divine government for the world is dualistic, the defenders of the *sacerdotium* held that it is monistic. This is the ultimate issue. The two positions are absolutely irreconcilable. When clearly understood they are mutually exclusive. The deductions drawn from each were entirely logical, and even the extreme conclusions of both the papalists and the imperialists must be conceded if we grant their premises. Furthermore, this great issue, in varying form but in essentials unchanging, has never been entirely absent from the political thought of the western world since the eleventh century at least, and down to the present time, though more prominent in certain epochs than in others. The epoch of John XXII and Lewis of Bavaria saw the last great phase of the contest over it which was to be fought out amid medieval conditions and ideas; the very possibility of so thorough-going a dualism as Marsiglio's is a sign of their passing. This epoch marked the culmination of the struggle on its theoretical side. By the year 1332 practically everything had been said that could be said on either side, granting the assumption of the solidarity of Christendom conceded in some degree by all. As in the pleas and rejoinders, the rebutters and surrebutters of the old English common-law pleading, the long argument had at length been "boulted out" and brought to the direct joinder of a clear and definite issue. Nothing of importance was later added on either side because there was nothing to add. On the papal side, for a hundred years or more after the middle of the fourteenth century there is no contribution of consequence, a fact that may be partially accounted for by the existence of the Great Schism of the West and the general scandal it created; on the side of the secular authority a few writings worthy of mention appeared, but in theoretical or even historical importance they are scarcely comparable with those which have just been reviewed.

The two of seemingly greatest significance before the era of the councils are the *Somnium Viridarii*,[1] written probably in 1376 or 1377 in France and appearing also in a French version, *Le Songe du Vergier*,[2] which, to judge from the frequent citations of it, exercised a considerable influence on the development of later Gallicanism; and, secondly, the writings of John Wycliffe. From both the theoretical and the strictly historical point of view, the purely political aspects of Wycliffe's writings are generally given a somewhat higher rating by modern historians than the evidence seems to warrant.

It was the philosophical, or more properly the strictly theological aspect of his great *Summa* and of the separate polemical tracts written in his last years against the Pope, which drew out the answers of adversaries in his own time, and entitle him now to a place in the history of European intellectual development. In the polemical tracts he identified the Pope with the Anti-Christ of the Apocalypse, and this unquestionably was one source of the similar identification so common in the anti-papal writings of the sixteenth and seventeenth centuries; but the political importance of this may easily be overrated. The doctrine of Dominion, the pivot on which his whole philosophic system turns, has usually been considered his great contribution to the development of political thought, but there is scarcely one significant point in it which had not already been elaborated again and again in writings resulting from the great controversy within or concerning the Franciscan order.[3] Wycliffe's practical interpretation of this doctrine is, of

---

[1] In Goldast, *Monarchia*, I, pp. 58–229.

[2] *In Traitez des droits et libertez de l'Eglise Gallicane* (1731), vol. ii.

[3] An account of some of these forgotten books is given in Cardinal Bellarmine's *De Scriptoribus Ecclesiasticis*, Venetiis, 1728, pp. 461–505. There is another in *A New History of Ecclesiastical Writers*, translated from the French of Louis Ellies du Pin, Dublin, 1723, vol. ii, pp. 517–537.

course, far different from that of Egidius Romanus,[1] but there are
few of his most fundamental conceptions which had not been fully
anticipated by Egidius more than a half century before. Of the
many writings on this subject in the interval between them probably the most important are those of Richard Fitzralph, Archbishop
of Armagh and primate of Ireland.[2] A comparison of Wycliffe's
statements with the chief of these, the *De Pauperie Salvatoris*, will
show at a glance how little there was really new in Wycliffe's
central doctrine of dominion, though the practical inferences
drawn from it by Wycliffe are different, in many cases, from those
of all his predecessors.[3] The portion of Wycliffe's *Summa* which
deals most directly with man's civil relations is the part entitled
Tractatus de Officio Regis,[4] and it contains some of his most characteristic political views. The duties of a king are treated in the
normal fashion. As king it is his chief business "to take thought
for the prudent government of his realm," and this consists in "the
institution (*institucio*) of laws few and just, in an administration
of them wise and exact, and in general in the protection of the
status and the right of each of his liege men"; and laws are more
essential to the community than the king, for they provide a perpetual and inflexible remedy more generally for the wrongs of every
man.[5] The laws of England excel the imperial laws because they
are fewer and leave greater scope for the exercise of equity.[6] The

[1] *Ante*, p. 250.

[2] On Fitzralph and his writings, see the admirable account by Reginald Lane Poole, in
the *Dictionary of National Biography*. Fitzralph's sermon preached before the Pope at
Avignon in 1357 is printed in Goldast's *Monarchia*, vol. ii, pp. 1391–1410, under the title
Defensio Curatorum. The first four books of his much more elaborate work on the same
subject, *De Pauperie Salvatoris*, is printed from a manuscript in the Bodleian Library as an
appendix to Mr. Poole's edition of Wycliffe's *Divine Dominion*. As early as 1433 Peter
Payne, an Englishman, and one of the spokesmen of the Hussites in the Council of Basel,
pointed out that Wycliffe was not the originator of the doctrine of dominion. *Johannis de
Ragusio Tractatus quomodo Bohemi Reducti sunt at Unitatem Ecclesiae* (*Monumenta Conciliorum Generalium Seculi Decimi Quinti*, vol. i, Vienna, 1857, p. 269). See also *A History of
the Papacy* by M. Creighton, vol. ii, p. 97.

[3] Wycliffe's most concise statement of his doctrine of dominion is to be found in the
opening chapters of his *De Dominio Divino* (Johannis Wycliffe, *De Dominio Divino Libri
Tres*, ed. by Reginald Lane Poole, London, 1890). In the preface to this edition Mr. Poole
gives an excellent summary of the theory. He gives another in *Illustrations of Medieval
Thought*, chap. x. For others, see Professor Lorimer's translation of Lechler's *John Wycliffe
and his English Precursors*, p. 254 *et seq.*; W. A. Dunning, *A History of Political Theories,
Ancient and Mediaeval*, pp. 260–265. An account of Wycliffe's views on Church and State
including a summary of the *De Officio Regis* is given by Herbert B. Workman, *John Wyclif*,
vol. ii, p. 3–30, Oxford, 1926.

[4] Johannis Wyclif, *Tractatus de Officio Regis*, edited by Alfred W. Pollard and Charles
Sayle, London, 1887.

[5] *De Officio Regis*, p. 55.

[6] *Op. cit.*, p. 56.

king is bound to the strictest observance of justice toward his subjects under the mandate of God to him as his chief vicar, and in
secular things is more bound to his subjects than they are to him.[1]
In case of necessity to the king or the realm, but only in such case,
the king may take the goods of laymen and clergy alike, but he
should not wrongly appropriate the lands of his vassals, nor transfer
them or permit their transfer to the dead hand.[2]   His jurisdiction
extends to all parts of his realm and over all his subjects in every
case affecting the peace of the kingdom.[3]   He is the vicar of God
in temporal matters, as the priest is in spiritual, and he should
put down rebellion.   He bears the image of Christ's Godhead, the
priest, that of his human character.[4]   In temporal matters his
power is greater than the priest's, as the priest's is greater than
his in things spiritual.[5]

"We hold that God himself instituted both powers immediately,
and not in the sense that one of them should institute or authorize
the other." [6]   England is bound to obey the Pope only so far as
Scripture directs, "and it is not deducible from Scripture that he
should dominate our realm secularly in temporal matters." [7]   On
the other hand, where the clergy fail in their duty, temporal lords
have power from God to use coercive force in "aiding the Church"
by correcting her abuses directly.[8]   In temporal matters the King
is greater than any of his priests and greater than the Pope himself.[9]   England is not subject to the Emperor and Roman law
is not better than the English law,[10] but we should know both the
canon and the Roman law in order that we may understand how
the Pope should be subject to Caesar as he formerly was.[11]

From these statements, taken more or less at random from the
De Officio Regis, it is evident that Wycliffe's views as to the nature
of the office of King are not different in any marked way from
those generally current in his time.   He is, of course, even in this
book, written before his extremer anti-papal views had developed,
always opposed to the political doctrine of the papalist writers
which subordinates the secular authority to the spiritual.   But
probably the most significant aspect of his book to the historian
of political thought is the continued insistence upon England's
independence of any "foreign" power spiritual or temporal and the

---

[1] *Op. cit.*, p. 79.
[2] *Op. cit.*, p. 97.
[3] *Op. cit.*, p. 119.
[4] *Op. cit.*, p. 13.
[5] *Op. cit.*, pp. 142–143.
[6] *Op. cit.*, p. 144.
[7] *Op. cit.*, p. 146.
[8] *Op. cit.*, p. 186.
[9] *Op. cit.*, p. 196.
[10] *Op. cit.*, pp. 189, 193–194.
[11] *Op. cit.*, p. 237.

consequent decrying of Roman law as compared with the law of England. Such repeated statements are not usually to be found in books written a century or even a half century before, and they are an interesting indication of the growing spirit of nationalism in western Europe, which, more than all the speculations of theorists, was soon to divert the political thought of Europe into new channels. Such statements as these of Wycliffe's, and the evidence of the English statutes of Provisors and Praemunire, coupled with the scandal of the Babylonish Captivity and the Great Schism, go far to explain the comparative ease with which an English king was able a century and a half later to outlaw the spiritual as well as the temporal jurisdiction of the Pope in England.

In order to make clear this long contest of the later middle ages between the two great powers contending for the mastery of Christendom, the central political problem of the age, it has seemed advisable for the time to disregard almost all other political aspects of the period. It becomes necessary now, therefore, to take a hasty glance backward at a few of the more important developments in the political thought of the age following the Investiture controversy, which were too remotely connected with the struggle of "Church and State" to be included in an account of its successive stages.

Of the varied forms of the amazing intellectual activity combined in the "renaissance of the twelfth century," all contributed in some degree to the enrichment and the stimulation of political thought; the recovery of the ancient classics, the revival of jurisprudence and its application in both state and church, the rise of universities, the rediscovery of Aristotle's speculations, the remarkable growth of representative institutions, and the beginnings of nationality and constitutionalism, to name no others.

The history of these and other separate manifestations of this remarkable cultural advance of course belongs elsewhere, and even their influence on theories of the state can only be illustrated incidentally here in passing, but even one who only follows the main channels of political thought cannot fail to mark as he passes the entrance here and there of successive tributary streams. He must, for example, note the effects of the classical revival in the copious Roman illustrations of John of Salisbury, including many from Roman law; in the following century he will discover in St. Thomas Aquinas a theory, foreign to the older thought, of the origin and growth of political institutions, borrowed from Aristotle; he will find texts of Justinian furnishing as never before the chief offensive weapons against the Papacy in the fourteenth century, and in the next a reflection of the development of institutions of representation in the theories of the conciliar party concerning the nature of the universal Church. A truer and more vivid appreciation of these successive additions to the general political thought of the West, as well as of their relative importance and proper sequence, can probably be got from a careful study of the contemporary writers themselves than from any isolated attempt to draw general conclusions from the mass of evidence they furnish. But we shall miss the main channel if we lose ourselves in an attempt to trace to its source every tributary stream. If, therefore, a writer adequately sums up a great movement of thought, his theory must often suffice here to illustrate the less comprehensive ones made by others.

As such an illustration of the political thought of the West as it was at the close of the investiture conflict and before it felt the full influence of Aristotle, no other contemporary statement is comparable with the *Policraticus* of John of Salisbury. It has been called by one competent modern scholar "the earliest elaborate mediaeval treatise on politics";[1] by another, "the first attempt to produce a coherent system which should aspire to the character of a philosophy of politics."[2] John of Salisbury, says Rehm, is "the first representative known to us from the middle ages of the organic theory of the State as a theory of its law,"[3] the "first systematizer of the law of the world as one state."[4]

[1] John Dickinson, *The Statesman's Book of John of Salisbury*, "Introduction," p. xvii.
[2] R. L. Poole, *Illustrations of Mediaeval Thought*, 2d. ed., p. 204, quoted by Dickinson, p. xvii.
[3] *Geschichte der Staatsrechtswissenschaft*, p. 168.
[4] *Op. cit.*, p. 182, note 3. The text of the *Policraticus* used here is the excellent one in two volumes published at Oxford in 1909, *Joannis Saresberiensis Episcopi Carnotensis Policratici sive De Nugis Curialium et Vestigiis Philosophorum Libri viii*, edited by Professor C. C. J. Webb. An English translation of all parts of this rather miscellaneous book important for the history of political thought is given by Professor John Dickinson, *The Statesman's Book of John of Salisbury*, with a valuable introductory essay on the author's theories and their place in the history of political thought (New York, 1927). Among other modern accounts of value are C. Schaarschmidt, *Johannes Saresberiensis*, Leipzig, 1862; Paul Gennrich, *Die Staats-und-Kirchenlehre Johanns von Salisbury*, Gotha, 1894; Ernst Schubert, *Die Staatslehre Johanns von Salisbury*, Berlin, 1897; *John of Salisbury and the Policraticus*, by Professor E. F. Jacob (*Social and Political Ideas of Some Great Mediaeval Thinkers*, ed. F. J. C. Hearnshaw, New York, 1923), pp. 53–84; and portions of vols. iii and iv of Carlyle's *History of Medieval Political Theory in the West*, and of R. L. Poole's *Illustrations of Mediaeval Thought*, 2d ed., London, 1920.

He is a systematizer rather than an innovator. None before him in the medieval period had such a knowledge as his of the political institutions and ideas of the ancient world and none had so wide an outlook upon those of his own time or so comprehensive a theory to account for all. But while his organic theory of the nature of the political community marks a distinct advance in political speculation, the concrete doctrines of the *Policraticus* concerning the nature and extent of the obligations of subjects and the duties and rights of governors remain practically the same as for its predecessors. There is the same assumption of the unity of Christendom as the central principle of its theory of the state, the same insistence upon the divine character of kingship carrying with it great prerogatives and even greater burdens. To John of Salisbury the fact that a true king is no less than God's vicar makes it all the more evident that a tyrant is no other than a vicar of the Devil who must be treated as such; it accounts in large measure for his acceptance of tyrannicide as a practical and even necessary measure. The vileness of a tyrant is in inverse proportion to the majesty of which he falls short. To John as to his predecessors the king exists for the sake of the people, not the people for the king; his chief duty next to the protection of the Church is the maintenance of peace and the securing of justice, and for these heavy duties he must have powers correspondingly great; but the *Policraticus* shows no more indication than its precursors of any conception of a "constitutional" sanction for their proper exercise. The responsibility of the king is for his people, but it is owing primarily to God and it is God who will enforce it.[1] "Vengeance is mine, I will repay, saith the Lord." Nor is this in conflict with John's acceptance of tyrannicide, for the slayer of a tyrant is nothing if not an agent, often an unwitting agent, of divine retribution. In this absence of all constitutional sanctions, the normal restraints upon a king are internal and moral. He should "put a bridle" on himself. The king is under the law which makes him king. If he exceeds or breaks this law on which all his legitimate authority rests, then, as Isidore of Seville said as far back as the seventh century, *ipso facto* he ceases to be king. A king is king only by ruling, but no official arbiter exists competent to decide whether a ruler remains a king or has become a tyrant. The king himself bears the heavy responsibility of determining what he may

[1] Dickinson, *The Statesman's Book of John of Salisbury*, "Introduction," p. xliv.

do and what he may not, and he can share it with none; but God will hold him responsible for his choice, and if it should be wrong God's retribution must inevitably follow, sometimes even in the form of tyrannicide. This is the explanation of the fact that so many treatises "On the Government of Princes," from Seneca to Bossuet, consist to so large an extent of moral rather than political precepts. They are usually concerned more with "the instruction of princes"[1] than with the nature of political relations, and the *Policraticus* is on the whole no exception to the general rule, though it does undoubtedly go far beyond any contemporary or earlier work in its endeavor to furnish a philosophic basis for these current political doctrines.

This basis, whether it is his own or not, is a truly organic theory of the world state, and it is probably the chief contribution of John of Salisbury to political thought. A commonwealth, he says, is a certain body which is endowed with life by the benefit of divine favor, which acts at the prompting of the highest equity, and is ruled by what may be called the moderating power of reason. "The place of the head in the body of the commonwealth is filled by the prince, who is subject only to God and to those who exercise His office and represent Him on earth, even as in the human body the head is quickened and governed by the soul.[2] The place of the heart is filled by the Senate, from which proceeds the initiation of good works and ill. The duties of eyes, ears, and tongue are claimed by the judges and the governors of provinces. Officials and soldiers correspond to the hands. Those who always attend upon the prince are likened to the sides. Financial officers and keepers (I speak now not of those who are in charge of the prisons, but of those who are keepers of the privy chest) may be compared to the stomach and intestines. . . . The husbandmen correspond to the feet, which always cleave to the soil. . . ."[3] "Between a tyrant and a prince there is this single or chief difference, that the latter obeys the law and rules the people by its dictates, accounting himself as but their servant. It is by virtue of the law that he makes good his claim to the foremost and chief

[1] "*De Instructione Principum*" is the title of such a work by Giraldus Cambrensis, John of Salisbury's contemporary. It is edited by George F. Warner for the *Rolls Series*, London, 1891, and its contents are what might be expected from the title.
[2] Elsewhere he speaks of the prince as one who "bears the person of the *universitas* of those subject to him." *Policraticus*, IV, 3.
[3] *Ibid.*, V, 2, Dickinson's translation.

place in the management of the affairs of the commonwealth and in the bearing of its burdens; and his elevation over others consists in this, that whereas private men are held responsible only for their private affairs, on the prince fall the burdens of the whole community. Wherefore deservedly there is conferred on him, and gathered in his hands, the power over all his subjects, to the end that he may be sufficient unto himself in seeking and bringing about the advantage of each individually, and of all; and to the end that the state of the human commonwealth may be ordered in the best possible manner, seeing that each and all are members one of another."[1]

Whatever be true of his treatment, these specific political institutions and ideas of which John treats were neither new nor strange to the thought of western Europe in the twelfth century. From Isidore of Seville in the seventh century, through Jonas of Orleans and Hincmar of Rheims in the ninth, and earlier writers in John's own century, such as Hugh of St. Victor and Hugh of Fleury, the same general conception of the king's prerogatives and responsibility may be traced. John of Salisbury's real originality lies in his comprehensiveness and his systematization, not in his particular political doctrines.

It is sometimes implied, if not said, that the doctrine of tyrannicide is an exception to this general rule, and it is undoubtedly true that most of the advocates of it in the sixteenth century referred to John as authority for their own views. But, as Professor Jacob has said, some modern writers have placed more emphasis on tyrannicide as a part of John's theory than he himself would have done.[2] It must be admitted that he does place more emphasis on the need of it than St. Thomas does in the next century on its disastrous effects, and he makes full use of the biblical and classical examples illustrating his thesis. In fact he puts the case for tyrannicide more clearly and he states it more emphatically than any other writer before the sixteenth century. But it was nevertheless incidental rather than central in his theory of secular government and he was by no means the first to hold or to express the general principles of which it is the logical outcome. Tyrannicide, in truth, had been implicit in current political thought ever since the acceptance of Isidore's dictum that one is a king only so

[1] *Policraticus*, IV, I.
[2] In *The Social and Political Ideas of Some Great Medieval Thinkers*, p. 69.

far and just so long as his acts are kingly. It always was and always remained a doctrine of tyrannicide, never of regicide, and the very glory of true kingship which so marks the theory of John of Salisbury and of all in his age, tends also by inevitable logic to widen the gulf between this and its opposite. Seldom has the majesty of kings been so high, as in the political literature of which John of Salisbury is the last great representative; or the debasement of a tyrant so low.

Such a difference in the theoretical aspects of monarchy could not but have an effect upon the current views concerning its actual administration. But so long as there was no "public authority" competent to prevent or punish the tyranny of a king who was legally "absolute"; so long, in other words, as men were unable to devise or to conceive of any legitimate administrative machinery in a monarchy which is not the king's and under his personal control — and John himself shows no sign of any such conception; so long as the king was confined to his proper sphere only by his own moderation or by obstacles which are not "constitutional" in character; indeed so long as no nation was thought of in a political sense which included the possibility of its having other organs beside the king and independent of him; just so long also it was natural that men should continue to recognize the occasional necessity for the removal of a tyrant even by private hands. The doctrine of tyrannicide is the logical outcome of the coupling in current political thought of the ideas that the king is always legitimately an autocrat, and may become an actual tyrant.

John was not the first to entertain such ideas, but his is the clearest and fullest exposition of them in medieval Europe, and the first which makes explicit many aspects of the theory not so definitely expressed before, including that of tyrannicide. In this sense, and probably in no other, can John of Salisbury be properly called the author of the doctrine of tyrannicide.

If, on the whole, John of Salisbury is the most important single figure in the development of the theory of the state during the twelfth century, in the thirteenth it is probably St. Thomas Aquinas; and no better index could be found of the great and comparatively rapid advance in political speculation between the middle of the twelfth century and the beginning of the last quarter of the next, than a comparison of the system of the *Policraticus*, probably the most perfect and the most complete single summation

of the political speculations of the past centuries, with the views
on law, justice, and government expressed in the voluminous
writings of St. Thomas Aquinas. Not that John of Salisbury was
unaffected by the profound changes in the environment of his own
day, nor that St. Thomas made any distinct break with the thought
of the past : few political writers have been more susceptible than
the former to the changing moods of political thought, and nothing
but a caricature of St. Thomas's views could result from representing him as a Descartes seeking a new foundation for philosophy.
The fundamental differences between the two men are essentially
differences between the thought of the earlier middle age and the
later, and in no medieval period did these differences develop so
rapidly or produce an effect upon political speculation so profound
as in the short span between the appearance of the *Policraticus* in
1159 and the death of St. Thomas in 1274.

A few of the factors in this change have been briefly noticed
already, but the one whose influence was greatest in shaping the
new tendencies in the political thought of St. Thomas was undoubtedly the fusion of the matured speculations of Aristotle with
traditional doctrines concerning the origin, the legitimacy, and the
nature of the social and political relations of men under the providence of God, a fusion which entailed an infinity of nice distinctions
in accommodating a pagan philosophy to the Christian cosmology,
the work of an intellect of the highest order. The power, the
receptiveness, and the boldness of St. Thomas's intellect can only
be appreciated through a consideration of the magnitude of his
task, and the monumental character and lasting influence of his
achievement. He was not the first to appreciate the importance
of Aristotle's political thought. Albert the Great, his master, who
survived him, was earlier in the field and influenced him greatly,
so was the great English Franciscan, Robert Grosseteste, bishop of
Lincoln, William of Auvergne, whom Professor De Wulf has called
"the first great philosopher of the thirteenth century," [1] and a

[1] Maurice De Wulf, *Histoire de la philosophie médiévale*, vol. i, p. 323, Louvain, 1924.
This book gives one of the best accounts of the predecessors and contemporaries of
St. Thomas. Another, containing elaborate bibliographies, is Friedrich Ueberweg's *Grundriss
der Geschichte der Philosophie der patristischen und scholastischen Zeit*, 10th edition edited by
Dr. Matthias Baumgartner, Berlin, 1915. An excellent account of St. Thomas's general
philosophic system — indispensable for an understanding of his politics — is *The Philosophy
of St. Thomas Aquinas* by Étienne Gilson, translated by Edward Bullough, Cambridge, England, and St. Louis, 2d ed., 1929. For a bibliography including the editions of St. Thomas's
works and the commentaries on them, see Mandonnet and Destrez, *Bibliographie thomiste*,
Kain (Belgique), 1921. In *Des écrits authentiques de S. Thomas d'Aquin* (second edition,

number of others; but of them all St. Thomas was greatest, and the subtlety, the profundity, and the comprehensiveness of his writings contributed to make them the principal medium through which the political ideas of Aristotle were reincorporated in the thought of the West in the later thirteenth century. But notwith-

Fribourg (Suisse), 1910) Professor Mandonnet gives an account of St. Thomas's writings and discusses the intricate problems arising out of the variations in the surviving medieval catalogues. A later treatment of these questions is given by Professor Martin Grabmann, *Die echten Schriften des Hl. Thomas von Aquin*, Münster i. W., 1920 (*Beiträge zur Geschichte der Philosophie des Mittelalters*, band xxii, heft 1–2).

The modern commentaries on St. Thomas's theories of law and politics are many, constantly growing in number, and of varying value. Of the works of St. Thomas himself, those most directly concerned with politics are his commentaries on the *Ethics* and *Politics* of Aristotle; parts of the great *Summa Theologica* (especially Prima Secundae Partis, Quaestiones xc–xcvii, on law; and Secunda Secundae Partis, Quaestiones LVII–LXI, *De jure et justitia*); and probably a portion of the *De Regimine Principum*. The commentaries on Aristotle are, and were intended to be, merely explanatory. They therefore contain few contributions by St. Thomas himself, but are indispensable for an understanding of his other political works. The edition used here is in volume twenty-one of the great folio edition of St. Thomas's works published at Parma, 1862–1873. Of the commentary on Aristotle's *Politics* the part ending with Bk. III, chap. vi, was the work of St. Thomas; the remainder was by his pupil, Peter of Auvergne (M. Grabmann, *Welchen Teil der aristotelischen Politik hat der hl. Thomas von Aquin selbst kommentiert? Philosophisches Jahrbuch der Görres-Gesellschaft*, 28 band, 3 heft, Fulda, 1915, pp. 373–379). St. Thomas's authorship of any part of the *De Regimine Principum* has been questioned, mainly on internal evidence. (See *e.g.* J. A. Endres, *De Regimine principum des hl. Thomas von Aquin, Festgabe zum 60. Geburtstag Clemens Baeumker*, Münster i. W., 1913, pp. 261–267.) It is agreed generally that only the first portion of the book was written by him, the rest probably by Tholommeo of Lucca, and the end of St. Thomas's part has been placed in the fourth chapter of the second book. (See Grabmann, *Die echten Schriften des hl. Thomas von Aquin*, pp. 216–219.) The edition of the *De Regimine* used here is in *S. Thomae Aquinatis Opuscula Selecta*, vol. iii, Paris, 1881, pp. 254–429. Of the *Summa Theologica* there are many editions. On Albertus Magnus, see especially G. von Hertling, *Albertus Magnus, Beiträge zu seiner Würdigung*, 2d ed., Münster i. W., 1914 (*Beiträge zur Geschichte der Philosophic des Mittelalters*). The most important politically of his works, his commentary on Aristotle's *Politics*, is printed in vol. viii of his collected works edited by Borgnet, Paris, 1890–1899.

For the general influence of Aristotle on the development of political thought and some discussion of the modern literature, see especially G. von Hertling, *Zur Geschichte der aristotelischen Politik im Mittelalter* (*Georg Freiherr v. Hertling historische Beiträge zur Philosophie*), Kempten u. München, 1914, pp. 20–31. The pioneer in the modern study of this subject was A. Jourdain, in his *Recherches critiques sur l'âge et l'origine des traductions latines d'Aristote*.

The publication in 1872 of the text of William of Moerbeka's Latin translation as a part of Franz Susemihl's 1st ed. of Aristotle's *Politics* was a noteworthy contribution to the study of medieval political thought. The Aristotle known to practically all the great theorists of the thirteenth and fourteenth centuries — the important period when the incorporation of his political thought with the general theory of the West took place — was the Latin text of the *Politics* translated by William of Moerbeka. For many generations, before it was superseded by the translation of Leonardo Bruni and by an increasing knowledge of Greek, it remained the chief medium through which the *Politics* of Aristotle was known to western Europe. No adequate study of the political thought of the period can possibly be made without its help. It is printed under the name of the "vetus versio" parallel with the later translation of Leonardo Aretino in the edition of St. Thomas's commentary on the *Politics* published at Parma and in the Paris edition of the commentary of Albertus Magnus, but Susemihl's text is preferable. The old translation of the *Nichomachean Ethics* is to be found in the same volume of St. Thomas's works.

standing his reception of Aristotelian ideas, St. Thomas was a man of his time, and it was the habit of thought at that time to conceive of the state primarily in terms of law, not law in terms of the state. The foundations of his political theory must therefore be sought in his conception of the nature and source of law, and of the relations of its various manifestations one to another. It is no accident that in the *Summa Theologica* these questions are treated at greater length than any other subject directly connected with political relations, and St. Thomas's remarkable discussion of them is not the least of his claims to greatness.

"A law (*lex*)," he defines, as "some ordinance of reason for the common good promulgated by him who has the care of the community"; [1] it is nothing else than "a precept of practical reason in a prince who governs some perfect community" — perfect in Aristotle's sense of completeness and comprehensiveness as compared with the household.[2]

If so, and if this world is governed by God's providence, then it is manifest that the whole community of the universe is ruled by divine reason; and so this reason, this principle of the governance of things, existing in God as the rationale of the universe, has the character of *lex;* and since divine reason is not of time but eternity, we must call this a law eternal. God is the prince who has care of the whole world, and all true laws are manifestations of the essential principle of things, existing from eternity in God as divine reason, and employed through his will and providence as a "rule or measure" for the governance of all his creatures. In the magnificent phrase of Hooker, no doubt in part derived from St. Thomas himself: "Of law there can be no less acknowledged, than that her seat is the bosom of God, her voice the harmony of the world." [3]

This is the *Eternal Law* (*lex aeterna*), the source of all true law upon earth; it is the eternal counsel of God, and for St. Thomas, as for Cicero, it "did not become law when it was written but when it was made, and it was made at the same time as the mind of God." [4] All God's creation is subject to this law, and all parts of that creation "participate" in it in so far as they are capable

[1] *Summa Theologica*, Prima Secundae Partis, Quaestio XC, art. iv.
[2] *Ibid.*, Quaestio XCI, art. i. Most of the quotations and paraphrases which follow are taken from Quaestiones XC-XCVII.
[3] *Of the Laws of Ecclesiastical Polity*, Bk. I, chap. 16.
[4] *Ante*, p. 114.

of receiving an "impression" of it which inclines them toward the acts and purposes which it enjoins. Thus a rational creature is subject to divine providence in a special and more excellent way than an irrational, in that he becomes a sharer in that providence itself, consciously applying its precepts to himself and to others. He participates with God in eternal reason, and by this "light of natural reason" (*lumen rationis naturalis*) inclines toward the acts and ends which reason prescribes, and can discern the evil and the good. Natural law (*lex naturalis*) is "*the participation of a rational creature in the eternal law*"; it is nothing but a reflection in us of the light divine. "All knowledge of truth is but an irradiation of and participation in the law eternal which is unchangeable truth."

But according to the definition with which we started, a law, in the meaning usually accepted among us, is a precept of practical reason promulgated for the government of a political community. How, then, is this related to the law of nature? There is, says St. Thomas, a like process in both the speculative and the practical reason: both proceed from certain principles to certain conclusions; and just as in the speculative reason the conclusions of the various sciences, of which we have no knowledge implanted in us by nature, are deduced by us through a process of reasoning from indemonstrable principles naturally known; in like manner also human reason must draw out of the precepts of natural law, as from certain general but unprovable rules, the laws applicable to particular cases. These particular dispositions or conclusions found through human reason are called "human laws (*leges humanae*)," provided they conform to the other conditions which are of the nature of *lex*.

Even in the speculative reason man can of himself have no full understanding of the truth as it is in God, but only an imperfect comprehension of certain of its general principles through the fragmentary share of the divine wisdom implanted in him by nature. In the sphere of the practical his reason is an even weaker and more uncertain guide, for here he is dealing not with things that must be as they are, but with the contingent and the variable; and so human laws have not the infallibility of the demonstrative conclusions of the sciences; nor is it necessary that they should, for a measure to be a true one need not always be infallible and certain in an absolute sense, but only so far as a rule or measure of such a character may be. All men, through the illumination of God, have a knowledge of the great principles of natural law and a natural inclination to observe them; but "human laws," unlike the eternal principles from which they are taken as fallible conclusions drawn by the practical reason to fit the changing needs of men, these cannot be known intuitively. He who has care of the community must therefore make them known, and human reason must also add to them sanctions which the ruler shall enforce. Promulgation of a human law, then, becomes a prerequisite to its effectual operation. For practical needs, it is not enough that a law be "an ordinance of reason for common utility": it must be "promulgated," and promulgated by one with authority — "by him alone who has the care of the community." For St. Thomas, however, as for all others in the middle ages, there is a vast difference between this promulgation of a law and the making of it. But if so, what shall we make of the famous Justinianian maxim, *Quod principi placuit legis habet vigorem?* "It is necessary," St. Thomas says, "that the will concerning the things commanded be a will controlled by some reason if it is to bear the character of a law," and so the maxim *voluntas principis habet vigorem legis* is to be understood. "Otherwise the will of the prince would be iniquity, rather than law."

Will, he says in another place, like anger or concupiscence, is an appetitive power (*vis appetitiva*) in distinction from a cognitive (*potentia cognoscitiva*), but it is a *rational* appetite (*appetitus rationalis*), not a sensuous one (*sensitivus*).[1] There is no true will but a rational will, and no promulgation by any prince of anything else can ever result in true law. This is the philosophic form of the constitutional doctrine by which St. Thomas's great contemporary Bracton adapts the same famous text of Roman law to the conditions of the thirteenth century.[2]

But even the most rigorous deductions from the principles of natural law, St. Thomas hints, must in their promulgation meet the other requirements conditioning human law, and the chief of these requirements, he says in the definition of a law with which he begins, are two in number: a true human law must be "for the common good (*ab bonum commune*)," and the authority under which it is promulgated must be no less than that which belongs to him who has the care of the whole community. Under the first of these requirements, St. Thomas fully incorporates in his

---

[1] Secunda Secundae Partis, Quaestio LVIII, art. iv.   [2] *Ante*, pp. 195-196.

theory of the state the familiar distinction fundamental in all medieval thought between the true king, and the tyrant who consults his own good in place of the good of his subjects. The enactments of such a tyrant are not laws, but "perversions of law"; they are "acts of violence" (*violentiae*) rather than laws. In his discussion of the second requirement, we find the clearest indication contained in the *Summa* of St. Thomas's theory of the relation of the law to politics. For an understanding of this relation it is necessary to remember his insistence upon the practical importance in human law of a coercive power (*vis coactiva*), which in essence is a power to punish. It is freedom from this coercive effect of law which alone renders a prince *legibus solutus*, for from law considered as a directive force (*vis directiva*) no prince can ever be free; and every prince worthy the name will subject himself to it voluntarily. This power to punish is also the highest stretch of positive political authority possible, and therefore the badge of supreme jurisdiction. Private persons may counsel or reward; none but the one "who has the care of the community" may lawfully punish. Who, then, may rightfully exercise this supreme power; in other words, who should have the care of the community? St. Thomas's answer to this fundamental question is one of the most significant political statements in the *Summa*. "The ability to compel is possessed by the multitude or by a public person who has the right to inflict penalties, and for this reason he alone can make laws." "But properly a law is first and foremost an ordinance for the common good, and the right to ordain anything for the common good belongs either to the whole multitude or to some one who acts in place of the whole multitude; therefore the authority to establish a law pertains either to the whole multitude, or it pertains to a public person who has the care of the whole multitude"; for here, as everywhere, it is for him whose end it is, to ordain the means to that end.[1]

It is apparent that the type of human government here most favored by St. Thomas is a true *res publica*, in form somewhat like that of the Roman republic, or one in which the people (*multitudo*) has entrusted the supreme government of the state to a single ruler who has the "care" of or responsibility (*cura*, *sollicitudo*) for it all. The latter form — and the latter was the form of chief importance in the thirteenth century, essentially the same whether elective or

[1] Prima Secundae Partis, Quaestio XC, art. iii.

hereditary — is a monarchy founded on the law eternal and created by the people for the common utility of all, and especially to secure peace, the chief earthly prerequisite to human good.   Its ruler or prince is therefore a true king, with vast powers, especially the power of judging and punishing offences, and with a responsibility of equal or greater weight.

This, however, for St. Thomas as for John of Salisbury, is no "constitutional" monarchy of the modern type in which this responsibility of the prince is regularly enforceable by other independent agencies of the community.   So far as my knowledge goes, the first and the sole clear advocacy before the Conciliar period of a theory of "limited" monarchy in any strict sense resembling the latter form occurs in Book I of the *Defensor Pacis*.[1] The responsibility of St. Thomas's prince is of a different order. His prime responsibility is to God, the author of the law on which all his authority rests; and, in a general, or even in a loose political sense, he might be said to be responsible also to "the multitude" which raised him or his house to the throne and might conceivably sweep them away for acts of tyranny.   But in the strictly legal sense he is "absolute" in the ordinary administration of human law in his realm, within this sphere he is without a superior or a

[1] In one place in the *De Regimine Principum* (Bk. I, chap. vi) St. Thomas intimates that a king may be checked or punished "by public authority," but only in the unusual cases where by the constitution of the state "an authority exists in some superior to take action concerning the king on behalf of the multitude," a provision which was not normal if ever existent in medieval monarchies, and not considered normal by St. Thomas.   All his examples of it are from ancient times.   Furthermore, he evidently regards this as an exceptional remedy only to be used, even where applicable, in case of tyranny of the worst description, such as that of the Tarquins. . . .   In his commentary on Aristotle's *Politics* (I, i) St. Thomas clearly shows that he fully understands the nature of such a monarchy "limited" in the modern sense.   In fact he there gives as concise and accurate a definition of it as has ever been framed.   As distinct from "regal rule," existing where the ruler has "full" or absolute power (*plenariam potestatem — plenariam*, not *arbitrariam*), the limited monarch is one who has only "a power restricted by *certain laws of the state*" (*potestatem coarctatam secundum aliquas leges* CIVITATIS, or, as he puts it in the next paragraph, SECUNDUM LEGES POSITAS PER DISCIPLINAM POLITICAM).   See Appendix II.   This is a limitation existing in the constitution or positive law of the state itself, not merely in the general obligation of all rulers to obey the dictates of justice; yet, notwithstanding this clear understanding of it, St. Thomas apparently does not advocate it as the form of monarchy best suited to meet the needs of the commonwealth.   His preference seems to be for a pure monarchy in which the king is "absolute."   In the part of the *De Regimine Principum* generally attributed to him, he declares that normally it pertains to a king "to be over all human offices and to direct them through the authority of his rule."   *De Regimine Principum*, I, xv. "The common natural rule is by one."   *Ibid.*, I, ii.

Where no "public authority" exists competent to punish the ruler, and this ruler is in fact a tyrant, the only available course is to remove the ultimate cause of tyranny which is the iniquity of the people themselves.   Removal of a tyrant by private men St. Thomas condemns, but chiefly on grounds of expediency: the evils produced by the remedy are invariably worse than the disease itself.   *De Regimine Principum*, I, vi.

peer, and is responsible to no man. Of human law, in the sense
of coercive force, St. Thomas says he is wholly free, a monarch
"legibus solutus" — the equivalent of Bracton's legal dictum
that no writ runs against the king. But, on the other hand, all
the king's official acts are subject to the direction of law, and if he
is a true king and not a tyrant he will profess willingly, as did
Theodosius and Valentinian, that he is under the law which makes
him king. In secular relation to his subjects, the king is "absolute," and he ought not to be "arbitrary"; but the sanctions which
maintain this equilibrium are not the sanctions of modern "constitutional law." In an aphorism much quoted and apparently
much admired, Lord Acton declared that "S. Thomas Aquinas was
the first Whig," but with what meaning I cannot even guess. If
he had in mind a legal limitation of the monarch, St. Thomas was
no Whig; if only a moral one, he was certainly not the first. The
statements of his *Summa*, epitomized above, in fact constitute one
of the most masterly analyses of civil relations surviving from
medieval times, but the specific political doctrine they set forth —
as distinct from the theory of the origin and justification of government — is the normal thought of the later middle ages, which might
be illustrated without end from other contemporary sources from
the thirteenth to the sixteenth century. Nor is this doctrine a
new one in respect of the source and extent of political authority;
from Cicero to John of Salisbury the political literature is full of
assertions of a similar kind, though seldom accompanied by arguments so cogent or distinctions so subtle, as those of St. Thomas.

Monarchy, then, seems the form of government preferred above
others by St. Thomas, under a monarch of great actual power if
and when he acts under the directive force of law. This is the
doctrine of the extracts given above from the *Summa*, and it is
fully confirmed by the statements of the portion of the *De Regimine
Principum* generally attributed to St. Thomas by modern critics,
on the basis of the evidence of the oldest manuscripts and catalogues of St. Thomas's works.[1]

[1] In one article of the *Summa*, however (Prima Secundae Partis, Qu. CV, art. i), occurs a
statement of St. Thomas which at first sight seems to indicate a decided preference for a
mixed form of government instead of the pure monarchy approved of in the part of the
De Regimine Principum just referred to, especially in Bk. I, chap. ii; and so complete does
the discrepancy between these two passages appear to some critics, that they consider it
proof of the impossibility that both could have come from the same writer, and therefore
sufficient ground for deciding against St. Thomas's authorship even of the first part of the
De Regimine Principum. See, for example, Jos. Ant. Endres, *De Regimine principum des*

This choice of pure monarchy as a form of government was a deliberate one, and in making it St. Thomas was fully aware that he was not altogether in agreement with Aristotle, "the philosopher." To Aristotle, and to Tholommeo of Lucca, or whoever finished the *De Regimine Principum*, a monarchy was not a truly "political" government, because in it there were no true "citizens" ruling and being ruled in turn, but only "subjects," who were always ruled and never ruling. The latter author held that we are not free unless we can participate in the government under which we live and have a legitimate part in its control. Free government to him is self-government and it can be nothing less. Therefore when the community, even voluntarily, has conferred all its *imperium* and *potestas* upon one, that community has lost its freedom and its members in becoming *subditi* have ceased to be *cives*, and share somewhat with actual *servi* in the condition of being subject to arbitrary will instead of to a law of their own choice. Can there ever be "free" government which is not self-

hl. Thomas von Aquin, in *Festgabe zum 60. Geburtstag Clemens Baeumker (Studien zur Gesschichte der Philosophie*, Supplementband), Münster i. W., 1913, p. 261 *et seq.*, especially pp. 263–265. There are several reasons for rejecting such a view, entirely aside from the evidence of the manuscripts and catalogues. One important ground urged by Endres for the rejection of the *De Regimine* as a genuine work of St. Thomas is that it was unfinished by him and must therefore be contemporaneous with the *Summa* which St. Thomas left uncompleted at death, a fact which, it is thought, would make a common authorship of both works less probable. But as Mandonnet well says, the unfinished state of a manuscript of St. Thomas is not in itself sufficient proof that this was necessarily a result of the author's death (*Bibliographie thomiste*, pp. xix–xx). There were other reasons, not always sufficiently noted by the critics, why some of the many incomplete works of St. Thomas were left unfinished. It is by no means certain, then, that the *Summa* and the *De Regimine* come from precisely the same period in St. Thomas's life. There is a difference of opinion as to which king of Cyprus the latter was addressed to.

But even assuming that it was St. Thomas's death which accounts for the incompleteness of both works, it is much more important that the supposed discrepancy between the two passages from them, noted above, seems insufficient to prove the argument based upon it. The statement of Quaestio CV diverges almost as much from those in Quaestiones XC and XCI of the *Summa* itself, as from the political views expressed in the *De Regimine*, as a comparison will make clear. We must, if necessary, interpret one part of the *Summa* by help of another, and to do so here would seem to me to show that it is far from certain that St. Thomas, in Article one of Quaestio CV — an article dealing primarily with the legislation of the Old Testament, or "old law" — means to express a clear preference for mixed government over pure monarchy as the form best suited for the polities of his own age and his own part of the world. On a careful reading it further appears that the "popular" element in a mixed monarchy, which St. Thomas is assumed to deem to be requisite in all states, is sufficiently provided for in the Article in question, by mere election of the monarch; a view which necessarily implies little more than the preference, often expressed at the time, for elective rather than hereditary kingship, between which there is no essential difference so far as the character and extent of royal authority are concerned, as St. Thomas's continuator points out in later portions of the *De Regimine Principum*. On the whole, it is pure monarchy, whether elective or not, which seems to me to be St. Thomas's matured choice as the general form of royal government best adapted to the needs of Europe in the thirteenth century.

government ? The question involved was no less than this, and a more momentous does not exist in politics. St. Thomas was thoroughly acquainted with all the answers given to it, in his time and before. Yet he deliberately chose to be the "subject" of a true but "absolute" king and in so doing thought himself none the less a free citizen. His ideal was a *regimen for* the community but not necessarily *of* it, as the one best fitted to secure the highest attainable welfare of each and of all within it, and this he considered more truly according to the organic principles of nature than a polity in which the due relation of the body to the head was disregarded, and probably also its true relation to the heart. He preferred, in other words, to accept Bodin's definition of citizenship instead of Aristotle's — or rather Bodin accepted his — and it no longer included participation in government as a requisite to freedom. John of Jandun might, in a qualified sense, be termed a "Whig," and Tholommeo of Lucca may have been in theory a democrat, but St. Thomas Aquinas was neither; he was the greatest of all contemporary exponents of pure monarchy.

As a philosopher and theologian he had weighed it carefully and approved of it because it seemed, of all forms of the state, most in accord with the divine economy to which all human government must conform, the closest possible approximation to the divine plan; as a student of history and politics he preferred it because he considered it further from tyranny than any of the intermediate forms of the state, the form under which men were most likely to be truly "free." The philosopher may possibly be entitled to say that he was wrong, the political historian may be qualified to say whether his theories have stood the test of practice, the historian of thought can only record the fact that contemporary opinion was overwhelmingly in his favor and that the keenest observers of political phenomena remained of that opinion for nearly five hundred years more. It held the field practically until the French Revolution. To be good, government need not be self-government, St. Thomas thought. None can say whether he would have continued so to think if he could have foreseen the entire development of representative institutions which was only beginning in his day, and none should ignore the vast difference that representation makes in any just comparison between competing theories and his.

If the statements above, chiefly concerning the source and

nature of law in general and the character of a government based
on law, show St. Thomas's debt to his great predecessors such as
Cicero and St. Augustine,[1] other passages in the *Summa*, especially
those dealing with natural law in particular and the possibility of
change in its application, and with justice, are equal proof of the
profound influence of Aristotle in shaping the course of his thought
and infusing into it certain great constructive ideas hitherto lacking in the political theory of the West, if not actually inconsistent
with it.

St. Thomas's fundamental distinction, noted above, between
the unchangeable principles of the law of nature and the fallible
and mutable but necessary deductions that may be drawn from
them, also serves to make clear most of his important discussion —
which must be omitted here — of the application of that law to
actual conditions, and the changes permissible in this application,
through custom, enactment, or dispensation. Under the question
whether all acts of virtue are according to the law of nature, he
says we may consider these acts in either of two aspects: as
dictates of natural reason to which man conforms as invariably as
heat is produced by fire, in which sense they are all subject to
natural law; or, on the other hand, according to their several
varieties, as when we speak of separate acts of virtue as they are
in themselves. If looked at in the second way, all acts of virtue
are not of the law of nature, for many acts are virtuous to which
in the beginning we were not by nature inclined. Men have come
to a discovery of them only through the questionings of reason,
and have thus found them to be "conducive to the good life." [2]
They are in fact additions made through human experience and
by human law to the intuitive principles with which man was
originally endowed; and similar additions, but "above" nature,
have also been made for man's welfare in the revealed word of God
or "divine law." Historically it is the negative aspect of all this
which is probably of greatest importance: the statements above
give at least a partial answer to the all-important question, What
is it to be "against nature"? and St. Thomas's answer is different
from any given in the middle ages before the thirteenth century.
No one before that time would have thought of saying what he

---

[1] For a useful collection of the statements of St. Thomas's predecessors concerning natural
law, from the time of the Roman jurists to his own, see Dom Odon Lottin, O. S. B., *Le droit
naturel chez saint Thomas et ses prédécesseurs*, Bruges (1926).

[2] Prima, Secundae Partis, Quaestio XCIV, art. iii.

says here.   There is one sense, he tells us, in which we may speak
of a thing as "natural," or "according to nature": namely, when
we mean merely that its contrary does not exist in nature.   For
example, we may say man is naked "according to the law of
nature" because nature gave him no clothing.   In precisely the
same sense, and in no other, can *communis omnium possessio* or
una libertas [phrases of Isidore of Seville] be said to be a part of
the law of nature (here *jus naturale*): private property and slavery
were not produced by nature but "by the reason of men for the
utility of human life"; they are, however, not changes in or vio-
lations of the law of nature nor even subtractions or "departures"
from it; but are necessary *additions* to it, consistent with its principles, "conducive to the good life," and made by human law
among all nations to meet enlarging legitimate needs as men
gradually advanced out of primitive barbarism toward the consummation of their earthly development in the "perfect community" of the state.[1]

But "the prime cause of servitude," St. Augustine says, "*is
sin!*"[2]

Even to an unpracticed eye the differences are obvious between
St. Thomas and the author of the last part of the *De Regimine
Principum*, written more than a quarter-century after St. Thomas's
death.   St. Thomas's mind is more orderly than his continuator's
and the expression of his ideas clearer.   There is also a considerable difference of emphasis and occasionally inconsistency between
the political parts of the *Summa Theologica* and the latter part of
the *De Regimine Principum*, although the influence of Aristotle is
almost equally marked on both.

The method of the second is in general more historical and
descriptive and less analytical than St. Thomas's; and, except for
its development of one important political idea — possibly suggested by St. Thomas himself,[3] the idea of dominion, its place
in the history of political thought is probably owing less to its own
vigor or originality than to the fact that it was generally attributed
in after-times to St. Thomas himself.

In the course of his discussion of monarchy — much in the
manner of Aristotle — the author comes in turn to the advantages
to a monarch of wealth, and then adds that monarchy must be

[1] Prima, Secundae Partis, Quaestio XCIV, especially art. v.
[2] *De Civitate Dei*, XIX, chap. xv.   [3] See *ante*, p. 259, note 2.

supported not only by wealth but by ministers. He quotes King Solomon, "I have possessed slaves and handmaidens and a household great beyond measure," and comments that anything which is possessed seems to be under the dominion of the possessor. It seems best, therefore, to discuss the ministers possessed by a king with particular reference to the nature of dominion. With this rather forced introduction he plunges abruptly into a consideration of the various kinds of dominion. The two principal forms of it which one may have over "his ministers" are, according to Aristotle, the "political" and the "despotic." A "political" *dominium* exists in a region or province, a city, or a *castrum* — he seems never expressly to include any higher political unit — where the government is according to its own statutes, whether the administrator be one person or more. Under a "political" régime the administrators or "*rectores politici*" have none of the arbitrary power (*arbitraria potestas*) which characterizes the government of a king; they are required to rule according to the form of government handed down to them or under control of the will of the people. They are, as the author says, "bound by the laws (*legibus astringuntur*)," and by this he means very definitely their own particular customs and statutes and not merely law in its wider and more general sense. Nor is this obligation in their case, as in a king's, a merely moral one : they must take oath to obey these laws and their observance of them is enforced by penalties.

Such is the actual character of a *dominium politicum*, but the word "*politicum*," he says, is commonly applied to polities where the government is in more than one person. These are called "political" from the Greek *polis* because there is a plurality or city, since this form of government properly pertains to cities, as may be seen in Italy especially, and as it formerly was in Athens. Provinces, on the other hand, are usually under regal government ; and as a general rule men of high spirit, with boldness of heart and confidence in their own intelligence, can be governed under no form of government except the "political," understanding political to include aristocratic. This is the form of government actually prevailing in Italy, and especially in Lombardy, where men are of high spirit and hence less tractable, and in Italy therefore regal government cannot exist except in those places where lords have established and maintain a tyranny.

In chapter ten of Book III the author gives a four-fold classification of *dominia*, the sacerdotal and regal, the purely regal (which includes the Imperial), the "political," and the "economical." It is apparent that for him the purely regal and the political are mutually exclusive and that the political form can never be "despotic," while the regal is sometimes a complete despotism, if not always despotic in some respects, a despotism being a *dominium* in which the subjects are treated rather as slaves than as citizens, a form necessary and legitimate in backward parts of the world where men have neither spirit nor intelligence enough to be citizens of a free state.

A regal *dominium* the author never expressly defines, but he seems to consider it a government of one ruler with "arbitrary power (*potestas arbitraria*)," who in his administration of justice is bound by no existing laws, since the rules for the decision of particular cases are "in his breast" and that which pleases him is held to be law. Such a form of government is inferior to the political, if we compare *dominium* with "the uncorrupt status of human nature called the state of innocence, in which there was no royal government but a political, because there was then no dominion, which implies servitude, but preëminence and subjection in disposing and governing the multitude, in accordance with the merits of each one." Regal government came about and persists on account of the corruption of nature.[1]

Such statements are unusual in the later thirteenth century and for that reason very interesting. It is apparent that the Italian author of this portion of the *De Regimine Principum* has a decided preference for a government on the model of the communes of Italy and an antipathy to every form of monarchy as a *dominium* unfitted for Italians or for men of like spirit anywhere. A king in

[1] The four forms referred to above are exactly those used by Wm of Moerbeka in translating the four of Aristotle's *Politics* (I, 1, 2), πολιτικόν, βασιλικόν, οἰκονομικόν, δεσποτικόν. Compare also St. Thomas's comments on this passage in his commentary on the *Politics* (Appendix II).

Apparently the continuator differs from St. Thomas chiefly in his assumption that a king's power is in its nature "arbitrary," whereas St. Thomas held it to be only "absolute." Being "arbitrary," it is also necessarily "despotic," and therefore inconsistent with "political," both of which characteristics St. Thomas denies to be true of real kingship. St. Thomas believed a limited, non-despotic monarchy to be possible, though he preferred a pure monarchy, which he considered non-despotic also. His continuator thought that all monarchy being arbitrary must be despotic. There can therefore be no limited monarchy, for the essence of monarchy itself is arbitrary rule. A "limited" monarchy is a contradiction in terms. As a consequence, for him *all* limited governments must be non-monarchical, and no other could be free. The whole difference between the two views really lies between the two words "absolute" and "arbitrary."

reality exercises a power not only "absolute" but truly "arbitrary," and the condition of his "subjects" can never be anything but servile compared with that of free "citizens" under a "political" régime.   If all forms of dominion must fall under one or the other of Aristotle's two classes, "political" and "despotic," it is clear that for him regal dominion is invariably despotic.   It may be legitimate but is always more or less servile, and, as he hints, in actual practice it is often scarcely distinguishable from a tyranny.

This evident dislike of all monarchy — notwithstanding a little occasional lip-service — is in flat contradiction of the statements contained in the first part of the same treatise and furnishes further proof, if more were needed, of the dual authorship of the book.   It is also contrary to the main current of political speculation at the time.

For these reasons the continuation of the *De Regimine Principum* is one of the most unusual political writings of its age and of great value on account of its recognition of existing institutions, both democratic and feudal; but it may well be doubted whether it has an importance in proportion if we consider it in the light of its influence on the contemporary growth of political thought. One possible reason for a lack of influence is a certain amount of confusion in the author's thought and expression, another may lie in his failure boldly to apply his favorite principles of government to the highest political units of the realm and the Empire.   But when all is said, it is well to remember that the principle central among them all — that the members of a free state must be true citizens in the Aristotelian sense and have a part in its control — this remained at the end of the middle ages the dominant theme of the last of the great medieval theorists, Nicholas of Cusa; and in modern times it has become the commonplace of all political thought.

Among the writings of the thirteenth century there is probably no more striking proof of the revolution suddenly wrought in the development of political speculation by the recovery of Aristotle, than the treatise of Egidius Romanus, *De Regimine Principum*. Though its author was a canonist and an Augustinian — he was later head of the order — this book, written in or before 1285, is permeated from end to end with Aristotelianism.   To say, as the Roman jurists and the Christian fathers after them for ages had said, that the *jus gentium* is a degradation of the *jus naturale*, or

THE LATER MIDDLE AGES

a departure from it, according to Egidius, is "to speak barbarously" (*ruditer loqui*).[1] Such institutions as slavery or private contracts are not contrary to nature; they are additions to or developments of it. It is as absurd to consider them with the lawyers (*juriste*) as against nature as it would be to hold that the wearing of clothes is against nature merely because it was not done in the most primitive times. The utility of men has required the introduction of many new institutions and rules by human law as additions to the primitive ones, but these are not against nature simply because not primitive, the product of human law. Nothing is truly against nature unless it is contrary to the dictates of natural reason. The mere fact that in the beginning men were born free, does not make of slavery an institution "against nature."[2] In like fashion private property and the institutions of government, because they developed later, are not worse but better than the institutions which preceded, since they are a fuller unfolding of man's nature, for man is by nature "a being civil and political."

That this is pure Aristotelianism is obvious; what a break it marks with the political thought of the western world in the preceding fifteen centuries and more, and what a sudden break, may be appreciated by comparing it with the views on the same matters expressed by John of Salisbury in his *Policraticus*.

As its title indicates, the *De Regimine Principum* of Egidius Romanus is not wholly nor even primarily a discussion of the nature of the state: its theme is the regimen of princes. It is one of the most important early examples of a general type of political writing which appeared with increasing frequency up to the end of the period of the Enlightenment in the eighteenth century. The best examples from the thirteenth century are the *De Regimine Principum* begun by St. Thomas Aquinas and dedicated to the King of Cyprus; and this book with a similar title, written for the instruction of the heir to the French Crown by Egidius Roma-

---

[1] *De Regimine Principum*, Bk. III, part ii, chap. xxxi. I have used the edition published at Rome in 1482.

A French version of the treatise, of the late thirteenth or early fourteenth century, was published in 1899: *Li livres du gouvernement des rois* ed. by Samuel Paul Molenaer, New York. In his introduction, the editor gives a full account of the book, and in "Appendix C," a list of the editions of it, the last in 1617.

[2] *De Regimine Principum*, III, ii, xxxi. The same distinction enforced by the same illustration is made by Saint Thomas Aquinas, *Summa Theologica*, Prima, Secundae Partis, Quaestio XCIV, art. v. *Ante*, pp. 334-335.

nus, then his tutor, before the death of King Philip III in 1285.
The long series really culminates in Bossuet's *Politique tirée de
l'Écriture Sainte*, though there are numerous later examples. The
works of this type are as a general rule tiresome to the last degree.
"Almost always there are the same general ideas, the same vague
counsels, the same impersonal observations; in this medley of
commonplaces, copied one from another it is difficult to single out
one work which shows any trace of interest or originality." [1] The
majority of these books are more suggestive of Hannah More than
of Machiavelli; and yet, properly speaking, the list of them would
be incomplete if it did not include *The Prince* itself, as well as the
brilliant dialogue of Buchanan, the *Monarchia Hispanica* of Cam-
panella, and the *De Rege* of Mariana.

The *De Regimine Principum* of Egidius has some of the defects
and many of the merits of most works of this kind. It is divided
into three books and only one of these is concerned with the strictly
political activities of the king. The first is ethical, the second
"economical" (dealing with the king's family and household) and
it is significant that the references to Aristotle far outnumber all
others even in Book I. Book III, with which we are concerned
here, is divided into three parts, the first of which treats of the
question what good or end is served by the community of the household, of the *civitas*, and of the realm; the second and most important deals with the government of a *civitas* or realm in time of
peace; and the third with the same government but in time of
war, an interesting treatise on warfare and defence, closing with
one chapter on the navy.

The main conclusions and even much of the arrangement of
parts I and II of Book III are taken with little change from Aristotle's *Politics* and therefore need not be repeated in detail. As
in the *Politics* the discussion begins with a discussion of the good or
end which the community of the *civitas* or of the realm is by its
nature destined to fulfil. Each of these two political units is a
true community (*communitas*) or *koinonia*, and it is the purpose of
part I, as it was of Book I of the *Politics*, to prove that this community is "according to nature"; as "natural," in fact, as the
household and the village out of which it evolves. And the fundamental reason for it all is the same as Aristotle's. "There is,"
says Egidius, "inborn in all men by nature, an impetus (*impetus*)

[1] Lacour-Gayet, *L'éducation politique de Louis XIV*, 1st ed., p. 23.

toward such a community as that of the *civitas*.[1] By nature man
is a being political and civil (*polliticum animal et civile*).[2] In chapter III he undertakes to prove that this is true in general notwithstanding the fact that some men actually live apart from the
state (*non civiliter vivere*) ; and here he adds to the Gods, who for
Aristotle were above, and to the beasts, which were below the
state, the "religious," a class regarded in the middle ages as "civ-
illy" dead. To adapt Aristotle's ideas to his own time, one more
addition was necessary and this Egidius makes in chapter V, in
which he proves that everything which in the *Politics* is found to
be true of the *civitas* is equally true of the highest and most comprehensive community of his own day, the *regnum*, of which the *civitas*
is a part.[3] A *civitas* is a community (*communicatio*) whose end is
the good and virtuous life of the citizens, a life perfect and self-
sufficient; a realm is a great multitude composed of many nobles
and freemen living a life of virtue under the government of one
best man as under a king."[4] The same "formal cause" is thus
operative in both, but for Egidius the realm, not the *civitas*, has
come to be the final consummation of man's political life. It is
significant that he makes no mention whatever of the other community regarded by many as the most comprehensive of all, the
Empire; but he was writing in France, for the edification of its
future king. This however does not necessarily imply any insin-
cerity on his part, for nothing in any of his surviving writings
indicates that he was ever an Imperialist or a Germanist.

Next follows, in the order of the *Politics*, an interesting discussion
of alternative theories, Plato's especially, which it is unnecessary
to summarize here. Egidius criticises the same features of Plato's
Republic that Aristotle does and in much the same way. He
favors Aristotle's unity as against Plato's uniformity, and agrees
with "the philosopher" in condemning the community in property,
wives, and children, and the military training of women. The
chief positive contribution of Egidius, if he can be said to make any
beyond a remarkable adaptation of Aristotle, is contained in the

[1] *De Regimine Principum*, III, I, cap. i. In omnibus hominibus est quidam naturalis
impetus ad communitatem civitatis. St. Thomas Aquinas, Commentary on Aristotle's
Politics I, 2. Natura quidem igitur impetus [ὁρμή] in omnibus ad talem communitatem :
qui autem primus instituit, maximorum bonorum causa. Translation of William of Moerbeka. F. Susemihl, *Aristotelis Politicorum Libri Octo*, 1872, p. 10.
[2] Egidius Romanus, *De Regimine Principum*, Bk. III, part i, chap. ii.
[3] Book III, part ii, chap. xxxii.
[4] *Ibid.*, chap. xxxiii.

thirty-six chapters of Part II in which he treats of the manner of ruling a *civitas* or *regnum* in time of peace. He here indicates the usual medieval preference for monarchy over all other forms of the state mentioned by Aristotle, and he argues at length in favor of the hereditary monarchy and against the elective. One of his reasons for preferring the former was that it was better suited to ensure the good of the subjects because it was founded in ancient custom and was therefore more according to nature. "For custom is a sort of other nature, wherefore forms of government originating in custom become quasi-natural." [1] This reflects the view which he sets forth elsewhere at greater length, that additions made by human law — which he normally regards as customary law — are not necessarily against the law of nature. To reach such an Aristotelian conclusion as this, he, of course, has to repudiate the definition of natural law given by Ulpian and adopted by the authors of Justinian's *Institutes* which identifies it with animal instinct. This he does by making a fourfold classification of law, into the *jus naturale, jus animalium, jus gentium,* and *jus civile,* thus distinguishing sharply between the law of man and that of the lower animals.[2]

In discussing the duties and functions of the prince Egidius devotes much space — much more proportionally than the *Politics* — to the difference between monarchy and tyranny, to the obligation of a prince to be a king and not a tyrant, and to the means he must employ to do so.

The bulk of this interesting discussion of politics is devoted to the functions and above all to the duties of the prince; but the author adds further chapters on the necessity of the king's taking counsel in the administration of his realm, the matters on which such counsel should be had, and the character and position of those from whom it should be received. This discussion is followed by another on the duties of the king's judges, and this part of the book concludes with a section on the duties of the people.

In sum, the king is "head of the realm" (*caput regni*).[3] In a sense he is law personified, for law is, as it were, an inanimate prince, and the prince a living law; and insofar as the animate is higher than the inanimate, to this degree the prince is above the law. To doubt, then, whether the prince should be just and impartial is to

---

[1] Book III, part ii, chap. v.   [2] Chap. xxiv.   [3] Chap. xxxv.

doubt whether a rule is truly a rule; and without an even rule all things would be in disorder.[1]

It is thus in the very nature of a true king to rule justly, and it is therefore the duty of every prince so to rule, and to strive to make his subjects good and virtuous. If he fails in this he is no king but a tyrant. If he does it — and apparently *only* if he does — then it is the subjects' duty to reverence and obey him, to avoid all occasion for his anger, and to be careful "not to transgress his ordinances and precepts"; "for it is worst of all for a realm to forsake the royal ordinances and the lawful precepts and not to be ruled by the king." [2]

A general survey of the political and intellectual development of the period between the close of the investiture struggle and the end of the middle ages leads to the impression that as a whole it was an epoch of ecclesiastic controversy in which the writings on "Church and State" constituted the chief stimulus to active political thought, furnished the principal concrete issue upon which it turned, and determined the general form of its expression. For most of the period, therefore, it is in writings concerned with this great controversy that we have found our main literary source of new political ideas and the chief illustration of habitual ones. But as we have seen the great controversy is divided chronologically into several distinct struggles each with its own peculiar sources of friction, and between these periods of intense controversial activity lie intervals of comparative quiet when for a brief period the chief purpose of political writing is neither to refute any particular "heresy" nor to drive its supporters out of court, but rather to survey in calmer spirit the whole complex of social and political relations and find a firm foundation upon which they can rest. Between the middle of the twelfth century and the end of the thirteenth we find such a period, when for a little time political works are sometimes more systematic than polemical, and John of Salisbury in truly philosophic spirit can sum up the thought of past centuries and St. Thomas lay a firm foundation for that of the centuries to come.

But the interval was comparatively short, and from the renewal of the old strife in the persons of Boniface VIII and Philip IV to the end, the current of political thought is found again flowing through the rapids of controversy instead of the quieter pools,

[1] Bk. III, part ii, chap. xii. [2] Chap. xxxiv.

and the charts we must follow are writings in support of a cause, such as the *Summa,* so called, of Augustinus Triumphus or the *Defensor Pacis.* To this, in the fourteenth century, there is only one exception important enough to be noted. We find here and there, in the technical writings of the jurists of this period, useful indications of contemporary thought entirely unoriginal and unsystematic, but the more valuable politically because they are usually unbiassed by championship of either side in the great controversy of the age. On incidental political questions they are cool, detached, and occasionally a little cynical.

The general name of "commentators" has been given by modern historians to the civil lawyers of this general period because the briefer "gloss" or note explanatory of Justinian's text customary with their predecessors in the law school of Bologna and elsewhere, had grown under their hands into an extended discussion of points of law for which the words of the original Roman law-book often served only as an introduction.

It was this, of course, which later laid them open to the attacks of the purists of the humanistic revival such as Cujas, who could only refer to them as "donkeys." Neither their Latin nor their law was classical, and it was easy to pick out "howlers" in plenty from their references to ancient history.

But it is in these very characteristics that we find their chief importance for the history of political ideas. Unlike their predecessors the Glossators of the twelfth and thirteenth centuries, the primary object they had in mind in their writings was not the clarification of a law of the sixth century, but an application of the principles of Roman jurisprudence to the laws actually existing in the fourteenth.

"The task to which they addressed themselves was a new one, and a greater one than anything attempted by their predecessors, the task namely of building up, on the foundations furnished by the Glossators, a Roman law which might be applied in actual life and which, as such, might serve (in the first instance for Italy) as a living *common* law." [1] The earlier Glossators are of vast

---

[1] *The Institutes,* by Rudolph Sohm, translated by J. C. Ledlie, 3d ed., Oxford, 1897, p. 141. This book is valuable for the whole subject and more sympathetic toward the Post-Glossators than the monumental work of Savigny, which, however, after a century still remains the standard account of medieval Roman law, *Geschichte des römischen Rechts im Mittelalter* 2d ed., 7 volumes, Heidelberg, 1834 ff. A good brief statement is given in English by Sir Paul Vinogradoff in *Roman Law in Mediaeval Europe,* New York, 1909, new ed. edited by Professor de Zulueta.

importance in the general history of political thought, but none
of this is owing to any information they can give us of how men
were actually thinking about the state at the time they were
lecturing on the law of ancient Rome. These Post-Glossators of
the fourteenth century, on the contrary, just because they were
practical lawyers dealing with the legal problems of their own time
have an interest for the historian of political thought in direct
proportion to the "barbarism" of their law. The greatest of them
was Bartolus, and the most important for politics,[1] but no one at
all acquainted with this juristic literature will expect to find in his
writings many positive contributions to political thought. One
does find, however, some invaluable indications of the nature and
the practical effects of some of the political ideas generally held
in the fourteenth century. In his discussion, for example, of the
status of litigants in a city with *merum et mixtum imperium* he
illustrates the contemporary political meaning of that ancient
legal phrase and shows the widespread practical effects of the
great dilemma of the middle ages between the theory of the
universality of Roman law and Roman sovereignty on the one
hand, and on the other the undeniable independence of that law
and authority enjoyed in fact, not by great realms only, such as
France and England, but in considerable measure by "free cities"
scattered over many parts of the "Roman" territory.[2] Only one
small work of his, *On Tyranny (De Tyrannia)*, attempts to deal at
all systematically with any political problems, and even in it his
purpose is as always that of the practical lawyer only.[3] Its chief
interest for us lies in the clear distinction he makes there, and
apparently one then generally accepted, between an usurper,
(*sine titulo*) and a ruler with legitimate authority who by acts of
misgovernment has forfeited his right to rule, a distinction which
was to receive its greatest illustration later in the religious divisions
of the sixteenth century.

By the middle of the fourteenth century the medieval phase of

---

[1] See *Bartolus and the Development of European Political Ideas* by J. N. Figgis in *The Divine Right of Kings*, 2d ed., Cambridge, 1914, pp. 343–372; and, above all, the brilliant study by Mr. C. S. N. Woolf, *Bartolus of Sassoferrato*, Cambridge, 1913.

[2] The passages from the commentary of Bartolus on the *Code* which illustrate these jurisdictional problems and constitute the real beginnings of the important branch of modern law termed "private international law" or "the conflict of laws," have been translated by Professor J. H. Beale, *Bartolus on the Conflict of Laws*, Cambridge, Mass., 1914.

[3] This has been translated into English by Professor Ephraim Emerton, *Humanism and Tyranny*, Cambridge, Mass., 1925, pp. 119–154.

the ancient conflict of Church and State had practically come to an end. Opponents of papal claims could add nothing of importance to what Marsiglio had already said, so long as medieval habits of thought persisted; and on the other side, the scandal of the "Babylonish captivity," followed by the worse scandal of the great schism, had for the time estopped men from defending the exclusive claims of an institution which in actual practice had fallen so low. But the very depth which the Papacy had sounded in this period, now brought to the fore another great question which was not new but was to remain the central political issue almost to the end of the middle ages, the problem of the true constitution of the Church itself.

The history of political thought in the period of the Great Councils of the Church in the first half of the fifteenth century constitutes its last great medieval phase. It is the last time that these political problems were to be agitated in an intellectual world which still started with the assumption that Christendom is and must be one single *regnum* under the governance of God; and possibly the chief interest for the historian of thought in the attempts of the Councils to solve these problems lies in the conflict which there comes to light as never before between the old medieval idea of unity, and the new demands for recognition of ideas which had grown out of the institutions of national states now passing out of the stage of infancy and becoming dimly conscious of their "national" rights and powers.

The so-called Babylonish captivity had lasted almost seventy years, from 1309 to 1376. In the latter year Pope Gregory XI returned from Avignon to Rome, but on his death two years later and the election of the Italian Urban VI, the French party in the College of Cardinals, which had become the dominant party during the long residence at Avignon, withdrew from Rome and elected a French Pope who took the name of Clement VII. Devout men were now shocked by the unseemly conflict which followed between two men, each claiming to be the vicar of Christ and rightful head of the universal Church, while the adhesion of the European states to one or the other of them was dictated by motives purely political and worldly, and wholly selfish, and the spiritual mission of the Church seemed to be utterly ignored.

The application of the extreme doctrine of the *plenitudo potestatis* of the Pope to this unfortunate state of facts created an *impasse* from which there seemed no way out except through a voluntary withdrawal of one Pope or both, which in the circumstances could scarcely be expected. In 1409 a Council convoked at Pisa by the cardinals adopted the revolutionary remedy of deposing both popes and choosing another, who assumed the name of Alexander V, but as neither of the deposed popes would renounce his rights, there were now three popes, each claiming of right an exclusive jurisdiction over all Christendom for which he was answerable to God alone. The scandal became so great that John XXIII, successor to Alexander, was finally forced reluctantly to summon the Council of Constance in 1414, and thus the great political question of the age was brought to a direct issue.

This question was not a new one and there is nothing really new in the arguments employed before the Council or during its sessions, but never before had these arguments been expressed with such heat or at such length as now. The essential point in the contention of the reformers was their assertion of the competence of a universal Council of the Church to adjudicate a disputed claim to papal authority, with its important corollary that the jurisdiction of this Council is higher than that of any Pope.

The position of the Conciliar party may probably be illustrated best by the acts of the Councils themselves which gave official expression to their views as to the true constitution of the Church universal.

In 1409 the Council of Pisa, as a "universal synod representing the Church universal," had deposed Benedict XIII and Gregory XII as "notorious schismatics."[1] In 1415, at its fifth session, the Council of Constance agreed to a declaration far more general and far-reaching, "Probably the most revolutionary official document in the history of the world," in the opinion of the late Dr. Figgis,[2] "A General Council constituting and representing the Catholic Church, has authority immediately from Christ which everyone in existence of whatsoever status or dignity, even of papal, is bound to obey in those things which pertain to the faith, the extirpation of the said schism, and the reform of the Church in head and in members."[3] In October 1417 the Council issued another decree which, had it become permanent, might have had

---

[1] Mirbt, *Quellan zur Geschichte des Papsttums*, 4th ed., p. 227.
[2] *From Gerson to Grotius*, 1st ed., p. 35.   [3] Mirbt, *op. cit.*, p. 228.

practical results even more important. Its provisions included
the summoning of councils at regular intervals of ten years "forever," and guarantees of their independence of papal control
through prorogation or removal from one place to another. In
1439 these two decrees of the Council of Constance were reaffirmed
in the Council of Basel and refusal to accept them was branded as
heresy.[1]

Our knowledge of the political thought of this time comes mainly
from the voluminous writings in defence of these principles written
between the beginning of the schism and the final victory of the
Papacy over the Council in 1448.[2]

Chief among them are the writings of Gerson during the Council
of Constance and the *De Concordantia Catholica* of Nicholas of
Cusa defending the acts of the Council of Basel, easily the greatest
of fifteenth century political writings, and one of the most interest-

[1] Mirbt, *op. cit.*, p. 233.

[2] The literature relating to the councils of the fifteenth century is large. Of the official
acts of the councils a judicious selection is given in Mirbt, *Quellen zur Geschichte des Papsttums und des römischen Katholizismus*, 4th ed., Tübingen, 1924, pp. 227–243, *passim*. The
Acta Concilii Constanciensis edited by Heinrich Finke, four vols., Münster i. W., 1896–
1928, now supersedes, for the official documents of Constance, the *Magnum Oecumenicum
Concilium Constantiense* of Hermann von der Hardt, six vols., Frankfort and Leipzig, 1697–
1700, though the latter remains valuable for some of the pamphlets reprinted there. For the
Council of Basel, the older *Consilia* of Mansi, vols. 29–31, and *Amplissima Collectio* of
Martène and Durand may be consulted, together with the *Monumenta Conciliorum genera-
lium saeculi decimi quinti*, Vienna, vol. ii, 1873, and J. Haller, *Concilium Basiliense: Studien und
Quellen zur Geschichte des Concils von Basel*, seven vols., 1896–1910. Among the histories of
the councils it is unnecessary to mention any beyond, *A History of the Papacy during the
Period of the Reformation*, by Bishop Creighton, vols. i and ii, Boston, 1882; Hefele's
Conciliengeschichte; and the early volumes of Pastor's great *History of the Popes* (English
translation).

On the political aspects of the councils much less has been written in modern times. The
brief chapter by Dr. John Neville Figgis in his *From Gerson to Grotius*, 1st ed., Cambridge,
1907, is the most brilliant and valuable summary extant, to which I am much indebted.
He has dealt with a part of the subject also in *Politics at the Council of Constance (Transactions of the Royal Historical Society)*. Mention should also be made of chap. x in Professor
W. A. Dunning's *History of Political Theories Ancient and Mediaeval*. Among contemporary
pamphlets, see Cardinal Zabarella's *De Schismatibus Authoritate Imperatoris Tollendis*, in
Schard, *De Jurisdictione, Autoritate, et Praeeminentia Imperiali*, Basiliae (1566), p. 688;
the *De Potestate Imperatoris et Papae* of Antonius de Rosellis (printed in Goldast's *Monarchia*,
vol. i, p. 252 ff), and the writings of Henricus de Langenstein and others, especially of Petrus
de Alliaco (Pierre d'Ailly), in the appendices to vols. i and ii of the complete works of Gerson
edited by Louis Ellies du Pin, Antwerpiae, 1706; together with others printed in the collection of von der Hardt referred to above. The *De Ortu et Authoritate Imperii Romani* of
Aeneas Sylvius (later Pope Pius II) is in Schard, *op. cit.*, p. 314. The five volumes of the
Opera Omnia Joannis Gersonii, edited by du Pin, contain all Gerson's writings on the coun-
cil. The *De Concordantia Catholica* of Nicholas of Cusa is given in Schard, *op. cit.*, p. 465.
For an admirable estimate of Cusanus, a select bibliography, and a brief summary of the
De Concordantia, see *Nicolas of Cusa*, by Professor Ernest F. Jacob (*The Social and Political
Ideas of Some Great Thinkers of the Renaissance and the Reformation*, edited by F. J. C.
Hearnshaw, p. 32); the fullest modern account of Nicholas of Cusa is by Edmond Vansteen-
berghe, *Le Cardinal Nicolas de Cues*, Paris, 1920.

ing of the later middle ages.[1] The *De Concordantia*, though written in support of a cause, was none the less a comprehensive summation of the political thought of the later middle ages, as the *Policraticus* of John of Salisbury was of the earlier. Each came at the end of an era, and each summed it up. The *De Concordantia* marks the last phase of a development of thought whose first phase is best illustrated by St. Thomas. As Dr. Figgis says, "It is almost the last book which treats Christendom as a single organic system, in which a complete theory of politics, whole and parts, is set forth."[2] But though the theories of the conciliarists are not novel their expression of these theories and their application of them to the changing political conditions of the time are second to none in historical importance or in their actual influence upon subsequent political thought. It was ideas much older than Gerson's which survived in modern Gallicanism, but a study of the whole movement will show that his formulation of these ideas constituted one of the chief precedents for all later assertions of the "Gallican liberties" in France, and in fact for all later constitutionalism wherever it is to be found. The discussions of Constance, as Dr. Figgis points out — and it is equally true of the political writings in support of them — were "far more purely political than those of the Middle Ages, because they were not concerned with the conflicts between ecclesiastical and spiritual authority [though Gerson does deal incidentally with these at considerable length], but with the depositary, the functions, and the limits, of sovereign power in a perfect society."[3] "They did not anxiously argue from the State to the Church or *vice versa*, but from the idea of a society to its consequences."[4] "Arguing from the precedent of constitutional States," the conciliar theory "decides upon the best form of government in general, and lays down the lines which controversy took until Whiggism succumbed to the influence of Rousseau."[5] "Now the belief of the Conciliar writers, which was derived really from the facts of the political world of their day but based in argument on appeals partly to Aristotle and partly to the Mosaic system, was that this constitution [the most perfect possible because the one prescribed by Christ for

---

[1] The space here allotted to the conciliar period is wholly incommensurate with its great importance, but greater brevity seemed possible because there is so little really new in the essentials of the theories advanced at the time.

[2] *From Gerson to Grotius*, 1st ed., p. 59.
[3] *Ibid.*, p. 55.
[4] *Ibid.*, p. 54.
[5] *Ibid.*, p. 50.

his Church] was a πολιτεία, a mixed, or as later writers have
called it, a limited monarchy, in which while the monarchical
principle is preserved the danger of tyranny should be removed
by the power of a small body of permanent advisers, a contin-
ual council, and ultimately checked by a large representative
assembly." [1]

It was the illimitable *potestas* claimed during the schism by
each of the rival popes as his exclusive right which made the
healing of the schism appear so hopeless.   For one brief period,
however, the scandal became so notorious that it overrode the
theories of the canonists.   For the moment they were silenced
though not convinced by the claim of the conciliar party that all
authority existed only for the edification of the Church and must
be resisted however legitimate, when it was found actually tending
to the Church's destruction.   The Councils resulted and the unity
of the Church was at length restored, but the very fulfilment of
this part of the conciliar programme made the other part unattain-
able.   The scandal which made the councils possible was caused by
the schism, not by the extravagance of papal claims, and therefore
when the former was removed the latter proved to be too firmly
entrenched in the law and custom of the Church to be attacked
successfully; the short revolutionary period of the councils was
followed by "the Papalist reaction," a phrase aptly characterizing
political conditions to the end of the middle ages, so far as these
were concerned with the problem of Church and State.   In the
failure of the councils and in its causes, Dr. Figgis says, "are to be
discerned at once the grounds of the religious revolution [the
Protestant revolt of the sixteenth century], the excuse for ultra-
montane ideals, and the general tendency to autocracy in all
States." [2]   As to the Reformation and ultramontanism, there can
be no doubt; for autocracy in secular politics the case does not
seem to be quite so clear.   To say that "Eugenius IV is the fore-
runner of Louis XIV" is impliedly to ascribe to the revived *plenitudo potestatis* of the Pope a somewhat greater rôle as a factor in the
growth of secular absolutism in Europe after the fifteenth century
than seems warrantable.

The weakening of feudalism and the growing strength of monarchy as the focus of the new national feeling, at least in the most
centralized of the states of the West, would seem to be forces potent

---

[1] *From Gerson to Grotius*, p. 50.   [2] *Ibid.*, p. 35.

enough ultimately to bring about autocracy without the help of canonist doctrine or papal power. As to the Papacy itself, the truth of Dr. Figgis's observation is proved both by official pronouncements and by other writings. Among the latter probably the most important in the fifteenth century is the *Summa contra Ecclesie et Primatus Apostoli Petri Adversarios* of John of Turrecremata.[1] The title indicates accurately the purpose and the contents of the book. Its size and comprehensiveness warrant the title of *Summa*, and it is clearly intended not only as a refutation of the heresies of Wycliffe and Hus to which considerable attention is given, but even more as a direct answer to the contentions of the conciliarists concerning the relative powers of Pope and Council. So far as this latter question is concerned — and it was the chief question in dispute at the time — this book of John of Turrecremata may be considered as probably the chief and the most authoritative presentation of the official view of the Papacy, the fullest statement of the principles of "the Papalist reaction." As might be expected, it is uncompromising in its denial of the validity of the decrees of the Councils of Constance and Basel, and in its assertion of the superiority of the Pope to any Council and of his power to annul or dispense with its decrees. It is therefore at first sight surprising to find, on the question of the relation of the papal jurisdiction to that of secular rulers, a moderate view much closer to the doctrine of Innocent III or of Cardinal Bellarmine in the sixteenth century, than to the extreme views of Augustinus Triumphus or Alvarus Pelegius or to the majority of papal defenses in the later fifteenth and early sixteenth centuries.

But if the "ultramontanism" of the restored Papacy justifies the word "reaction" in describing its ecclesiastical theory, the phrase "age of the concordats," sometimes applied to this period, is equally accurate as an indication of its actual practice in dealings with the secular governments of the time. With the exception of France, from which the conciliar principles had come and where they were more deeply rooted than elsewhere, the states of western Europe were in the main content to drop the question of the general constitution of the Church and oppose no serious objection

---

[1] I have used the edition published at Rome in 1489, apparently the *editio princeps*. Many extracts from it are printed in Gieseler's *Compendium of Ecclesiastical History* (English translation), Edinburgh, 1853, vol. iv, p. 425 ff.

to the papal theory, provided some clerical abuses were remedied and a few regalian rights guaranteed within their own dominions. Thus the Papacy by a concordat or treaty with each state could make such concessions of this kind as were necessary without any apparent impairment of the theory of its own plenitude of power. They were concessions only. But they were concessions guaranteed by a bilateral document in the nature of a treaty, which implies two treaty-making powers. The concordats were in fact the price the Papacy paid for its victory over the councils and it was a price heavier than appeared at the time. They were a tacit acknowledgment of the sovereignty of national states and they mark the virtual end of the medieval theory that Christendom in its secular aspect is one great state as in its spiritual it is a single Church. From such an admission the logical inference must come sooner or later that the Church is *in* every nation instead of embracing all nations, and this can ultimately mean only that its functions are primarily spiritual and that its participation in secular matters is never justifiable except for a spiritual end — *ad finem spiritualem*. Cardinal Bellarmine's sixteenth century doctrine of the indirect power of the Pope in secular matters was not new in principle, but it had a new "international" application for which there had been less occasion before the late medieval period. The concordats made the theory of the indirect power a logical necessity, the only possible alternative to Gallicanism in Catholic Europe. By the beginning of the seventeenth century the doctrine of the papal plenitude of power which opposed the Gallican principle of its purely spiritual character, in practically every part of Europe which remained Catholic, had been softened into the claim of a right to mingle in secular matters only where spiritual needs imperatively demanded it; the fourteenth century doctrine that the Pope was temporal lord of the world, even of the Christian world, was gone forever. The principal factor in this great theoretical change was the emergence of national states so strong that their independent sovereignty could not safely be denied, and the concordats of the fifteenth century were a tacit admission of the fact and probably a principal cause of the subsequent change in theory. It was probably an early appreciation of this which led John of Turrecremata to couple his theory of papal omnipotence in matters spiritual with a power only indirect in matters temporal, but the majority of contemporary papal champions had not his keenness of sight, and it was only after the Council of Trent and the appearance of Cardinal Bellarmine's epoch-making *Disputationes* that this doctrine became general.[1]

France alone of the important nation-states of western Europe was still too firmly committed to the conciliar principles to make the concessions implied in a concordat with a Pope. Her solution of the problem, through the independent enactment of an assembly of the clergy of France summoned by King Charles VII, the Pragmatic Sanction of Bourges in 1438, constitutes the chief land-mark in the early development of the so-called "Liberties of the Gallican Church." [2]

When we turn, in the history of political thought in the fifteenth century, from the ecclesiastical to the secular field, we find comparatively few striking new developments and no very important literary sources, but the institutional growth was going steadily on which was slowly transforming the political world. On its intellectual side probably the political development of greatest importance was the gradual preparation of Germany for the reception of Roman law which was accomplished in the sixteenth century.[3] Of the books in which the development of the time may be traced, one of the most important was the *Libellus de Cesarea Monarchia* of Peter von Andlau which appeared in 1460.[4] It had been preceded by some fifteen years by the short treatise of Aeneas Sylvius, *De Ortu et Authoritate Imperii Romani*, and both followed at an interval of more than a century the important work of Lupold von Beber.burg. But Lupold wrote when nationalism was just beginning to influence political thought; it is more prominent in these two constitutional writers of the fifteenth century. The work of Aeneas is important as "the first study of the nature and

[1] The most important of the concordats, but typical in its provisions, is the one concluded at Vienna between Pope Nicholas V and the Emperor Frederick III in 1448. It is printed in Zeumer, *Quellensammlung*, p. 221; Mirbt, *Quellen* (4th ed.), p. 238; and elsewhere.

[2] The text of the Pragmatic Sanction of Bourges is given in Isambert, *Recueil général des anciennes lois françaises*, vol. ix, pp. 3–47.

The best account of it is in the admirable study by Noël Valois, *Histoire de la Pragmatique Sanction de Bourges sous Charles VII*, Paris, 1906, which includes a valuable appendix of illustrative documents.

[3] The account of the Reception which I have found most satisfactory is *Die Ursachen der Rezeption des römischen Rechts in Deutschland*, by Georg von Below, München und Berlin, 1905. It is preceded by a valuable critical examination of the earlier modern works on the subject.

[4] Printed in the *Zeitschrift der Savigny-Stiftung* (Germ. Abteilung xii, pp. 34–103; xiii, pp. 163–219). The fullest account of it is by Dr. Jos. Hürbin, *Peter von Andlau*, Strassburg, 1897.

content of sovereignty," [1] though the analysis of the conception was to wait for more than a century before it was made by Bodin, while Aeneas deals with it only in the concrete form of the institutions of the Empire. He differs from Peter von Andlau chiefly in treating the Empire as Roman, while Peter considers it as essentially German. For this reason there seems some justification for calling the *Libellus de Cesarea Monarchia*, as Hürbin does, the first attempt to treat of German constitutional law.[2]

Probably both these books are more important constitutionally than politically. The writings of Sir John Fortescue have an importance of both kinds, but this is probably owing to the use made of them in later constitutional crises in England, and to the indications they give of contemporary habits of thought, rather than to any great power of political analysis on the part of the author.

Next to Bracton, among medieval English writers on law and politics, the author probably most quoted in the great struggles of the seventeenth century was Sir John Fortescue, Chief Justice of the Court of King's Bench under Henry VI; and, as in Bracton's case, supporters and opponents of prerogative both claimed him as a champion of their own constitutional doctrines.[3] This impartiality resulted not alone from the proneness of controversialists always to force a one-sided meaning of their own into earlier precedents; it came in part from the apparently two-fold character of Fortescue's thought itself and from the inability of men of a later generation any longer to reconcile political conceptions which the medieval mind was still capable of harmonizing. The seventeenth century could see nothing but antagonism between powers which Fortescue thought of as working in concert; through the change of political conditions the earlier harmony had become a strident discord. For Fortescue, though writing late in the fifteenth

---

[1] Rehm, *Geschichte der Staatsrechtswissenschaft*, p. 197.

[2] *Peter von Andlau*, p. 184. See also Rehm, *Geschichte der Staatsrechtswissenschaft*, p. 182, note 6.

[3] Their quotations were all from the *De Laudibus Legum Angliae*, the only work of Fortescue's then in print. *The Governance of England* was first printed in the eighteenth century, and the *Natura Legis Naturae*, never before Lord Clermont's edition of Fortescue's works which appeared in 1869. References to many of these quotations is made by Miss Caroline A. J. Skeel, in a paper included in the *Transactions of the Royal Historical Society* for 1916 (Third Series, vol. x, pp. 77–114) on *The Influence of the Writings of Sir John Fortescue.* For an additional modern discussion of Fortescue, see Miss A. E. Levett, *Sir John Fortescue,* in *The Social and Political Ideas of Some Great Thinkers of the Renaissance and the Reformation*, edited by F. J. C. Hearnshaw, pp. 61–85.

century, was still distinctly medieval in thought, and the feudal conception of the state which he retained could accommodate *jura regalia* with the rights of subjects in a way not possible for men to whom feudalism was no longer even a memory or at best only "the badge of their ancient slavery." [1]

No word is more prominent in the political part of Fortescue's works than *dominium*, and the feudal doctrine of dominion is the key to his whole theory of the state. Now the essence of the theory of dominion is a hierarchy of rights and powers all existing in or exercisable over the same objects or persons, and the fundamental relationship of one power to another in this hierarchy is the superiority of the higher to the lower, rather than a complete supremacy in any one over all others. Historically as well as etymologically the "sovereign" (*superanus*) was in many respects superior before he became supreme. Every baron, says Beaumanoir, is "sovereign" in his barony, but the king is sovereign over all and of his own right has control over the whole of his kingdom.[2] Barons within their own fiefs have powers similar to the king's, as his in his own kingdom are similar to the Emperor's, but these powers are not to be exercised against the king.[3] The king's right is greater than all others, but only because he alone has custody (*garde*) over all the realm with obligations and powers correspondingly wide. Richard Fitzralph, Archbishop of Armagh, expressed these ideas with unusual clearness in his *De Pauperie Salvatoris*, written about the middle of the fourteenth century, and a quotation from him may prove helpful in understanding the thought of his century and the next.

"*Richard:* Since there are then several rights of dominion over a single thing any one of which belongs to one person alone, as a baron has his own dominion over one barony, his lord the earl has his dominion over the same barony, his duke has *dominium* belonging to him over the selfsame barony, and even his king has a regal dominion to him belonging; so it follows that each one of these has ownership (*proprietas*) of such a barony. Yet no one doubts, I think, that one who has ownership of anything whatsoever may make use of that thing without legal wrong (*injuria*) to anyone else, and so it follows that each of these may have use

---

[1] The phrase is Milton's, *The Tenure of Kings and Magistrates.*
[2] *Coutumes de Beauvaisis*, edited by Salmon, § 1043.
[3] *Ibid.*, § 1510.

of the barony without injury to any of the others; and likewise any of the superiors mentioned above may, as it seems, without legal wrong to the baron receive the revenues of the barony and use them as he sees fit — which is not true."

"*John:* So it seems to follow, though I don't see how that can hold good, because the baron can use and ought freely to have the use of the revenues of the barony, and not his superior lords except with his consent."

"*Richard:* You are wrong in adding that statement. For if the baron should intend to prevent his king's, his duke's, or his earl's enjoyment of the use proper to the dominion of either in the revenues of the barony, then the baron would be doing an injury to his lord, for his lord's right of use in things subject to him by his own right of dominion is just and proper.

"In a word, if the earl, the duke, or the king should summon the baron to his parliament or to a just war in which they have a common concern, and should decree a reasonable stipend for a certain number of knights to be paid out of the revenues of the baron for the conduct of the common war, he would do that justly, and the baron could not resist without doing him an injury; and the like is true in many other cases. And so the king, the duke, and the earl, in his own case may freely use the revenues of the barony and even the very person of the baron, yet they have no ownership in the revenues of the barony or in the body of the baron, though each of them does have over the barony a *dominium* belonging to him. It follows therefore that not every right of dominion belonging to one person alone is or can be called ownership."

"*John:* So I see, since the *dominium* of the aforesaid superiors, although a *dominium* belonging to them individually, in respect of the barony, is not full and entire, for not one of those superiors can grant or sell that barony nor perform any act of lordship in the barony, completely or generally as the baron can." The latter form of dominion alone then, he thinks, is properly called *proprietas*, and not the less complete rights of the superior lords. But Richard hastens to add a correction.

"For everything belonging to one there is a corresponding *proprietas:* so, as each of these persons has a *dominium* of his own, in each of them exists one *proprietas*. But perhaps you do not notice that there is one *proprietas* of dominion (*proprietas dominii*), another *proprietas* of the thing dominated (*rei dominate proprietas*)." The superior lords, he says, have the former alone, the *proprietas dominii*, the baron in addition has the ownership of the barony (*proprietas baronie*) or proprietary right in the thing dominated, and this gives him a fuller use of it than that enjoyed by the superior lords who have only a *proprietas dominii*. In general, "the proprietas over distinct things is the immediate and entire dominion over those things." [1]

This is a long extract and somewhat technical, but it serves to make clear some fundamental political ideas of the later middle age, including Fortescue's. It is noteworthy that the *dominium* of the king, according to Fitzralph's statement, though higher in degree, is exactly the same in kind as that of the duke or the earl. It is evident that Fortescue's *dominium regale* which so dominates all his political thought is of much the same kind. "As a piece of land which is given to me is called my right (*jus*), so the power which is given to the king is properly named the king's right." [2] In feudal fashion, the king's royal power is regarded as a quasi-private right over the persons and property of his subjects, existing side-by-side with, and in close relation to other proprietary or dominical rights not inconsistent with it which others enjoy over the same persons or property. With this in mind, we have one key to Fortescue's *dominium regale* and may hope to understand his *dominium politicum et regale*, and it becomes easier to appreciate the causes of the failure to apprehend his true meaning in the seventeenth century and afterward, when feudalism was a thing of the past.

In light of the statements above we may consider Fortescue's famous classification of monarchical government which appears in slightly varying form in all his works. In one of his writings, Fortescue mentions three kinds of lordship, *dominium regale*, *dominium politicum*, and *dominium despoticum*,[3] where, as Mr. Plummer surmises, "by *dominium regale* he probably means a limited, and by *dominium despoticum* an absolute monarchy." [4]

[1] *Ricardi Armachani De Pauperie Salvatoris*, Lib. I, cap. ii, in *Johannis Wycliffe De Dominio Divino*, edited by R. L. Poole, London, 1890, pp. 279–280.

[2] *De Natura Legis Naturae*, Part I, chap. 27, *The Works of Sir John Fortescue, Knight*, edited by Thomas (Fortescue) Lord Clermont, London, 1869, vol. i, p. 218.

[3] *The Declaracion upon Certayn Wrytinges, Works*, vol. i. p. 533.

[4] *The Governance of England*, edited by Charles Plummer, Oxford, 1885, p. 169. I am unable to agree with some of the principal conclusions in the valuable introduction to this book, but wish to acknowledge my great indebtedness to it.

In the *De Natura Legis Naturae* the author speaks of three forms
of rule and calls them respectively *dominium regale*, *dominium
politicum*, and *dominium politicum et regale*; [1] meaning, as
Mr. Plummer thinks, by the first "absolute monarchy," by the
second, "republican government," and by the third, "the mixture
of the two" "which is constitutional monarchy." [2] In the *De
Laudibus Legum Angliae* the classification is practically the same
as in the *De Natura Legis Naturae*, [3] and in the *Governance of England* two kinds of kingdoms are referred to, a *dominium regale* in
which the king "mey rule his peple bi suche lawes as he makyth
hym self. And therfore he mey sett vppon thaim tayles and
other imposicions, such as he wol hym self, withowt thair assent";
and a *dominium politicum et regale*, where the king "may not rule
his peple bi other lawes than such as thai assenten unto. And
therfore he mey sett vpon thaim non imposicions withowt thair
owne assent." [4]

Before attempting to explain these terms or to criticise Mr. Plummer's explanation, it is necessary to add another statement of
Fortescue himself. In the *De Laudibus* he says in answer to a
question of the Prince, "Wherefore, to give a brief answer to that
question of yours concerning the different powers which kings
claim over their subjects, I am firmly of opinion that it arises solely
from the different natures of their original institution. . . . So the
kingdom of *England* had its original from *Brute* and the Trojans,
who attended him from *I aly* and *Greece*, and changed into a
lordship both political and regal (*in Dominium Politicum et Regale
prorupit*)." [5]

In support of his most fundamental distinction, that between a
dominium regale and one *regale et politicum*, Fortescue cites especially the *De Regimine Principum* of St. Thomas Aquinas and the
book with the same title by Egidius Romanus. In neither of these
books can acceptance be found of any form of government that
bears much resemblance to a "constitutional" or "limited"

[1] Part I, chap. xvi, *Works*, vol. i, pp. 77, 205.
[2] *The Governance of England*, p. 83.
[3] Chaps. 9-14, *Fortescue De Laudibus Legum Angliae*, edited by A. Amos, Cambridge,
1825, pp. 26-46, 218-223.
[4] *The Governance of England*, chap. i, p. 109. In the *De Natura Legis Naturae* the king
with *dominium politicum et regale* is said to rule "secundum leges quas cives *instituerunt*."
Part I, chap. xvi, *Works*, vol. i, p. 77. In the original *instituerunt* is not in italics. I have
inserted them to emphasize the past tense.
[5] Cap. xiii.

monarchy, though the difference between political and despotic government is well understood and that between monarchy and tyranny discussed at great length.   We are driven to the conclusion reached by Lord Clermont and Mr. Plummer that Fortescue drew the most valuable part of his speculations "from his own experience of the government of England"; but, on the other hand, his own definite statements repeated in all his works, leave no doubt whatever that he considered these speculations to be essentially those of the *De Regimine Principum* of St. Thomas and of Egidius.   Did he then misunderstand these authors, or may we possibly have been somewhat misunderstanding him?   When he says that *dominium politicum et regale* is to be found in principle in the *De Regimine Principum*, and we can find nothing of "constitutional monarchy" there, may it be that *dominium politicum et regale* for Fortescue does not quite mean "constitutional monarchy" in our sense of the term; and if so, wherein does his meaning differ from ours?[1]

Modern "constitutional" or "limited" monarchy means somewhat more than a mere "rule of law": it implies necessarily the existence of some organ or organs of government with an authority not derived from the king.   It is, in the words of Mr. Plummer's definition of Fortescue's *dominium politicum et regale* quoted above, a mixture of absolute monarchy and republican government.   The

[1] If the interpretations given above (pp. 329-333, 335-338) of the political thought of St. Thomas and the continuation of his *De Regimine Principum* are accurate, it is apparent that Fortescue adopted from the latter his terms *dominium politicum* and *dominium regale*, but not his third form of government, the *dominium politicum et regale* which for him best fits the English constitution.   As we have seen, the continuator of St. Thomas was an anti-monarchist and his *dominium regale* was "despotic" and incapable of mixing with a *dominium politicum*.   Fortescue, on the other hand, like St. Thomas, was unquestionably a monarchist and his *dominium politicum et regale* was certainly not despotic.   Tholommeo of Lucca, therefore, in all probability furnished Fortescue with his terminology, but not with his theory of the state.   That is, in general, the orthodox theory of monarchy prevalent in Fortescue's days, held, as I have tried above to show, by both St. Thomas and Egidius Romanus, and set forth both in the *De Regimine Principum* of Egidius and in St. Thomas's part of the other work with the same title.   Fortescue gives no hint of seeing any inconsistency between St. Thomas and his continuator, and possibly he found none, but he could not follow both.   The assumption that he agrees in theory with Egidius and St. Thomas seems to account satisfactorily for all his statements; the assumption that he is following the political views of Tholommeo is an impossible one if my reading of the *De Regimine Principum* is correct, for it would make Fortescue's theory decidedly anti-monarchical and that it certainly was not.   The only solution of this riddle which satisfies me lies in the belief that Fortescue is using the phrases *dominium regale* and *dominium politicum* in a sense consistent with the political ideas of his time and with the monarchical doctrine of St. Thomas and Egidius Romanus.   This alone makes possible the mixture of the two in Fortescue's *dominium politicum et regale*, but it is a sense contrary to any "republicanism" whether of Tholommeo of Lucca or of modern interpreters of Fortescue.

king is not restricted merely negatively by laws defining or limiting his legitimate sphere of action: he is hampered positively in the actual exercise of his governmental functions by a competing authority which within its limits is as valid as his own. Nothing less than this can be meant by a true mixture of absolute monarchy and "republican government." But no such mixture is advocated in the writings of St. Thomas or Egidius cited by Fortescue, little of it could, I believe, have been drawn by him, "from his own experience of the government of England," and there is no real indication anywhere in Fortescue's writings of the existence of such an idea in his own mind. Mr. Plummer is doubtless right in identifying *dominium regale* with monarchy "absolute" in some sense, he seems as certainly wrong in saying that by *dominium politicum* Fortescue meant "republican government." To Fortescue the government of England was in his own day a *regimen politicum et regale*. It had been merely *regale* in the mythical period of Brute which Fortescue accepted as historical, and was then a *regimen despoticum* not unsuited to the manners of that age; and *regal* it remained, for the Lancastrians were heirs of Brute's regalian rights and England was an hereditary monarchy. But Fortescue, like all the theorists of his age, was an Aristotelian as well as a monarchist, and in the thirteenth chapter of the *De Laudibus*, he shows how in time political government "broke out" (*prorupit*) in England and in other monarchies, as men advanced in political capacity. The political government which thus arose Fortescue defines in the words of Cicero reported in St. Augustine's *City of God* as "a body of men joined together in society by a consent to right, by an union of interests, and for promoting the common good." In the "body politic" so created it is inevitable that "one part must govern and the rest be governed," but such government must be according to the "right" in consent to which the state exists; the king is the head of the body politic, but "the law, under which the people is incorporated, may be compared to the nerves or sinews of the body natural." "And as the bones, and all the other members of the body preserve their functions, and discharge their several offices by the nerves; so do the members of the community by the law. And as the head of the body natural cannot change its nerves or sinews, cannot deny to the several parts their proper energy, their due proportion and aliment of blood; neither can a king, who is head of the body politic, change the laws thereof, nor take from the people what is theirs by right against their consents. . . . For he is appointed to protect his subjects in their lives, properties and laws; for this very end and purpose he has the delegation of power from the people; and he has no just claim to any other power but this."[1] Therefore, in England, which is a body politic, the king "may not rule his peple bi other lawes than such as thai assenten unto. And therfore he mey sett vpon thaim non imposicions withowt thair owne assent."[2] These laws or sinews of the state, Fortescue says in chapter fifteen of the *De Laudibus*, so far as they are merely human in origin, consist of the laws of nature, customs, or statutes; "but the two former, when they are reduced into writing, and made public by a sufficient authority of the Prince, and commanded to be observed, they then pass into the nature of (*in naturam mutantur*), and are accepted as, constitutions or statutes, and, in virtue of such promulgation and command, oblige the subject to the observance of them under a greater penalty than otherwise they could do."

From all this it is plain that the king is "under the law," which, on its negative side, means that his rights are bounded by the existence of other rights in the hands of subjects. But is this properly a "constitutional" or "limited" monarchy? Does it of necessity imply any popular control over the king in his government, or a definition of citizenship in any way similar to Aristotle's, under which citizens shall rule and be ruled *in turn*? Bodin later objected to that definition and on the ground that it was inconsistent with the "absolute" monarchies of western Europe in the middle ages and afterward. It is true that Fortescue denies the right of the king to change the laws of the state, to obstruct the subjects in "the discharge of their several offices," or to deprive them of "their due proportion and aliment of blood"; but these restrictions we are now in little danger of overlooking though they often were overlooked in the seventeenth and eighteenth centuries. What we at present are most likely to forget is the fact that for Fortescue England's government was both "political" *and* "regal,"

---

[1] *De Laudibus Legum Angliae*, chap. xiii.

[2] *The Governance of England*, chap. i, p. 109. Fortescue is evidently thinking primarily of the assent to parliamentary grants when he thus speaks of the "lawes" which the people "assenten unto." The obvious and striking exercise of a "despotic" regal power consisted in the levying of "imposicions" without consent as in France, and it was in this chiefly that Fortescue believed a difference existed between the monarchies of France and England.

a *dominium politicum* ET *regale :* that by becoming a *regimen politicum* it did not cease also to be something of what it was before. Under the law of England even in Fortescue's time there were still *jura regalia* as well as rights of the subject, and the law gave to the members no authority to interfere with the head of the body politic in the discharge of his proper office or to deny him his "due proportion and aliment of blood." His rights were secured against the encroachment of his subjects by the same law which deprived him of the right to abridge their liberties or immunities, and the subjects had no more authority to alter that law in their interest than the king in his. Like the franchises of his subjects the king's administration was a *liberum regimen,* a "free" government. The "estate," or at least the power of the king, thus remained a *dominium regale,* and within the sphere of his royal administration he was without a superior or an equal and legally "absolute," though the *dominium politicum* which had "broken out" since the days of Brute had deprived him, in theory at least, of his former arbitrary or "despotic" power; thus leaving "regal" no longer, as before, synonymous with "despotic," but substituting the directive force of law for the king's unbridled will even in the performance of his "office," as well as recognizing the *jura* of subjects by which that office's scope was limited. Some of the rules of nature and custom which guaranteed these rights of both king and subject might be "changed into the nature" of constitutions or statutes through a formal promulgation which the king alone could make and must make only with the subjects' consent, but promulgation did not imply that either a king or his people might re-define, or abridge, or obstruct a right belonging to the other.

England was thus still a *dominium regale,* but it was now also a *dominium politicum,* and the royal office was hedged in by other rights guaranteed to subjects by laws "such as they assenten unto," or "have established." This is certainly a government "under law," but it is scarcely helpful to define it without qualification as a "constitutional" or "limited" rule, mixed of absolute monarchy and "republican government."

In Fortescue the chief practical limitations on kingship are the negative limitations of law familiar to the medieval mind and enforceable as most things were in the feudal period, when enforceable at all, almost entirely through remedies applicable for the securing of proprietary rights. In modern times, as in ancient, governments are generally limited practically in a much more positive way, by the actual infusion of a popular element among the organs of government themselves. In the middle ages, in short, government was *limited*, in modern times it is also *controlled;* and a fruitful source of later constitutional struggles is to be found in the attempt positively to prove or to disprove a traditional right of *control* of government on the basis of medieval precedents which themselves contemplate nothing beyond its *limitation.* A failure to draw a distinction between these two must always result in serious misunderstanding not only of the whole of political thought in the later middle ages, but of many periods since, when medieval constitutional precedents were in dispute.

CHAPTER VII

CONCLUSION

Probably nothing in Jean Bodin's great treatise on politics has been more severely handled by modern English writers than his statement that the English monarchy of the late sixteenth century is an absolute monarchy differing in no essential way from that of France at the same period.[1]   Dr. John Cowell, a good Englishman even though a professor of Civil Law, writing a generation after Bodin, reached a conclusion in some ways similar, and for his pains had his book condemned by the King under pressure from the House of Commons.   Were these men as completely deceived concerning the nature of the English monarchy and of "absolute" monarchy in general as most modern historians insist?   For answer we must look back to the conception of monarchy prevailing in the later middle ages, which still colored political thought in the sixteenth century, and, it must be admitted, is not always understood by constitutional historians of today, who are oftentimes almost as naïve in their interpretations of medieval precedents as some of their predecessors in the seventeenth century.   Applying to medieval times our own modern notions, we are too ready to assume that when a thirteenth century publicist declares, as Bracton did, that the King is "under the law," he had in mind a "constitutional" ruler of the modern type.   By a constitutional king we mean one whose power even if not his person is controlled by other agencies or organs in the state, one whose governmental acts may be brought to book through the "responsibility" of the king himself or of his appointees associated with him in their practical operation.   A king who is irresponsible we think of as "absolute."   So he is, and so he was thought to be in the middle ages.   Their kings were actually both irresponsible and absolute, and absolute because irresponsible.   But the middle ages made some distinctions which we have lost or ignored.   The power of a king was "absolute" and practically irresponsible, but

[1] For example, Sir William Holdsworth, *A History of English Law*, vol. iv, p. 194.

it was not "arbitrary." The medieval king was an autocrat *de jure*, but he was not a despot, and if he abused his lawful power he might become a tyrant, something different from either. "What the king has willed has the force of law" only when that will is expressed in a particular way, and for certain purposes. As these limitations were usually expressed, the king is bound by the law of God and the law of nature, and sometimes the latter was considered the same as the customary "common" law of the land. "Custom is a sort of other nature," Egidius Romanus asserted in the thirteenth century, and in the middle ages generally men tended to identify the law of nature with the ancient *coutume*, much as some of the Roman jurists had identified it with the *jus gentium* centuries before, and as St. German in the sixteenth century identified it with the "law of reason" or Sir Edward Coke in the seventeenth with "the perfection of reason" which the ancient English common law embodied, a principle which Lord Camden declared late in the eighteenth century was "engrafted in" the English constitution. "Custom is the common law of those who use it," declared Pierre Grégoire in 1572,[1] and as late as 1628 Sir John Davis could say, "Therefore as the *lawe of nature*, which the Schoolmen call *Ius commune*, and which is also *Ius non scriptum*, being written onely in the heart of man, is better then all the written lawes in the world to make men honest and happy in this life, if they would observe the rules thereof: So the *customary law* of England, which we doe likewise call *Ius commune*, as comming neerest to the lawe of *Nature*, which is the root and touchstone of all good lawes, and which is also *Ius non scriptum*, and written onely in the memory of man . . . doth far excell our *written* lawes, namely our Statutes or Acts of Parliament."[2]

When a medieval king is sworn to treat such a law as beyond his competence to create or abridge, and when he actually treats it so in his administration, we, with our modern notions of "sanction," are all too ready to assume that this means no more than a check self-imposed by the king upon himself. But men of the middle ages did not so regard it.

One of the best proofs that these limitations were considered to be and actually were in some degree legal and practical and not merely "moral," truly coercive and not simply a "bridle" which

[1] *Praeludia*, Lugduni, 1587, p. 63.
[2] *Le Primer Report des Cases et Matters en Ley*, London, 1628, "A Preface Dedicatory."

the king placed upon himself in refraining voluntarily from acts which he might legally do, is the fact that the sanction of these limitations did not rest in "legalized rebellion" alone, but often lay to some extent also within the power of officials of the state and was actually exercised by them in cases where they were convinced that the "absolute" power of the king in administration had exceeded its bounds and trenched upon the customary rights of the people. This would naturally appear most clearly in a control over royal enactments actually exercised by those officials or bodies whose participation was a regular and necessary part of the formalities of promulgation. In this way monarchy was more or less restricted "by tying the instruments it was to act by." [1] In England, for example, this "tying" was ultimately brought about by the requirement that all "statutes" must be made by the king with the coöperation of the Lords and the Commons. In France, we have numerous proofs of the practical effectiveness of such checks, in the refusal of the Parliament of Paris and of other *Parlements* in the realm to register ordinances of the king. Without registration, it was held, no royal ordinance was binding.[2] If the *Parlement* refused to register, it is true, the king might order them to do so in a *lettre de jussion*, and finally compel them in a *lit de justice*, in which the king in person through an exercise of his "absolute" administrative authority for the moment superseded, by his presence in the *Parlement*, the jurisdiction of all judges deriving authority from him, somewhat in the way the jurisdiction of the Roman republican magistrates was suspended on the appointment of a dictator, or the rights guaranteed in some modern states are occasionally placed in temporary abeyance by a "suspension of the constitution." Even in this extreme case registration by the *Parlement* could not be dispensed with; it was obtained, often under formal protest, only at the oral command of the king in person, and by virtue of his supreme authority.[3] There are numerous instances of important modifica-

[1] Sir Roger Twysden, *Certayne Considerations upon the Government of England* (Camden Society), p. 111.

[2] Guy Coquille, *Institution au droit des François*, p. 2, in the 2d vol. of Coquille's collected works, published at Bordeaux in 1703.

[3] These French conflicts between the "absolute" jurisdiction of the king and the prescriptive rights embodied in the "constitution" have a curious parallel in England as late even as Stuart times. For instance, in 1628 Charles I wished to remove Sir John Walter from his place as Chief Baron of the Exchequer, but was unable to deprive him of his proprietary right in an office held *quamdiu se bene gesserit*, and never made any attempt to do so; but the king by an exercise of his "absolute" administrative authority did issue an order forbidding

tions practically forced upon the king by the *Parlement's* refusal
to register, and Bernard de la Roche-Flavin, the early historian of
the *Parlements*, mentions cases in which the royal *lettres de jussion*
were repeatedly ignored.[1] This requirement of registration was a
very real, even though an incomplete check upon the king, and a
check that was external and even "constitutional" in its character.
In the *Parlement* Claude de Seyssell saw a body constituted to
enforce *la justice*, one of the three "bridles," "by which the
supreme power of kings is checked."[2] The necessity for registration was, according to Chancellor Pasquier, "the chief restraint"
upon the King of France.[3]

Thus the medieval king was "absolute" and irresponsible, but
he was "limited." There were things beyond his legitimate power
and if he overstepped that power his acts were *ultra vires*. In a
feudal age it was natural to bring all these things under the usual
conceptions of tenure, or as we should say, of "property." This
property which a subject had of legal right in the integrity of his
personal status, and the enjoyment of his lands and goods, was
normally beyond the reach and control of the King. The rules
governing transactions concerning them came from immemorial
custom, the *coutume* which kings did not make and could not
destroy, but were bound to preserve and enforce. No one was
bound by a royal decree which infringed it, such a decree might
lawfully be disobeyed, and the feudal régime recognized the sanction of the withdrawal of allegiance and the further possibility of
legal rebellion or private warfare. At the opening of the fourteenth
century John of Paris declared that neither Pope nor King could
take a subject's goods without his consent.[4]

the Chief Baron to sit thereafter as a judge in the court, and this order was strictly obeyed
to the end of Walter's life. On this and other similar cases, see especially Samuel Heywood,
A Vindication of Mr. Fox's History, London, 1811, *Appendix No. I;* also C. H. McIlwain,
The Tenure of English Judges, American Political Science Review, vol. vii, no. 2, p. 217, May,
1913.
[1] *Treze livres des Parlemens de France*, Liv. XIII, chap. viii, no. 11, p. 686, of the first
edition, used here, Bordeaux, 1617. I owe the reference to Esmein, *Histoire du droit français*,
11th ed., p. 585.
[2] *La grant monarchie de France*, first published in 1519, and now rare in any edition. I
have used the Latin translation by the German historian John Sleidan, published at Leyden
in 1626. The quotation above is at page 22.
[3] *Les Recherches de la France*, Liv. II, chap. iv. (*Les Œuvres d'Estienne Pasquier*, Amsterdam, 1723, vol. i, p. 66.) For some modern accounts of the registration of royal ordinances
in France, see Esmein, *loc. cit.;* Viollet, *Histoire des institutions politiques et administratives
de la France*, vol. ii, pp. 196–198; Chénon, *Histoire générale du droit français*, vol. i, pp.
527–529.
[4] *Ante*, p. 265.

If we consider this sanction of private war as mere lawless violence, there was comparatively little legal remedy for a King's
arbitrary acts extending beyond his legal rights. But the middle
ages did not so consider it. The *Diffidatio* and if necessary the
feudal rising, was the normal and not illegal manner of obtaining
rights unlawfully withheld. It was, then, the legal fact that the
King's rights as overlord did not make him sole proprietor of his
subjects' lands and goods, that they were beyond his legitimate
authority to take, to destroy, or disturb, and the further fact that
his vassals were within their lawful rights in renouncing his authority and openly defying him if he did so; it was this which
explains the nature of medieval kingship and the way in which it
was in course of time made subject to the control of the people.[1]
But while we recognize this we must remember that within his
proper sphere the king was absolute. In the "civil power" he
had no peer and no associate, much less a superior, and in its
exercise he was irresponsible. *A* King may do wrong but in so
doing he is no king but a tyrant; *the* King can do no wrong. And
the royal authority must not be repudiated. Even "the error of
the prince creates right" of a kind, and furthermore, as Bracton
says,[2] no writ runs against the King. This dilemma was not
peculiar to the middle ages. So long as the individual feels that he
is the ultimate judge of the rightfulness or wrongfulness of his own
actions, so long as "private judgment" is admitted — and it was
admitted in the middle ages as much as now in some spheres —
so long there will be the possibility of a clash between his ideas of
right and those imposed by authority. Which shall he obey? It
is little wonder that contemporaries gave answers that seem inconsistent, it is less wonder that historians have misunderstood their
answers.

Modern conceptions of a corporate or collegiate sovereign organ
in the state requiring the coöperation of its parts and thus involving
the negative or positive check of one part by another, the develop-

---

[1] "It was never doubtful that the highest Might, were it spiritual or were it temporal,
was confined by truly legal limitations. . . . A fugitive glance at Medieval Doctrine
suffices to perceive how throughout it all, in sharp contrast to the theories of Antiquity,
runs the thought of the absolute and imperishable value of the Individual" . . . Gierke,
Political Theories of the Middle Age (Maitland's translation), pp. 74, 81–82. See Gierke's
whole passage, which discusses these points in masterly fashion, *op. cit.*, pp. 73–100. "It
pertains to Princes," says Egidius Romanus, "to guard well the laws through the civil
power" (*De Regimine Principum*, Bk. III, part ii, chap. i).

[2] *De Legibus et Consuetudinibus Angliae*, Lib. I, cap. viii, fol. 5 b.

ment and extension of representative institutions, and the replacement of the feudal relation by that between ruler and subject — all these have operated to reduce the frequency of crises demanding a settlement of such questions by the *ratio ultima* of force, but they have only reduced it, they have not removed them. Men never need invoke the sanction of force if they have at hand adequate legal means of controlling their rulers and giving full protection to the rights of each as well as the rights of all.

But such perfect means have never yet been found, the tyranny of one, or of a few, or of the majority, is still a possibility which can at times be obviated in the end only by force, and we properly recognize a political though not a legal "right of revolution" as the ultimate remedy for legalized wrong. What we forget is that this differs from the medieval sanction of private war only in being needed less often and in involving wider collective action when it does occasionally occur.

The advocacy of such extra-legal or even illegal sanctions has always appeared when men were driven by oppression — sometimes when they were led by reasons less adequate — to the conclusion that the constituted authorities afford no protection for the rights, or actually obstruct the duties founded upon a higher law, whether the fashion of the time was to term this the law of God, the law of nature, the law of reason, or "the rights of man"; and of such a law men in authority are no better judges than others. The individual opinion or conscience is the ultimate test in all cases, and this has been the occasion of most of the great political writings in history. They have been appeals to "public opinion," because in the end that opinion will decide, by legal means if they exist, by revolution if these fail. Thus the political thought of most of the sixteenth century may be summed up in terms of this old dilemma, in the form then uppermost, a hesitation between two texts of Scripture: "Let every soul be subject to the higher powers" and "We must obey God rather than man." In a different form the problem is with us still. Honest and well-meaning men are often doubtful of their duty today in the face of a rule prescribed by the highest authority yet against their definition of that authority or their conceptions of right. Had it not been so we should probably have had no American Civil War. Were it not so now, we should be closer to unanimity concerning a sumptuary law inserted among the fundamental rules of the American federal constitution. And when we find some sincere men seriously proposing — rightly or wrongly — a "nullification" of such laws as the only safeguard of right or liberty, we are not far from the normal medieval habit of mind in which private warfare was recognized as the ultimate sanction of law. It has always been admitted more or less explicitly that the individual sense of right must be the ultimate interpreter of all law, the final arbiter to judge whether it is binding or not; but when this sense of right results in outward acts affecting others, the community for its own protection has thought it necessary to limit such acts and to empower its agents to maintain these limits if need be by force. Under all forms of the state, and in all periods of their history, the preservation of the proper balance between private judgment and constitutional authority has proved the deepest and most perplexing of all political problems. Authoritarians have left but little scope for the former, libertarians would always cut down the latter to the smallest proportions, and in some periods the authoritarians prevail, in others, their opponents; but, as Aristotle said, the voluntary actions of men belong to the realm of the contingent, not of the absolute, and the rules controlling them fall within the province of the practical, not of the speculative, reason.

No political philosopher has ever dared to set up permanent markers bounding the respective fields of liberty and authority, and none need ever try.

We should be the last, therefore, to point the finger of scorn at the middle ages because they left unsolved a problem which is still beyond our power to solve. We shall never understand them unless we bear constantly in mind, that then as now, respect for constituted authority might at times come into conflict with ideas of right and law. So long as the idea of sovereignty was yet in abeyance and law considered as immemorial custom, this conflict naturally appeared as one between royal authority and the "private" law, which at that time was in the main the law of fiefs.

It is this antithesis between the supreme authority of the King and the sanctity of private right, which explains the fact that the historical development of modern constitutional liberty has come through the power of the purse. Taken together they explain it. If either one of them is neglected that development becomes incomprehensible.

The principle that "supply and redress of grievances go hand-in-hand" is the key to modern constitutional development, and when it was accompanied by the decline of the king's feudal revenues, the growth of representative institutions, and a feeling of national solidarity, it tended to make real and effective the limited, as well as the national, character of kingship.　The point in greatest need of emphasis is that in the beginning this balancing of redress and supply is based on two correlative assumptions equally important: first, that redress must be bought: it cannot be legally forced; and second, that supply must be asked: it cannot be legally taken.[1]　But this means that, save for the rights guaranteed by the "private" customary law, the king is the sole and "absolute" ruler of his kingdom.　Every medieval king was in one sense a "limited" monarch, and every one was recognized as truly "absolute."　His legitimate power was autocratic but not "despotic."　Some statements of Lupold von Bebenburg and the author of the *Defensor Pacis* may seem to attribute a true "constitutional" control of the *populus* over the king, but these were probably made with reference only to the Empire or with the precedents of the Roman republic particularly in mind.　The normal medieval idea of a king limited him strictly to his proper sphere of action, and recognized all known means of enforcing this limitation, such as the coronation oath, excommunication, and ultimately "legalized rebellion"; but in his "office" (*officium*) it left him alone and supreme and answerable to none.　In England the king's solemn oath at his coronation to guard and enforce the ancient customary laws "which the mass of the people have chosen" (*quas vulgus elegerit*) [2] is not really inconsistent with Bracton's assertion that the king has no peer on earth, and Bracton also says, "Those things which concern peace and jurisdiction . . . belong to none but the Crown alone and the royal dignity." [3] John Locke used his words with more discrimination than we usually do when he said "that even absolute power . . . is not arbitrary by being absolute." [4]　If we disregard a few occasional difficulties introduced into Bracton's statements by the "*addiciones*" made by later hands in the manuscripts of his great work,

---

[1] "Cur sua consilia non communicabit
A quibus auxilia suplex postulabit?"
The Song of Lewes, Lines 929–30.
[2] *Rot. Parl.*, III, p. 417 B.
[3] Lib. II, cap. xxiv, fol. 55, b.　The whole chapter is important.
[4] *Two Treatises of Government*, Bk. II, chap. xi, § 139.

the supposed contradictions in his assertions which have so puzzled modern interpreters usually turn out not to be there.

There are several ways in which a modern historian may approach an important but baffling text like Bracton's. When he finds in it assertions apparently inconsistent and even contradictory, seeming now to support a theory of limited monarchy, now an absolutism; he may do, and sometimes does, as the English party leaders did in the seventeenth century, choosing such texts as support his prejudices and ignoring the others, a method scarcely worthy of an impartial student. Or he may conclude that these apparent inconsistencies are simply evidences of a confusion of mind on the part of the author, and they will therefore have little influence on his own interpretation of history. This seems the usual method, less partisan but little more intelligent than the other. In the third place, he may begin with the assumption that an inconsistency in the text of an able and well-informed man like Bracton is probably apparent only, at least in respect to the institutions of his own time, that it may possibly be owing to our own defects and not the original author's, and might be explained if we could but recover the point of view of the author himself, and read out of our minds for the moment the later development of institutions and the ideas about them, which may have rendered their earlier nature and operation incomprehensible to us now. If the third of these methods were followed thoroughly, the political conceptions of Bracton would reappear, I believe, and prove to be not only accurate but entirely consistent.

In the middle ages a king must be "absolute" in administration if he is to fulfil his obligation to preserve the law and ensure peace and justice. "It is expedient," says Egidius Romanus, "that he have a fullness of civil power (*habundare in civili potentia*) in order to be able to control those who would rise in revolt and disturb the peace of the realm." [1] "Justice cannot be maintained in a realm if transgressors of the just are not punished by the civil power." [2]

---

[1] *De Regimine Principum*, Bk. III, part ii, chap. vi.

[2] *Ibid.*, Bk. III, part ii, chap. xv.

In the middle of the fifteenth century Nicholas of Cusa gives an interesting illustration of the persistence of this notion of the absolute and unhampered power of a ruler in administration and applies it to the law of the Church. After asserting the superiority over the Papacy of a General Council which "represents" the whole Church universal, he adds that it is very doubtful whether this superiority extends to the "exercise of administration"; not on account of any weakness of the Council, but because that would really be a contradic-

When the medieval kingship began to outgrow the narrower limits just indicated, modern constitutionalism began. As the needs of national kings gradually came to outstrip their feudal revenues the only recourse was to ask for voluntary grants, and thus the needs and the grants in supply became "national" in scope, and the redress of grievances by which these grants were bought also took on a wider and more national character.

Most of this is the commonplace of constitutional history, but one aspect of it is sometimes forgotten, or rather two. If the king in all cases could appropriate *de jure* his subjects' goods without their consent, this constitutional development would have been impossible and is now incomprehensible. That is probably understood well enough. What is not so generally understood is the fact that the subjects would have had no need to buy redress if they could always demand it as a right. Redress was in large measure voluntary on the king's part, supply was in the main voluntary with the subject. Each was given in return for the other, and when the feudal *curia* melted into the national Parliament this feudal *quid pro quo* turned into the grant of the nation, in return for royal assent to petitions of national scope. The beginnings of all this are incomprehensible if the king is not "absolute" within his sphere of action, that is, without a superior, associate, or companion, to whom he is in any manner responsible. The proof that it is true is written all through the official documents of western Europe in the later middle ages, in the Spanish kingdoms, in France and Germany, and in England.

In France, says Viollet, even up to 1789 the King's ordinances rarely touched the "private law."[1] It is the people who made that law, declared Guy Coquille even at the end of the sixteenth century.[2]

"To Kings belongs authority over all men, to subjects ownership."[3] This "authority over all men," an authority supreme and to be shared with none, is attested as fully in medieval precedent as the proprietory rights of the King's subjects, but it is

tion in terms, "for the Papacy in essence is nothing else than an unlimited power of administration (*papatum in libera administrandi potestate tantum consistere*)." *De Concordantia Catholica*, Lib. II, cap. xviii. Schard, *De Jurisdictione*, p. 549.

[1] *Histoire des institutions politiques et administratives de la France*, vol. ii (Paris, 1898), pp. 199–202.

[2] Viollet, *op. cit.*, II, p. 205.

[3] "Ad Reges enim potestas omnium pertinet: ad singulos, proprietas." *Fr. Hotomani, Quaestionum Illustrium Liber*, Quaestio I, p. 14 (1576). This is a quotation from Seneca's *De Beneficiis*.

usually ignored or misunderstood in modern times. I shall here give mainly English illustrations of it, because among us England is generally assumed — entirely without foundation before the fourteenth century, at least — to be more "constitutional" than every other part of western Europe.

After Henry III had been declared of sufficient age to act for himself, the English magnates, lay and ecclesiastical, in a Parliament in 1223 demanded of him a confirmation of the Great Charter and the Charter of the Forest, granted by the regents in the King' name in 1217. One of the King's oldest and most experienced councillors, William Brewer by name, advised the King to refuse because these liberties, extorted by force "ought not of right (*de jure*) to be observed." [1] Archbishop Langton, the spokesman of the magnates, did not see fit to deny this doctrine, though he might have questioned the fact of violence in the reissue of 1217; he was content in his reply to upbraid Brewer only for endangering the peace of the realm. In the actual reissue of the Charter made in 1225 the correctness of Brewer's dictum seems to be assumed. The King declares officially that he has granted and conceded the liberties demanded, of his own free and good will (*spontanea et bona voluntate nostra*) and that "in return for this concession and grant" (*pro hac . . . concessione et donatione*) the magnates "have given" (*dederunt*) him a fifteenth part of all their moveable property.[2]

This is good constitutional doctrine. "There is no one who may presume to withstand a royal decree which has been made for the good of the peace," declared the author of the *Dialogue of the Exchequer*, in the reign of Henry II.[3] No charter could bind the King in matters within his authority, no subject could question his power. "There should be and there can be no adjudication concerning royal charters *or the acts of Kings*," says Bracton, and it belongs to no private person to dispute them.[4]

---

[1] Matthew Paris, *Chronica Majora* (Rolls Series) III, pp. 75–76.

[2] Stubbs, *Select Charters* (9th ed.), p. 350.

[3] *De Necessariis Observantiis Scaccarii Dialogus*, edited by Hughes, Crump, and Johnson, Oxford, 1902, Lib. II, cap. x, p. 139. The passage from which this extract is taken is a good illustration of the conflict which sometimes arose in the medieval mind between the conception of the inviolability of the subjects' property and that of the absolute authority of the King. The author confesses that he is "disturbed" by the forfeiture to the King of a felon's chattels in apparent violation of the right of the felon's lord, but he feels bound to say, nevertheless, that the King's decree requiring it must be obeyed.

[4] *De Legibus et Consuetudinibus Angliae*, Bk. II, chap. 16, fol. 109 a. For expressions of the same view of the English monarchy by Gregory IX, and of his opinion that the English King's coronation oath bound him to try to regain rights of the Crown which had been alienated, see Rymer's *Foedera* (Record Commission), vol. i., pp. 229, 234.

In 1253, as the Barons' War was becoming imminent, all the precaution possible against a violation of the charters is to provide for a penalty of excommunication. The clearest indications of the lawfulness of the King's "absolute" power comes during the general period of the war itself, when the lawfulness of the participation of the barons in the King's administration was a point directly in issue. The celebrated *Provisions of Oxford* which had conceded that participation, St. Louis in 1264 declared to be "in greatest derogation of the regal right and honor," whereas the King should have "full power and unhampered control in his realm and the things pertaining thereto," (*quod dictus rex plenam potestatem et liberum regimen habeat in regno suo et ejus pertinentiis* [sic]),[1] — "the ancient and accustomed liberty and plenitude of free royal power in matters extra-judicial as well as judicial" as the papal legate defined it in commanding the barons to restore it to Henry III.[2]

In conceding such power to Henry, however, the French King was careful to explain : "we do not wish or intend by the present ordinance to derogate in anything from the privileges, charters, liberties, enactments, and laudable customs of the realm of England, which were in existence before the time of these provisions [of Oxford]."

Such a decision was the only one possible for a conscientious and impartial arbiter in touch with the political conceptions of his time.

It is true, of course, that this view of the King's "absolute" administrative authority was not without its opponents, in both theory and practice, in medieval England, nor without its opponents now. The opposition barons in 1215 forced King John to assent to a provision of Magna Carta which created a committee of twenty-five of their own number to exercise powers that none but the King had exercised before,[3] and the Charter was defended on principle by Archbishop Langton and other learned and influential men.[4] The provisions of Oxford,[5] though a similar "blemish-

[1] Stubbs, *Select Charters*, pp. 395–397.
[2] Rymer's *Foedera* (Record Commission), vol. i, p. 447.
[3] Stubbs, *Select Charters*, 9th ed., pp. 301–302.
[4] But Professor Powicke contends with good reason that Langton's support of the Charter resulted from his sympathy with the baronial demands only "so far as they professed to be a statement of custom or a request for its observance. . . . He was with equal certainty out of sympathy with the appeal to force." The provision interfering with the king's administration was not of his making, was opposed to his views, and was added at a time when he had ceased to have any control or influence over the barons' actions. F. M. Powicke, *Stephen Langton*, Oxford, 1928, pp. 124–125.
[5] Stubbs, *Select Charters*, p. 378 *et seq.*

ing" of the royal authority, were defended by some, as in the contemporary political poem known as *The Song of Lewes*,[1] and the political principles underlying the *Provisions* seem to have been accepted by at least one thirteenth century annotator of a Bracton manuscript, and by the author of *Fleta*.[2]

Yet Innocent III had annulled John's charter as a "loss of regal right" (*regalis juris dispendium*),[3] and St. Louis had declared the similar interference with Henry III's authority in the Provisions of Oxford "in greatest derogation of the royal right and honor" (*juri et honori regio*).[4]   The future was with the claims of Simon de Montfort and the author of the *Song of Lewes*, but it was in the thirteenth century a far distant future; and though our natural sympathies are on their side, this should not blind us to the fact, attested as I believe by the weight of contemporary evidence, official and non-official, that the decisions of Innocent III and St. Louis were strictly in accord with existing precedent and with the best and most generally accepted constitutional opinion of the thirteenth century in England and elsewhere.   The King was recognized to have of right "*plenam potestatem et liberum regimen*" in the words of St. Louis, and *liberum regimen* — "free government" — meant a rule unhampered by any outside restraint, and it meant nothing more.

---

[1] *The Song of Lewes*, edited by C. L. Kingsford, Oxford, 1890.
"Ex predictis omnibus poterit liquere,
Quod regem magnatibus incumbit videre,
Que regni conveniant gubernacioni,
Et pacis expediant conservacioni."

Lines 951–954.

[2] For the well-known *addicio* to the text of Bracton (folio 34) concerning royal charters referred to here and above at page 196, in which it is asserted that the King has a superior in his *Curia*, see the introduction of Professor Woodbine to his edition of Bracton, *Bracton de Legibus et Consuetudinibus Angliae*, edited by George E. Woodbine, vol. i (New Haven, 1915), pp. 252, 332–333, 378; F. W. Maitland, *Bracton's Note Book* (London, 1887), vol. i, pp. 27–33.   The statement in *Fleta* is as follows (Bk. I, chap. 17, p. 17): "Nemo enim de facto Regis praesumat disputare, nec contra factum suum venire; verumtamen in populo regendo superiores habet, ut legem, per quam factus est Rex, & curiam suam, videlicet Comites & Barones."   It is not impossible that the *addicio* to Bracton's text may have come originally from the manuscript formerly owned by the author of *Fleta* himself, and have been his work; but the apparently later date of the one known old manuscript of *Fleta* preserved among the *Cotton Mss.* would seem to preclude any fruitful attempt to verify such a guess by a comparison of manuscripts.

In another *addicio* (folio 171), possibly inserted later in his manuscript by Bracton himself, as Maitland thinks, we seem to find a recognition of the fact that some of his contemporaries are holding a theory of the supremacy of the Curia, but there is nothing in the note to indicate that Bracton agreed with such a view, while many passages of undoubted authenticity in the text assert the contrary theory with greatest clearness.

[3] Charles Bémont, *Chartes des libertés anglaises*, pp. 41–44.
[4] Stubbs, *Select Charters*, pp. 395–397.

In the *Dictum de Kenilworth* issued on the King's behalf as his terms of peace to the defeated barons at the war's close in 1266, the same doctrine is affirmed — "We declare and provide that the most serene prince Lord Henry, illustrious King of England, should hold his dominion, authority and regal power, should fully enjoy, and freely exercise them without let or contradiction of anyone whomsoever, whereby the royal dignity may be hurt contrary to the approved rights and laws and the customs of the realm long established." [1]

This document was probably inspired in part by Prince Edward who became king some six years later, and it expresses well the conception of kingship which recent English historians attribute to Edward I in preference to the more "constitutional" views which Bishop Stubbs credited him with a generation or more ago. Even the discredited Edward II, after the victory over his baronial opponents at Boroughbridge, reverts to the claims of 1266 in the *Statute of York* of 1322, and this time more explicitly than ever before. This famous statute has been the subject of much modern discussion and difference of opinion,[2] but the general intent of its provisions seems clear enough. It contains a rehearsal of the famous ordinances enacted in 1311 by Parliament in the King's name but under control of the opposition barons, and a finding that in these "the royal power was restrained to the blemishing of the King's sovereignty and against the estate of the Crown," and that not according to "the oath which our said lord the King made at his coronation." The statute therefore abolishes the ordinances and further enacts "that forever hereafter, all manner of Ordinances or Provisions, made by the subjects of our Lord the King or of his Heirs, by any Power or Authority whatsoever, *concerning the Royal Power* (*sur le poair real*) of our Lord the King or of his Heirs, or *against the Estate* of our Lord the King or of his Heirs, or against the Estate of the Crown, (*ou countre lestat nostre dit Seigneur le Roi, ou de ses Heirs, ou countre lestat de la Coronne*), shall be void and of no Avail or Force whatever; but the matters which are to be established *for the Estate* of our Lord the

---

[1] *Statutes of the Realm*, I, p. 8, *et seq.* The prelates and magnates in whose name these articles of pacification were issued further implore the king, appealing to his sense of duty (*pietas*) — *but to nothing more*, to observe the liberties of the Church, and the charters of liberties and of the forest, which he is bound by his own express oath to keep and preserve.

[2] Mr. G. T. Lapsley in *English Historical Review*, No. xxviii, p. 118 ff.; Professor T. F. Tout, *The Place of Edward II in English History*, pp. 150–151; Mr. James Conway Davies, *The Baronial Opposition to Edward II*, Cambridge, 1918, part ii, chap. x.

King and of his Heirs, and *for the Estate* of the Realm and of the
People, shall be treated, accorded, and established in Parliaments
by our Lord the King, and by the Assent of the Prelates, Earls,
and Barons, and the Comminalty of the Realm; according as it
hath been heretofore accustomed." [1]   The sentence just quoted
seems to make three separate prescriptions : first, that no subjects
of the King may enact any provisions whatsoever which in any
manner even *touch* the King's *power or authority;* second, that
they cannot enact any valid ones *against* the King's *estate* (presumably such as the provisions of the late ordinances touching the
King's Wardrobe); third, that fiscal matters concerning the King
and the realm alike must be enacted by the King with assent of
what later would be called the Lords and the Commons in Parliament.   The first of these provisions has been obscured by the
supposed greater importance of the last, but it is with this first
provision alone that we are concerned here.   No subjects of the
King even in Parliament may concern themselves in any way with
the King's authority, or what James I later called his "public
prerogative." [2]   This seems to be a reassertion of the principle of
the *Dictum de Kenilworth*, that the King's authority is not to be
questioned.

Whether the King himself might surrender or "blemish" this
royal authority or not, the Statute does not say, but Edward III
in 1341 revoked some earlier provisions already assented to by him,
on the ground that they were "against our royal rights and prerogatives," [3] no doubt "a piece of atrocious duplicity" as Stubbs
calls it, entirely characteristic of Edward III, but not for that
reason necessarily without the support of precedent or opposed
to contemporary political ideas.   For questionable actions men will
try to give reasons which they think likely to carry conviction —
for such actions even more than for others.   It seems clear that
as early as 1266 at least, the "public prerogative" of the King was
regarded in England, and presumably in France as well, as in
some sense a "fundamental law of the monarchy" and beyond the
power of the King's subjects to change "by any Power or Authority
whatsoever."

---

[1] 15 Edward II, *Statutes of the Realm*, vol. i, p. 189.   The italics are mine.
[2] A principle acted upon by Queen Elizabeth when she forbade debate in the Commons
concerning religious matters which belonged exclusively to the "Supreme Governor."
[3] *Rot. Parl.*, II, p. 131 a, no. 42.   For Stubbs's comments see *English Constitutional
History*, vol. ii (4th ed.), pp. 407-410.

The monarchy existed for the sake of the people, was originally created by them, and the fundamental rules governing its transmission and extent were a part of the people's customary rights as inviolable as the rules of the private law protecting their own seisin.

Possibly this doctrine that the rights of the Crown could not be abridged even by the king himself was not universally accepted in England in the time of Edward III, and Stubbs may be justified in his strictures on the king's actions; but there is some room for doubt. In 1176 Henry II instructed his itinerant justices to enforce the rights pertaining not only to him but "to his Crown" as well (*et ad coronam suam*).[1] Pope Gregory IX warned the English king in the next century that the coronation oath required him to recover all royal rights which had been alienated.[2] In 1301, Edward I himself officially recognized the principle that his own competence to assent to changes in the bounds of the forests was strictly limited to those which could be made "without blemishing his oath and without disinheriting the Crown,"[3] and one of the chief grounds for the annulment by the Statute of York of the ordinances of 1311 was that these ordinances, though they had, of course, formally received the royal assent, "of our free will," were not according to "the oath which our said lord the king made at his coronation."[4] It is a curious fact calling for further investigation, that in no surviving contemporary form of the medieval English coronation oath is there to be found any provision touching the inalienability of regalian rights; and yet the statements just cited, and a number of others, seem to leave no doubt that in the thirteenth and fourteenth centuries at least, the English king at his coronation did take some kind of solemn engagement under oath not to dismember his realm nor to "blemish" the rights of his Crown, possibly an addition to the regular oath somewhat analogous to the declarations against transsubstantiation which English sovereigns made for two centuries in modern times. Early in the thirteenth century, more than a century before Edward III, an English writer had made the following significant statement: "The King of right ought to preserve and defend all the lands and honors, all the dignities and rights and

[1] *Assize of Northampton*, cap. 7, Stubbs, *Select Charters* (9th ed.), p. 180.
[2] *Ante*, p. 374, note 4.
[3] Palgrave, *Parliamentary Writs*, vol. i, p. 104, no. 44.
[4] *Statutes of the Realm*, vol. i (1322), p. 189.

liberties of the Crown of this realm in entirety and in their whole integrity without diminution"; [1] and Bracton declared a little later, "Those things which pertain to jurisdiction or the peace, and those things relating to these, belong to no one but the Crown alone and the royal dignity. Nor can they be separated from the Crown, since they are of its essence. For it belongs to the Crown to do justice and pronounce judgments, and to preserve the peace; and without these the Crown can neither exist nor endure. Moreover neither rights of this kind nor jurisdictions can be alienated to persons or to fiefs, nor can they be held by a private person — neither the use nor the execution of the law — unless the right has been granted him from above as a delegated jurisdiction. And it cannot be so delegated as not to remain in the King himself as a matter of course." [2]

In the reign of Edward I the author of the important legal treatise passing under the name of *Fleta* held that "ancient manors *or rights annexed to the Crown* the king shall not alienate, but every king is bound to restore to his Crown those which have been alienated"; [3] and in *Britton*, another law-book of the same reign, a like doctrine is set forth: "Kings also may not so alien the rights of their crown or of their royalty as not to be revocable by their successors." [4]   In 1366 Parliament formally declared that King John's cession of England and Ireland to Innocent III as overlord was null and void, because "neither the said King John nor any other could bring himself or his realm or his people into such subjection without their assent, and as it appears by many proofs, that if this was done it was done without their assent and against the King's oath at his coronation." [5]

The same idea underlies chapter xiii of the famous *Golden Bull* of the Emperor Charles IV promulgated in 1356,[6] and it is expressed a few years later with the greatest clearness in France by the Gallican author of the *Songe du Vergier:* No king may grant away his sovereignty, transfer it, or renounce it; it is

---

[1] *Leges Anglorum Saeculo XIII Ineunte Londiniis Collectae*, Liebermann, *Gesetze der Angelsachsen*, vol. i, p. 635. For an account of this book, see Liebermann, *Ueber die Leges Anglorum Saecuto XIII Ineunte Londiniis Collectae*, Halle, 1894.

[2] Lib. ii, cap. xxiv, fol. 55 b.

[3] *Fleta*, Londini, 1685, Lib. I, cap. 8, p. 3.

[4] *Britton*, edited by Francis Morgan Nichols, Oxford, 1865, Bk. II, chap. iii, section 3 (vol. i, p. 221).

[5] *Rotuli Parliamentorum*, vol. ii, p. 290, no. 8. There is an interesting discussion of this whole question in Selden's *Dissertatio ad Fletam*, chap. x, section iv.

[6] Zeumer, *Quellensammlung zur Geschichte der deutschen Reichsverfassung*, p. 170.

inseparably annexed to the Crown. If a lord wishes to transfer his fief and his men to another, the vassals may oppose and prevent it, for it is to the advantage of subjects not to change their lords when they are good and acceptable.[1] In 1418 or 1419 the inalienability of the Crown of France, the fundamental and unchangeable character of the rules governing its extent and transmission, and the inability of any king to renounce or to alter the succession, were asserted in most definite form in the remarkable tractates of Jean de Terre Rouge (Johannes de Terra Rubea).[2]

Even as early as the middle of the thirteenth century the English Bracton makes a significant statement to which historians have given scant attention. The keeping of the peace and the administration of justice, he says, "cannot be separated from the Crown, *because they make the Crown what it is.*" [3] The same doctrine was asserted in France about Bracton's time in *Li livres de jostice et de plet:* "The prince is not above the law, but the law above the prince, *for it confers upon him such privilege as he possesses.*" [4]

In the fifteenth century Aeneas Sylvius applies this theory to the Empire, and denies the validity of all grants made by Emperors in derogation of the imperial sovereignty,[5] an argument which imperial writers had been using for more than a century before against the papal interpretation of the Donation of Constantine.

For France, the constitutional doctrine was admirably summed up in the sixteenth century by the celebrated jurist Pierre Rebuffe: "From the discussion preceding I am led to ask the question whether the King of France can alienate the things belonging to the realm, and Baldus . . . concludes that he cannot, in the abdication of all his jurisdiction, dignity, and dominion, and retaining nothing for himself, for this would be a blemishing of his government or realm, and this the king cannot do. Even if he should retain for himself the *dominium directum,* it would not be valid if it

---

[1] *Le songe du vergier*, Liv. II, chap. ccli, *Traitez des droits et libertez de l'église gallicane* (1731), tome ii. I am indebted for reference to this passage to the valuable essay of André Lemaire, *Les lois fondamentales de la monarchie française*, Paris, 1907, p. 47.

[2] For these, see especially Lemaire, *op. cit.*, chap. i, vii. The tractates were reprinted by Francis Hotman as an appendix to his *Disputatio de Controversia Successionis Regiae*, 1585.

[3] Lib. II, cap. xxiv, fol. 55 b.

[4] Liv. I, 2, 3, edited by Rapetti, Paris, 1850, p. 6.

[5] *De Ortu et Authoritate Imperii Romani*, cap. xv–xvi, Schard, *De Jurisdictione*, pp. 321–322.

tended to the hurt or disadvantage of the realm." [1]   The constitution of the realm embodied in ordinances made for its conservation, says du Haillan, no king could think of violating, and should he do so his command would not be obeyed, particularly in those things concerning the royal domain and patrimony which a king cannot alienate except under necessity and with consent of the Estates.[2]

"The Kingship is a dignity, not an inheritance," declared Philippe Pot in the Estates General at Tours in 1484.[3]   "Kings are heirs, not of kings, but of the kingdom." [4]

It seems, then, that the normal thought of western Europe in the thirteenth century and afterward — as much in England as elsewhere — placed the rights of the Crown beyond even the "absolute" king's power to abridge or to alienate; it certainly placed them out of the reach of any of the king's subjects or of any assembly of them.   Possibly more significant still is the contemporary definition of royal authority which excludes it from any interference with a subject's property but at the same time recognizes its absolute character within the sphere allotted to it.[5]   Such

[1] *Feudorum Declaratio*, Lugduni, 1566, p. 483.   Such statements could be multiplied indefinitely from the writings of the French jurists.   Many of them are referred to, applying to Spain and the Empire, as well as to France, in Choppin's great work, *De Domanio Franciae*, Lib. II, Tit. I (3d ed., Paris, 1605).

[2] Bernard de Girard, Seigneur du Haillan, *De l'estat et succez des affaires de France*, Paris, 1571, folio 82.

[3] Journal of Jean Masselin, edited by A. Bernier, Paris, 1835, p. 146.

[4] Adam Blackwood, *Pro Regibus Apologia*, cap. xii (1580), *Adami Blacvodaei Opera Omnia*, Paris, 1644, p. 69.

[5] A noteworthy example of the persistence of these medieval ideas in England occurs in the case of Willion *v.* Berkley, determined in the court of Common Pleas in the third and fourth years of Queen Elizabeth, in which it was declared that " altho' by the Common Law the King has many Prerogatives touching his Person, his Goods, his Debts and Duties, and other personal Things, yet the Common Law has so admeasured his Prerogatives that they shall not take away nor prejudice the Inheritance of any. . . .   The King's Prerogative by the Common Law cannot prevail against such a Custom as stands with the Right of Inheritance of another."   Plowden's *Commentaries*, p. 236.   Many other similar statements might be added.   Sir William Holdsworth quotes some of these (*A History of English Law*, Boston, 1924, vol. iv, p. 202), but the conclusions he draws from them are very different from the ones set forth above.   The view here set forth is essentially the position of Sir Matthew Hale in his *Reflections* on Hobbes's *Dialogue of the Common Laws of England*, printed by Sir William Holdsworth (*History of English Law*, vol. v, p. 500) : "The Laws of the Land," he says, "and the Oath of Supremacy teach us, that the King is the only Supreame Governour of this Realme. . . .   These are the greate Jura Summi Imperii that the Laws of this Kingdome have fixed in the Crown of England, Butt yett there are certaine Qualifications of these Powers."   Sir William Holdsworth's comment is that Hale "in his criticism of Hobbes, quite misunderstood his theory of sovereignty.   He interpreted sovereignty as meaning only a supremacy, which was not incompatible with the supremacy of Parliament or the law in their several spheres" (*Some Lessons from our Legal History*, New York, 1928, pp. 127–128).   Hale in fact had ventured to differ from "Hobbes, the one Englishman who had really grasped the theory."   In all this it seems evident that Sir Matthew

a combination of ideas now usually regarded as mutually incompatible was made in the *De Officio Regis* of Wycliffe,[1] and it was still retained apparently in the fifteenth century. When we examine with care the praise given by Sir John Fortescue to the principles of the *dominium politicum et regale* exemplified for him so perfectly in the English constitution but absent as he thinks from the *dominium regale* found in France,[2] or the similar observations of the French chronicler Commines;[3] we find nothing in either writer to conflict with the usual medieval view that the King was "absolute" within his proper sphere. Both writers in contrasting France and England in the fifteenth century have in mind primarily *les impôts permanents* which the French king had long been taking without consent of the Estates as no English king could do. Neither was thinking of the regular administration of the king. To both, the French monarchy seemed a despotic though not necessarily a tyrannical government, a *dominatus* or *monarchie seigneuriale* in which the goods of the subject were legally at the disposal of the monarch. In this lay the difference between the two kingdoms; it was not a difference between the "absolute" administration of France and the "constitutional" monarchy of England; in government, in its strict sense, both realms were "absolute." The King "has supreme jurisdiction in his realm" declared Jean Bouteiller, quoting the opinion of the great Italian jurist Baldus.[4]

The Humanistic revival of Roman law in the sixteenth century undoubtedly brought some change in these ideas. Esmein has shown how the truly absolutist Roman doctrine of monarchy affected the monarchy of France,[5] and Maitland in a brilliant lecture [6] has proved that even in England the outcome of the struggle between the two legal systems was not as certain as was formerly supposed. With the revived study of Roman law came

Hale understood Hobbes fully as clearly as Sir William Holdsworth does, but strongly disliked that of which Sir William as strongly approves. Apparently the latter is still "beneath the shadow of the Austinian idol."

[1] *Ante*, pp. 316–317.

[2] *The Governance of England* by Sir John Fortescue, Kt., edited by Charles Plummer, Oxford, 1885; Fortescue, *De Laudibus Legum Angliae*, text and English translation, edited by A. Amos, Cambridge, 1825.

[3] *Mémoires de Philippe de Commynes*, edited by B. de Mandrot, Paris, 1901, Liv. iv, chap. 1; Liv. v, chap. xix.

[4] *Somme Rural*, edited by Charondas le Caron, Paris, 1611, Bk. II, Title I, p. 646.

[5] *La maxime* PRINCEPS LEGIBUS SOLUTUS EST *dans l'ancien droit public français* (*Essays in Legal History*, edited by Paul Vinogradoff, Oxford, 1913, pp. 201–214.)

[6] *English Law and the Renaissance*, Cambridge, 1901.

the restoration of the Roman idea of indivisible ownership in place of the feudal conception of its partibility, as we have seen;[1] and it was natural that a Romanist such as Dr. Cowell, Regius Professor of the Civil Law at Cambridge, should define a subsidy in his law dictionary, as a levy ordinarily granted by Parliament but within the King's right to take without consent if he chose.[2] The same view as Cowell's had already been expressed by the King of the Scots in his *Trew Law of Free Monarchies*[3] (by which he meant monarchies free of control, the *liberum regimen* of St. Louis, and somewhat more); and by the celebrated jurist of Toulouse, Pierre Grégoire, in his *De Republica*, first published in 1578.[4] For these men the monarchies of England, France, and Scotland were *Seigneuries* (*dominatus*) of their lords, the kings. They were monarchies not merely "absolute" in the proper medieval sense: they were "economical" (in the primary meaning of that term) and "despotic";[5] somewhat like the government of the ancient *paterfamilias* over his household — though, of course, they were not tyrannical.

Under the influence of the feudal conception of the proprietary character of all rights, a tendency had appeared in some medieval theorists, and now persisted among these neo-Romans, to identify such a despotic or "economical" régime with the "arbitrary" though not tyrannical government of a king, who as lord of his kingdom is legitimately under the control of no law but his own will: a "despotism" had come to be thought of by them simply as a legitimate form of government not based upon law, thus differing from both the political and the "economical" rule of Aristotle, who held that the household is as much a régime of law as the state itself, though he argued against Plato that its law is different from that of the state, and less perfect, because its subjects are in part slaves, instead of the freemen who alone can constitute the higher political community of the *polis*.

[1] *Ante*, p. 181, note 2.
[2] *The Interpreter* (eds. of 1607 and 1637), *s. v. King, Parliament, Subsidy*, and *Prerogative*.
[3] First published in 1598. *The Political Works of James I*, Cambridge, Mass., 1918, pp. 53–70.
[4] *Dn. Petri Gregorii Tholozani, De Republica Libri Sex et Viginti*, Francoforti, 1609, Lib. XXIV, cap. v, § 3. "Nam & sine consensu populi, potest jure suo princeps tributa imponere & exigere, sed ut paterne subditos moneat, causam necessariam esse, ex qua cogatur propter utilitatem publicam, ab illis subsidia petere." On Pierre Grégoire, see A. Lemaire, *Les lois fondamentales*, pp. 128–133; Georges Weill, *Les théories sur le pouvoir royal*, pp. 171–174.
[5] See Aristotle's *Politics*, I, i.

Such an arbitrary régime was recognized as possible in medieval political theory, but it was then thought scarcely fit even for serfs, who possessed some rights theoretically protected by the custom of the manor, and much less for vassals, who had undoubted proprietary right in their *tenementa* and their *contenementa*. For some of these more modern devotees of Roman law, however, the revival of the Roman conception of indivisible ownership and the decline of vassalage tended to transform the royal lord of the middle ages into a "despot" who *ought* to be benevolent, but nevertheless lawfully enjoyed absolute proprietary rights over the goods and the persons of all his subjects. Compelled by the logic of the revived Roman doctrine that there could be but one owner of a given thing, the upholders of the seignorial or despotic monarchy placed these proprietary rights in the monarch exclusively, and emphasized the medieval precedents drawn from the royal demesne, on which the king had always claimed and usually exercised the right to exact a tallage without consent; while they conveniently forgot the unmistakable precedents on the other side. True, their opponents in England in 1628 were clearly going beyond medieval precedent when in the *Petition of Right* they quoted from the so-called statute *De tallagio non concedendo* the assertion that the King could levy no tallage without consent; but these supporters of prerogative were guilty of an even worse offence in conceding to the King the right to dispense with assent to aids or to other novel exactions which, as Edward I had solemnly affirmed, the people had given "of their own grant and good will" and should never be taken "but by the common assent of all the realm, and for the common profit thereof."

The revival of Roman law principles and the obscuration of feudal conditions and conceptions, in short, led one party to treat the whole realm as royal demesne to be tallaged at will, while they led the opposite party to regard it as consisting exclusively of the "estates" of the King's vassals or subjects, over which regalian rights were to be reduced to a minimum. Each party had plausible medieval precedents to cite and each was guilty of citing them unfairly, but the one-sided claims of the defenders of prerogative were more illiberal and oppressive in their practical tendency than the contentions of their opponents, and constituted in reality a more fundamental departure from the general spirit of medieval institutions and ideas.

Toward the end of the sixteenth century there were some who were thus beginning to hold a "seigneurial" or despotic conception of monarchy, and in the next century the number greatly increased; but no blunder could be more serious and none has been more frequent than the assumption that Jean Bodin was one of this number. In his own day Bodin was accused of holding these arbitrary views, and even now he is regarded by most English and American historians of political thought as one whose theories fall short in nothing but logic of the slavish political doctrines of Hobbes.

In a letter prefixed to the later editions of his *République* he refutes this charge, and his refutation is as valid in answer to his modern detractors as to his contemporaries. He protests with some heat and with justice that almost alone among the defenders of monarchy in his time he allows his "sovereign" no proprietary right in the subjects' lands and goods, and his own courageous defence of this liberal principle in the Estates of Blois in 1576 [1] is proof that in him it was no mere academic doctrine, but a reasoned and sincere conviction.

To Bodin, then, and in after years to others like him, such as Eliot, Twysden, Philip Hunton, and Sir Matthew Hale in England, the French monarchy, the English monarchy, and, in fact, every monarchy of the highest type existing in a free state, must needs be "absolute" if it is to effect its great purpose of securing and enforcing peace and justice; a monarchy founded in law and based on ancient custom, in which the "sovereign" is free from ordinary law but bound by those fundamental rules which define his authority in the state; and in every monarchy of this highest type these fundamental rules include the medieval principle that the subjects' goods are their own, to be taken by the ruler only "by the common assent of all the realm and for the common profit thereof." [2]

Thus for Bodin England and France were essentially alike, both were "royal monarchies" and "absolute," and neither was "des-

---

[1] Bodin's own journal of this meeting of the Estates, giving his speeches, is printed in *Des états généraux et autres assemblées nationales*, edited by Charles Josef Mayer, vol. xiii (La Haye, 1789), pp. 212–315. For a modern account of his activity in the assembly, see R. Chauviré, *Jean Bodin*, Paris, 1914, pp. 52–68.

[2] The phrase comes from the *Confirmatio Cartarum* assented to by Edward I in 1297 — "par commun assent de tout le roiaume, et a commun profist de meismes le roiaume." Stubbes, *Select Charters*, 9th ed. p. 491. Compare the similar statements in Beaumanoir (Salmon's edition, §§ 1103, 1043, 1499, 1513, and 1515).

potic" or "seignorial." Was he entirely wrong in thinking
England "absolute" and France not "despotic"? Later developments in both countries have made the answer somewhat difficult.
The English civil wars of the seventeenth century roughly threw
English political thought permanently out of its true orbit and
substituted a theory of might for a theory of law; and the English
theory of sovereignty, as well as the American theory derived from
it, has been eccentric ever since in its adherence to the ideas of
Hobbes and Austin — a costly aberration, which lost for England
one great colonial empire and would soon have lost another if practice had not fortunately departed from theory just before it was too
late, and even within the realm had practical results scarcely less
serious in their character. It furnished a basis for justification of
the enactment or the retention by an unreformed Parliament of
oppressive class legislation such as the combination acts, religious
disabilities, the suspension of the habeas corpus act, and much more.
The extension of the suffrage has fortunately removed all serious
danger of further exploitation of this despotic theory for the ends
of any social or economic class, but the theory itself is still generally
accepted, and it is not inconceivable that the future may find
some new mischief for it to do.

This fatal identification of sovereignty with might is the
damnosa hereditas of the English civil wars, but the beginnings of
the departure from medieval thought which led to it go back
much further, and before the Long Parliament the more extreme of
the Parliamentary party were placing a one-sided emphasis upon
the fixity of the *coutume* in the medieval precedents and thus
developing Coke's doctrine of the supremacy of the common law
to the exclusion of the precedents for the King's administrative
supremacy; whilst their opponents in some cases were asserting
with the same lack of discrimination a complete royal supremacy
over every part of the common law itself. Later, under the stress
of war, these opposing and one-sided but not yet wholly immoderate
claims gave way to extremer views; on the one side, to a radical
republicanism which had no precedent whatever in medieval
England, and on the other, to the advocacy of a "despotic"
monarchy like that of Filmer's *Patriarcha*, which the political
thought of the middle ages had recognized only to repudiate.
In France the medieval precedents were similarly obscured and the
great ideal of *la monarchie tempérée* was superseded in practice at

least, in the long period of the Bourbon personal monarchy which lasted till the Revolution.

Bodin's is a more moderate and a more medieval political conception than the theories of monarchy which thus replaced it, but it may well be doubted whether the views of any other theorist had such an influence on the political ideals of thoughtful and moderate men between 1576 and 1640, as those of Jean Bodin.

The significant thing in his thought, which originally provoked even if it does not justify this long digression, is the fact that in his famous difference between a royal monarchy which is "absolute" and a seignorial monarchy which is "despotic," he retains a medieval distinction which later political developments have obscured; and, above all, that in his description of the royal "absolute" monarchy he mirrors far more faithfully than many writers of a later day the true political thought of the later middle ages in some of its most important aspects — more faithfully perhaps than he does the thought already becoming current in his own time.

It was natural perhaps that Bodin's followers of the seventeenth century, such as Loyseau, de L'Hommeau, and Lebret, should emphasize the evident absolutist tendencies of his thought to the exclusion of some of its more liberal elements drawn from medieval precedent; but there is less excuse for any view so one-sided in a modern historian than in a publicist of the time of Henry IV or Louis XIII. The more liberal parts of Bodin's conception of kingship are a heritage of the middle ages; the development of the absolute monarchy into an arbitrary one is a modern achievement.

True kingship was never absent from the medieval mind even in the period we think of as most feudal,[1] but no doubt the idea of it as well as the actual authority of kings was deeply affected by the fact that every king was feudal lord or *dominus* as well as *rex;* and many of his people, feudal vassals as well as subjects. In the mass of changing reciprocal rights and obligations existing between a medieval king and his people it is not always easy to distinguish clearly between the ones arising solely out of feudal custom and those based upon the relation of king and subject — Henry II of England demanded an oath of fealty from his knights,

[1] Achille Luchaire, *Histoire des institutions monarchiques de la France*, 2d ed., Paris, 1891, vol. i, pp. 47-59.

but he exacted it "even from rustics." At one time the actual relations will seem more feudal, especially in the royal demesne, at another more national or constitutional. But we know that feudalism at length gave way to nationalism, or was merged with it, and the king of the feudal age became the national monarch of modern times. And with the passing of feudal conditions the full understanding of those conditions passed too, and we can only recover it now in part by a painful effort to rethink the thoughts of men long dead who lived their lives in the midst of conditions in many ways radically different from our own. Maitland's remark that it was Sir Henry Spelman who introduced feudalism into England is only partly justified. A good many have not made its acquaintance. As we begin to know it better it may possibly appear that it was precisely because England remained in some ways more feudal than any other country, that the actual limits of her King's authority in time became narrower than elsewhere; and we may be inclined more than formerly to attribute England's remarkable and unique advance toward representative self-government in part to extra-constitutional causes, or to political conceptions which were general, rather than to an original constitutionalism inherent in English institutions as such. Among the many debts we owe the middle ages, the debt to feudalism is not the least.

One of its most signal services in the development of modern liberty lay in the actual checks it imposed upon the arbitrary acts of the king, in excluding him from interference with the private rights of his subjects. It thus drove him eventually to bargain with them for the supply necessary for the conduct even of the ordinary business of government. It is probably, therefore, a principal source of the extreme individualism of most modern political thought as it is of modern constitutionalism, of the prominence of compact in so many phases of its development, and of its constant tendency to place emphasis upon the rights rather than the duties of the governed. In general the historical influence of feudalism has tended to set off the individual against the state, and to restrict the sphere of the latter. While admitting the great services which feudalism rendered in this way we must recognize the unavoidable defects in modern political thought resulting from it, especially the tendency to break up the organic unity of the state. A sovereign who bargains with his subjects is in a sense distinct from them. To a degree unthought of in earlier ages, the King or the "government" is thought of in modern times as outside the state, and either above or below it, but scarcely of it. As a whole, modern political thought has been atomistic rather than organic, and in this there has been loss as well as gain. It was this loss, no doubt, which led to the extreme reaction in certain quarters, as expressed in the nineteenth century in the political philosophy of Hegel and his followers.

Among the characteristics of political thought to which we attach the word "modern" none is more important than the conceptions, closely related to each other, of sovereignty, of the responsibility of the ruler, of adequate public sanctions for the enforcement of this responsibility, and of nationality. The first of these conceptions, "sovereignty," which in its only correct and modern meaning is *legislative* sovereignty, could not and did not assume its distinct and definite form until "legislation" itself in its modern sense had become so frequent that it forced itself upon the attention of men, and this "legislation" is not the medieval "finding" of a precept whose binding force comes from its supposed conformity to universal reason or to immemorial custom, but the modern *making* of a rule recognized to be law only because of the authority of the organ of the state, whether King or Assembly, by which it is promulgated. Until there is a State, standing prominent before the eyes of men with its reciprocal public relation of ruler and subject, instead of the mere quasi-private relationship existing between the individual vassal and his overlord, there can be no such organ by which national law can be *made;* until national law can thus be made, there can be no true "legislation"; and until there is true "legislation" of this more modern type, there can be no real conception of legislative sovereignty. Bodin with reason made the claim that he was the first of political philosophers or jurisconsults to give a clear analysis of the conception,[1] and Sir Frederick Pollock is justified in saying that this analysis could scarcely have been made at any time earlier than it was.[2]

---

[1] *De Republica*, Lib. I, cap. viii (Paris, 1586, p. 78).

[2] *An Introduction to the History of the Science of Politics*, London, 1900, p. 46. Bodin himself did not reach his final conclusions on this important subject at once. In his *Methodus*, written in 1566, some ten years before the more famous *République*, he finds the essence of a commonwealth in the *summum imperium*, which the French call *suverenitas*, but of the five parts into which he then divides it, he declares this to be the chief (*praecipua*) : "the creation of the highest magistrates and the defining of the function of each" (*in summis magistratibus creandis, & officio cuiusque definiendo*). *Methodus ad facilem historiarum cognitionem*, Paris, 1572, chap. vi, p. 261. But in the *République*, which first appeared in 1576 in French, and in 1586 in Latin, this is changed, and he clearly recognizes the primacy

The chief historical prerequisite to the growth of a conception of sovereignty is the existence of a "nation," with a governmental organ competent to *make* true law. In the later middle ages, such nations, such governmental organs, and such law, were rapidly taking shape in many parts of western Europe: the basis of fact for the modern theory of sovereignty was already there in incomplete form. But as we have seen it is almost a law of the development of political thought that political conceptions are the by-product of actual political relations, and oftentimes in history these relations have changed materially long before this change attracted the notice even of those most affected by it, or became a part of their unconscious habits of thought, much less of their political speculation, when they had any. The beginnings of sovereignty are to be found in the later middle ages, but the formal recognition of it had to wait for a clearer apprehension than yet existed of the significance of the appearance of nationality, the greatest of all the factors which were remaking the political life of the West and changing it from a medieval into a modern world. In the spirit of the middle ages, as Viollet says, "the sovereign power had been instituted not to change the law but to ensure its respect," and if men actually altered it "it was by uncon-

---

of legislation in sovereign power. *"Hoc igitur primum sit ac praecipuum caput maiestatis, legem universis ac singulis civibus dare posse."* *De Republica, Libri Sex,* Paris, 1586, Bk. I, chap. 10, p. 153.

"Et par ainsi nous conclurons que la premiere marque du Prince souverain, c'est la puissance de donner loy à tous en general, & à chacun en particulier." *Les Six Livres de la République,* Paris, 1577, p. 161. The unusual character of these newer views of Bodin may be appreciated by comparing them with the statement of the great French jurist Charondas le Caron, made as late as 1587: "La principale marque de souveraineté est la droite & souveraine administration de la Justice." *Pandectes ou digestes du droit françois,* Lyon, 1593, p. 3.

"Il est facile de conclure que la Justice est la premiere marque de souveraineté: car d'icelle depend la puissance de faire Loix & les casser pour le bien & salut de la republique, qui contient la conservation de l'estat du souverain, & la tranquilité des suiects: instituer & destituer les officiers, cognoistre des appellations de tous les magistrats: & distribuer les loyers & honneurs & les peines." *Ibid.,* p. 5. The older view was retained also by the Chancellor Michel de l'Hôpital, in his *Traité de la réformation de la justice."* "En somme, il fault tenir pour la plus certaine maxime d'estat, et ne me lasseray point de le repétér souvent, que le principal office des roys et princes soubverains, est de judger et faire justice: veoire mesme par plusieurs passaiges de l'Escriture, se peult justifier que ce mot de judger signifie régner et commander absolument." *Œuvres inédites de Michel de l'Hospital* (Paris, 1825), vol. i, p. 38. There is no improbability in the suggestion of Sir Frederick Pollock that the theory of Sir Thomas Smith expressed in his *De Republica Anglorum* may have been influenced by Bodin, but it is important to note the fact, pointed out by the late Dr. Julius Hatschek, that it was the theories of the *Methodus,* not those of the *République,* which Smith adopted. Julius Hatschek, *Englisches Staatsrecht* (Tübingen, 1905), vol. i, pp. 602–608. Dr. Hatschek's book deserves more attention than it has ever got from English readers. See also the same author's *Englische Verfassungsgeschichte* (München and Berlin, 1913), pp. 364–377.

sciously stretching it" : they never so much as admitted even to themselves that they were making changes in the ancient *coutume*.[1] Though it may not have been admitted, however, or even consciously done, this "stretching" process was more and more effecting real changes in the ancient customary law to keep pace with developments in the social and economic order which were probably never more rapid than in the latter part of the medieval period. Under the guise of interpretation these changes ultimately became so radical and so frequent that men awoke at length to the fact that one of the principal functions actually performed by the King, and the one above all others that most clearly set him above every inferior officer as the embodiment of the nation's supreme authority, was not the interpretation or the enforcement of law, but the *making* of it. The provision of the English coronation oath as it appears in the earliest surviving pontificals, that the people are to live in peace under the king's "judgment" (*nostro arbitrio*);[2] the fourteenth century theory that "the first and highest act of royal power is *to judge*," as Alvarus Pelagius put it; these are giving place to the theory formulated in a later age by Bodin, that the head and front of sovereignty consists in the authority to give laws to citizens all and sundry;[3] which, after all, is but a return to the older theory of the Roman jurists, to the "antique-modern" view as Gierke aptly terms it, that the interpretation of law belongs to him who has promulgated it (*conditor*). Adjudication has become once more, as in ancient times, accessory to legislation, not *vice versa*.

The full development of the idea of sovereignty belongs to the historian of modern, not of medieval, political thought, but the latter is warranted perhaps in indicating those elements in the political thought of his own period which tended to postpone the appearance of the idea till modern times, and also in pointing out the factors which must be considered as the earlier unconscious preparation for its appearance. Chief among the latter, conducive to a theory of sovereignty, is the idea of nationality, growing gradually into a sentiment of national unity. The complete expression of this sentiment is not to be found before the sixteenth century but its beginnings and much of its growth fall within the

---

[1] *Histoire des institutions politiques et administratives de la France*, vol. ii, p. 199.
[2] L. G. Wickham Legg, *English Coronation Records*, p. 15.
[3] *Ante*, p. 391.

later medieval period and they are its greatest contribution to our modern stock of political ideas.

As we trace this growth backward toward its beginnings, we come at length to a time in the depth of the feudal period when scarcely any signs of a true national feeling can be discerned at all, at least among the governing class. Human relations are determined mainly by tenure, and tenure knows little of distinctions of race or nation. It is doubtful if a single "King of the English" in the twelfth century could speak the language of the mass of his subjects. If a De Lucy or a Glanvill, each a chief justiciar of the realm of England under Henry II, had been asked whether he was French or English, he would have been hard pressed to give an answer, even on the assumption that he understood the question. The disaffected English barons in 1215 had few qualms of nationality in proclaiming a Dauphin of France King of England. It is for the writer of intellectual or constitutional history to show how these things changed, the history of political thought is concerned only with the reaction of that thought to these changes.

However we characterize it, as the decline of feudalism, the substitution of the relation between King and subject for that between lord and vassal, or the growth of the spirit of nationality, there is abundant evidence, clear and unmistakable, that by the end of the fifteenth century a change almost revolutionary in its character had taken place in many parts of western Europe. The rights and revenues of an eleventh century king would not take long to enumerate if we left out what belonged to him as *dominus;* his successor of the fifteenth century was still "Our lord the King" but the title "lord" was fast becoming an empty one. His importance was owing to his being the head of the nation to whom his subjects of every grade were bound in an equal obedience enforceable by national law. The chief developments in the theory of monarchy in the later centuries of the middle ages are the result of the growing feeling of patriotism, and of its concentration upon the king as the nation's political centre and the embodiment of its law. It was much the same whether the national Estates met often or not. The fact that an English *Statute* might require the assent of the Lords and a representative Commons where a French *Ordonnance* required only registry by magistrates in the *Parlements,* though it was a difference of the greatest moment, was not such an one that we are warranted in thinking that England had a constitution while France had none.   In both countries the King was the political centre and embodied the political ideal.   They were more alike politically than unlike.   Only by reference to such facts can we understand the words of the publicist of the sixteenth century.   In England France, Spain, and every other country where feudal decentralization had given way before the national ideal, their language is much the same, and the developments of the later middle ages which lay behind this common ideal of a national king were everywhere more nearly alike than patriotic modern historians are sometimes ready to admit.

If I were asked which of the famous maxims into which the political thought of the world has at times been compressed is the one which on the whole best comprises the living political conceptions of the later middle ages, my choice, I imagine, would be rather unexpected, and not in all cases accepted, but it is one which my study of this period makes me willing to defend.   It is the aphorism from Seneca's *De Beneficiis*, "Ad Reges enim potestas omnium pertinet: ad singulos, proprietas" — to kings belongs authority over all; to private persons, property.

APPENDIX I

(From page 29, above)

ABSOLUTE AND PARTICULAR JUSTICE

I am aware that this identification of Plato's distinction between general and particular justice with that made apparently by Aristotle is very likely to be questioned. My reasons for making it may be briefly stated as follows:

In the book on Justice where the distinction is stated most explicitly, which stands in the same form and extent as number four in the *Ethica Eudemia* and number five in the *Ethica Nicomachea*, justice is spoken of as of two kinds, partial and complete (τὰ μὲν ὡς μέρη τὰ δ'ὡς ὅλα. *Eth. Nic.*, V. 1130 b.). This seems to be intended as the primary classification, and the two kinds are usually called by modern commentators, "general" or "absolute," and "particular" or "relative" justice. But the meanings given by the author to these two kinds seem somewhat indistinct and confusing, if not at times inconsistent, and the modern commentaries reflect the same uncertainty. Elsewhere in the same discussion the just is defined as "the lawful and the fair" (τό τε νόμιμον καὶ τὸ ἴσον,) and the unjust, "the unlawful and the unfair" (τὸ παράνομον καὶ τὸ ἄνισον. *Eth. Nic.*, V, p. 1130 b). Further on, a somewhat different classification is made between the just in a general sense (τὸ ἁπλῶς δίκαιον) on the one hand, and on the other the just in a political or civic sense (τὸ πολιτικὸν δίκαιον) as existing "among people who are associated in a common life with a view to independence, and enjoy freedom and equality whether proportionate or arithmetical" (*Eth. Nic.*, p. 1134 a), or in the sense of the despotic justice prevailing between master and slave (δεσποτικὸν δίκαιον) and of the paternal justice exercised by the father over his children (τὸ πατρικόν) (*Ibid.*, p. 1134 b). This political or civic justice in its turn is subdivided into natural justice (τὸ φυσικόν) "which has the same authority everywhere and is not dependent upon its being adopted or not"; and conventional (τὸ νομικόν) whose origin makes no difference, provided only it be enacted (*Eth. Nic.*, V, p. 1134 b).

According to the Sophists, if the statements of Plato and Aristotle may be trusted, there is no higher kind of justice to be found among men than this conventional justice based merely upon positive laws, and as variable as those laws themselves. It is this view that Plato combats with vigor in the *Republic*. The writer of this book of the *Ethics* takes a position on this question not fundamentally different from Plato's, but he expresses it differently and with great caution. The Sophistic view, he says, has some truth in it, but it is not altogether true. Among the gods it is not true at all, and though it is the fact among men that justice varies, it is not true that no justice can be found which is according to nature. As one might expect in the sphere of the contingent within which all human conduct falls, there will be variations among men in natural rules as well as conventional, but these variations are no proof that these rules as a whole are not according to nature; just as one may train himself to be ambidextrous though "naturally" we are right-handed. "Similarly, such rules of justice as exist not by nature, but by the will of man, are not everywhere the same, as polities themselves are not everywhere the same, *though there is everywhere only one naturally perfect polity.*" (*Eth. Nic.*, pp. 1134 *b*–1135 *a*.) The word here used to indicate this conventional justice is νομικόν in contradiction to φυσικόν. This is clearly a word far different in meaning from νόμιμον which was used earlier to mark off what was lawful from what was merely fair (ἴσον). Whatever be the cause, it is apparent in this whole discussion that the point of view is not always the same. What then is the real relation intended, if there is any single one, between these respective divisions of law into complete and partial; lawful and fair; political and despotic, paternal, or economic; natural and conventional? Are these pairs all coördinate one with another, or are some of them subordinate to others? Are they the same in basis, or if not, are they based on differences equally fundamental?

From the entire discussion — which is rather rambling and disjointed — it appears that the whole of justice is that based on the law of a naturally perfect polity and of no other, and there it cannot but be whole and wholly natural as well, even though based in part on positive enactment; while actual polities will approximate this justice just in so far as they approximate this natural perfection.

The laws of these polities, therefore, if just, will be so because of the "natural" justice to be found in part in them, for there is such a justice shared to some extent by all actual polities not completely depraved, a universal which like all universals is to be found in every particular and nowhere else. This is the answer of the *Ethics* to the greatest of all the questions about justice, and in the main it is the same answer that Plato also gave to the Sophists. The distinction between the lawful and the fair, though very important, is less fundamental and has to do with the mere extension of justice rather than with its objective reality, and the same is true *mutatis mutandis* of the distinction between political and paternal justice. "Particular," as compared with "general" in this discussion, then, may be so-called because it does not extend to all virtue, as fairness, for example, compared with lawfulness, but only to relations between individuals; or because it does not extend to *all* these relations, as in the case of paternal justice; but in its deepest meaning "particular" justice signifies a justice based merely on the law of actual states, compared with the whole of justice — existing by nature in a perfect state. All these different distinctions are found here, but they are not all of the same kind or of the same importance. It seems scarcely adequate or even accurate, then, to say, as Sir Paul Vinogradoff does, that by general justice Aristotle means merely "a complex of all the rules formulated by the State as legally obligatory for the members of the community," and by particular justice, "the set of rules which govern relations *between* the members of the community." (*Historical Jurisprudence*, II, p. 45.) Mr. W. L. Newman's statement excels this only in caution : — ". . . what the laws prescribe (or ' normally constituted laws,' at all events) is there [in the Fifth book of the *Nicomachean Ethics*] said to be universally just." (*The Politics of Aristotle*, II, p. 390). One is tempted to ask whether all laws so prescribed are *ipso facto* "normally constituted." The answer of both Plato and Aristotle would, I think, have been an unhesitating "No."

To Aristotle, as to Plato, the most fundamental question connected with justice was its objective reality. He was as much concerned as Plato in proving against the Sophists that it was no mere variable human device, but rather a natural and universal characteristic of man as man. It may vary in the extent of its application, but important as this is, such variation is to Aristotle as much as to Plato a less important thing than the establishment of the fundamental fact of its "natural" character.

APPENDIX II

MONARCHY "ABSOLUTE" AND DESPOTIC, AND TYRANNY

ὅσοι μὲν οὖν οἴονται πολιτικὸν καὶ βασιλικὸν καὶ οἰκονομικὸν καὶ δεσποτικὸν [εἶναι] τὸν αυτόν, οὐ καλῶς λέγουσιν (πλήθει γὰρ καὶ ὀλιγότητι νομίζουσι διαφέρειν, ἀλλ᾿ οὐκ εἴδει τούτων ἕκαστον, οἷον ἄν μὲν ὀλίγων, δεσπότην, ἄν δὲ πλείονων, οἰκονόμον, ἄν δ᾿ ἔτι πλειόνων, πολιτικὸν ἢ βασιλικόν, ὡς οὐδὲν διαφέρουσαν μεγάλην οἰκίαν ἢ μικρὰν πόλιν· καὶ πολιτικὸν δὲ καὶ βασιλικόν, ὅταν μὲν αὐτὸς ἐφεστήκῃ, βασιλικόν, ὅταν δὲ κατὰ τοὺς λόγους τῆς ἐπιστήμης τῆς τοιαύτης κατὰ μέρος ἄρχων καὶ ἀρχόμενος, πολιτικόν· ταῦτα δ᾿ οὐκ ἔστιν ἀληθῆ). δῆλον δ᾿ ἔσται τὸ λεγόμενον ἐπισκοποῦσι κατὰ τὴν ὑφηγημένην μέθοδον. ὥσπερ γὰρ ἐν τοῖς ἄλλοις τὸ σύνθετον μέχρι τῶν ἀσυνθέτων ἀνάγκη διαιρεῖν (ταῦτα γὰρ ἐλάχιστα μόρια τοῦ παντός), οὕτω καὶ πόλιν ἐξ ὧν σύγκειται σκοποῦντες ὀψόμεθα καὶ περὶ τούτων μᾶλλον, τί τε διαφέρουσιν ἀλλήλων, καὶ εἴ τι τεχνικὸν ἐνδέχεται λαβεῖν περὶ ἕκαστον τῶν ῥηθέντων.

Aristotle, *Politics*, I, I, 2–3 (p. 1252 a).

William of Moerbeka translated this passage as follows:

Quicunque quidem igitur existimant politicum et regale et yconomicum et despoticum idem, non bene dicunt (multitudine enim et paucitate putant differre, sed non specie horum unumquodque, puta si quidem paucorum, patremfamiliae, si autem plurium, yconomum, si autem adhuc plurium, politicum aut regale, tamquam nihil differentem magnam domum aut parvam civitatem: et politicum et regale, quando quidem ipse praeest, regale, quando autem secundum sermones disciplinae talis secundum partem principans et subiectus, politicum: haec autem non sunt vera): manifestum autem erit quod dicitur intendentibus secundum subiectam methodum. sicut enim in aliis compositum usque ad incomposita necesse dividere (haec enim minimae partes totius), sic et civitatem ex quibus componitur considerantes videbimus et de hiis magis, quidque differunt ab invicem, et si quid artificiale contingit accipere circa unumquodque dictorum.

— *Aristotelis Politicorum Libri Octo*, Ed. Franciscus Susemihl, Lipsiae, 1872, pp. 1–3.

The commentary of St. Thomas Aquinas on this passage is in part as follows:

Civitas autem duplici regimine regitur: scilicet politico et regali.   Regale quidem est regimen, quando ille qui civitati praeest habet plenariam potestatem. Politicum autem regimen est quando ille qui praeest habet potestatem coarctatam secundum aliquas leges civitatis. . . .

Quando enim ipse homo praeest simpliciter et secundum omnia, dicitur regimen regale. Quando vero secundum rationem talis scientiae in parte praesidet, id est secundum leges positas per disciplinam politicam, est regimen politicum; quasi secundum partem principetur, quantum ad ea scilicet quae eius potestatem subsunt; et secundum partem sit subiectus, quantum ad ea in quibus subiicitur legi.

— *Sancti Thomae Aquinatis, Opera Omnia*, Parmae, 1867, vol. xxi.

ὅτι μὲν οὖν ἔχει τινὰ λόγον ἡ ἀμφισβήτησις, καὶ οὐκ εἰσὶν οἱ μὲν φύσει δοῦλοι οἱ δὲ ἐλεύθεροι, δῆλον, καὶ ὅτι ἔν τισι διώρισται τὸ τοιοῦτον, ὧν συμφέρει τῷ μὲν τὸ δουλεύειν τῷ δὲ τὸ δεσπόζειν καὶ δίκαιον καὶ δεῖ τὸ μὲν ἄρχεσθαι τὸ δ' ἄρχειν, ἣν πεφύκασιν ἀρχὴν ἄρχειν, ὥστε καὶ δεσπόζειν, τὸ δὲ κακῶς ἀσυμφόρως ἐστὶν ἀμφοῖν (τὸ γὰρ αὐτὸ συμφέρει τῷ μέρει καὶ τῷ ὅλῳ καὶ σώματι καὶ ψυχῇ, ὁ δὲ δοῦλος μέρος τι τοῦ δεσπότου, οἷον ἔμψυχόν τι τοῦ σώματος κεχωρισμένον δὲ μέρος [τοῦ σώματος]· διὸ καὶ συμφέρον ἐστί τι καὶ φιλία δούλῳ καὶ δεσπότῃ πρὸς ἀλλήλους τοῖς φύσει τοιούτοις ἠξιωμένοις, τοῖς δὲ μὴ τοῦτον τὸν τρόπον, ἀλλὰ κατὰ νόμον καὶ βιασθεῖσι, τοὐναντίον)· φανερὸν δὲ καὶ ἐκ τούτων, ὅτι οὐ ταὐτόν ἐστι δεσποτεία καὶ πολιτική, οὐδὲ πᾶσαι ἀλλήλαις αἱ ἀρχαί, ὥσπερ τινὲς φασίν. ἡ μὲν γὰρ ἐλευθέρων φύσει ἡ δὲ δούλων ἐστίν, καὶ ἡ μὲν οἰκονομικὴ μοναρχία (μοναρχεῖται γὰρ πᾶς οἶκος), ἡ δὲ πολιτικὴ ἐλευθέρων καὶ ἴσων ἀρχή. ὁ μὲν οὖν δεσπότης οὐ λέγεται κατὰ ἐπιστήμην, ἀλλὰ τῷ τοιόσδε εἶναι, ὁμοίως δὲ καὶ ὁ δοῦλος καὶ ὁ ἐλεύθερος· ἐπιστήμη δ' ἂν εἴη καὶ δεσποτικὴ καὶ δουλική, δουλικὴ μὲν οἵαν περ ὁ ἐν ταῖς Συρακούσαις ἐπαίδευσεν (ἐκεῖ γὰρ λαμβάνων τις μισθὸν ἐδίδασκε τὰ ἐγκύκλια διακονήματα τοὺς παῖδας), εἴη δ' ἂν καὶ ἐπὶ πλεῖον τούτων μάθησις, οἷον ὀψοποιητικὴ καὶ τἆλλα τὰ τοιαῦτα γένη τῆς διακονίας, ἔστι γὰρ ἕτερα ἑτέρων τὰ μὲν ἐντιμότερα ἔργα τὰ δ' ἀναγκαιότερα, καὶ κατὰ τὴν παροιμίαν " δοῦλος πρὸ δούλου, δεσπότης πρὸ δεσπότου." αἱ μὲν οὖν τοιαῦται πᾶσαι δουλικαὶ ἐπιστῆμαί εἰσί· δεσποτικὴ δ' ἐπιστήμη ἐστὶν ἡ χρηστικὴ δούλων, ὁ γὰρ δεσπότης οὐκ ἐν τῷ κτᾶσθαι τοὺς δούλους, ἀλλ' ἐν τῷ χρῆσθαι δούλοις. ἔστι δ' αὕτη ἡ ἐπιστήμη οὐδὲν μέγα ἔχουσα οὐδὲ σεμνόν· ἃ γὰρ τὸν δοῦλον ἐπίστασθαι δεῖ ποιεῖν, ἐκεῖνον δεῖ ταῦτα ἐπίστασθαι ἐπιτάττειν.

— Aristotle, *Politics*, I, 6–7 (p. 1255 *b*).

William of Moerbeka translates this thus:

Quod quidem igitur habet quandam rationem dubitatio et non sunt hii quidem natura servi, hii autem liberi, palam, et quod in quibusdam determinatum est quod tale, quorum huic quidem expedit servire, huic autem dominari et iustum est et oportet hoc quidem subici, hoc autem principari quo nata sunt principatu principari, quare et despotizare, male autem inutiliter est ambobus (idem enim expedit parti et toti et corpori et animae, servus autem pars quaedam domini, veluti animatum aliquid corporis, separata autem pars corporis: propter quod et expediens ali-

quid est et amicitia servo et domino ad invicem hiis qui natura tales
dignificantur, hiis autem qui non secundum hunc modum, sed secundum
legem et violentiam passis contrarium) : manifestum autem et ex hiis,
quoniam non idem est despotia et politica neque omnes ad invicem principatus, sicut quidam aiunt. hic quidem enim liberorum natura, hic
autem servorum est, et yconomica quidem monarchia (ab uno enim regitur omnis domus), politica autem liberorum et aequalium principatus.
despotes quidem igitur non dicitur secundum scientiam, sed eo, quod
talis sit, similiter autem et servus et liber : scientia autem utique erit et
despotica et servilis, servilis quidem, qualem quidem qui in Syracusis
erudivit (ibi enim accipiens quis pretium docuit ancillaria ministeria
pueros), erit autem utique et ad plus horum disciplina, velut pulmentaria
et alia talia genera ministrationis, sunt enim alia aliis haec quidem hono-
rabiliora opera, haec autem necessariora, et secundum proverbium,
"servus ante servum, dominus ante dominum." tales quidem igitur
omnes serviles scientiae sunt : despotica autem scientia est quae [est]
usiva servorum, despotes enim non in possidendo servos, sed in utendo
servis. est autem haec scientia nihil magnum habens neque venerandum :
quae enim servum oportet scire facere, illum oportet haec scire praecipere.
— Susemihl, *op. cit.*, pp. 24–27.

The next passage is an entire chapter of the *Dialogus* of William of Occam
(*Pars III, Tractatus I, Liber II, Cap. VI,* Goldast, *Monarchia,* vol. II, pp. 794–
795), the fullest and clearest discussion of these important distinctions that I
have found in the political writings of the fourteenth century.

"*Magister:* Politiarum autem duae sunt species primae : sicut & duae
sunt species propriae principatuum sive praelationum, & principantium
sive praelatorum seu rectorum. Omnis enim principatus aut ordinatur
principaliter ad bonum seu conferens commune bonum, scilicet principantis & principantium & etiam subiectorum : aut non ordinatur ad
bonum commune. Si ordinetur ad bonum commune, sic est principatus
temperatus & rectus. Si non ordinatur ad bonum commune, est principatus vitiatus & transgressio : quia est corruptio & transgressio principatus temperati & recti atque iusti. Politia igitur omnis, aut est tem-
perata & recta : vel est vitiata & transgressa. Politiae autem temperatae
& rectae tres sunt species principales & impermixtae. Prima est, quando
principans est unus, & vocatur *regalis monarchia:* in qua dominatur unus
solus propter commune bonum, & non principaliter propter propriam
voluntatem & conferens. Et huius modi politia secundum Arist. *8 Ethic:*
est optima secundum optimum modum ipsius, sunt enim ipsius modi
plures, secundum ipsum, *3 poli. c. 16* sed potissimus ipsius modus videtur,
quando aliquis regnat & principatur in regno, non secundum legem, sed
secundum voluntatem suam. Quod quidam sic intelligunt. Ille dicitur

principari & regnare secundum voluntatem suam, & non secundum legem,
qui regnat propter commune bonum omnium & nullis legibus humanis
pure positivis vel consuetudinibus alligatur: sed est supra omnes huius-
modi leges, licet legibus naturalibus astringatur. Et ideo talis rex non
habet iurare nec promittere se servaturum quascunque leges vel consuetudines humanas introductas, licet expediens sit ipsum iurare, quod
leges naturales pro utilitate communi servabit, & quod in omnibus quae
spectant ad principatum assumptum commune bonum intendet, non
privatum. *Talis rex potest dici habere plenitudinem potestatis respectu,
scilicet eorum, quae bonum commune respiciunt, non privatum. Talis
autem principatus differt a principatu tyrannico: quia ille est propter commune bonum, differt etiam a principatu despotico, quia principatus despoticus est principaliter propter bonum proprium principantis, quemadmodum
dominum bestiarum & aliarum rerum temporalium est propter bonum possi-
dentis.* Principatus autem regalis est propter bonum commune, & ideo
non dicitur proprie principatus despoticus, & tamen rex talis est quodammodo Dominus omnium, sed aliter quam in principatu despotico: quia
in principatu despotico principans habet tantum dominium, quod potest
uti suis servis & bonis aliis quibuscunque, quae ad suum pertinent principatum talem, non solum propter bonum commune, sed etiam propter
bonum proprium, dummodo contra legem divinam vel naturalem nihil
attentet. Sed principans in principatu regali praedicto non potest uti
subiectis & bonis eorum qualitercunque sibi placet propter bonum proprium, & ideo sibi non sunt servi, sed naturali libertate gaudent: quia ad
naturalem libertatem spectat, ut nullus possit uti liberis propter utilitatem utentis, sed non est contra naturalem libertatem, ut quis rationa-
biliter utatur liberis ad bonum commune: cum quilibet teneatur bonum
commune praeferre privato.

Discip. Secundum ista principatus despoticus esset maior & perfectios
tali principatu regali: quia maiorem potestatem includeret, principans
enim despotice potest uti servis & bonis eorum propter utilitatem tam
communem quam privatam, rex autem nisi propter utilitatem communem, igitur est maior & perfectior.

Magist. Respondetur, quod principatus despoticus est quodammodo
maior: quia ad plura quodammodo se extendit, sed ex hoc ipso est imperfectior, seu quia bonum multorum est melius, quam unius bonum: seu
quia detrimentum boni multorum nullam perfectionem sed imperfectionem importat. In principatu autem despotico est detrimentum multorum ex hoc ipso, quod despotes potest uti sibi subiectis & bonis eorum
ad propriam utilitatem, & ideo talis potestas maior imperfectionem boni
melioris, scilicet boni multorum includit. Propter quod principatus
despoticus non solum qui est unius patrisfamilias in una domo, sed qui
esset unius regis in uno regno: & per consequens qui est unius impera-

toris in toto orbe, esset simpliciter imperfectior principatu tali regali.
Praeter istum principatum regalem sunt alii principatus regales diver-
simode deficientes ab isto: convenientes tamen in hoc, quod sunt Monarchiae quaedam. Quidam enim principatus unius Monarchiae deficit ab
isto, quantum ad intentionem boni communis, quia scilicet non est insti-
tutus totaliter propter bonum commune, sed etiam propter bonum proprium, & talis principatus regalis aliquid habet de principatu Tyrannico
vel despotico: & est quodammodo mixtus ex principatu despotico, tyrannico, & regali. In quantum enim quo ad aliqua intendit bonum commune: & in quantum unus solus principatur, habet aliquid de principatu
regali. In quantum vero bonum proprium etiam intendit, habet aliquid
de principatu tyrannico & despotico, & ideo est quodammodo mixtus ex
principatibus illis, unde & aliquis principatus regalis & tyrannicus vocatur
ab Aristo[teles]. Principatus autem unius interdum deficit a saepe dicto
principatu regali quantum ad potestatem, quod scilicet non habet illam
plentitudinem potestatis, quam habet principatus regalis praefatus. Et
talis principatus regalis dicitur secundum legem, quia licet unus principetur, modo tamen principatur secundum voluntatem, sed quibusdam
legibus & consuetudinibus humanitus introductis astringitur, quas tenetur
servare, & ipsas se servaturum iurare vel promittere obligatur, & quanto-
plures tales leges & consuetudines servare tenetur, tanto magis recedit a
memorato principatu regali, & ideo forte his diebus non est in universo
orbe talis principatus scilicet primus regalis. Secundum Aristot[eles]
nullus est dignus tali regno, nisi sapientia & virtute & bonis omnibus tam
corporis quam animae, quam etiam exterioribus bonis, scilicet amicis &
divitiis, superexcellat. Aliter enim timendum est, ne ad tyrannidem se
convertat, unde & propria bona debet habere vel ex se vel ex assignatione
illorum quibus praeest, ut bona liberorum nequaquam sibi appropriet,
nec etiam quoquomodo accipiat, nisi evidens utilitas vel manifesta neces-
sitas hoc exposcat. Isti principatui regali etiam summae opponitur
tyrannis, quae est transgressio & corruptio eius, quae est prima species
& pessima politiae vitiatae, quia tyrannis non intendit bonum subiectorum, nisi per accidens, sed principaliter intendit bonum proprium, sive
bonum proprium sit bonum etiam aliorum, sive sit malum ipsorum.
Fiunt autem tyranni secundum Aristo. 5 Politi. c. 8. saepe ex Demagogis,
sunt autem Demagogi, ducentes populum secundum voluntatem suam de
beneplacito populi, non tanquam reges aut Domini vel Tyranni seu ius
regendi populum aut imperandi habentes: sed quasi procuratores & con-
cionatores seu monitores instigant populum ad illa, quae populo placent
id est quibus populus credit, & ideo Arist. vocat eos *4 Politic. c. 3.* adula-
tores, tales enim saepe, postquam sibi unierint populum, incipiunt propter
potentiam tyrannizare: & etiam involuntariis dominari. *Fiunt etiam*
Tyranni nonnunquam ex regibus, quia, ut dicit Aristo. 8 Ethicorum,

malus rex tyrannus fit, si enim secundum legem incipiat principari in-
voluntariis propter bonum proprium, fit tyrannus, si incipiat principari
voluntariis propter bonum proprium, fit proprie despotes. Cuius prin-
cipatus nonnunquam Tyrannis ab Aristotele vocatur, propter similitudinem
magnam ad despoticam: non tamen Tyrannis proprie est despotia, sicut
ex supradictis patere potest. Ex praedictis colligi potest, quod princi-
patui regali, praesertim potissimo, non solum Tyrannis proprie dicta, sed
etiam principatus despoticus aliquo modo opponitur, vel est principatus ita
disparatus, ut nullus unus principatus possit esse regalis & despoticus
respectu eorundem: quo tamen aliquis dominetur regaliter, & aliquis despo-
tice, inconveniens non videtur.[1]

To these might be added the definitions of Bodin in the sixteenth century:

Donc la Monarchie royale [*Monarchia regalis*, in Bodin's own Latin
version], ou legitime, est celle où les sugets obeissent aux loix du Monarque, & le Monarque aux loix de nature, demeurant la liberté naturulle,
& proprieté des biens aux sugets. La Monarchie seigneuriale [Latin
Dominatus], est celle où le Prince est fait Seigneur [*dominus*] des biens &
des personnes par le droict des armes, & de bonne guerre, gouvernant ses
sugets comme le pere de famille ses esclaves. La Monarchie tyrannique
[*Tyrannis*], est où le Monarque mesprisant les loix de nature, abuse des
personnes libres comme d'esclaves, & des biens des sugets comme des
siens.

— *De la République, Liv. II, Chap. II.* edition of 1177 (French), p. 200;
edition of 1586 (Latin), p. 189.

[1] The Italics are not in the original.

INDEX

DATE DUE

NOV 8 '74			
NOV 18 '75			
DEC 15 '76			
			DEMCO 38-297